THE WASHINGTON, D.C.
BOOK OF
FACTS & FANCIES,
CAPRICES & CURIOSITIES

The Insider's Guide to the Passions, Possessions and Pleasures of the Power Elite in the Nation's Capital

by

James Jennings Sheeran

Published by
Palm Beach Publishing Group©

i

Library of Congress Cataloging-in-Publication Data
1. Washington   2. Personalities   3. Lifestyle   4. Society
I. Sheeran, James Jennings   II. Title

1993 93-092634
ISBN 0-9622977-4-7
ISSN 1071-1562

Printed in the United States of America

First Edition (November 1993)

1 2 3 4 5 6 7 8 9 10

This book is dedicated

with admiration,

gratitude and affection to

the Spirits of Washington

Past, Present and Future.

May they conquer

the problems

of this world, and

create a land of plenitude

where people

can live gracefully

amid peace and pleasure.

CONTENTS

Preview: Most popular surname * Original social classes * Cave Dwellers credentials * Cave Dwellers vs Nouveaux * Wealthiest residents * Most beautiful people * Foremost brunettes/redheads/blonds * Most wanted autographs * Advanced-age super-achievers * Most club memberships * Lady Rainmaker * Grande Dames * Best dressed women, men, couples * Socially desirable people * "Green Book" significance * Most homes owned * Eligible singles * Most enduring marriages * Nicknames * Maiden names * Best dancers * Most distinguished moustache * Most energetic resident * Washington Class.

Preview: Elitists * Most popular personalities * Formidable communicators * Foremost actionaries * Choicest seats * Status symbols * Most celebrated business woman * Dynamic duos * Most power * Salaries * Income taxes * Democratic insider * "Conger" touch * Political satirist * Most accomplished woman * Poet laureate * Liaison * Most visible association executive * WETA * Queen of "Discovery" * Most influential P.R. man * Prominent Senator * Banking/Racing * Military backround * Foremost cartoonist * "Wonder Woman" * Photographers * Washington Schadenfreude * Washington Philosophy.

Preview: Fame and fortune * Hollywood insiders * Museum cable network * Far-flung architect * Most listened to radio personality * Most noted horse woman * Virginia rancher * Iron-pumping congressman * GM Director * CEO of animals * WASPs * Father and son * Prominent investigator * Kennedy family mystique * Mega-lawyer * Gold winners * Mr. Manners * Songstress/theologist * Friend to lost souls * Highest court * Political columnist * Doctor to the stars * Sir Denis Thatcher Society * Mayor of Capitol Hill * Real winners' homes * Ultimate material girls.

Preview: Importance of galas * Registered charities * Most giving archangels * Greening of a socialite * The Chairman * A chairman's inner thoughts * Charitable donations * Most prestigious charities * Charity event efficiency * Cost of galas * Trends in fundraising * Ball gowns * Dress code * Ball jewelry * Ball transportation * Songs at galas * Best orchestras * Ball menus * Washington debutantes * A-List parties * Favorite party planners * Foremost caterers * Cost of private party * Most lavish wedding * Washington characters.

ACKNOWLEDGEMENTS

A book like this cannot be written in a vacuum; it is the result of hundreds of interviews seeking the insights and opinions of many of Washington's most prominent residents and professionals. It is also the subjective expression of the Author in that much of the material presented is purely a matter of personal perception. As in many literary works that entertain yet are considered reference books, there is a fine line between fact and fiction; we beg your indulgence for whatever fine shadings we, personally (and in some cases, presumably) have placed on certain **Facts & Fancies**. While every effort has been made to assure accuracy, no responsibility can be assumed by the author or the publisher for errors or misinterpretations.

In view of the foregoing, we gratefully acknowledge the many sources who gave so generously of their understanding and knowledge of Washington; they are listed in the Contributors section.

INTRODUCTION

Hundreds of thousands of people have come to Washington in hopes of "conquering" it in one way or another. Some have businesses; some are desirous of climbing the ultimate social ladder; some take a fling at government and some just want to enjoy a lifestyle that is apparently more elusive than it seems.

Most of them have departed in high dudgeon and low pocketbook. When they go, the common reason is "They just didn't understand the Nation's Capital."

Is Washington so incomprehensible?

The Washington, D.C. Book of Facts & Fancies, Caprices & Curiosities is a collection of information that explores and explains the peculiarities, the perceptions, the possessions that make the Town what it is: **unique**, for better or for worse.

It is a peek inside the palaces, an analysis of its personalities, their passions and occasional perversions. It is a discovery of the power-elite in business and government, and an expose of the pecking order by which most people live.

It can be used as a handbook for those who wish to join or to conquer society or it can be read just for the fun of it. Much of its "wit and wisdom" is universal to human nature.

But most of all, this is an insiders' commentary on an enclave that has fascinated all manner of folk ever since Congress created the glittering legend of **WASHINGTON** in 1800. The author has observed its foibles with enthusiasm, with bemused wonderment, and sometimes with exasperation, but always with affection!

May you enjoy Washington, as it is presented, too.

CHAPTER I

THE LUCKIEST PEOPLE IN THE WORLD
(Washington Players, Partisans & Pilgrims)

Regal, resplendent and radiant,
Mrs. Evangeline Bruce and Oscar de la Renta.

Photo: J.R. Black

1. **WHAT IS THE MOST POPULAR SURNAME IN WASHINGTON?**

Many seem to think that the most popular name in Washington is "Darling," but based on registered voters in the area, **Smith** is the surname most frequently represented. Not far behind are **Miller, Adams, Jackson, Jones, Brown, Johnson** and **Davis.**

As for the first names, way back when, the most popular names were Jonathan, Christopher, Anthony, David and John, Emily, Elizabeth and Jessica. Lately, first names like Tiffany, Samantha, Alexandra, Katherine and Jennifer; Daniel, Ashley, Jason, James, Albert, Michael and Alexander are the winners.

2. **WHAT WERE THE ORIGINAL SOCIAL CLASSES IN TOWN?**

Five levels in the social pyramid were evident:
1. **The Rich-Rich Old Guard or Cave Dweller:** old money, old names, big houses, blueblood; not easy to reach out and touch (but could be done by membership in the right clubs). Very reserved with roots tracing back to Mayflower and railroad/oil money, basically non-mixers.
2. **The Nouveaux:** striving for status, the seekers, big supporters of politicians and charities, publicity-anxious; no matter what, never escalated to Rich-Rich status.
3. **The Marginals:** fair amount of money, fair ambition, fair prowess on the golf links and in the boudoir; working feverishly to climb into "nouveau riche" status.
4. **The Ethnics:** keep to their own interests and groups, partly by design, partly involuntarily, original enough to create their own space, clubs, restaurants, social pyramids.
5. **The Singles:** at one time, men-on-the-make, now includes ladies of all ages and proclivities; a growing category, one with unique entree to higher classes as escorts, companions or possible candidates for marriage.

(Interesting to note: the classes have not changed appreciably over the decades; if anything, activity among the Singles has intensified and the Marginals have moved on to other locations, basically frustrated by the Social Pyramid.)

3. **WHAT CREDENTIALS MAKE ONE A "CAVE DWELLER"?**

A more inappropriate name for world-class sophisticates who have enjoyed the galaxy of human experiences at the highest levels, would be hard to find; **Cave Dwellers** as a name, despite its historical relevance to the **Old Guard**, connotes all the wrong things about those who dwell in the nation's Capital.

The origin of the term is unknown, but it dates back a century or so when some bright social observer decided to lay an accolade on those pioneers who created and massaged Washington society to its current *ne plus ultra* status. In a strict sense, a Cave Dweller is someone born to a patrician family and bred in the Capital dating back 75-100 years; someone born to the manner with an abnormal love of the Capital and the perseverance to tolerate revolving administrations and social aspirants. In other cities, the **Old Guard** is equivalent to a **Cave Dweller**, but despite nomenclature, members of that sacrosanct classification do, usually, have great breeding, genes and a special *joie de vivre* (even if it is conservatively concealed).

Credentials include the right **birthplace** (Columbia Hospital for Women), **schools** (St. Albans, National Cathedral Visitation Convent), **charities** (Smithsonian, Symphony, Corcoran), **hangouts** (Chevy Chase, Sulgrave or Cosmos Clubs, Occidental), **churches** (Georgetown Presbyterian or St. Matthew's); and as the Game gets played out, even the proper **undertaker** (Gawler's) and **cemeteries** (Oak Hill or Rock Creek) are *de rigueur*.

WHAT IS THE MAJOR DIFFERENCE BETWEEN WASHINGTON "CAVE DWELLERS" AND THE "NOUVEAUX"?

	"CAVE DWELLERS"	NOUVEAUX
Art	Hunt prints, landscapes, family portraits in oil, English prints, Monet, Old Masters, Renoir	Picasso, Chagal, Miro, elaborate bronze and marble statues, family photos in small sterling frames
Autos	American made autos — station wagons, sedans, jeeps, old Rolls, and Bentleys, antique classics (15 years or older)	New Rolls, Mercedes, Volvo station wagons, Range Rovers, Ferraris, BMWs, Jaguars
Charities	National Symphony, Smithsonian Institution, Corcoran Gallery of Art, Phillips Collection, Washington Home	Traveler's Aid, Washington Opera Company, Hospital for Sick Children, Thrift Shop Centers, "Disease" causes
Churches	Christ Church, St. Matthew's, St. John's Episcopal, Holy Trinity, Washington National Cathedral	Washington National Cathedral, St. Patrick's Episcopal, First Baptist
Clubs	Alibi, Sulgrave, Cosmos, Chevy Chase, Metropolitan	Georgetown, Pisces II
Dress (Women)	Favorite outfits dating back several years; Adolfo, Blass, Chanel, Beene, de Ribes, Feraud, Galanos, prized Lilly's, Givenchy, Herrera, Simpson, St. John, St. Laurent, Trigere, de la Renta	Newest styles, latest designs etc., designer sweats and jeans; Karen, Klein, LaCroix, Mackie, McFadden, Scaasi Ungaro, Versace

Dress (Men)	Navy Blazer a la Brooks Bros. tan or gray straight legged cuffed pants, button-down shirts, Hermes tie, shawl-collared tuxedos, LeBow gray flannels, cashmere sweaters, linen trousers, Belgian loafers	Navy Blazer a la Bloomie's, Armani shirts, Club check jackets, Nicole Miller tie, baggy pants with cuffs, double-breasted tuxedos, ruffled shirts, Banker's tweeds, Banks and Flusser designs
Drinks	Scotch, martinis, bourbon, cognac, French wine	Vodka, champagne, imported beers, domestic wines
Favorite Fabrics	Printed cottons, silk, cashmere, linen (natural)	Silk charmeuse, colored linen, cashmere blends, sweats
Hobbies	Bridge, gin rummy, tennis (white attire), golf, backgammon, polo, hunting, fishing on shore	Polo, golf, tennis (pastel or colored clothing), backgammon, thoroughbred racing
Home Locales	Chevy Chase, New York, Newport, Saratoga, Alexandria (Old Town)	Washington, Hamptons and condos in "in" locations (Aspen)
Jewelry	Treasured family heirlooms, pearls, solitaire diamond engagement rings, gold wedding bands, cameos	Tennis bracelets, large stones set in "high" mountings, gold chains, sapphire engagement rings, multi-rings worn together, Cartier "Love" bracelets, nugget and faux jewelry
Orchestras	Gene Donati, Lester Lanin, Peter Duchin, Miles Davis	Howard Devron, Miles Stiebel, "Doc" Scantlin
Pets	Labradors, golden retrievers, German shepherds, dachshunds, canaries	Shar peis, poodles, Yorkies, lhasa apso, exotic parrots
Public Image	Avoids press, abhors paparazzi	Has PR agent—wants as much public exposure as possible
Society Families	Bruce, Duemling, Biddle, Charles, Roosevelt, Alsop, Fritchey, Graham, Harriman, Blair, Kiplinger, Shouse, Phillips, Mellon	Kay, Altman, Allbritton, Bender, Carr, Coopersmith, Haft, Lee, Marriott, Ourisman, Zlotnick, Redmon, Rosenthal, Kraft, Bernstein

"Cave Dwellers" in Washington are becoming a somewhat endangere species; some blame locked-in trust funds with low interest rates set up year ago, poor personal executors, inflation; whatever the cause, the prognosis fo the survival of this species is questionable, Financially, those who have ha everything (background, breeding, proper education, glamorous lives) are now in a position of meager existence (meager only by Washington standards and not by the standards of those in authority and status based on heritage and ancestry; unfortunately, this status can't buy exorbitantly priced material goods that are so much a part of today's Washington *nouveau* society (but, on the other hand, ancestry is priceless and can't be bought or earned). The question has recently become — who carries more status in Washington? One who was born into the "right" family, living without extravagance yet belonging to the *in* clubs because of joining when initiation fees were lower (or non-existent), or one who through individual hard work and personal achievement has created life in the "grand style" (the former style of the Cave Dweller)?

WHO ARE THE WEALTHIEST WASHINGTONIANS?

According to the latest survey by *Forbes Magazine* ("The Forbes Four Hundred") the area has an abundance of rich and super-rich residents. The following are the most visible:

BILLIONAIRES

John Werner Kluge, Charlottesville (VA), 78, $5.5 billion; communications, varied businesses;

Forrest Edward Mars, Jr., McLean (VA), 61, $2.5 billion, candy, snacks, real estate;

Edgar Miles Bronfman, Charlottesville (VA), 63, $2.4 billion, liquor and wines;

Paul Mellon, Upperville (VA), 85, $1.2 billion; inheritance, banking, real estate;

MILLIONAIRES

Jack Kent Cooke, Middleburg (VA) and DC, 79, $900 million, real estate, investments, sports;

Laszlo Nandor Tauber, Potomac (MD), 77, $500 million, real estate;

Alice Francis du Pont Mills, Middleburg (VA), 79, $350 million, inheritance;

B. Francis Saul II, Chevy Chase (MD), 60, $300 million, real estate; financial operations;

Joe Lewis Allbritton, DC, 67, $290 million, broadcasting, banking, insurance.

Some of the great family fortunes which have representatives in the CapCity area are: **Bingham** (newspapers, $400 million); **Graham** (communications, $565 million); **Kennedy** (real estate, $350 million); **Marriott** (hotels, real estate, $660 million); **Rockefeller** (oil, real estate, $5.5 billion).

Katharine Graham is undoutedly the wealthiest woman in the area with a personal fortune estimated in the $250-$350 million range. When the late **Mitzi Newhouse** passed away a few years ago, her estate was estimated at $8 billion which put her in league with Queen Elizabeth (worth $8.1 billion) and Queen Beatrix ($5 billion).

For the record, the richest man in America is **William Henry Gate**
(Seattle, WA, age 36) founder of Microsoft Corp.; net worth at $6.3 billion
The richest man in the world is **Yoshiaki Tsutsumi** (Japan, 59) owner of th
Seibu empire; net worth at $22.5 billion.

The greatest concentration of wealth in the world is in the US. Famil
dynasties control staggering fortunes. Among leaders are (billions): Walto
($25.3); Mars ($9.2), du Pont ($8.6), Newhouse ($7.0), Buffett ($6.6).

6. **WHO ARE WASHINGTON'S MOST BEAUTIFUL PEOPLE?**

By any measurement, Pamela Harriman fits the specifications (she wa
selected by *People Magazine* in May '93 as one of the 50 Most Beautifr
People in the World). In her league are: **Princess Michael of Kent, Marylo
Whitney, Dina Merrill, Wendy Raines, Gahl Burt, Betsy Davis, Nanc
Dickerson Whitehead, Buffy Cafritz, Deeda Blair, Lynda Carter, Coki
Roberts, Robin Chandler Duke, Pat Cummings, Debbie Dingell, Nir
Ferguson, Nina Pillsbury, Lynda Webster, Allison Paley, Alexandra d
Borchgrave, Tandy Dickinson, Gabriele Steers** and **Marlena Cooke**.

For the guys, the "hunks" are: **Robert McCormick Adams, Jac
Valenti, Bud Palmer, David Mulford, Michel Duchamp, Christophe
Rebman, Nash Whitney Schott, Bill Bryant, Fritz Allen Korth, Bo
Schieffer, J. Carter Brown, Arnaud de Borchgrave, Lloyd Bentsen, Bo
Gray, Leo Daly, Geoffrey Davis, Gordon King, Donald Graham, Orri
Hatch, Rusty Powell, John Ray, William Webster, William Colby an
Chris van Roijen.**

7. **WHO ARE THE FOREMOST BRUNETTES/REDHEADS/BLOND
IN WASHINGTON?**

If the past is mutable, and it is – we change it all the time – imagine th
conceivable changes inherent in hair coloring. An endless spectrum of ton;
possibilities exist; but here/now, the social scene in Town presents thes
formidable Ladies and colors:

Brunettes   Lynda Robb, Susan King, Nancy Opalak, Sarah Gewir;
                    Jane Edmonson, Constance Morella, Freida Wallison,
                    Nina Totenberg, Cathie Black, Elayne Bennett, Flavia
                    Biancheri, Heidi Berry, Anne Sidey, Helen Curtin, Patric
                    O'Brien, Deena Clark, Giselle Theberge.

Redheads   Lady Fairfax, Mary Margaret Valenti, Jane Sloat,
                    Marlene Malek, Mariana Grove, Didi Cutler, Buffy Cafrit
                    Arianne Huffington, Aniko Gaal Schott.

Blonds　　Pamela Harriman, Jean Kennedy Smith, Lea Thompson, Laura Bode, Ina Ginsburg, Donatella Andreani, Karen Newman, Judith Terra, Dianna Kay, Pattie Pusey, Brownie McLean, Mary Haft, Michele Rouse, Pat Cummins, Aliki Bryant, Margaret Hodges, Penne Percy-Korth, Lea Frohnmayer, Pat Scheiffer, Gayle Hyman, Margot Howar, Susan Firestone, Belinda Hidalgo, Pat Dixson, Palmer Graham, Wanda Baucus, Pat Oxley, Grega Daly, Jill Gore, Mary Frances Smoak, Barbara Nevin Gray.

8.　WHAT ARE THE MOST SOUGHT-AFTER AUTOGRAPHS IN TOWN?

Naturally, sightseers and non-administration locals go for the big scrawl — President/Vice-President, top Cabinet guys and dolls, Senators and assorted other power-players. When Jackie comes back, she's mobbed; same for the Reagans. Their signature goes to big-time collectors. Kissinger rates well; Schwarzkopf is a #10 as is Liz Taylor and Colin Powell.

Top cats and administration bigwigs go for showbiz lettering — Madonna, Schwarzenegger, Streisand, Selleck, Greg Peck, Pavarotti, Domingo, Warren Beatty, Shirley MacLaine, Sinatra, Redford and Streep. The late Helen Hayes, when she visited CapCity was a living legend with autograph seekers galore (and her own theater in the Library of Congress).

9.　WHO ARE THE CAPITAL'S "ADVANCED-AGE" SUPER-ACHIEVERS?

Col. Edward deTreville Ellis (at 103, unbelievable! One of Ike's classmates at the Point); **Renee Kraft** (like the Eveready Battery, she just goes on-and-on); **Catherine Filene Shouse** (in the mid-90s and every bit a Queen; the First Lady of Wolf Trap); **Lolo Sarnoff** (Arts for the Aging, her discovery, befits this woman of locomotion); **Jack Kent Cooke**, (ubiquitous, uncommonly involved — watch out world, here I come, again!); and **John Kluge** (irresistible force in everything).

10.　WHAT WASHINGTONIAN BELONGS TO THE MOST CLUBS?

The most fraternal of gents in Town (residing at 3320 Volta Pl. NW), **Eugene Myers** (USAF-Ret.) pays dues in a number of places. Among them are: Beach, Everglades, Sailfish and Society of Four Arts in Palm Beach; Explorers, Harvard, Metropolitan, Wings (NY); Minneapolis Club (MN); Field Country, City Tavern, National Aviation, St. Andrews Society (DC); Royal Scottish Automobile, NEW (Scotland); ESU.

11.　WHO IS NOW CONSIDERED THE "LADY RAINMAKER" IN WASHINGTON?

What you see depends on where you're standing; **Pamela Harriman**

Impeccable,
incandescent Lady—
Pamela Harriman.

Photo: J.R. Black

has always been standing in the right place at the right time and at the right level. The daughter of a British lord who became an American citizen in '71 when she married her third husband, Averell Harriman (after being wed to Randolph Churchill and Leland Hayward), the former Pamela Digby has always had plenty of social topspin; her career as a professional Democrat (with designations as empress, doyenne, party duchess, PAC leader—which under her aegis raised about $20 million—now as power broker) has rarely been equalled by anyone, much less a woman; her impeccable demeanor and beauty is all the more remarkable for its timelessness, and her contribution to world society just can't be matched by any single person (whole contingents might suffer by comparison). She is the all-time immutable, indisputable class act, a maximum example of the perfect Lady Rainmaker.

12. WHO ARE THE GRANDEST OF THE GRANDE DAMES HOLDING FORTH IN TOWN?

In a Town with wall-to-wall hostesses, all sophisticated, cosmopolitan and competitive, these are the stand-outs (although each would deny same, preferring a low-key somewhat passive role):

Polly Fritchey (a genuine CapCity insider, knower/keeper of secrets, now married to a Fourth Estater, charming nonetheless)

Katharine Graham (always a power, at whatever!)

Jennifer Phillips (formerly married to developer Conrad Cafritz, now major art patron and beguiler; wife of Laughlin Phillips)

Deeda Blair (elegant international hostess, local champion of cancer funding)

Evangeline Bruce (great democrat, anglophile and far-flung socialite, now addressing the problems of runaway and troubled children)

Susan Mary Alsop (elegant, advocate of many causes, always up to snuff in whatever she does)

Ruth Buchanan (got the message through her husband's role as Ike's Protocol Chief; knows the domestic ropes and soundly impresses her international chums)

"Oatsie" Charles (witty and wise with a Newport/Alabama humor—only

18

Dame to have a DC street named after her grandfather—Oates St. NE)

Estelle Gelman (a pillar for several causes, get-it-done now Lady, no-nonsense and lots of philanthropy; recently named President, American Cancer Society - DC Div.)

Margaret Hodges (inexhaustible cancer fighter and world-class persuader, tools off to Jamaica to regroup occasionally)

Mary Patterson (proof that octogenarians can pull off the impossible — backer of scores of charities, most notably her own Marpat Foundation).

And, of course, **Pamela Harriman**, rich and rare, who transcends categories.

13. WHO ARE WASHINGTON'S BEST DRESSED WOMEN, MEN AND COUPLES?

The Winner's Circle is owned by those who follow cogent little dictates and fashions—the keystones to access, success, and a full life. In CapCity, being a fastidious and elegant dresser opens eyes, doors and invitation lists. On a comparative basis, Townies are sartorially superior and certainly rank with the world's elite in terms of being fashionable. Based on a survey of major fashion outlets in Town, here are the chosen ones (most are well-known in the community, support our Town via charitable activities, buy "locally" whenever feasible, and are workers/doers; they are admired and represent a dynamic force):

WOMEN

Deeda Blair, understands the power of high-fashion, near perfection in detail; always elegant and proper. (On International Best Dressed List)

Aniko Gaal Schott, enjoys updated classics with a twist, is highly individualized with great sense of style and flair.

Monica Greenberg, understands fashion in technical way, likes clothes with drama and swing.

Jacqueline Leland, very chic, European looks,put-together with precision.

Evangeline Bruce, internationally acclaimed for good looks and extraordinary flair; considered very chic. A big Blass and YSL fan.

Nini Ferguson, always elegantly and appropriately dressed, the epitome of sophistication and charm.

Dianne Kay, understands what works perfectly, has overall good taste and a neatly "seasoned" look.

Marion Rosenthal, conservative elegance, regal looking, the classic advocate of superb taste in fashion.

Sarah Gewirz, displays excellence in selecting her wardrobe, wears clothes regally and has a willowy appearance.

Kay Graham, wears designer fashions beautifully, loves Blass, Oscar de la Renta; gracious in every way.

Other: Among Ladies—best dressed professionals are **Lynda Carter** and

Andrea Mitchell; and, known as fabulously groomed, fastidious and immaculately presented are **Baroness Garnett Stackelberg, Grace Bender, Gahl Burt, JoAnn Mason, Ina Ginsburg, Ruthie Leffall, Sarah Warfield Clark, Elizabeth Dole** (the mistress of understatement) and **Anne Stock. Grega Daly** and **Carol Foley** are generally perfectly turned out with a sublime balance of clothing, jewelry, accessories; **Elizabeth Bagley** presents a striking "head-turner" image of classy chic; **"Bunny" Mellon** (who some years ago spent about $150,000/yr. on fashion) has the most extensive wardrobe of conservative elegance.

The owner of the most hats and shoes is **Renee Kraft.** Owner of the most Bob Mackie gowns is **Alexine Jackson.** Lady with the most coiffed hair is **Ina Ginsburg.** Most *avant garde* dressers are **Norma Kline** and **Novella Samperton.** Lady with the most femininely athletic body (and clothes to match) is **Kathy Valentine.** Owner of the most Chanels, Blass and Ungaros is **Estelle Gelman.**

Dorcas Hardin was the Capital's best dressed retail fashion expert (now retired).

MEN

Leo Daly, wears blazers and formal wear exceptionally well; lean, suave, neatly assembled.

William Webster, urbane, stately looks, great formally or informally, well tailored.

True Davis, international look, great flair, has individual style.

Clem Conger, sophisticated, an advocate of the professional look, always on the mark.

Gordon King, the look of today's Washington; his uniform is Belgian shoes, no socks, white trousers, striped shirt with white collar and sweater (over the shoulder).

Kyle Samperton, typifies Washington in its halcyon day, sporty, tasteful, loves outrageous colors (pink, chartreuse, magenta), the fast-forward look.

J. Carter Brown, refined, sports the "traditional" international look.

Robert Keith Gray, elegantly understated, subdued but classy.

Paul Simon, conservative, strictly business look, clean cut, tight.

John Warner, refined, balanced styles, tends to be formal yet dashing. Always well turned out in town or country.

Marion Smoak, custom-tailored to present a perfect balance of the dashing and debonair.

Robert J. Higdon, immaculately tailored, can pull off any clothing assignment with ease.

William Cafritz, very proper but flexible, a real turn-on in English threads.

George Stephanopoulos, young, with-it look, style-under-pressure (on nominee list for International Best Dressed).

COUPLES

The Arnaud de Borchgraves; internationally stylish, a classy "old guard" look befitting their rich heritage.

The Malcolm Endicott Peabodys, exquisite taste, understand the power of low-key.

The Brice Clagetts, distinguished look, tastefully conservative.

The **Ben Bradlees**, have a "young at heart" look reflective of their zeal in living life to the fullest, both open to new styles, but mainly preppie.

The Brian Bernsteins, classic American looking couple, sensitive, careful about their traditional yet adventurous look.

Peggy and Kenneth Crosby, perfect in protocol and propriety of dress, very fashionable yet disciplined.

The William Seidmans, always appropriately dressed for the occasion, adaptable, fitting, stylish.

Nancy and Rusty Powell, he's dapper, perfectly put together (including a straw hat), she has a tailored, enduring look.

The Leo Dalys, debonair, trim, make every fashion more fashionable.

Sharon and Jay Rockefeller, he's conservative, wears neatly tailored clothing, she prefers contemporary chic styles; both right on the money. Our Town's regal couple, tall, genteel; stylish clothing accentuates their stature.

Also very much up to snuff in a sartorial manner are **Buffy and Bill Cafritz, Ruthie and LaSalle Leffall, Margot and Edmond Howar** and **JoAnn and John Mason**.

These Washingtonians join the illustrious ranks of their counterparts on a global basis. The International Best Dressed List, coordinated by **Eleanor Lambert**, and now in its 55th year, annually selects those who dress exceptionally well. Among the Ladies are: **Princess of Wales, Brooke Astor, China Machado, Jane Dudley, Nina Griscom, Anne McNally** and others. For the men, best dressed winners are: **King Juan Carlos** of Spain, designer **Bijan, Peter Jennings, Paul Newman, Mark Hampton, Count Frederic Chandon, Massimo Ferragamo** and **Paul Wilmot**.

The International Best Dressed List was started in 1940 by fashion promoter Lambert (born in Crawfordsville, IN, daughter of a circus owner) and has been a driving (if not serious) force for stylish people since; through the years fashion editors—Eugenia Sheppard, Diana Vreeland, Ernestine Carter and Hebe Dorsey have been influenced by the list which has included icons like Babe Paley, Gloria Guiness, C.Z. Guest, Slim Keith, Marella Agnelli, Anne Bass, Betsy Bloomingdale, Evangeline Bruce, Denise Hale, Pilar Crespi, Jacqueline de Ribes, Nan Kempner, Helene Rochas, Paloma Picasso, Jacqueline Onassis and Jayne Wrightsman.

· WHO ARE THE MOST SOCIALLY DESIRABLE PEOPLE?

Once you are inside the Circle, the big city becomes a small town. These are the Centri-people: **Liane and Martin Atlas, Catharina and Livingston Biddle, the Malcolm Endicott Peabodys, Pamela Digby Harriman, Douglas and Susan Hurley Bennett, Estelle Gelman, J. Carter Brown,**

Evangeline Bruce, Ruth Buchanan, Peggy Cooper Cafritz, F. Dav
Camalier, Oatsie Charles, Ann and John Fitzpatrick, Katharine Gra
ham, the Ben Bradlees, the Warren Christophers, Letitia Baldrig
Carol and Robert Foley, Bitsey Folger, June and John Hechinger, Pa
Dixson, Wilhelmina and Wallace Holladay, Gogo and Austin Kiplinge
Mary Patterson, the Clayton Fritcheys, the Clement Congers, the Wi
liam Cafritzes, Anne and Elliot Richardson, the Brice Clagetts, John an
Joy Safer, Richard and Hanne Merriman, Carter and Lisa Cafrit
Ambassador and Mrs. Robert Gelbard, Ambassador and Mrs. Alexand
Watson, Carol and Peter Kaplan, Bill and Jan Prutting, Ruth Nob
Groom, the Williamson Stuckleys, Donna and Jack Pfleiger, Caroli
and David Boutte, the Colin Powells, Jorge Carnicero, the Willia
Websters, Mariana and Brandon Grove, Hani and Cheryl Masri, Magg
and James Wimsatt (Administration and Embassy desirables will be pr
sented in another chapter).

In 1990, in its 15th-Anniversary issue, the late much-missed publicatio
Dossier highlighted the "400" in Town -- the "People, the Parties and the Politics
Although much has changed in the years since then, here's a compilation of tho
who made the grade as the elite "400" (note, a few of these listees have gone c
to another world, and many have left Town, so there is built-in inaccura
in the following): Joan Ambrose, Carolyn Amoit, Grace Bender, Sondra Bende
Diane Bernstein, Norman Bernstein, Albert Beveridge, Madzy Beveridge, Di
Beyda, Catharina Biddle, Liv Biddle, Jean Ann Bostwick, Jim Brady, Sus
Brady, Jeannette Brophy, Ray Brophy, Carter Brown, Marnell Bruce, Barba
Burris, Aliki Bryant, Dan Callahan, Giuseppe Cecchi, Mercedes Cecchi, Wa
Chamberlin, Adelaide Clark, Clem Conger, Nina Corby, Judy Cox, Ke
Cushenberry, Sally Davidson, Trudy Davis, David Deckelbaum, Barbara
Franceaux, Marion Denby, Dale Denton, Jill Denton, Evelyn DiBona, Mart
Lyn Dippell, Roselyn Epps, Jean Fangboner, Bud Fantle, Gerry Fantle, Mar
Feinstein, Adrienne Arsht Feldman, George Ferris, Nancy Ferris, Linda Fisk, B
Fitzgerald, Sally Fogarty, Bitsy Folger, Neal Fox, Jedy Frank, Gerald Freed, Ca
Freeman, Susan Fuge, Morty Funger, Norma Lee Funger, Bernard Gewi
Alma Gildenhorn, Melody Gilsey, Ina Ginsburg, Herbert Haft, Gloria Ha
Joan Harlan, Stephen Harlan, Sara Hayes, Theo Hayes, John Heching
June Hechinger, Joe Hennage, June Hennage, Frankie Hewitt, Gra
Hobelman, Cheray Hodges, Luther Hodges, Ed Hoffman, Billie Hollada
Pam Howar, Ray Howar, Marta Istomin, Paula Jeffries, Edna Jones, R
Judd, Alan Kay, Dianne Kay, Gil Kinney, Susan Koehler, Bob Kogc
Arlene Kogod, David Lloyd Kreeger, Dorothy Lapadula, LaSalle Leffa
Ruthie Leffall, Malinda Lindsay, Ken Luchs, Susan Luchs, Mary A
Lundgren, Clark MacGregor, Virginia Mars, JoAnn Mason, John Maso
Julia Mailliard, Marlene Malek, Donna Marriott, Cathy Martens, Ceci
McGhee, George McGhee, Bill McSweeny, Dorothy McSweeny, Han
Merriman, Maggie Miller, Skippy Miller, Beth Montgomery, Stephen Mo

gomery, Sally Nevius, Mollie Ottina, Betty Lou Ourisman, Mandy Ourisman, Marjorie Parker, Jackie Pendleton, Jennifer Phillips, Laughlin Phillips, Bob Pincus, Tanya Potter, Lydia Preston, Kelley Proxmire, Lisa Pumphrey, Carrie Queenan, Joan Quigley, Anne Richardson, Sharon Percy Rockefeller, Beth Rocks, Evie Rooney, Nancy Rosebush, Bob Rosenthal, Marion Rosenthal, Marta Ross, John Safer, Joy Safer, Novella Samperton, Lolo Sarnoff, Pat Schieffer, Nina Selin, Gretchen Poston, Jerry Principato, Marjorie Principato, Bill Quinn, Bette Quinn, Becky Rogers, Paul Rogers, Michele Rouse, Randy Rouse, Carl Rowan, Vivien Rowan, Diane Sappenfield, Aniko and Nash Schott, Ron Sappenfield, Farol Seretean, Jan Shepard, Taz Shepard, Francie Smoak, Joe Smoak, Francis Spalding, Sigrid Spalding, Gaby Steers, Newton Steers, Deecy Stephens, Connie Valanos, Helen Valanos, Ann Vanderpool, Wynant Vanderpool, Julia Walsh, Bennetta Washington, Walter Washington, Bob Washington, Nola Washington, Frankie Welch, Rose Saul Zalles, Evelyn Zlotnick, Sidney Zlotnick, Secretary of the Treasury Jim Baker, Susan Baker, Secretary of Commerce Malcolm Baldrige, Midge Baldrige, Secretary of Education William Bennett, Elayne Bennett, Senator Lloyd Bentsen, B.A. Bentsen, Senator Albert Gore, Tipper Gore, Senator Fritz Hollings, Peatsy Hollings, Marine Commandant P.X. Kelley, Barbara Kelley, Senator Paul Laxalt, Carol Laxalt, Attorney General Ed Meese, Ursula Meese, Congressman Bill Nelson, Grace Nelson, Senator Sam Nunn, Colleen Nunn, Senator Larry Pressler, Harriet Pressler, White House Chief of Staff Don Regan, Ann Regan, Chief of Protocol Lucky Roosevelt, Archie Roosevelt, Senator Ted Stevens, Cathy Stevens, Congressman Guy Vander Jagt, Carol Vander Jagt, Ambassador Dan Terra, Judy Terra, Senator Malcolm Wallop, French Wallop, Senator John Warner, Secretary of Defense Cap Weinberger, Jane Weinberger, USIA Director Charlie Wick, Mary Jane Wick, Congressman Sidney Yates, Adeline Yates, Senator Ed Zorinsky, Cece Zorinsky, Davis Camalier, Roberta Freer, Webb Hayes IV, Knight Kiplinger, Todd Kiplinger, Donna Lefeve, Nancy Lurton, Christopher van Roijen, Swedish Ambassador Wilhelm Wachtmeister, Countess Ulla Wachtmeister, Cypriot Ambassador Andrew Jacovides, Pam Jacovides, Turkish Ambassador Sukru Elekdag, Ayla Elekdag, Italian Ambassador Rinaldo Petrignani, Anne Petrignani, Austrian Ambassador Thomsa Klestil, Edith Klestil, Greek Ambassador George Papoulias, Emily Papoulias, Netherlands Ambassador Richard Fein, Monique Fein, Australian Ambassador Rawdon Dalrymple, Ross Elizabeth Dalrymple, French Ambassador Emmanuel de Margerie, Helen de Margerie, Penny Abramson, Barby Allbritton, Joe Allbritton, Stuart Bernstein, Wilma Bernstein, Sally Chapoton, Esther Coopersmith, Estelle Gelman, Barbara Gordon, Pamela Harriman, Margaret Hodges, Alexine Jackson, Penne Korth, Bob Linowes, Millie Mailliard, Betty May, Ernie May, Audrey Mars, Abe Pollin, Irene Pollin, Nancy Shipley, Jane Sloat, George and Cecilia McGhee, Ken and Susan Luchs, Susan Fuge, James Wyngaarden, Mary Wilkens, Frankie Welch,

Walter Heacock, Carol Kaplan, David Beal, Helene de Margerie, Steve Martindale, Kelley Proxmire, Kyle Samperton, Penni Alison, Val Cook, Laurie Firestone, Suzy Minkoff, Gerald Freed, Katherine Beall, Everet Hutchinson, Molly Mitchell, Mary Heron, Davis Camalier, Muffie Potter Nakamura Kanzaburo, Al Haig, Helga Orfila, Bill Hunter, Chris Hunter, We and Karen Williams, Leni Muller, Marshall Coyne, Barbara Luter, Bes Abel, Renee and Wyatt Stewart III. (Note: this list aptly demonstrates how short is the "Limelight Longevity" of most Washingtonians—with an ever evolving administration, business fortunes/misfortunes and the general ca prices of life, no one is guaranteed much time in grade as a leader/VIP celebrity/winner!)

15. **WHAT IS THE SIGNIFICANCE OF THE "GREEN BOOK" IN WASHINGTON?**

The Social List of Washington, D.C. has, since 1930, been the instru ment by which prominent Washingtonians are given their social validity About 400 pages of Capitol Hill, Diplomatic Corps, Organization of th American States, administration and federal officials, and Social personage are listed (some 5,200 names); 111 pages of advertising and miscellaneou dignitary listings, protocol procedures and maiden names flesh out the 51 page Green Book (it has a green suede cover) which is priced at $68 annuall to subscribers (some 6,000 personages). Published by Thomas J. Murray i Kensington, MD each fall, a Green Book listing only identifies names c listed, maiden name of spouse and children's names plus address and phon number. To the CapCity climber, the book is indispensable; it is a caree guide and a phone book, although many dwellers prefer not to be liste simply because it publicizes/categorizes them.

A sample (and fictitious) listing follows:

MORNINGSTAR, Mr. and Mrs. James Peter
(Carol Anne Sheen)
"   **Mr. James Peter, Jr.** - at
Middlesex
3443 Hawthorne Street   (16)
202-111-2222
and
"Casa Jennings"
Holly Lane
Remsenburg, NY 11960
(516) 325-1234

By way of contrast, the *Social Register* (published by Forbes Ente prises) lists 28,000 names, addresses, phone numbers, alma maters, cl

24

memberships and yacht locations of leaders in 12 US cities. It was founded in 1912 by Louis Keller and became the property of the late Malcolm Forbes in '76. It comes out each November at a cost of $85/copy.

The *Social-Index Directory* of Palm Beach, FL and the Bahamas lists 1,908 residents—names, addresses (at various homes), clubs, colleges, offspring and yachts or airplanes. It has 50 pages of ads, lists of officers at the major clubs and organizations, a separate section on maiden names and a social calendar for the year. October publication at $50/copy.

16. WHO, IN THE GREEN BOOK, HAS THE MOST HOMES AWAY FROM HOME?

The Honorable and Mrs. Charles A. Camalier, Jr. list four homes (in Bethany Beach, DE; Montross, VA; Willsboro, NY; Naples, FL), in addition to their local abode on Belmart Road in Potomac. The Camaliers also have the lengthiest listing in the Green Book — three inches of detailed copy.

The **longest** letterman in the book is **Von Streeruwitz** (14 letters) versus others with slightly fewer digits such as Van Rensselaer, Hollingsworth and Crittenberger. (Note: another 14-letter name—Choumenkovitch, Miss Milena—also appears).

The **shortest** name award goes to a number of three-letter names like May, Law, Kay, Cox, Poe, Lee, Cox and others.

The family listed as having the **most children** is **Mr. and Mrs. Thomas Augustine Nolan, Jr.** with seven offspring (Miss Martha Hogentogler, Mr. Thomas Augustine, III, Mr. William Chester, Mr. Peter David, Mr. Matthew Worthington, Mr. James Robertson and Mr. Michael Gormley).

(Note: almost all listings in the Green Book are of residents in the NW section of Town.)

17. WHO ARE THE CAPITAL'S MOST ELIGIBLE SINGLES?

Nothing succeeds like address, and all these single Washingtonians have the proper topography:

Steve Wyatt, Congressman Charles Wilson, Senators John Warner and Chris Dodd, Joseph Tydings, Robert Early, Steve Stricklan, John Damgard, Chris van Roijen, George Stephanopoulos, Michael Winston, Gerson Nardlinger, Samuel Verts, J. Carter Brown, Patrick Daly, Ken Riegle, Randy Major, Bob Corby, Armando Chardiet, John Gerstenfeld, Sonny Montgomery, Sydney Epstein, Peter Jacobs, Jay Dixson, Duncan Dixson, Al Friendly, Boyden Gray, Preston Brown, Jamie Gore, Richard Haase and Franklyn de Marco.

Eligible Ladies include: Giselle Thebege, Nini Ferguson, Vicki Bagley, Mary Frances Smoak, Cheryl O'Donnell, Joan Nichols, Amy Dresh, Roberta Zoritelli, Pat Dixson, Shawn Bernhardt, Linda Hahn, Sassy St. Louis, Lindsey Stroud, Nancy Bagley, Jill Gore, Kate Maginnes, Tandy Dickinson and Virginia Warner.

18. WHAT ARE SOME OF THE MOST ENDURING MARRIAGES IN TOWN?

Richard and Lois England (Hechinger Company; supporters of Goodwill Industries and American Red Cross);

John and June Hechinger (UN Representative and general gooddoers, married in 1947);

Austin and Gogo Kiplinger (Kiplinger Letter and Foundation, and National Symphony);

Bill and Donna Marriott (hotels, multi-charities);

Elliot and Anne Richardson (presidential favorites and world travelers);

Robert and Letitia Hollensteiner (scholarship, diplomacy, etiquette, romance and motion);

Jack and Mary Margaret Valenti (czars of filmdom and many charitable interests);

Fred and Marlene Malek (originals, activists, uncommon charity to common causes);

Stuart and Wilma Bernstein (munificent and outgoing, friends to all);

Bob and Arlene Gelbard (great sense of civic responsibility in/out of government);

James and Maggie Wimsatt (long-time supporters of good causes and observers of the social circuit);

Paul and Becky Rogers (a zeal for democratic representation and devotion to family, country and causes);

Jack and Carey Miller (Nixon's former attorney and his Lady living the good life);

Bill and Aliki Bryant (all-around Town supporters and friends of the elite):

Ray and Jeanette Brophy (involved in any number of important causes, always there when needed).

19. WHAT WASHINGTONIANS HAVE NICKNAMES?

Appellations are important in Town; often, as the name goes, so goes the person. Here are a few titillating designations: Ann "Bitsey" Stone, Selwa "Lucky" Roosevelt, William "Wild Bill" Regardie, Margaret "Maggie" Wimsatt, Letitia "Tish" Baldrige, Martha "Stormy" Byorum, Mildred "Brownie" McLean, Byron "Whizzer" White, Caspar "Cap" Weinberger, Antonin "Nino" Scalia, Mrs. Robert "Oatsie" Charles, Mandell "Mandy" Ourisman, Corinne "Cokie" Roberts, Mary Louise "Go Go" Kiplinger, Anita Marie "Buffy" Cafritz, Christopher "Kit" Bond, Wiley "Buckie" Buchanan, Jr., Mabel "Muffie" Brandon, Earl A. "Rusty" Powell III, Benjamin "Benjy" Bradlee, Tony "Bear" Bradlee, Pierre "Plucky" Salinger, Frederick "Frecky" Vreeland, Endicott "Chub" Peabody, John "Buck" Chapotan, Mrs. Joe "Barby" Allbritton, Gabriele "Gabi" Steers, Mrs. Hale "Lindy" Boggs,

Mrs. Ernest "Buffie" Ives, Edward "Ted" Kennedy, Charles "Chuck" Percy, Mrs. George "Obie" Shultz, Tammenons "Tommy" Bakker, Mrs. Hans "Baby" Thomsen, Mrs. James "Candy" Van Alen, Mrs. William "Kitsy" Westmoreland, Thomas "Tip" O'Neill, Mrs. Paul "Bunny" Mellon, Dan "Rosty" Rostenkowski and Ernest "Fritz" Hollings.

20. WHAT ARE THE MAIDEN NAMES OF WASHINGTON'S MOST PROMINENT WOMEN?

ACHESON, Mrs. Dean	(Alice Stanley)
ADAIR, Mrs. E. Ross	(Marian Wood)
ADAMS, Mrs. Robert	(Ruth Salzman)
ALBRIGHT, Mrs. Madeleine	(Madeleine Jana Korbel)
ALLBRITTON, Mrs. Joe Lewis	(Barbara Jean Balfanz)
ALSOP, Mrs. Susan Mary	(Susan Mary Jay)
AUCHINCLOSS, Mrs. John Winthrop	(Audrey Maynard)
BAKER, Mrs. Howard H.	(Joy Dirksen)
BAKER, Mrs. James A.	(Winston-Susan Garrett)
BERNSTEIN, Mrs. Stuart Alan	(Wilma Janice Estrin)
BIDDLE, Mrs. Livingston Ludlow	(Catharina vanBeek Baart)
BILLINGTON, Mrs. James Hadley	(Marjorie Anne Brennan)
BORK, Mrs. Robert Heron	(Mary Ellen Pohl)
BRENNAN, Mrs. William Joseph	(Mary Walter Fowler)
BRINKLEY, Mrs. David	(Adolph-Susan Benfer)
BRUCE, Mrs. David K. E.	(Evangeline Bell)
CAFRITZ, Mrs. William Norman	(Wilkes-Anitamarie Boffa)
CALIFANO, Mrs. Joseph A.	(Byers-Hilary Paley)
CHAPOTON, Mrs. John Edgar	(Sarah Mason Eastham)
CHARLES, Mrs. Robert Horne	(Leiter-Marion Saffold Oates)
CHENEY, Mrs. Lynne V.	(Lynne Vincent)
CLAGETT, Mrs. Brice McAdoo	(Knop-Diana Wharton Sinkler)
CLARK, Mrs. Deena	(R. Constandina Speliakos)
CLIFFORD, Mrs. Clark McAdams	(Margery Pepperrell Kimball)
CONGER, Mrs. Clement Ellis	(Lianne B. Hopkins)
COOPERSMITH, Mrs. Jack	(Esther Lipsen)
deBORCHGRAVE, Mrs. Arnaud	(Alexandra Darielle Villard)
FRITCHEY, Mrs. Clayton	(Wisner-Mary Ellis Knowles)
GEWIRZ, Mrs. Bernard Samuel	(Sarah Ruth Myers)
GRAEBER, Mrs. George Kenneth	(Betty Beale)
GRAHAM, Mrs. Katharine	(Katharine Meyer)
HAIG, Mrs. Alexander Meigs	(Patricia Antoinette Fox)
HALABY, Mrs. Najeeb Elias	(Jane Allison Coates)
HARRIMAN, Mrs. W. Averell	(Hayward-Churchill-Pamela Beryl Digby)
HECKLER, Honorable Margaret M.	(Margaret Mary O'Shaughnessy)

HERTER, Mrs. Christian A.	(Cameron-Catherine Hooker)
HOLLADAY, Mrs. Wallace Fitzhugh	(Wilhelmina Cole)
HOLLENSTEINER, Mrs. Robert	(Letitia Baldrige)
IKARD, Mrs. Frank Nevill	(Brumley-Jayne Keegan)
JACKSON, Mrs. Aaron Gordon	(Helen Alexine Clement)
KELSO, Mrs. Frank B.	(Landess McCown)
KIPLINGER, Mrs. Austin Huntington	(Mary Louise Cobb)
KORTH, Mrs. Fritz-Alan	(Penne Ann Percy)
KRAFT, Mrs. Alvin A.	(Renee Zlotnick)
KREEGER, Mrs. David Lloyd	(Carmen Felicia Matanzo y Jaramillo)
LAXALT, Mrs. Paul	(Carol Bernardini)
MAILLIARD, Mrs. William S.	(C. Millicent Fox)
MARRIOTT, Mrs. John Willard	(Donna Rae Garff)
MARS, Mrs. Forrest E.	(Deborah Adair Clarke)
MELLON, Mrs. Paul	(Lloyd-Rachel Lambert)
MORGAN, Mrs. Edward Pierpont	(Joan N. Norton)
MUDD, Mrs. Roger Harrison	(Emma Jeanne Spears)
MULDOON, Mrs. Joseph A.	(Caroline Curtis)
MUSKIE, Mrs. Edmund S.	(Jane F. Gray)
OATES, Mrs. Hugh Franklin, Jr.	(Mary Katharine Withers)
OBOLENSKY, Mrs. Alexis N.	(Selene Rountree-Smith)
PENNINGTON, Mrs. William Carter	(Marcia Moss Lewis)
PHILLIPS, Mrs. Laughlin	(Cafritz-Jennifer Stats)
PILLSBURY, Mrs. Philip Winston, Jr.	(Caroline Elizabeth Hannaford)
POWELL, Mrs. Lewis Franklin, Jr.	(Josephine Pierce Rucker)
REED, Mrs. Joseph Verner	(Marie M. Byers)
REHNQUIST, Mrs. William Hubbs	(Natalie Ann Cornell)
REYNOLDS, Mrs. Percival Livingston, Jr.	(Quinn-Merrilyn Bardes)
RICHARDSON, Mrs. Elliot Lee	(Anne Francis Hazard)
ROGERS, Mrs. William D.	(Suzanne Rochford)
ROOSEVELT, Mrs. Archibald Bulloch	(Selwa Carmen Showker)
SAFER, Mrs. John	(Scott-Joy Sherin)
SAFIRE, Mrs. William	(Helene Julius)
SARNOFF, Mrs. Stanley Jay	(Lili-Charlotte Dreyfus)
SCALI, Mrs. John Alfred	(Denise Yolande St. Germain)
SCALIA, Mrs. Antonin	(Maureen McCarthy)
SCHLESINGER, Mrs. James Rodney	(Rachel Mellinger)
SCHOTT, Mrs. Nash Whitney	(Aniko Gaal)
SEIDMAN, Mrs. Lewis William	(Sarah Marshall Berry)
SHOUSE, Mrs. Jouett	(Dodd-Catherine Filene)
SHRIVER, Mrs. Robert Sargent, Jr.	(Eunice Kennedy)
SIDEY, Mrs. Hugh S.	(Anne Trowbridge)
SLOAT, Mrs. Jonathan Welsh	(DeGraff-Jane Eva Roberts)
SMOAK, Mrs. Marion H.	(Mary Frances Meister)

SPENCER, Mrs. Samuel	(Byrne-June Beakes)
STACKELBERG, Mrs. Constantine	(Gardiner-Garnett Butler)
STRAUSS, Mrs. Robert S.	(Helen Jacobs)
SUTER, Mrs. William K.	(Jeanie Bogart)
TAFT, Mrs. Robert, Jr.	(Joan McKelvy)
THEBERGE, Mrs. James Daniel	(Giselle Fages Repetto)
TROWBRIDGE, Mrs. Alexander Buel, Jr.	(Hutzler-Eleanor Kann)
TYDINGS, Mrs. Joseph Davies	(Keyser-Rosemary Elliot)
UPTON, Mrs. Thomas Graydon	(Ann C. Nash)
VALENTI, Mrs. Jack Joseph	(Mary Margaret Wiley)
van der BURGH, Mrs. Charles E.	(Marielle M. Nijdam)
van ROIJEN, Mrs. Peter Portner	(Beatrice Sterling Frelinghuysen)
VAN SLYCK, Mrs. DeForest	(Katharine Gamble Rogers)
WALSH, Mrs. Thomas Michael	(Montgomery-Julia Curry)
WARNKE, Mrs. Paul Culliton	(Jean Farjeon Rowe)
WEBB, Mrs. James Edwin	(Patsy Aiken Douglas)
WEINBERGER, Mrs. Caspar Willard	(Jane Dalton)
WELCH, Mrs. John J., Jr.	(Louise Patricia Joyce)
WHITE, Mrs. Byron Raymond	(Marion Lloyd Stearns)
WILSON, Mrs. Don Whitman	(Clardy-Patricia Ann Sherrod)
WIMSATT, Mrs. James McSherry	(Margaret Louise Sampson)
ZLOTNICK, Mrs. Sidney Somers	(Evelyn Durez)

1. WHO ARE THE TOWN'S BEST DANCERS?

Alan Simpson (Wyoming Senator and one of the tallest gents in Town at 6'7") moves with the utmost grace (he is also a great M.C.); so do decorator **Bob Waldon**, car merchant **Mandy Ourisman**, Louisiana's **John Breaux**, **Mario di Paolo** of the Beethoven Society, **Herbert H. Haft**, man of many lives; Senator **Orrin Hatch** (Utah), **John Ray**, DC City Councilman-at-large, *Newsweek* columnist **Hugh Sidey, Livingston Biddle, Stuart Bernstein, Sheldon Fantle** (People's Drugs), Dallas oilman **Bill Lee** and TV-legend **Walter Cronkite**.

When matched with the ballroom experts like **Nina Totenberg, Betsy Reid, Colleen Nunn, Donna McLarty, Marcia Carlucci, Betty Beale** and husband **George Graeber, Grace Bender, Barbara Duncan, Melody Gilsey, Mary Richardson, Suzanne Gralow, Sarah Gewirz, Jane De Graffe Sloat, Susan Brinkley, Jacqueline Leland, Gloria Haft, Deborah Siebert, Ellen Proxmire, Kate Michelman, Pat Schroeder, Aniko Gaal Schott, Elizabeth Bagley, Elsie Hillman**, and naturally, **Pamela Harriman**, dance cards will be joyfully filled.

Probably still dancing, wherever they are, are some of the deceased ballroom legends of the era: Jack Kennedy, Bobby Kennedy, Edward Bennett Williams, Lyndon Johnson and David Lloyd Kreeger (a violinist of some repute and Benny Goodman devotee).

22. WHO SPORTED THE MOST DISTINGUISHED MOUSTACHE IN RECENT WASHINGTON HISTORY?

In a league by himself for several decades, was Statesman **Dea**
Acheson, who distinguished himself with the Truman Administration i
many ways and in many roles (mostly as Secretary of State). His statel
presence (and credentials from Groton, Harvard, Wall Street and the Easter
Establishment) embellished by a veddy anglo-moustache, gave him ju
enough pizzazz to confront any friend or foe. He will always have a historic
lock on "most memorable moustache" of the times. (His wife — Alice — sti
lives on Cathedral Ave. in the District).

Tom Dewey tried hard to make his upper lip look as stern as his rigorou
demeanor, but somehow it didn't project the right message; **Walter Cronki**
was one of TV's first moustached anchors, and, in his case, it all cam
together perfectly (his visage as he announced the death of JFK on TV wi
always be one of the era's most poignant visual memories).

23. WHO IS WASHINGTON'S OLDEST, MOST ENERGETIC AND VISIBLE RESIDENT?

As intrepid and dynamic as human beings come, **Catherine Filene Shou**
(somewhere in the mid-90s) zips around Town spreading good will and espou
ing causes with a zeal unmatched; she is a tableau of "firsts"—first woma
appointed to the DNC (from Massachusettes), first woman to receive a Maste
from Harvard in Education, first Lady of many charities, first woman to institu
a job training program at a federal prison (the first such program for women) an
of course, the first woman to have the vision and resources to help found Wc
Trap, the first national park devoted to the arts (in '66, she donated her Vienn
VA farm to Uncle Sam). She is one of the few women in the US to be honore
with the Medal of Freedom (from President Ford in '77). She is currently involv
with—on the board of, or just promoting—Kennedy Center, Marymount Cc
lege, the Washington Opera and Wolf Trap Foundation Associates.

24. WHAT IS WASHINGTON CLASS?

Any man who wears a plaid suit with a striped shirt, checked tie ai
polka-dotted handkerchief–and looks great–has CLASS (especially wh
most guys spend 20 minutes picking the wrong tie). It's indefinable, but i
there.

In a Town where Class abounds, it's easier to see it than define it; easi
to sense Class than understand it; and it's quite impossible to clone it, imita
it or get it by osmosis. CLASS is in a Class by itself.

Here's what true Washington CLASS is:

CLASS never makes excuses. It takes its hits, learns from experience ai
is always ready for the next confrontation.

CLASS is very considerate of others. It knows that good manners nothing more than a series of petty sacrifices, small "gives" in anticipation of modest receipts.

CLASS can walk with kings and keep its virtue, and talk with the masses via a common touch that reaches everyone.

CLASS bespeaks an aristocracy that has nothing to do with lineage or wealth. The most affluent blue-blood can be devoid of Class while the descendant of an Irish fisherman may ooze Class from every pore.

CLASS knows whether to congratulate or to commiserate in every situtation; there is never a loss for words nor is there any automatic rejoinder. Class is basically quiet, soft, sure.

CLASS knows you can never abuse the system without some form of punishment; there are no miracles, and the Marines aren't coming.

CLASS never runs scared. It is sure-footed and confident in the knowledge that you can meet life head on and handle whatever comes along.

CLASS regards the "New Tycoonery" with disdain, and knows that little monkeys follow big apes without much analysis; thereby condoning greed and assuring ostracism for all.

CLASS never tries to build itself up by totaling others; Class is already up and does not strive to look better by making others look worse.

CLASS understands that people who have had the same surgery like to compare scars; and keeps its distance from private dalliances.

CLASS realizes that there is no such thing as a do-it-yourself Rex Harrison Kit; and works at self-perfection rather than perfecting the style of others.

CLASS refutes the concept that life is a tragedy wherein we sit as spectators awhile, then act out our own part in it. Class believes a person is what he/she does.

CLASS realizes that there are no draws in games of power.

CLASS is aware of (but protests) the normal sequence in most projects; Exultation; Disenchantment; Confusion; Search for the guilty; Punishment of the innocent; Distinction for the uninvolved.

CLASS realizes that the higher you climb the pyramid the more southern exposure you have.

CLASS knows there is no better way to flaunt power than to appear equal when dealing with inferiors.

CLASS recognizes that it isn't proper to serve five o'clock tea at all hours.

CLASS understands that the more you complain, the longer God lets you live.

CLASS assumes that it is wasted energy to have a battle of wits with an unarmed person.

CLASS recognizes a certain truism in the credo of Napoleon: "My power is dependent on my glory, and my glory on my victories. My power would fall if I did not base it on still more glory and still more victories.

Conquest made me what I am; conquest alone can keep me there." Class
however, predicates life on victory for humankind, not victories over it.

CLASS knows that money doesn't talk, it swears!

Finally, CLASS appreciates the fact that this life kneels before the next

Altruist, humanitarian, best friend to the world—Margaret Hodges.

CHAPTER II

SOCIOLOGY, STATUS & SAVOIR FAIRE
(Spirit, Style & Success)

Photo: J.R. Black

Mrs. William McCormick "Deeda" Blair, Jr.—elegant, elysian, elitist.

25. WHO ARE WASHINGTON'S ELITISTS?

Some of the Old Dukes, Grand Dames, Boulevardiers and Eterna Winners always seem to be in style to flash their elite demeanors in all the right places. In this category and on the scene today are:

Power financier **John Safer**; Demo/scholar **Patrick Moynihan**; warrior/statesman **Colin Powell**; Lady of etiquette and world-class social arbiter **Letitia Baldrige**; **William Brennan**, liberalist super-judge; **Paul Volcker** mighty persuasive (when in Town) even as a retiree from the FRB; **Elizabeth** and **Robert Dole**, always upfront for their convictions and always taken seriously; **Sally Quinn**, who almost matches Big Ben for longevity and clout; dynamic dynasties a la the **Mars**, **Grahams**, and **Marriotts**; mogul performing arts master **James Wolfensohn**; man-about-the-universe **True Davis Jack Kent Cooke**, undeniably a master at the money game; **Lucky Roosevelt** former and always Chief of Protocol; grande dame **Ella Poe Burlington** publisher and former NATO official **Philip Merrill; Bunny** and **Paul Mellon** have the franchise on charm and civility; former Defense chief **Harold Brown** classic Cave Dwellers **Amy** and **Huntington Block**, Librarian/Congress **James Billington** and **Marjorie** and philanthropists **Mary** and **Sidney Dillon Ripley**

Elitists, too, in the conduct of their professional and personal lives are **Warren Christopher**, many things to many people, currently CEO of State **MacNeil/Lehrer**, without peer in clarity of communication; **Cokie Roberts**, "Hill's Angel" and straight, incisive media spokeslady; **John McLaughlin**, ponderous (and righteous) talkshow power; **George Bush**, by whatever barometer, still kingly and honorable; **C. Boyden Gray**, ethic guru, lawyer and Town patrician; **Robert Strauss**, former USSR/US conduit, current power-player everywhere; **Senator Lloyd Bentsen**, long-time popular federal honcho, now TreasSec; **William Rehnquist**, mega-conservative Chief Justice, forever proper and reserved; **Prince Bandar bin Sultan al-Saud**, Saudi Arabia connection, likable, wheeler-dealer of the first magnitude; **Bob Woodward**, journalist, author, always first with the most in reporting; **Joseph Moakley**, House Rules Committeeman from Massachusetts, a real mover/shaker on the floor.

26. WHO ARE THE CAPITAL'S MOST POPULAR PERSONALITIES?

Once the game is over, the king and the pawn go back into the same box but while the game is being played, some people give it such life-force that they automatically rise to the top. Among our most popular Townies are mega-athlete **Cal Ripken**, columnists **George Will** and **Dave Barry**, reporters **Bob Woodward** and **David Broder**, writers **Tony Kornheiser** and **Ton Boswell**, civil rights man and top lawyer **Vernon Jordan**, architect **Leo Daly**, **George Stevens**, co-chair American Film Institute, author and talk show habitue **Kitty Kelley**, Doonesbury, Ladies Who Lunch **Diana McLellan**, **Susan Watters** and **Maureen Dodd**, legend **"Tip" O'Neil** promoter **Abe Pollin**, negotiator **Tommy Boggs**, society doctor **Ronal**

Paul, Townie's **Dick** and **Lynne Cheney,** policy expert **Strobe Talbott,** Fellows program boss **Brooke Shearer, Bob Strauss** of USSR and consultant fame, journalist and intellect **Tim Russert,** communicator **Johnny Apple,** General **Colin Powell,** restorer/diplomat **Clem Conger,** Senators **Simpson, Dodd, Kennedy, Rockefeller, Bradley, Bond** and **Warner,** do-gooders **Buffy** and **Bill Cafritz, Oatsie Charles, Val Cook,** lawyer **Lloyd Cutler,** all-around good guy **George McGovern,** Kennedy Center founder **Roger Stevens,** Canada Ambassador **John G.D. de Chastelain** and **Mary Ann,** *Post* publisher **Donald Graham,** Smithsonian secretary **Robert McCormick Adams,** French Ambassador **Jacques Andreani** and **Donatella, Sir Robin Renwick,** Ambassador from Great Britain and **Lady Annie Renwick,** VIPs **Sargent** and **Eunice Kennedy Shriver,** timeless **Fritz** and **Peatsy Hollings,** egghead **Norman Ornstein,** comm/consultants **Ed** and **Sherrie Rollins,** humorist **Art Buchwald,** commentator and sage **David Brinkley** and **Susan,** and former Marine top gun **P.X. Kelley.**

7. **WHO ARE THE MOST FORMIDABLE "COMMUNICATORS" IN TOWN?**

FDR in one of his classic quips noted — "Why should two bald men fight over a comb?" — that type of acute observation made him one of the great mass communicators of our time; **JFK** hit the heartbeat of Americans, too, and in his time (especially after the televised debates with Nixon in '60) delivered some immortal lines.

Ronald Reagan was the perfect #10 in the '80s scoring with every argument; his Hollywood background gave him the showmanship and aplomb to face, and face down, any and all audiences. **Clinton** is a master speaker.

On the chicken dinner circuit today are a number of convincing orators: **Ted Kennedy** and **Patrick Moynihan** offer believable and compelling copy; **Dick Cheney** has that fresh can't-tell-a-lie directness; **Colin Powell** dares listeners to challenge him in a soft, authoritative way; **Mario Cuomo** masters words and nuances and powers forward with glibness; **Jim Baker** carries a verbal tune well with logical and pragmatic offerings; **Jesse Jackson** has a certain rhythm in his dialogue that gets affirmative nods; **Pat Schroeder** scores with sincerity and credibility; **Dick Gephardt** gets across effectively with a boyish exuberance as does **Les Aspin; Jack Kemp** projects an image of substance and charisma; **Pat Buchanan** is so firm in his convictions that people have no chance to be dissuaded; socialites **Pam Harriman** and **Georgette Mosbacher** (ex-Townie) beguile and charm and court and cajole audiences (from one to 100) to the point of surrender; and **Bill** and **Buffy Cafritz** present the perfect double-punch in their salesmanship.

Among other highly-articulate motivators in Town are: political strategists **Mary Matalin** and **James Carville, David Gergen** (communication coach to the lofty), columnist/commentator **Michael Kinsley,** *Nightline* anchor **Ted Koppel,** C&P Telephone boss **Delano Lewis,** broadcasters **Al**

Hunt and **Judy Woodruff**, Hoya leader **Leo O'Donovan**, film produce **Gerald Rafshoon**, Attorney General **Janet Reno**, film impresario **Jac Valenti** and *US News* newsmaker **Mortimer Zuckerman**.

28. WHO ARE CONSIDERED THE TOWN'S FOREMOST ACTIONARIES?

Like the Nike ad message — "Just Do It!" — an actionary use locomotion to satisfy the demands of any job, assignment or project. Friend clients, suppliers, anybody within earshot are drafted and used to fill th manpower requirements. The thrust is to consummate, quickly and effec tively, whatever challenge awaits.

Among the top-flight "Do It" people in Town are: Crystal City's **Rober Smith**; **Jack Valenti**, czar of motion pictures; *Post* publisher **Dona Graham**; jock enthusiast **Jack Kent Cooke**; racehorse and art buff **Jo Allbritton**; KPMG Peat Warwick's DC boss **Joseph Ball**; art lovers **Rober** and **Louisa Deumling**; all-arounders **John** and **Debbie Dingell**; the one-an only **Kay Shouse**; DC's pontiff equivalent **Father James Cardinal Hicke** local developer **Stuart Bernstein**; lawyer/activist **Joe Rauh**; National Th ater prexy **Donn B. Murphy**; telecaster **Roger Mudd**; celebrity restaurate **Duke Zeibert**; humankind supporter **Ethel Kennedy**; homerun hitter/lobb ist **Tommy Boggs**; the **Ben Bradlees**, scribes; lawyer/financier **James W Jones**; Howard U. CEO **Franklyn Jennifer**; WETA's **Sharon Rockefelle** Avenel community developer **Anthony Natelli**; **Calvin Cafritz**, Found tion-eleemosynary to the tune of several million/annum; **Pat Dixson**, re estate expert; **James Wolfensohn**, highly mobile Kennedy Center Chai man; Smithsonian **Robert McCormick Adams**; radio personality **B Mayhugh**; resurrector of stately conditions **Clem Conger**; **Eunice Shrive** relentless archangel, and general luminaries **Mark Leland, Maurice Tobi** Mayor **Sharon Pratt Kelly,** the **Bruce Babbitts** and **Margaret Hodges**.

29. WHO HAVE THE CHOICEST SEATS ON OPENING NIGHT AT THE NATIONAL THEATER?

Sociologists have a ball trying to codify a pecking order for first nighte at the National Theater; there is no formalized seating arrangement, but, always, a certain authority quotient is visible to astute observers. Here generally who rates the best upholstery:

Naturally the Prez and his entourage have a box that commands viewin and being viewed; the Secretary of State rates orchestra, a few rows bac ditto for top Embassy Chiefs (most notably the British and USSR Ambass dors); the boys from the Shubert Organization (**Bernie Jacobs**, president an **Gerald Schoenfeld**, chairman) aren't likely to sit in Row W; visitin producers, scribes, directors, theater personalities are presented with prim seats as a *quid pro quo*; steadies like Senators **Kennedy, Dodd, Bradle Hatch, Laxalt** (ex) and **Congressmen Downey, Jones, Markey** get upfro treatment; critics (**Hap Erstein** and **Ms. Lloyd Rose**), occupy similar Row G seats on opposite aisles since they competitively vie for best-read reviews; other media hitters like **Kay Graham, Hodding Carter, Chris Wallace, Ann Compton, David Brinkley, Judy Woodruff** and **Al Hunt, Jim Lehrer** and **Robert MacNeil** don't need opera glasses to catch the action from their vantage point/seats. Rounding out the select seating are a few theater professionals (**Frankie Hewitt**, Ford Theater; **Martin Feinstein,** Washington Opera; **John B. Adams**, Chairman, and **Donn B. Murphy**, President, National Theater Corporation). Often humorist **Mark Russell** plops down in Row D to get new material from a Justice of the Supreme Court (**Sandra Day O'Connor** is a frequent attendee) or member of Congress.

30. WHAT ARE THE MOST SIGNIFICANT SOCIAL STATUS SYMBOLS IN WASHINGTON?

Results have a way of informing the world much better than words; these possessions are a function of results:

* Having homes in Washington, Switzerland, Palm Beach, an apartment on Park Avenue, and summer residences in the Hamptons and Nantucket (and maybe a ranch in Montana).

* Donating a million dollars to a charity anonymously.

* Belonging to the prestigious clubs during the winter plus similar clubs in the appropriate summer locations.

* Driving a Range Rover in addition to owning a Rolls, Ferrari, Jaguar convertible and a Honda Accura.

* Wearing the most expensive "tiara" to the International Red Cross Ball in Palm Beach.

* Having a household staff of at least six live-ins.

* Owning your own stable of polo ponies.

* Wearing a 15 ct. diamond ring while playing tennis.

* Having your own five-star chef.

* Wearing ordinary "blue jeans" with a $3,000 sport coat.

* Hosting a dinner party with many celebrities in attendance and not inviting or informing the press.

* Buying only the couture collections of important designers.

* Chairing the most balls of the season.

31. WHO IS THE CAPITAL'S MOST CELEBRATED BUSINESSWOMAN (EVEN IN RETIREMENT)?

On a no-question, no-discussion, no-doubt basis, **Katharine Graham** is the area's most celebrated businesswoman, and maybe, most celebrated every other kind of woman.

Upon the death of her publishing husband (Philip Graham) at age 46 she joined the working-person ranks and steadily, through either her ruthless and imperious nature (as implied in the recent book — *Power, Privilege, and the*

Post, an unauthorized bio by Carol Felsenthal) or smarts and salesmanship made the *Washington Post* one of the dominant publications in the world. With a top management team, which she assembled over the years, and several smart acquisitions — magazines, cable TV and cellular telephones — the company is positioned to become as successful as it is powerful and ubiquitous (more embassies around the world take the *Post* than any other US newspaper). Although Kay Graham recently named her son Donald as successor, her influence will not quickly fade; wherever she goes, her celebrity focuses on her exploits as a publisher (the publisher most instrumental in ending the political career of then-President Richard Nixon, via Watergate in '74) and her general influence on everything that affects the Capital.

As for retirement: Check the Kennedy Center or National Gallery of Art or American Heart Association gala or an affair at the British Embassy — she'll be there, giving it everything she's got!

32. WHO ARE THE TOWN'S MOST DYNAMIC DUOS?

Quite outside of good looks, perfect breeding and manners, and a belief in creating your own myths, certain social imperatives are obvious in certain people; for whatever reason, and by whatever vicissitude, these characteristics usually make people highly mobile, visible and desireable to others. Among the most dynamic couples in Town are: **Bruce and Hattie Babbit** (he: IntSec, she: Ambassador to the Organization of American States), **Ruth Bader Ginsburg** and **Martin Ginsburg** (Supreme Court Justice/top attorney), **Alan Greenspan** and **Andrea Mitchell** (Fed Chair/NBC White House correspondent), **Bob and Elizabeth Dole** (Senator/Red Cross prexy), **Cathleen Black** and **Tom Harvey** (Newspaper Assoc. CEO/CPB counsel), **Richard and Jane Gephardt** (House leader/leader of the house), **Al and Tipper Gore** (refreshing, straight, fun-loving products of the political system), **Marian Wright Edelman** and **Peter Edelman** (Children's Defense Fund boss/aide to many), **Tim Russert** and **Maureen Orth** (NBC bureau chief/*Vanity Fair* scribe), **Strobe Talbott** and **Brook Shearer** (F.O.B.s and policy works), **Al Hunt** and **Judy Woodruff** (media establishment prime movers), **James and Suzanna Woolsey** (leaders of CIA/National Academy of Sciences), **William and Elayne Bennett** (administrator and Town fixtures—always there, always in demand), **Paul and Leezee Nitze** (popular the way we were, and are), **Kerry Kennedy Cuomo** and **Andrew Cuomo** (R.F.K. Memorial chief/H.U.D. Assistant Secretary), **Joseph Duffey** and **Anne Wexler** (USIA Director/top lobbyist), **Bob Barnett** and **Rita Braver** (lawyer-agent/CBS White House reporter), and **John and June Hechinger Sr.** (retired, gracious always welcome old-line Townies).

33. WHAT WASHINGTON WOMEN WIELD THE MOST POWER?

Smart money suggests you never go up against the Pope in church.

proceedings; a comparable verisimilitude applies to any liaison or type of needing/wanting or form of bonding with these heavy-artillery Ladies:

Meg Greenfield — whose *Washington Post* editorial page power is numbing; **Jeane Kirkpatrick** — sweet, affable, a nun with a switchblade; **Heather Foley** — boudoir time with Speaker of the House can be awesome; **Kitty Kelley** — big buck literary assassin, happily confined to books and talk shows; **Pam Harriman** —holds immense pecking order due process; **Nina Totenberg**— long term mistress of downside subtleties, sacred/scary fixture in Town; **Ellen Sigal**—big in land development, can create and terminate with the best of them; **Patsy Ticer** — first Lady Mayor of Alexandria, and superb tight-rope walker; **Maureen Dodd** — her *New York Times* fraternal support makes access to anywhere easy, and access wins every time!; wizard economist **Laura Tyson;** children-defender **Marian Edelman;** HHSSec **Donna Shalala; Letitia Baldrige** — although removed from designated hitter status, still has high-charged resources and firepower, especially with the social set.

4. **WHAT ARE SOME OF THE HIGHER SALARIES IN WASHINGTON?**

It's a territorial imperative that athletes don't compare salaries with TV anchors who don't discuss money with leveraged-buyout buffs who refuse to talk monetary stuff with authors who, in turn, don't want to know what lawyers, brain surgeons or arbitragers make. Outside of everybody in Town knowing what you make, what you make is your own business. Definitely private!

In recent years, **Ben Bradlee** of the *Post* has picked up about $1.2 million per; **Allen Murray** of Mobil has an annual take of around $3.5 million; **Cathleen Black**, top gun at the Newspaper Association of America is salaried at $600,000 (which makes her highest Lady earner in Town); Black & Decker chief **Nolan Archibald** received $1.3 million in salary with beaucoup more in stock options ($15 million); **Cal Ripken Jr.'s** (Orioles) contract calls for some $35 million over five years; O's **Glenn** and **Storm Davis**, brothers to the end, get about $5 mil/season jointly; author **Tom Clancy** cleans up every few years with a blockbuster book, netting him about $10 mil; Riggs former CEO **Joe Allbritton** takes home about $1 million/ year; law firms like **Hogan & Hartson** pay each partner $365,000 (highest earnings were $440,00 for each principal at **Arnold & Porter**); average income of Gannett's five top executives was $775,000 each; Georgetown Med's chairman and professor of surgery **Robert Wallace** made $729,000; his associate **Nevin Katz** scaled in at $504,000. To compare societal value — **Bruce Babbitt** as president of the League of Conservative Voters got all of $1; DJ jerk **Howard Stern**, malice mouth, took in over $2 million last year!

35. WHAT ARE THE PROJECTED INCOME TAXES ON THE THREE MOST INFLUENTIAL POLITICAL LEADERS (UNDER THE NEW TAX PLAN)?

	CLINTON	BUSH	PEROT
1992 taxes	$66,225	$111,319	$15.8 M
1993 taxes under Clinton plan	70,208	123,951	19.5 M
Dollar change	3,983	13,632	3.7 M
Percent change	6%	12%	23%

36. WHO IS CONSIDERED THE CONSUMMATE DEMOCRATIC INSIDER?

The former Press Secretary to Robert F. Kennedy, **Frank Mankiewicz** ha: been in Washington several decades and for the last 10 years has been called "M Democrat" by his colleagues at Hill & Knowlton Public Affairs World-wic (where he serves as Vice Chairman), a public relations firm dubbed as the "Pow House" during the Reagan years because of its considerable leverage in gettin things done in the Capital.

Mankiewicz suggests he isn't a lobbyist but does talk to his friends on the Hi now and then, and that money has taken over politics in the US. His awareness « how the power struggle takes place has assured him of a stable and senior positic at Hill & Knowlton, one of the world's largest public relations firms (owned t WPP group in London) with billings in the $100 million range.

37. WHAT IS THE "CONGER" TOUCH?

In the early '60s, **Clement E. Conger** was Deputy Chief of Protocol for th State Department and decided that his contribution to Capital history would t the furnishing of the then recently completed entertainment rooms — the eighth floor Diplomatic Reception Rooms (plus offices and a ceremonial room on th seventh floor) at the Department of State Building. Over the years, the Cong Touch was evident in the 5,000 objects he procured to make the complex of room as elegant 18th-and-19th-century American-style as possible; his touch extend to private individuals, corporations and foundations, all convinced that his effc was truly historic — donations at the $30 million range followed and, today, th Diplomatic Reception Rooms have objects and antiques valued at $60 millio

Rewarded for his efforts by President Nixon, in '70 Conger was asked serve as Curator of the White House; there he did a reprise (raising anoth $15 million) and refurbished sections of the classic "home" so that it tod: looks much as it did in 1817, following its restoration after the War of 181 Early on in the Reagan Administration, Mr. Conger and Nancy Reagan h: words, which resulted in his dismissal. He took it smilingly, with : outpouring of support from his many friends.

Mr. Conger is still active on the local scene; a party-goer-and-thrower, and guest lecturer at many universities around the country. He lives in Alexandria, VA, Rehoboth Beach, DE and Delray Beach, FL.

38. WHO HAS BEEN THE LONGEST-RUNNING POLITICAL SATIRIST IN THE CAPITAL?

Mark Russell's first job was at the Merryland Club (L Street between 14th and 15th) where he played piano and told jokes while the Ladies shed their sequins; he went on to minimum fame at the Carroll Arms for a while, then maximum adulation at the Shoreham Hotel for 20 years. He has been sharpshooting at presidents, Capitol Hill, politicos and candidates and bureaucrats and the federal government for 40 years. Now at age 60, with an annual income of $1 million from performances, lectures, seminars and TV guest appearances, his wit is slightly more intellectual but not noticeably less caustic. Married to his second wife (Ali, 20+ years his junior) and living the good life in Cleveland Park, Russell continues to dominate the political satire field, with no heir apparent in sight.

39. WHO IS GENERALLY CONSIDERED ONE OF WASHINGTON'S MOST ACCOMPLISHED WOMEN?

She was a notable artist in oils and mosaics, a champion skeet-shooter, an Olympic swimmer and fencer, a scratch golfer, and a blue-ribbon winning equestrian.

Clare Booth Luce, at one time or another, was the youngest editor of the most sophisticated magazine of the day—*Vanity Fair*; she was a playwright—*The Women* was her most notable work; and a foreign correspondent in WWII who filed over 1,000 stories from the front; she was a congresswoman from Connecticut and Ambassador to the Vatican; she was a member of the President's Foreign Intelligence Advisory under Nixon, Ford and Reagan. She was a world-class intellectual, a polyglot raconteur whose wit was legendary. She often over-shadowed her legendary husband, *Time-Life* founder Henry Luce, and was star-quality wherever she went.

After the death of her husband, Luce retired to Hawaii but kept her Washington connection via an apartment at The Watergate. She died in '87.

40. WHO WAS THE YOUNGEST POET LAUREATE IN THE HISTORY OF THE US?

Rita Dove, a Pulitzer Prize-winning writer whose works reflect on the heritage of her family, is at age 40, the youngest Poet Laureate of the Nation, and the first African American to be chosen for the prestigious office.

She teaches poetry at the University of Virginia and won the Pulitzer Prize (in poetry) in '87 with a collection of poems based on her maternal grandparents themed *Thomas and Beulah*. She was chosen as Poet Laureate by the Librarian of Congress, James H. Billington.

Some predecessors of Ms. Dove are Robert Penn Warren, Richard Wilbur, Joseph Brodsky and Mona Van Duyn.

Originally, in England, a Poet Laureate was appointed by the monarch to serve for life and write verse for state occasions. In '86, the US began the appointment of a Poet Laureate (Warren) to serve on a yearly basis, and help the Library of Congress acquire important works of poetry.

41. WHAT IS THE MOST RECENT WASHINGTON LIAISON TO BE FEATURED IN A BEST-SELLER?

In her new book — *Power at Play: A Memoir of Parties, Politics and the Presidents in My Bedroom* — legendary social chronicler **Betty Beale** lets the juice flow about her three-year affair with oft-office contender and darling of the toastmasters, statesman Adlai Stevenson.

Now seventy-something, married for 24 years to dapper George K Graeber, Mrs. Beale still makes the rounds, presses all the warm and winning flesh, and imparts words of maximum wisdom to her chums through the year The Adlai Affair was long ago and far away, but memories of the late lady's man still force a wistful Beale smile.

42. WHO IS THE CAPITAL'S MOST VOLUBLE AND VISIBLE ASSOCIATION EXECUTIVE?

Jack Joseph Valenti came to Washington with then President Lyndon Johnson in late '63; he's been here since, mostly as head of the Motion Pictur Association of America (a job which earns him some $500,000 yearly). His Texas roots and friendship with Johnson gave him office as advisor to th President, a job he parlayed into the motion picture CEO designation in '66 He is reputedly the only presidential aide to have lived in the White Hous (during the early turbulent days when Johnson took office following JFK' assassination) and has courted Washington's high-and-mighty over th decades to the point where he is not only a local, but international celebrit (at the Cannes Film Festival, he is one of the most sought-after deal-makers His rugged good looks and beguiling smile mark him as a senior macho ma (despite an elevation of only 5'6") but his life is nicely composed and balance with his wife, Mary Margaret. He's one of the few genuine insiders in th Capital, as well as the world.

43. WHAT MEGA-RICH FAMILY IS VITALLY INVOLVED WITH WETA - PUBLIC BROADCASTING?

In their 16-acre compound (The Rocks, in the Crestwood section **Sharon and Jay Rockefeller** discuss the ozone layer with their childre listen to Placido Domingo, Joan Sutherland and Willie Nelson, catch a occasional Redskin game and act like other normal families. The differenc might be that Sharon is an up-and-coming television entrepreneur (now hea of WETA public broadcasting which projects such shows as the *MacNeil/ Lehrer News Hour* and the documentary series *The Civil War* on your screen); husband Jay is a 54-year-old 6'7" US Senator from West Virginia (and potential presidential candidate), the family is composed of four squeaky-clean quite perfect offspring (ages 12 to 23, three boys, one girl) and the word "royalty" keeps entering their lives.

With good looks, unlimited cash flow (Jay's worth is estimated at $250 million), a bubbling presence and ambition that won't quit, the family of John D. Rockefeller IV will never die of irrelevance. They are, to a person, Royalish, clear-eyed, impeccably styled, perfect to audition for any role in anything but a sitcom. As head of WETA (TV and radio), Sharon sits on an operating budget of almost $50 million; she is making friends far and wide in her current role, and such alliances bode well for her husband if he elects to expand his universe beyond the hills of West Virginia.

Whatever, the Rockefeller name won't soon be forgotten.

44. **WHAT WASHINGTON WOMAN IS THE QUEEN OF "DISCOVERY"?**

Being the guiding light behind TV shows dealing with science, history, nature and lifestyle has given **Ruth Otte** (Mrs. Edward Huling) official recognition in Town as "Queen of Discovery"—in that the focus of her interests is a cable outlet known as the *Discovery Channel*, the nation's fifth-largest cable network.

With an MBA from Georgia State, Otte worked for Coke in Atlanta for a while, then journeyed over to **Warner-Amex** (*Nickelodeon* and the *Movie Channel*) and to fledgling *MTV* in '85; she starred with the red-hot channel for two years before joining *Discovery* (under the aegis of businessman John Hendricks) and helping develop a company which is now the darling of the TV industry. Recently, *Discovery* was voted one of the Town's most successful companies with 375 employees, about $220 million in gross sales and some 50 million subscribers (covering 70 percent of homes in the US). In '91 *Discovery* added the **Learning Channel**, broadening its base and initiating programming in classrooms.

In '87, Otte was named Cable Industry Woman of the Year; she continues to discover new formats for entertainment and education and like others in the industry, refuses to predict the future because of its dizzying growth. She does suggest, however, that like **nature**, it **knows no bounds**.

45. **WHO IS THE CAPITAL'S MOST INFLUENTIAL P.R. MAN?**

In a world of terminators, fast guns for hire, saboteurs, hitmen, henchmen and assorted professional killers, a 5'5" wisp of a man with white thinning hair, benign grin, polite to the extreme, 70ish and soft-spoken doesn't seem to be in the right arena. Yet, for over 30 years, **Robert Keith Gray**, the onetime young man from Hastings, NE has been a power unmatched in the game of verbal jockeying and championship-winning.

His various titles in his three decades of service in the P.R./lobbying/ selling game in the Capital have all been, at one level or another, Manager or Director or Supervisor or Vice-President or President or CEO or Chairman. He has played on the teams of Nixon, Reagan and Bush, and probably has hired more top aides to Presidents and other Cabinet officials than anyone in Town (Frank Mankiewicz, Jody Powell, Anne Wexler among them). His personal wealth is in the $30 million range, largely due to buyouts/sellouts, mergers/acquisitions, all of which he survived and capitalized on (although in one celebrated case, he landed a $10.7 million contract from the Justice Department to publicize the Immigration and Naturalization Service).

At one point ('74), Gray bid on the Adirondacks estate of Mrs. Marjorie Merriweather Post—"Topridge"—with an offer of $800,000 (the $5 million property was in decline and considered to be an unworthy real estate investment), but was outbid by Roger Jakubowski who made his fortune in carpeting. For years, Gray was Chairman of Hill & Knowlton Worldwide (now owned by London-based ad giant WPP Group), but split off to found his own firm—Gray & Company Communications. Today, he breezes along as always despite some bad press and the general ennui that comes with time.

46. WHAT US SENATOR IS IN THE HEADLINES FOR ESCORTING BEAUTIFUL WOMEN, REAL ESTATE DEALING OR PLAYING WITH THE EQUESTRIAN CROWD?

John Warner, in the Senate for ages (previously Secretary of Navy and head honcho at assorted other federal offices), former husband of Elizabeth Taylor and Constance Mellon (daughter of Bunny and Paul Mellon), is now dealing to sell off portions of, or all of Atoka Farms, his 557-acre Middleburg, VA estate (20-room, 1816 farmhouse, stables, storage building, four tenant houses, tennis courts, swimming pool in a barn and 400 head of cattle). Price tag is an ever diminishing $6.8 million. He continues to play with the equestrian set while diligently serving his Virginia constituency in the Senate and painting up a storm in Senate Room EF-100 (see Chapter XI) and escorting the Town's most dazzling women to openings and special events.

Atoka Farms was once almost 1,200 acres (one of the biggest spreads in nearby Washington) but in recent years **Jack Kent Cooke** and former conglomerateur (Litton Industries) and head of OBM (under Nixon) **Roy Ash** have accumulated some 600 acres.

Senator Warner wants to simplify his life-style with an apartment at Watergate and a 40-acre farm in Middleburg; and when the votes are in, he'll probably have his way. In the meantime, he attends lavish parties with ravishing women.

7. WHAT WASHINGTONIAN COMBINED TWO PASSIONS — BANKING AND THOROUGHBRED RACING — TO MAKE/LOSE FORTUNES?

Some 22 years ago **Joe Lewis Allbritton** peregrinated to the Capital from Houston where he had enjoyed a successful career in real estate and banking. His Washington magnet (at that time, '73) was the purchase of Washington Star Communications, a modest media complex (*Washington Star* newspaper, WMAL radio and TV—the local ABC affiliate, plus several TV stations and a radio outlet in Virginia). He did the deal for $35 million and moved his wife (Barbara Jean) and son to Foxhall Rd. (where he still lives, although his official voting residence is Houston and summers are spent in La Jolla). From that point on, the story gets interesting.

Allbritton became owner of the venerable Riggs National Bank (chartered in 1836, it was a piece of Washington history; the bank financed the US purchase of Alaska with $7 million in gold) and saw his investment triple over a six-year period, during which he became a major player in thoroughbred racing with the acquisition of Calumet Farms and its world-class stud "Alydar." But what goes up generally comes down; with the bust in the real estate boom in the '80s plus significant recessionary waves in most financial categories, the Allbritton fortunes seemed less than bright. Nonetheless a 5'3" maverick from Texas (Baylor University) with friends like Treasury Secretary Lloyd Bentsen, former Ambassador Robert Strauss, Jack Valenti, and continued ownership in Riggs (where he has installed Paul Hoffman as new CEO primarily to clean up Riggs's $320 million portfolio of nonperforming loans), WJLA-TV and Channel 8 (all-news cable) plus Lazy Lane Farm in Upperville, 1,762-acres of horse country (where his horse "Hansel" who won the '91 Preakness and Belmont was trained) keeps moving forward.

Just what the future plays out for Allbritton is unknown, but few friends would bet against his continued escalation. As Jack Valenti suggests, "Crisis is when Joe shines..."

8. WHO HAVE BEEN SOME TOP RANKING GOVERNMENT OFFICIALS WHO WERE FORMERLY IN THE MILITARY?

Might is often right in bellicose situations; but in the "private sector" might translates to power and power does, indeed, have its rank, so the relationship between military clout and civilian clout may be the same for some people. Here are a few:

Vernon Walters, diplomat, soldier and presidential aide (for Presidents Truman, Eisenhower, Johnson and Nixon) is a retired Army Lieutenant General; **James Baker**, former Treasury Secretary, was a Marine Corps officer; **Ben Blaz**, delegate from Guam, retired as a Brigadier General from the Marine Corps in '80; **Jeremiah Denton**, a Naval Academy graduate and Rear Admiral, spent nearly eight years as a prisoner of war in North Vietnam and following retirement was elected to the Senate; **Don Engen**, a retired

Admiral, was head of the Federal Aviation Administration; **John Glenn** Ohio Senator and retired Marine Colonel, is a WWII and Korean Wa aviation combat veteran (he was also one of America's first seven astronaut and the first American to orbit the earth); **Alexander Haig**, former Secretar of State and four-star General, was a powerful figure in the White Hous under two Presidents; **Robert McFarlane**, a career Marine, was the quie strong influence behind many of Reagan's key national security decisions fo nearly three years; Rear Admiral **John Poindexter** was Reagan's Nationa Security Adviser; **Don Regan**, formerly Reagan's right-hand-man, is Marine Corps combat veteran of WWII and retired Marine Corps office Senator **J. Robert Kerry** (NE) is a Congressional Medal of Honor winner– Army in Vietnam.

Most of our recent Presidents defended their country, too; **Truman** as Captain of field artillery in WWI; **Eisenhower** as Supreme Commander of Allied Powers in Europe; **Kennedy** as Naval Lieutenant; **Johnson** as Nava Commander; **Nixon** as Naval Lieutenant; **Ford** as Naval Lieutenant Com mander; **Carter** (an Annapolis grad) as Naval Commander and Aide t Admiral Rickover (Nuclear Submarine Program) and **Reagan** as US A Force Captain.

49. WHO IS THE FOREMOST CARTOONIST IN TOWN?

Doonesbury has been poking holes in the fabric of government politic for over 20 years via its creator **Gary Trudeau**; at one time or another all th Town's saints and sinners, exalted, magnanimous, admirable or abominabl overpoweringly virile, tyrannical or loving personages have been the focus o his razor-edge pencil. His cartoons dealing with matters of state get read an considered wherever important people gather; like the *Washington Post*, I has an incredibly broad reader-base (even the Pope is an avid reader). In th process of always opening up new aspects of himself, readers, too, begin little self-exploration. For his jolly efforts, Trudeau racks up about $1 millic a year.

Another cartoonist, dear to the hearts of Washingtonians, is *Herbloc* **(Herbert Block)**, who, too, has been making the rounds for many years; h intuitive renderings of public characters and insights to their thought pr cesses makes his work a work of art. Top funnyman at the *Post* since 194 his new book—*Herblock: A Cartoonist's Life* just hit the bookstores.

50. HOW IS "WONDER WOMAN" WORKING HER WONDERS IN THE CAPITAL?

Much beleaguered lawyer and BCCI connection Robert Altman had winning wife in actress and TV series star *Wonder Woman* **Lynda Carter** the messy court battle that pitted Altman against the government in the ca of scandal-ridden Bank of Credit and Commerce International (a unit BCCI Holdings, Luxembourg). A celebrated matter worldwide with maj players like Clark Clifford and law firm Skadden, Arps, Slate, Meagher and Flom (and Davids, Polk and Wardwell) involved, Altman needed all the help he could get. "Wonder Woman" defended her brash 47-year-old husband/ hero at every opportunity and was a rallying point for a group of concerned friends who donated about $100,000 for his legal defense. With legal bills churning out at a level of $50,000/week, the rally fit the demands effectively. Altman was recently acquitted.

Mrs. Altman continues to be spokesman for Maybelline and Lens Express and pulls in about $200,000/yr. from residuals on ongoing showbiz efforts. The Altmans live in luxury — a $2.5 million Potomac mansion (20,000 sq. ft., 12 bedrooms and 16 bathrooms, library, billiard room, etc., etc., etc.) and continue to be high profile in Town with regular lunches at Duke Zeibert's (with chum Larry King) and even a drop in at one of Clinton's inaug parties.

1. WHO IS THE DEAN OF PHOTOGRAPHERS ON THE SOCIETY AND EMBASSY SCENES IN TOWN?

For almost 35 years, **Albert Majic** has been the lens control of the grip-and-grin groups that frequent society and embassy flings. The Polish-born linguist (12 languages) and raconteur came to the Capital after serving with the Army in the Korean War. His $90 PX camera got him a few assignments around the campus and soon he developed a relationship with the Iranian Embassy which got him into diplomatic circles. He worked closely with Tongsun Park, and in time began getting insider info which he kept "inside"—and is today given high marks (for trustworthiness).

Over the years, he has photographed every head of state (he speaks Russian and was one of the few media people who had a cheerful in with USSR diplomats), President, member of Congress and visiting dignitary. His photo collection is valued at $250,000 but Mr. Majic has no interest in selling anything; he likes his work and continues to be a photographic presence at as many as four parties a night.

Bill Allard is another photographer super-star; his subject matter ranges from people to places to objects and intense studies of personalities. His long-term tenure with *National Geographic* instilled a sense of adventure and he now roams the globe in pursuit of something "essential," something that will bring new dimension to the world of graphics. Washington, a "city full of surprises," is one of his favorite shoot sites.

Society photographer **J.R. Black** knows the Town well and has been a favorite of socialites and event chairmen for many years; his work favors the dynamics of the lens and focuses on people in their unstaged-but-happy moments. Educated at George Washington U. and Stanford, Black began his career as a photog at the *Post*; he and wife Marianne are a twosome at most sociopolitical affairs, and are now engaged in video productions.

52. WHAT IS WASHINGTON "SCHADENFREUDE"?

A **neighbor** who has recently been listed on the *Forbes 400* is tooling down Rock Creek Parkway in his Rolls, passes you and your Chevy with a flip nod, and is suddenly the focus of a police siren. As he's pulled over by our local gendarme, you wheel by majestically with a faint salute. **One** of the more imperious Washington Chairmen, who has repeatedly ignored your good work at committee level, has her hair dyed to the latest rage-color of titian, but it turns out a sickly off-red, and can't be corrected for weeks because of a scalp problem. A **leading** Man in town who has been zealously courting a special, and very rich friend of yours, makes the headlines via an indictment in New York for stock fraud. **The** biggest and most ostentatious house in McLean is found to have life-threatening structural faults and is closed to its egotistical owner. **These** are the gleeful times and circumstances that give rise to **Schadenfreude**, that unyielding and limitless power we all have to bear the misfortune of others (with a quiet laugh, a deep sigh and a joyful lifting of the glass).

Throughout **history**, man had enjoyed a perverse appreciation of the failure of others; "the more my friends fail, the more success I feel" is the operative line. Schadenfreude is one of life's sweet consolation prizes.

For example, many of Manhattan's **queens of philanthropy** are the object of these feelings of pleasure derived from the humiliation of others. Toppled from the AAA society lists in the Big Apple was **Susan Gutfreund** for being too pushy and not pulling off her presumed knowledge of French well enough. **Gayfryde Steinberg** has been delisted for being tough and flashy, especially in arranging family birthday and wedding parties in the $million range. Many social elitists took secret pleasure at **Carolyne Roehm's** misadventure as a fashion designer ("Everybody knows her angel husband **Henry Kravis** was indulging her by financing what was sure to be another business failure"). Other icons like **Milken, Boesky, Leona Helmsley, Khashoggi, Imelda Marcos, Noriega** or on the local scene, **Antonelli, Allbritton, Donald Regan, John Sununu** and **Al Haig** gave rise to many gleeful moments for millions of people via their misfortunes, misalliances and misfires. The '80s was an era of perverse private joy produced by public comedowns of what-were-once-deemed as world-class leaders.

Schadenfreude, from the German **schaden** - "damage" and **freude** - "joy," was (according to Freud) a form of humor based on juvenile impulses, a silly little good feeling we got when one of our peers who was always winning this or that had a monumental failure. Where we once envied that person in his success, we began to feel inferior with too much triumph outside of our own sphere, and an inverse human equation set in. Where we originally were just cynical about a friend's failure, in time, we become overjoyed.

Envy is universal, too. Think of the sleepless nights you've known because one of your companions was promoted over you, or won the country club golf tournament, or was elected to the board of CBS; you may feel some elation in another's upward mobility, but there's an undeniable envy, too. Having **envy** for a friend or someone in your peer group can be especially disturbing in that you're

48

constantly around that person; envy for a VIP or television celebrity carries less pressure because of remoteness of contact. Same for schadenfreude; feelings are more intense if a friend is involved in the great gaffe.

Some people **set themselves up** as objects for schadenfreude. **Bruce Willis, Madonna, Mike Tyson, Richard Nixon** position themselves as targets; **Barbara Bush, Sister Theresa, Dina Merrill** and **Kay Shouse** conversely, are above the feeling. Even in their great and lasting success, people continue to root for them and are unfailingly supportive. That's largely a function of perception and an unassuming, low-key personality.

Too much **excellence** in a given category is also a basis for schadenfreude; the *New York Times*, Harvard, IBM, the Vatican, *Washington Post*, NYC high society and Hollywood are so-often credited with genius or sophistication that there's a natural turn-off. The public argues that no one can be that good and gloats over failure. Same for a dominant personality; when the longtime and thoroughly disliked head of Columbia Pictures, Harry Cohn, died, legions of entertainers breathed easier; and legions attended his burial services. Red Skelton commented on the massive crowd by saying: "That's show business, give the public what they want, and they really come out."

Although **schadenfreude** is a quiet, inner emotion, it often gets voiced at an embassy party, at a backgammon table or after a tennis game. People like to share the gratification they take at the setbacks of leaders/winners/major players. But wise people voice their rapture **softly**; by being too vocal and overstating your case, it's easy to become an object of schadenfreude, thereby giving others the pleasure you once had. Instead of your rejoicing in them, they are titillated by you.

"What goes around, comes around" is a verity with schadenfreude, too; in Washington the key to success is remembering that the greater the pride that precedes the fall, the less sympathy for the fallen.

53. WHAT IS THE WASHINGTON "PHILOSOPHY"?

The Capital has a unique blend of Oriental, European, South American and Middle-East cultures intermixed with historic Indian-and-Anglo origins, yet, somehow, when dealing with the esoteric side of life, **Latin** strikes a responsive chord. Often, a Latin idiom is used in matters of state or territorial imperatives. Here's some enlightenment (via Latin expressions/interpretations) about Washington life-at-large and philosophy:

DUM VIVIMUS VIVAMUS—While we live, let us live. The motto of Epicureans who believed that pleasure is the goal of morality, but defined life as one of honor, prudence, and justice (later corrupted to suggest self-indulgence).

NON EST VIVERE SED VALERE VITA EST—Life is more than just being alive. A suitable motto for those who want the ultimate self-fulfillment; who "want it all."

BIS VIVIT QUI BENE VIVIT—He lives twice who lives well.

Milton, in *Paradise Lost*, offered the same wisdom in these words: Nor love they life, nor hate; but what thou liv'st live well, how long or short permit to Heaven.

CARPE DIEM, QUAM MINIMUM CREDULA POSTERO—Enjoy today, trusting little in tomorrow. From Horace's *Odes*.

GAUDEAMUS IGITUR—Let us therefore rejoice. The opening words of a student song of German origin; the melody to the lyrics is the *Brahms Academic Festival* Overture.

NUNC EST BIBENDUM—Break out the champagne. Horace's call to merrymaking, literally "Now it's time to drink," from the *Odes*.

PLURES CRAPULA QUAM GLADIUS—More people die partying than fighting wars. A subtle reminder that excessive champagne takes its toll; overindulgence is more lethal than the sword.

FACILIS DESCENSUS AVERNO—The descent to hell is easy. A grim caveat that too much enjoyment has its down side, too. From Virgil's *Aeneid*, this thought cautions that it is easy to fall, but difficult to make one's way back up.

ARS AMATORIA—*The Art of Love*, a work by Ovid on the amatory art with full accounts of how to find and keep a lover. The first "how-to" book on passion.

AMO, AMAS, AMAT—I love, you love, he/she/it loves. The beginning of the paradigm of a first conjugation Latin verb in the present indicative. An expression well-known to man, an essential part of Everyman's verbal repertoire.

AMANTES SUNT ENTES—Lovers are lunatics. The foolish things lovers do are considered justification for this maxim. In *A Midsummer Night's Dream,* Shakespeare's Theseus put it this way: "The lunatic, the lover and the poet are of imagination all compact."

AMOR VINCIT OMNIA—Love conquers all. The famous line of Virgil, quoted by Chaucer in the prologue to *The Canterbury Tales*.

AMANTIUM IRAE AMORIS INTEGRATIO EST—Lovers' quarrels are the renewal of love. An old Roman proverb echoed by Robert Frost who chose as an epitaph: "I had a lover's quarrel with the world."

ALIS VOLAT PROPRIIS—She flies on her own wings. An independent spirit, she, who chooses her own destiny, pays her own way, and rejoices or suffers in her singularity.

QUO VADIS—Whither goest thou? The well-known, and painful question from *John*. The universal conundrum.

CHAPTER III

ANATOMY, APLOMB & ANTHROPOLOGY
(Martinets, Moguls & Mortals)

Photo: J.R. Black

Quintessential and consummate civility—Clement Ellis Conger.

54. WHAT BORN/BRED WASHINGTONIANS HAVE GONE ON TO FAME AND FORTUNE?

At any given function, there is always someone better, prettier, richer, smarter, younger, which has ruined many an evening. But there are often those of whom it is said: "I knew him when . . ." CapCity has a plenitude of locals who went for the gold, and got it! Here are some: Hollywood rajah **Warren Beatty**, a '55 grad of Washington-Lee High in Arlington (voted class pres, best all-around and variety show standout); Actress **Goldie Jeanne Hawn**, '63 Montgomery Blair High in Silver Spring homecoming co-chair (drama); Professional smiler **Kathie Lee Epstein**, '60 Bowie High in MD (cheerleader, drama); Feminist **Gloria Steinem**, '52 Western H.S. in District (class VP, archery queen); Writer **Benjamin Jeremy Stein**, '62 Montgomery Blair (thinker, Woodman of the World Award); Watergate historian/journalist **Carl Milton Bernstein**, '61 Montgomery Blair (U.N. Club, fledgling scribe); Conservative mouthpiece **Patrick Joseph Buchanan**, '56 Gonzaga H.S. in District (class pres, debating champ); Novelist **Pat Conroy**, '62 Gonzaga (football and wrestling); TV anchor **Connie Chung**, '64 Montgomery Blair (student council, debater); Power-Publisher **Donald Edward Graham**, '62 St. Albans (editor, class leader); Morning TV greeter **Katherine Anne Couric**, '75 Yorktown High, Arlington (homeroom pres, cheerleading); Gargantuan weatherman **Willard Herman Scott**, '51 George Washington High, Arlington (class pres, public speaking, drama); Investor **Warren Edward Buffet**, 1947 Woodrow Wilson H.S. (mathematician, scientist); Legislator **Edward William Brooks,** 1936 Dunbar H.S. in District; Drug czar **William Bennett**, '61 Gonzaga (general jock, toastmaster); Veep **Albert A. Gore**, '65 St. Albans (football captain, class leader); Observer **Anna Lou Liebovitz**, '67 Northwood High, Silver Spring (photography, drama); Hoya coach **John R. Thompson**, '60 Archbishop Carroll H.S. in District (varsity basketball), Miss Manners **Judith Perlman Martin**, '55 Woodrow Wilson H.S. (glee club). Actress **Shirley MacLaine** also metamorphosed from CapCity into her many beings/worlds.

55. WHO ARE HOLLYWOOD'S "INSIDERS" TO THE CLINTON ADMINISTRATION?

Many stars from Hollywood's galaxy descended on Washington during the Inauguration frolic; some made a statement, some just made it. Administrations generally have a sphere of showbiz influence, never taken too seriously (remember JFK and Lawford, Sinatra and Miss Monroe?) but good for some photo ops and entertainment. In Town, these days are some major players in the world of chachacha:

Lady Barbra Streisand, Robert De Niro, Warren Beatty, Shirley MacLaine, Sigourney Weaver, Angelica Huston, Jack Lemmon, Jack Nicholson, Sally Field, Richard Dreyfuss, Chevy Chase, Goldie Hawn, Christopher Reeve, Billy Crystal, Sam Waterston, John Ritter, Lindsay Wagner and **Diana Ross.**

One function stars star at, is fundraising. When Streisand opened her 24-acre ranch estate in Malibu to the aristocracy of Hollywood (at $5,000 per pop) to generate funds to combat any future Chernobyls, she raised $1.5 million by singing 17 songs. Via her various performances and royalties, Ms. Streisand takes in an estimated $10 mil/year; she funds her own foundation and distributes up to $1 mil annually to 64 organizations; most deal with civil rights, the environment and AIDS.

WHAT PROMINENT WASHINGTONIAN PRESIDES OVER THE FIRST "MUSEUM" CABLE NETWORK?

Director Emeritus of the National Gallery of Art, **J. Carter Brown** is a full-fledged, highly-worshipped museum-man. Putting in some tough years ('69-'92) as top gun at National gives him the credentials to do almost anything in the world of art.

Ovation Inc., a cable network devoted to high-quality theater, music, dance and visual arts, is what he chooses to do; the TV outlet goes on line in '94 to serve, hopefully, some 50 million homes. According to Brown, the "sky's the limit" in terms of programming—erudite offerings, fundamental instruction on art appreciation, events such as the Whitney Biennial, seminars, interviews, exhibits are all part of the creative mix to be served up. In his usual role as aloof and imperious commander-in-chief, Brown promises not to get into the day-to-day action, rather to sit somewhere up there in art heaven and give direction.

Incidentally, when Brown was impresario of National he took some heat for his romantic/friendship with Pam Harriman, who has been a generous benefactor of the museum—she donated van Gogh's *Roses* worth an estimated $50 mil in '91.

Truman Capote once said of Harriman: "There are people who though perhaps not born rich, are born to be rich." As for Brown, he was born to the manner—father was John Nicholas Brown, once dubbed by the press as "the World's Richest Baby"; his mother is the former Anne Kinsolving, whose father was Rector of Old St. Paul's Episcopal Church in Baltimore. The Brown family descended from the Browns of Providence, one of the illustrious Five First Families that have virtually divided Rhode Island up among themselves.

Brown was educated at Groton, Stowe School in England, Harvard and Harvard Business School, several European art schools, then, finally, at age 26 he took over as heir apparent to John Walker at the 20-year-old National Gallery, and the rest is history.

WHO IS WASHINGTON'S MOST FAR-FLUNG ARCHITECT?

Projects in the Netherlands, Bermuda, EuroDisney, Athens, Dominican Republic, Kentucky, La Jolla and Bel Air, Martha's Vineyard (Jackie O's summer playhouse) and South America keep **Hugh Newell Jacobsen** in

perpetual motion; he is a master at movement (both in his architecture a■
lifestyle) and has left his imprint on the world of design via white flowi■
lines as well as shock value stuff like solid black swimming pools.

Jacobsen lives in Georgetown and travels with the senior jet-set; h■
friends and fans number many of the Grande Dames in world capitals a■
many mega-rich **arrivistes** who want his touch in making a stateme■
(money be damned).

Married (wife Robin is a political activist) with three sons (all in so■
form of art), Jacobsen says of his existence: ". . . as with my wife, I nev■
can guess what's going to happen next. . ."

58. WHO IS THE MOST LISTENED TO RADIO PERSONALITY IN TH■ WORLD?

The Voice of America's **Willis Conover** broadcasts 12 one-hour pr■
grams each week on the subject of music—French vocals, American ja■
Brazilian street sambas, German opera, French torch songs, a little bit ■
everything musical. The world international audience in any given week ■
estimated at 15 million listeners, far and away the largest for a single sho■

Conover himself is a musician and favors American jazz, the only ho■
grown musical product in America. He observes: ". . .Jazz came about fr■
the interaction of two cultures, the Black American and the Europe■
American culture. They came together in this country and the result is a 2■
century musical language, with as many dialects as there are individu■
playing it."

Over the years, Conover had interviewed giants like Bing Crosby, Du■
Ellington, Ethel Merman, Ginger Rogers and Fred Astaire, Preside■
Eisenhower, Ford and Reagan and others; and has been the recipient of ma■
broadcast industry awards. He lives quietly in the District.

59. WHO IS THE AREA'S MOST NOTED HORSEWOMAN?

With a name like **Jane Marshall Dillon**, horsemanship is a natural; a■
so it is for founder and director of the Junior Equitation School in Clift■
VA—Jane Marshall Dillon.

Over a four-decade period, Dillon has given young riders the pro■
horseback training and imparted a sense of propriety while dealing with ■
subject of life. Her own dignified life is a model for the younger set, ma■
of whom come from non-riding families who want their offspring to le■
all the skills relevant to a horse-oriented community. Dillon quickly disp■
riding as a means to—rather horsemanship is an end unto itself . . . "a v■
graceful form of expression," she says.

Dillon's Clifton school (at Little Full Cry Farm) has credentials in its o■
structuring; just English enough, homey and unpretentious, complete yet ■
overpowering, subtle yet sophisticated, just enough social topspin to ■
impressive.

0. WHAT CAPITAL VIP OWNS AN AUTHENTIC WESTERN RANCH IN NEARBY VIRGINIA?

The late **J. Willard Marriott** bought 4,000 acres of land around Oventop Mountain outside Middleburg in '51 as a reminder of his early days in Utah; in time he turned the rugged woodlands and high meadows into an Old West ranch. Even now, 40 + years later, the acreage (comprising two ranches—"Fiery Run" and "Fairfield") function as a cattle ranch with cowboys riding about, quarter horses sauntering over the fields, sheep and longhorns grazing, and a mock ghost town where corporation picnics are staged (complete with chuck wagons).

Always pragmatic, the Marriott family makes the ranch pay its way— it provides beef for the corporation's restaurant business and is occasionally leased by corporations for week-long seminars, or by the movie folks for a shoot.

1. WHAT AGING AND ALMIGHTY CONGRESSMAN PUMPS IRON AND STUDIES TAE KWON DO TO AUGMENT HIS POTENCY?

In high school, **Thomas S. Foley**, Speaker of the House, was known as "Slim." But over a long and hazardous career on Capitol Hill (he's been in Congress since '65), both his youth and litheness have undergone something of a transition.

Today the overweight Democrat cycles to the University Club daily at 5 a.m. to pump iron and learn the rudiments of tae kwon do.

So far, so good; an 80-lb. reduction in overall weight, some newly defined pecs, bulging biceps, and a much happier Heather at his Capitol Hill home.

2. WHAT FORMER SECRETARY OF HEALTH AND HUMAN SERVICES IS THE ONLY AFRICAN AMERICAN SERVING AS A DIRECTOR OF GENERAL MOTORS?

Highly-esteemed African American **Dr. Louis W. Sullivan**, 60, is currently the president of Morehouse School of Medicine in Atlanta; from '89-'93 he was US Secretary of Health and Human Services and a major spokesman for the Bush Administration. He joined the GM Board last year as a member of the Audit and Public Policy Committees.

Additionally, he is a Director of Household International Inc., CIGNA Corporation and Bristol Myers Squibb Company.

Washingtonian J. Willard Mariott, Jr. also serves as a Director of GM.

3. WHAT CAPITAL LEADER IS CEO OF SOME 5,000 ANIMALS?

Courtship and mating are specialties of **Dr. Michael Robinson**, director of the National Zoo; in his role as CEO to over 5,000 walking, talking, chirping, demanding pets and animals and insects and reptiles, he sees a lot of mating, courting, seduction and reproduction. After all, what's a monkey to do on a lazy afternoon?

The son of a pet-store manager in England, Robinson earned a doctorate at Oxford under the careful eye of Nobel Prize-winning animal behaviorist Niko Tinbergen. He then picked up an option with Smithsonian's Tropical Research Institute and spent almost 20 years in Panama and other boondocks getting up to snuff on predator-prey relationships, secretion euphoria, animal cognition, and olfactory discrimination in pigs. It's all fascinating stuff, and Robinson can't learn enough about it. Says he: "All the problems facing humankind are basically biological—tribalism, territoriality, aggression. . . If you're going to be a cultured person in the 21st century, it will be really important to be biologically literate."

64. WHAT IS THE MYTHOLOGY OF THE "WASPS"?

A WASP can mean White-Anglo-Saxon-Protestant (as it generally does in reference to Cave Dweller or member of the Old Guard), or it can be **Woman Air Force Service Pilots**, an elite group who served their country during WWII by ferrying bombers, fighters and trainers around the US, thereby freeing male pilots for overseas duty.

During their heydey, WASPs were a power to be reckoned with; they had their own Walt Disney-designed insignia character (Fifinella, a Tinkerbell-like fairy with goggles and a leather helmet) and reported to a high command at the US Army Air Corps, predecessor to today's Air Force. During the period 1942-44, almost 1,100 WASPs patrolled the skies and delivered their goods; some not only ferried planes, but went on combat missions and towed targets for gunnery practice. Thirty-eight WASPs were killed during the war due to plane malfunctions or other accidents.

Practitioners of the Golden Rule—Senator Ted and Catherine Stevens.

After lots of hassling with the government, surviving WASPs were finally given their due, and in '84 got full VA benefits, and their proper place in history by being awarded the Victory Medal and the American Theater Medal.

65. WHAT FATHER AND SON SERVED IN CONGRESS SIMULTANEOUSLY FOR EIGHT YEARS?

The **Symingtons** have been on the Capital scene for several decades and have contributed admirably to our country's welfare.

Washington lawyer **James Symington** has a political heritage; great-grandfather John Hay was private secretary to Lincoln and Secretary of State under McKinley and Theodore Roosevelt; his grandfather James Wadsworth was a Senator and member of the House. His father **Stuart** was a Senator and Cabinet member (Eisenhower Adminstration); while a Senator, Stuart, and son James, a Congressman, shared eight years as legislators on Capitol Hill.

66. WHO IS THE TOWN'S MOST PROMINENT INVESTIGATOR?

In a Town where names like Yirchenko, spooks, Felix Bloch, "Dr. Gunn," the "plumbers," KGB and Watergate are part of the folklore, few people know **Terry Lenzner**, chairman of Investigative Group, Inc., a team of specialists at "discovering" the reality of any shady deal.

Lentzer came to Washington in '64 to work for the Justice Department; he got his first visibility in the media when he personally delivered a subpoena (for presidential testimony) to Nixon. Although he can function as a lawyer (Harvard graduate) his strength is mostly in excavating deeper than his peers in the pursuit of the real facts. In recent years, his firm has been called in on the United Way/Aramony mess, corruption surrounding the building of the Alaska Pipeline, Mike Tyson's rape-conviction appeal, and a number of SEC and merger/acquisition cases, plus international art thefts. Definitely not a member of Handshakers Supreme, his demeanor has caused a revolving door at IGI and kept Lenzner strapped for case time and a personal life. Nonetheless, in the style of G. Gordon Liddy, he charges forward, oblivious to the downside of a case and quite unwilling, as in the United Way fiasco, to show much charity to the defense.

67. WHAT IS SOME OF THE ALWAYS ENTERTAINING KENNEDY FAMILY MYSTIQUE?

WHEN JACKIE BOUVIER MARRIED JACK KENNEDY IN '53, ON WHAT BASIS WAS THE AUCHINCLOSS FAMILY SUPERIOR TO THE KENNEDY CLAN?

Mr. and Mrs. Hugh Dudley Auchincloss (Janet Auchincloss was Jackie's mother, divorced from Jack Bouvier, re-married to Hugh Auchincloss) were part of American society; the name Auchincloss had been associated with the high-and-mighty for seven generations, and through marriage had linked with such venerable families as the Rockefellers, Sloans, Winthrops, Saltonstalls, du Ponts, Tiffanys and Vanderbilts. By comparison, the Kennedys were *nouveau*.

WHY DID JACK BOUVIER (JACKIE'S FATHER, KNOWN AS BLACK JACK) MISS HER CELEBRATED WEDDING (STAGED AT HAMMER-SMITH FARM, THE AUCHINCLOSS COUNTRY ESTATE IN NEWPORT, WITH 1200 GUESTS IN ATTENDANCE)?

Since he was uninvited by his former wife, Janet, then Mrs. Hugh Auchincloss) to Jackie's wedding, Black Jack decided to defy protocol and gravity, and stayed drunk for several days during the wedding. It was his show of defiance. Word (to the press) was that he had flu. He subsequently died from living the too-good life and is buried in St. Philomena's Cemetery in East Hampton, NY; his headstone only bears the initials J.V.B.

JOHN KENNEDY'S BEST FRIENDS WERE KNOWN AS THREE-DECKER IRISHMEN. WHY?

Most came from neighborhoods of three-flat tenements in the poor waterfront district of Boston.

WHAT WAS THE HISTORICAL SIGNIFICANCE OF "HICKORY HILL," WHERE JOHN AND JACKIE KENNEDY LIVED IN THEIR EARLY MARRIED LIFE?

It had been the home of the late Supreme Court Justice Robert Jackson and during the Civil War had served as HQ for General George McClellan (it is now home to Ethel Kennedy and family).

ON WHAT BASIS DID KENNEDY'S BOOK *PROFILES IN COURAGE* WIN THE PULITZER PRIZE IN '57?

Although the book had merit, the longtime friendship between Joe Kennedy (John's father, the family patriarch) and Arthur Krock, *New York Times* columnist and member of the Pulitzer Board, played a vital role in securing the prestigious prize for then Senator John Kennedy. (Incidentally, at the time, Joe Kennedy was proclaimed the 11th richest man in America, with a fortune in the $400 million range).

WHAT WAS THE KENNEDY FAMILY CONNECTION TO CHARITY?

In 1946, the family established the Joseph P. Kennedy, Jr. Foundation, a memorial to the oldest son who was killed in WWII. The foundation was the first in the US to benefit the mentally retarded. Rosemary Kennedy, the third of the nine Kennedy children, was mentally retarded and lived at St Colette School in Jefferson, WI most of her life. Her sister Eunice (Kennedy Shriver) is especially close to the foundation and the cause and annually stages a special event at her Rockville estate for the handicapped.

BEYOND POLITICAL DIFFERENCES, WHAT WAS THE DISPARITY BETWEEN DWIGHT EISENHOWER AND JOHN KENNEDY?

There was a considerable "generation gap" at the time of Kennedy's ascension to the White House; he was 43, the youngest man ever elected to the office (also the first Roman Catholic to serve as President and the first President born in the 20th Century) while "Ike" at age 70 was the oldest man to serve as President. Since then Ronald Reagan at age 78 takes honors for oldest President.

WHAT WAS DESIGNER OLEG CASSINI'S ROLE IN THE KENNEDY ADMINISTRATION?

He was appointed Official White House Designer by Jackie Kennedy, creating clothes for her made exclusively in the US.

WHAT WAS JACKIE'S WARDROBE BUDGET IN HER WHITE HOUSE YEARS?

About $40,000 per year; in '60 she was elected "First Lady of Fashion" and one of the "Best Dressed Women of the World." Given the Kennedy wealth, her wardrobe allowance was a pittance.

WHAT WAS JACKIE'S FIRST YEAR EXPENDITURE FOR PERSONAL ITEMS?

Clothing, art, food and liquor, medical, jewelry, beauty salon and gift expenditures totaled over $105,000 as Mrs. Kennedy exercised her purchasing power in her first year as First Lady (Note: at the time, Kennedy was making a salary of $100,000 as President).

WHAT WAS JACKIE'S FEELING ABOUT THE PRESS?

"Minimum information given with maximum politeness."

HOW IS AUTHOR GORE VIDAL RELATED TO JACKIE KENNEDY ONASSIS?

Nina Gore, Vidal's mother and the daughter of a Senator, divorced Eugene Vidal and married Hugh D. Auchincloss; Gore Vidal was 10 years old at the time. The newlyweds moved into Merrywood, the Virginia estate overlooking the Potomac owned by Auchincloss where they lived for six years. When that marriage ended and Auchincloss married Janet Lee Bouvier (Jackie's mother), Gore met the Bouvier daughters, Jackie and Lee.

WHAT WAS JACKIE'S MOST EMBARRASSING FEATURE?

Size 10 feet, perhaps the biggest of any First Lady. (Smallest First Lady feet belonged to Nancy Reagan, who at barely 100 lbs., 5'4" and size four dress, hopped into size 5 highs as she made the rounds.)

WHAT WERE SOME OF THE GIFTS RECEIVED BY THE FIRST LADY FROM FOREIGN DIGNITARIES?

The trove was on the extravagant side: a $100,000 diamond, emerald and ruby necklace from the President of Pakistan; a $75,000 full-length leopar coat from Haile Selassie, Emperor of Ethiopia; $50,000 worth of assorte bracelets, pins and boxes from Prince Hassan of Libya; dozens of other gif ranging from $5,000 to $30,000 and all "keepers." (Note: US Presidents ar families are now very conservative about giving/receiving gifts since the are elected officials in a democracy, and would be spending taxpayer money in gift-giving.)

WHEN JACKIE AND HER SISTER LEE MADE THEIR CELEBRATE TRIP TO INDIA AND PAKISTAN, HOW MANY PEOPLE ACCOM PANIED THEM?

A total of 28 people made the journey; a hairdresser, personal maid, pre secretary, Jackie's favorite Secret Service man (Clint Hill, who was later shield her during the critical moments of the Kennedy assassination), 2 security guards and 64 pieces of luggage. The group traveled some 16,00 miles in 20 days and made headlines the world over.

HOW DID SISTER LEE FARE WITH MONEY AND POWER?

After a routine marriage to Michael Canfield, Lee Bouvier married Princ Stanislas Radziwill, a self-made millionaire and international celebrity. Sł became Princess Lee Radziwill and enjoyed his lifestyle which included large Georgian mansion in London near Buckingham Palace, a 12-roo Fifth Avenue apartment in New York, a Queen Ann country estate on 4 acres near Henley-on-Thames and a villa in Greece. At one point, he wa considered one of the richest men in England based on his ownership of a re estate construction firm.

WHAT ENTERTAINER MADE A QUICK FORTUNE IMITATING TH KENNEDYS, THEN JUST AS QUICKLY FADED INTO OBSCURITY

Vaughn Meader's record — "The First Family"— parodied Kennedy Boston twang and Jackie's debutante whisper. It sold millions of copies, b Meader's career was short-circuited by the Kennedy clout.

WHAT WAS THE BIGGEST "JIGGLE" DURING THE KENNED YEARS?

At a birthday party (May 29, '63), for Kennedy in Madison Square Garde (NYC), Marilyn Monroe, clad in the most diaphanous of gowns, sar "Happy Birthday" to the President. It was a performance seen around tł world and disparaged by the intelligentsia; Adlai Stevenson suggested h dress "looked like flesh with sequins sewed onto it."

HOW MANY FOREIGN NATIONS SENT DELEGATIONS TO ATTEN THE KENNEDY FUNERAL?

Led by France's President de Gaulle, 91 other nations were represente at the funeral in Washington.

AT THE TIME OF HIS DEATH, HOW MUCH WAS JOHN KENNEDY WORTH?

Although Kennedy was one of the wealthiest men ever to occupy the White House, his taxable net worth at the time of his death was only $1,890,640.

WHO ARE BURIED NEXT TO PRESIDENT KENNEDY AT ARLINGTON CEMETERY?

His two children — the daughter born dead in '56 and his son, Patrick Bouvier Kennedy, who only lived for 39 hours — share the Eternal Flame burial ground with their father.

WHAT IS CALLED "WIDOW'S WEEDS"?

The garments worn by the wives (and often friends or relatives) of state officials after their death; Jackie Kennedy wore black clothing for a year of mourning after her husband died.

HOW MUCH DID JACKIE KENNEDY'S MANHATTAN APARTMENT COST?

The five-bedroom, 23-windowed co-op at 1040 Fifth Avenue, with its own private elevator to the 15th floor, only cost $200,000. Today, its value is estimated at $1.3 million.

WHAT WAS THE BATTLE OF THE BOOK?

The Death of a President was written by William Manchester soon after Kennedy was assassinated; in some detail the author wrote about the First Lady's vanity, idiosyncrasies and abhorrent behavior. A number of Kennedy friends and consultants had read the manuscript and requested considerable revision. When Manchester refused to delete the "Jackie" parts, she started an elongated headline-grabbing war with the author, which resulted in modest changes in the manuscript (but most of the unfavorable portions had already been leaked to the press). *Death* was finally published (after serialization by *Look* Magazine) in '67, and became a best-seller.

WHEN JACKIE BECAME MRS. ARISTOTLE ONASSIS, WHAT DOMESTIC RESPONSIBILITIES DID SHE OVERSEE?

The new First Lady of Scorpios (the Greek island, shaped like a Scorpion, bought by Onassis in '71 for $110,000) oversaw 72 servants on the island; 10 servants as mistress of a villa in Glyfada; five servants in the Paris penthouse and the same in the Fifth Avenue apartment in New York, plus 38 servants in the hacienda in Montevideo. "Daddy O" provided handsomely for "Jackie O."

WHAT WAS THE "MILLION DOLLAR TRIANGLE"?

Photographers dogged the new Mrs. Onassis to the extreme; her exotic

lifestyle, filled with Valentino gowns, Halston dresses, Maximilian furs an
jewels by Zolotas, gave her entry to the Best-Dressed Hall of Fame, and dai
media coverage world-wide. Even as she went private, camera lense
zoomed in on her from thousands of yards away (on land, sea and air). Whil
sunbathing on Scorpios, she was photographed in full-frontal nude sequence
thus the "Triangle." The photo portfolio is still a collector's item.

HOW MUCH MONEY DID JACKIE FINALLY GET FROM ONASSIS'
ESTATE (AFTER HIS DEATH)?

Over $26 million is the figure most often used, which was a net of $2
million after taxes ($6 million to the IRS); the settlement was arranged b
Christina Aristotle (then only surviving child of Onassis) with the provis
that Jackie break all ties with the Onassis family and seek no further monetar
satisfaction.

68. WHO HAS BEEN WASHINGTON'S MEGA-LAWYER?

It's said he could deal his way out of anything, except getting old an
getting dead.

On August 13, '88, one of the great and terrible guys went on
immortality; legal magician **Edward Bennett Williams** died of cancer
Georgetown University Hospital. His life was a tableau of firsts, an
controversy, of business prowess and ill-tempered, anti-social behavior,
brilliant legal victories and insubordination, of intense friendships an
promises broken and kept, of giantism through it all. Williams was a dem
God to many and Satan to others, but he was always high-visibility, goo
copy, super-charged, bigger than life, a true one-and-only.

**69. WHAT WASHINGTONIANS, OVER THE YEARS, HAVE GON
FOR THE GOLD?**

A number of Townies have seen the glory of gold in winning an Olympi
event for the US; they have been standard bearers on athletic fields all ov
the world and still call Washington home. Some are:

Theresa Andrews, '84 gold medals in 100-meter backstroke and 44(
meter medley relay; **Edmund Sloane Coffin**, '76 gold medal for individua
and team equestrian three-day event; **Charlie Green**, '68 gold medal for 40(
meter team relay and bronze medal in the 100-meter sprint; **Harold Connoll**
'56 gold medal in hammer throw (held the world's record for nine years
Debra Holloway, '88 silver medal for tae kwon do, bantamweight; **Lynett**
Love, '88 gold medal for heavyweight tae kwon do; **Dick Steere**, '32 bronz
medal for team foil competition; **Charles Mooney**, '76 silver medal f
bantamweight boxing; and **Lawrence Hough** and **Anthony Johnson** '6
silver medal for crew pairs without coxwain.

Defenders of good causes and a great country—Marcia and Frank Carlucci.

"Wonder Woman" Lynda Carter Altman with Evan and Marie Galbraith—
solid citizens and supporters.

70. WHO IS MISS MANNERS' MISTER?

A man who appreciates double duty, has a double appreciation of lif

Thus, **Dr. Robert Martin**, molecular biologist at Bethesda's Nation
Institute of Health, **and** Managing Director of the City Stage Theat
Company has fulfilled his aspirations, twice!

Now, factor in the role he plays as Mister to "Miss Manners" (Judi
Martin, his wife, former theater critic for the *Washington Post's* Weeken
section and current lady of manners, "Miss Manners") and you see just ho
capable this gent is, and how zealous he is in pursuing multiples. A
successfully, so far. As VegasSpeak suggests—keep rolling all seven
mannerly Mr. Martin.

71. WHAT FAMED SONGSTRESS EARNED A DEGREE IN THEOLOGY AT GEORGETOWN (WHILE IN HER 60s)?

No one would expect less of the late **Pearl Bailey**, a strand of America
for four decades; by getting her degree in '85 at GU **and** at the same tim
writing a book (her sixth) **and** making her 10th movie **and** acting as Speci
Adviser to the US Mission to the UN **and** producing another (sure to be gol
record **and** triumphing on Broadway with an all-black cast of *Hello Doll*
she was simply doing what came naturally. Which is the story of her fabl
life.

Growing up in DC and being musically-divined from the beginnin
Miss Bailey remembered the Great Black Way—U Street's once-boomi
corridor of theaters, ballroooms and clubs, the Howard Theater, Club Ba
Republic Gardens and the Caverns—all for blacks in the era of leg
segregation.

In her final years Bailey lived in California; she died in '90 at age 72

72. WHO IS THE CAPITAL'S BEST FRIEND TO "LOST SOULS"?

Wherever you go, there you are! Sometimes you get there in an orderly manner, often you arrive by luck or help from the area's mapmaker—**Mark Turcotte**, boss at ADC, the people who publish the little black and yellow maps that so many Washingtonians won't leave home without!

ADC, under Turcotte's leadership, now produces 65 atlases covering all of the DC area plus Philadelphia, Baltimore, Richmond, Raleigh-Durham, Atlanta and the Tidewater lands. In any given year, several million maps are sold for car travelers plus about 400,000 navigation sheets (62 varieties) for sailors, boaters and fisherman.

ADC is now owned by Langenscheidt, a German complex that runs five other map operations in the US. With a growing population, better highway infrastructure and bargain rates at many tourist attractions, Turcotte is bullish about the future and the invariable need for maps—"Go four miles north on highway 7N, make a U-turn and go four miles south on highway 7N and guess where most people will be. Lost!"

73. HOW DID JUSTICE SANDRA DAY O'CONNOR GAIN ENTRY TO THE "HIGHEST COURT"?

The charming Justice recently programmed a daily aerobics workout for lady friends in the Supreme Court gym, winning women new privileges on the "highest court in the land," as the basketball court about the Supreme Court chambers is known.

For the record, **Justice O'Connor** makes $159,000 annually and could easily afford a private trainer, but in a democracy it's best to take advantage of public facilities. Her boss—Supreme Court Chief Justice William Rehnquist makes his decisions based on a salary of $166,200 (by way of comparison, Georgetown University School of Law Dean Judith Areen pulls down $152,500).

74. WHAT CELEBRATED POLITICAL COLUMNIST BEGAN BY WRITING RADIO SCRIPTS?

At Syracuse University, Dick Clark asked friend and contemporary **William Safire** to write some scripts dealing with music and dancing and the germ of an idea for a radio show. Later, the *American Bandstand* under Clark's tutelage became a national institution; and William Safire went on to become an institution writer (Nixon Administration) and something of a self-institution at the *New York Times* where his focus on semasiology and his theses "On Language" have propelled him into the super-star category among journalists.

75. WHO IS CONSIDERED "PORTRAITIST TO PRESIDENTS"?

When recent Presidents Ford, Reagan and Bush wanted their likeness for posterity, the signal was sent to New York-based **Everett Raymond Kinstler,** who over the years, has rendered portraits of some 42 cabinet members, administration officials and presidents. His works hang in the White House, the National Portrait Gallery, the Yale Club in NYC (where portraits of Yale University alumni William Howard Taft, Gerald Ford and George Bush are proudly displayed—with Yalie Bill Clinton as the next likely subject) and other galleries in the country.

Kinstler recently completed portraits of former Secretary of State James Baker and Defense Secretary Casper Weinberger; his last rendering of Gerald Ford is the ninth version since Ford left office in '77 and reflects the same man— "He hasn't changed much in 16 years. . . " notes Kinstler.

76. **WHAT YOUNG PROFESSIONAL RECENTLY SCULPTED WORKS FOR THE NATIONAL CATHEDRAL AND WAS PORTRAYED IN AN AD FOR DEWAR'S SCOTCH?**

About $500,000 worth of magazine ads in the last 12 months have shown a weary artist reclining against a wall in the shadows of the afternoon, after completing another sculpture. **Jay Carpenter** is that artist; he is a "Dewar' Profile," the subject of a series of color ads that depict winners taking a break from the Great Game with thoughts of a Dewar's on-the-rocks. In much the way that Absolut Vodka has championed new and unknown artists in its national ad campaigns, Dewar's has given expensive visibility to Carpenter (who has sculpted almost 500 works for the Washington National Cathedral). In the ads, the artist suggests that his future hope is "to truly keep on loving what I do. I hope I never adopt the attitude of another day, another gargoyle."

77. **WHAT FORMER AMBASSADOR'S WIFE ALMOST BECAME THE FIRST AMERICAN WOMAN TO SCALE MOUNT EVEREST?**

It was a gallant effort, but **Sue Cobb**, wife of Ambassador to Iceland Chuck Cobb, just couldn't manage the final peaks at the summit of Mount Everest; had she prevailed, Mrs. Cobb would have been the first woman to reach those forbidding heights. In Iceland, she is preparing for another try, serving up ice for guests at cocktail time and trying to outglare her crystal environment.

78. **WHAT IS THE SIGNIFICANCE OF THE SIR DENIS THATCHER SOCIETY?**

As the Laws of the Land change, with more femininity showing up at the top (of everything—corporations, government, spy-rings, etc.), the Laws of Servility also change.

And thus the **Sir Denis Thatcher Society**, a nonpartisan refuge for men who are married to politically prominent women. Founded by Charles Horner, husband of a former Under-Secretary of the Department of Health and Human Services, the society simply gives spouse recognition to those men who are invited to/then ignored at all the political parties where their mates have key speaking roles or some special interest.

Of the new members (103rd Congress), three of four female Senators are married as are 15 of the 24 new Congresswomen and one of the five women serving in the Clinton Cabinet; this leaves a lot of husbands holding the bag or the purse or the *Bible* as their mates get sworn in or photo-op'd or receiving-lined. According to humorist Ray Blount Jr. (his novel *First Hubby* profiles America's first First Husband), "Husbands are now in the category of backup spouse."

Each year, the Sir Denis Thatcher Society grows, and members are predicting the day ('96) when Bill Clinton becomes the newest advocate.

79. WHO IS THE UNOFFICIAL MAYOR OF CAPITOL HILL?

Sixty-something maverick, pundit, dreamer and schemer **Thomas V. Kelly** has held the Unofficial Mayor title for several decades; he's a born/bred Washingtonian having lived a good part of his life at 420 Constitution Ave. NE, a rambling 19-room dinosaur that recalls the good old days and the many changes in the Capital. His career as a reporter and feature writer for the old *Washington Daily News* was marked with success and his capacity to recall, then dramatize the days of old, make him a welcome drinking partner in the area where "Hill Rats" fraternize and galvanize for days to come.

80. WHERE DO SOME OF THE TOWN'S REAL WINNERS LIVE?

In a complex as diverse and as saturated with important people as Washington, there are few neighborhoods that **don't** have celebrity live-ins. So it is that almost anywhere in the area, one can saunter into a bar, exchange pleasantries and be safe in taking candy from a stranger, because in all likelihood, that stranger will be a power-circuit Washington insider. Here's where the elite hang out:

In **Kalorama**, you'll find Treasury Secretary Lloyd Bentsen, Senator Dianne Feinstein (CA), mediapersons James Reston and Nancy Dickerson, benefactors Gay and Stanley Gaines, and Senator Nancy Kassebaum (MI); on **Capitol Hill**, aces like Larry King, Senators Barbara Boxer (CA) and Patrick Moynihan (NY), House Speaker Tom Foley and NPR's Nina Totenberg live; **Cleveland Park** boasts publisher Donald Graham, sportsman Jack Kent Cooke, Commerce Secretary Ron Brown, talker John McLaughlin, tycoon Herbert Haft, *New York Times* reporter Maureen Dodd, defender Marian Wright Edelman, many media and press corps staffers and Mary Matalin, former Bush campaign manager; **Georgetown** harbors historian Susan Mary Alsop, Pamela Harriman (now Ambassador to France); newspaper heiress Joan Bingham, Kennedy Center founder Roger Stevens, former Senator Charles Percy (IL), scribes Sally Quinn and Ben Bradlee, H&H Services Secretary Donna Shalala, commentator Rowland Evans, former Defense Secretary Harold Brown; author Bob Woodward, Defense Secretary Les Aspin, former Senator Eugene McCarthy (MN), grande dame Oatsie Charles, protocol lady Lucky Roosevelt, CIA man William Colby, Senator Claiborne Pell (RI), cable TV and art mogul J. Carter Brown and patron Livingston Biddle; the **Gold Coast** features Mayor Sharon Pratt Kelly, Jesse Jackson, Jay Rockefeller and many of the African American aristocracy; **Adams Morgan** and **Dupont Circle** is the place of preference for mannerly Judith Martin, Senator David Pryor (AR) and Congressman Barney Frank (MA); **Alexandria** and **Arlington** house Justice Clarence Thomas, TV host Katie Couric, journalist Hodding Carter and members of Congress Pat Schroeder (CO), Jim Moran (VA) and Lee Hamilton (IN), plus General Colin Powell (who soon will move to his new $1.9 million home in McLean), Justice William Rehnquist, Senator Jesse Helms (NC) and Warren Burger, former Supreme Court Justice. In **Fairfax County (McLean, Clifton, Great Falls** et al in Virginia), residents include Senators Ted Kennedy (MA), Orrin Hatch (UT), Chuck Robb (VA), Supreme Court Justices Antonin Scalia, Byron "Whizzer" White and Anthony Kennedy, National Geographic Society prexy Gilbert M. Grosvenor, Congressman Dick Gephardt (MI) and mavericks G. Gordon Liddy and Pat Buchanan, advisor David Gergen and mega-restauranteur Jean-Louis Palladin.

81. **OVER THE YEARS, WHO RATE AS THE ULTIMATE MATERIAL GIRLS?**

Only the truly rich can afford to play at being poor in **Washington**, or anywhere in the world. Someone with zillions can live a threadbare, barefoot life of boring quietude and pull it off with aplomb. That's because the constancy and responsibility of being super-rich wears on the system and becomes a monster often described as "being resident of a gilded prison." **Simplicity is relief.** For most people, though, winning any social game requires hard-and-blood-letting play, massive assemblies of resources, fine-tuned intelligence, masterful strategy and a fearsome assault. The logistics of follow-up are no lark either; having attained anything near the stratosphere on the social pyramid implies only one sort of further mobility—**downward**. To the south. The place where gravity just naturally goes.

Yet those with the Jack Russell terriers, Hermes saddles, Rollers and Harley-Davidsons, model wives, homes in Santa Barbara and Bridgehampton, visitations to Canyon Ranch, polo teams and stables, somehow have mastered the esoteric of making it, and are enjoying an interlude of **social supremacy**.

One of the early-on great **Material Girls** was **Flora Payne**, daughter of an Ohio Senator, who married William Whitney, and thereby became co-partner of his $40 million Standard Oil fortune. She spent her days collecting European art for their Fifth Avenue mansion and organizing events for the Four Hundred. Her favorite line: "Money is the root of society."

Certainly a qualifier in the **Great Dame** category is **Mrs. Cornelius (Grace Wilson) Vanderbilt III**. Her marriage into the Vanderbilt dynasty prompted her father-in-law to cut her then husband out of his will (she came from "inferior" stock—her father made his fortune selling blankets to the Rebels in the Civil War); fortunately the couple was saved by a $6 million allocation from brother Alfred, who felt their father had acted injudiciously. Grace became "Her Grace" in early 1900s society.

Looking for **love** in all the **right places** was **Cordelia Drexel Biddle**, the product of a very proper upbringing in Philadelphia; she took the vows with tobacco heir Angier Duke, and the twosome moved forward in society and planned parenthood producing Anthony Biddle Duke (who later became an ambassador, and founder of Boys Harbor). Tiring of the Duke name, Cordelia subsequently married the architect of the Graybar Building—where the couple lived.

No one can accuse **Barbara Cushing** of seeking **megabucks**—she was just in the right place at the right time. The beautiful daughter (one of three)

Accomplished, alluring, artistic—Susan Firestone.

of Dr. Henry Cushing of Boston, she married Stanley Mortimer Jr., grandson of the co-founder of Standard Oil, then exchanged vows with the young-man-in-a-hurry Bill Paley, who founded CBS. Always the equivalent of royalty, always on the best-dressed list, always untouchable, "Babe" Paley was described by Truman Capote: "Her only problem, she was perfect."

Credentials. Credentials. To this day one of the most dynamic Democrats in the country is **Pamela Harriman**, who came through the ranks originally as the daughter of English baron Lord Edward Digby, then as an early wife of Randolph Churchill, and Mrs. Leland Hayword. During a brief interlude as a single, she had liaisons with Frank Sinatra, Edward R. Murrow, Aly Khan, Jock Whitney, Elie de Rothschild, Giovanni Agnelli and other top-drawer types; in '71 she married ex-New York Governor and advisor to presidents, Averell Harriman. Since his death in '86 (at which point, she received the bulk of his $75 million estate), she has earned the title "Queen Pamela" for her indefatigable work on behalf of dozens of causes, not the least of which is the Democratic Party. (See other chapters)

Brooke Astor, the former Brooke Russel of Portsmouth, NH is "**Queen Brooke** of New York" to most society crowds. When Vincent Astor, her third husband, died, she took control of the Vincent Astor Foundation and has since doled out millions to charities ranging from the Metropolitan Museum to the New York Public Library, which she almost single-handedly made into a chic and functional facility. By any standards, she is the Grand Dame of New York society.

Among some of the other prominent **Lady leaders** are Mrs. Joseph (Estee) **Lauder**, who made the name **Estee** synonymous with class and beauty; Mrs. Milton (Carroll) **Petrie**, blond-beauty, once married to playboy Marquess de Portago, now to Petrie Stores founder, Milton, one of society's true philanthropists; Mrs. Cornelius (Marylou) Vanderbilt **Whitney**, an original—author, artist, sportsman and business tycoon, whose interests are far-flung and inspired; and, Mrs. William (Pat) **Buckley**, First Lady of All Good Things, and the liaison between Seventh and Park Avenues, the Old Guard and all those rich and attractive Wannabees, junior and senior committees, fortune seekers and fortune cookies and on and on. She, too, is an original—proper Canadian-English upbringing, married to patrician and eminently quotable Bill Buckley, mother of journalist Christopher, a Lady who knows power, never forgets an obligation and starts each day with a smile.

Maybe most of these **Great Dames** married money, but it wasn't a capricious union, nor is the result of their duality easily dismissed. Billions have been swifted to various charities via their **good work**; those husbands still living seem chipper enough, the family tree continues to grow with dignity, and each Lady is proof that social contracts are viable, and can open the doors of the most exclusive clubs and social cliques, and further, open the gates to paradise right here on the hot Planet Earth.

CHAPTER IV

NOBLESSE OBLIGE IN ACTION
(Parties, Pastiche & Philanthrophy)

Photo: J.R. Black

**Mrs. Estelle Gelman, crusader for countless charities
and causes; an Original.**

82. HOW IMPORTANT ARE GALAS AND PARTIES IN THE CAPITAL?

Washington philosophy: What you do from 9 a.m. to 5 p.m. differs greatly compared to what you do from 5 p.m. to 9 a.m.

Thus, one might say, the Washington day begins over cocktails at an embassy or a penthouse or ivory tower; and fun is a secondary consideration in the social whirl. Amount of money raised, flags waved, contacts made, deals cut, connections advanced, affiliations secured are the major missions of any interpersonal relationships.

The social agenda in Town is set by the Oval Office; everything vital to one's career pivots around workings of the government, and embassy parties, glad-handing and wordsmithing are only devices by which one climbs the social-political pyramid. Although the elegant days of yore with roast beef and hovering servants and political idealism are gone, replaced by catered foods and the cacophony of ambitious self-promoters, business tycoons and distrusting imports, the Law of the Jungle still suggests the nocturnal hours are prime for consummation (although the majority of serious performers are in bed by 11 p.m.)!

This is not to dismiss power-breakfasts-and-luncheons as critical vehicles for making connections/deals. Both time periods are sure-fire means to an end, but are less formal (dress code) and don't have the same gallantry as the evening hours.

There still are traces of the authentic party when people meet to discuss "issues" or to welcome new power-players to Town, or to honor work-well-done by peers. And although there are still a privileged few (shrinking in quality and quantity) and a semblance of a golden age, Washington of the '90s is a slick, result-oriented, amenities-be-damned assemblage of human beings, that somehow, in some way, make it through the days and nights with enough dignity to be considered part of humankind.

Since the White House is the key in social affairs, the person occupying it has tremendous leverage in setting the stage: JFK set up a Camelot environment; Johnson had zip for polish; Nixon had no warmth and Carter no style; Reagan was showbiz and Bush the eternal preppie. Clinton doesn't promise much sophistication and it's likely that in the mid-'90s, the Town will be linked to the past in these ways:

DAYS OF YORE	TODAY
calling cards	business cards
cottage at Newport	condo at Aspen
Martha's Vineyard	Martha Stewart
clipping coupons	putting it on the VISA
good work	network
country club	health club
Bentley with driver	XJ6 with three-year lease
at homes	office parties

polo at Potomac	Polo by Ralph Lauren
Riggs	Nations
pheasant under glass	chicken anywhichway
Coco Chanel	St. John
utility bonds	junk bonds
seated dinners	buffet or barbeque
anonymity	publicity
stationery with family crest	car phone
equity	debt

Yes, parties and galas are important—vital, critical, the *sine qua non* of success in the Nation's Capital.

83. HOW MANY REGISTERED CHARITIES HELD FUNCTIONS IN WASHINGTON LAST YEAR?

Almost 150 charitable organizations held special events or fundraisers in the continuing effort to generate support/growth for their causes. Among them are:

Georgetown Children's House
Recordings for the Blind of Metropolitan Washington
Juvenile Diabetes Foundation, Capital Chapter
Jewish Foundation for Group Homes
Jewish Council for the Aging
American News Women's Foundation
Alexander Graham Bell Association for the Deaf
Royal Academy of Arts
Washington National Cathedral
United Cerebral Palsy of Washington
Save The Children
Girl Scout Council of Nation's Capital
Anchor Mental Health
American Diabetes Association, Washington DC Area
Georgetown University Medical Center's Perinatal Center
Hospice Care of DC
District of Columbia Jewish Community Center
National Symphony Orchestra
St. Albans Scholarship Endowment Fund
Epilepsy Foundation for the National Capital Area
National Kidney Foundation of National Capital Area
Young Benefactors of the Smithsonian Institute
US Committee Sports for Israel
Thrift Shop Charities
Independent Living for the Handicapped
Cystic Fibrosis Foundation
Catholic Charities of Archdiocese of Washington

CARE Inc.
Art for the Aging
The Phillips Collection
The Corcoran Gallery
American Heart Association, Nation's Capital Affiliate
Visiting Nurse Association
Cultural Center For Social Change
Washington Ballet
Lab School of Washington
National Capital Area Chapter of Leukemia Society of America
Samaritan Ministry of Greater Washington
Physicians Memorial Hospital Foundation
So Others Might Eat
March of Dimes Birth Defects Foundation
Concord Hill School
Washington Opera
Georgetown Family Center
National Multiple Sclerosis Society, Capital Chapter
Shakespeare Theater Guild
Hospital for Sick Children
Big Sisters of Washington
Oratorio Society of Washington
American Cancer Society
National Museum of Women in the Arts
Capital Area Community Food Bank
Campagna Capital Campaign
Wolf Trap Institute for Early Learning
Howard University Hospital
American Red Cross
Cathedral Choral Society
National Head Injury Foundation
Very Special Arts International
Arthritis Foundation, Metropolitan Washington Chapter
Pan American Development Foundation
Washington DC Literary Council
Boy Scouts of America
Potomac Community Library
Nature Conservancy
Washington Humane Society
International Visitors Information Service
Children's Hearing and Speech Center
Homemaker Health Aide Service
Metropolitan Police Boys and Girls Clubs
Choral Arts Society of Washington

US National Arboretum
DC Preservation League
Muscular Dystrophy Association
Leukemia Society of America
Washington Tennis Foundation
National Peace Foundation
DC Special Olympics
Kennedy Center Opera House
Hebrew Home of Greater Washington
Make-a-Wish Foundation
Marine Corps Reserve Toys for Tots
Georgetown Visitation Preparatory School
Fight for Children, Inc.
Bright Beginnings Homeless Child Development Center
Columbia Lighthouse for the Blind
Meridian International Center
International Eye Foundation
Salvation Army Women's Auxiliary
Washington Theater Awards Society
Youth for Tomorrow
USO of Metro Washington
Ronald McDonald House
Vincent T. Lombardi Cancer Research Center
United Nations Association
Capital Children's Museum
Woodrow Wilson House
Capitol Hills Arts Workshop
Project HOPE
SOS (Share Our Strength)
Weizmann Institute of Science in Israel
GROW (Garden Resources of Washington)
Eisenhower World Affairs Institute
Washington Humane Society
Jewish Social Service Agency
Pediatric AIDS Foundation
National Chamber Orchestra
Washington Performing Arts Society
Prevention of Blindness Society
Stop Child Abuse Now
Operation Smile International
National Aquarium
Cultural Alliance of Greater Washington
Washington Home and Hospice
March of Dimes

Friends of Art and Preservation in Embassies
YMCA
Catholic Charities of Washington
Parkinson Society of Greater Washington
Hebrew Home of Greater Washington
National Building Museum
DC Volunteer Clearinghouse
Folger Shakespeare Library
National Alliance to End Homelessness
McLean Symphony
Historical Society of Washington
Children's National Medical Center
Marymount University
Emergency Care for Kids
Independent Living for the Handicapped
District of Columbia Special Olympics
Washington Rehabilitation Center, Inc.
Planned Parenthood of the Washington Area
Garden Club of Washington, Inc.
Mental Health Association of Washington
Croquet Foundation of America
Zoological Society of Washington
Washington County Food Pantry for People with AIDS
National Italian American Foundation
National Wheelchair Sports Fund, Washington Chapter
American Ireland Fund
Israel Cancer Research Fund
A Living Memorial to the Holocaust Museum of Jewish Heritage
Animal Rescue League of the Washingtons, Inc.
Washington Community Chest/United Way
Albert Einstein College of Medicine Yeshiva University
Washington Chapter City of Hope
Hadassah Angel of Mercy
Brandeis University
Anti-Defamation League of B'Nai B'Rith
American Friends of Tel Aviv University

Collectively these charities raised approximately $70 million, up from the previous year; since tax legislation changes frequently, monies derived from various charities vary substantially. One factor is constant, however the direct correlation between liberal laws and liberal donations. When charity-funding is allowable as a tax deduction, such funding is liberal; when the law is strict, so is the eleemosynary instinct.

84. WHO ARE OUR TOWN'S MOST GIVING ARCHANGELS?

Outside of the federal government which seems to give and give and give irresponsibly and sans direction or accountability in the eternal search for Xanadu, our Town has some impressive archangels who serve life very well. They are the understated believers in mankind, who commit fully, quietly and sincerely, and in the process, work miracles for their contingents. Here are some:

Foundations like those of **Morris and Gwendolyn Cafritz, Eugene and Agnes Meyer, J. Willard Marriott** and **Philip Graham**; the late **David Lloyd Kreeger**, retired CEO of GEICO and major supporter of the National Symphony, Washington Opera and the Corcoran, was a virtual one-man army in his philanthropy; **Paul Mellon**, humanitarian and civic leader, a stalwart of the National Gallery of Art; **Henry Strong**, of the Hattie M. Strong Foundation, altruist and promoter of charities for the young (For Love of Children, Youth Awareness Program); **Catherine Filene Shouse** (daughter of the Lincoln Filenes of Boston department store fame) has dedicated most of her life to public service, specifically the National Symphony Orchestra, Kennedy Center and her own Wolf Trap Farm Park for the Performing Arts; the **Livingston Biddles**, longtime benefactors to the arts and civic endeavors; **James Rouse**, champion of housing for the less fortunate and creator of Enterprise Foundation, dedicated to solving the homeless problem, a king-among-men.

Other superpowers in generating funds for charities are: **Barby and Joe Allbritton, Sally Chapoton, Barbara Gordon, Audrey Mars, Frank and Candy Stroud, Peggy Cooper Cafritz, Oatsie Charles, Jane Sloat, Debbie Dingell, Eden Rafshoon, Joan Bingham, Donna McLarty**, the **Len Garments, Carla and Rod Hills, Millie Mailliard, Pennie Abramson, Alexine Jackson**, and one-of-the-greats of all-time **Estelle Gelman**.

85. WHAT IS THE "GREENING" OF A CAPITAL SOCIALITE?

One of Shakespeare's most brilliant passages "All the world's a stage" traces, with succinct eloquence, the cycle of human endeavor through seven ages, from infancy to dotage. Using Washington society as a stage, here are the **seven ages** through which a socialite lives/loves in a lifetime.

To pinpoint how/why one becomes "social" is difficult; it may be inherent, genetic, a function of ambition or a gregarious nature. But whatever the common characteristic, fledgling socialites can be spotted as soon as they can walk and talk. They listen to their elders, are curious about people and quick to comment, squirm in their seats when bored, are fastidious (even at age five) about clothing, and have a gifted young tongue. That is the **first age**.

During the latter part of this greening, a budding socialite attaches to a **mentor**, usually of the grandfather-or-mother variety, or an elegant aunt or uncle. Whatever the strange alchemy, a vital bond is forged and the wisdom of age is passed on to absorbing ears. Gossip, small talk about money and rank, cars, beautiful fashions, the importance of fulfillment, and personal grooming are all the focus of this **second age**, which initiates a lust for social recognition in the teenage years.

The **third age** is one of positioning on the social pyramid, and refinement. The socialite begins to perceive the **power structure**, and his/her placement; and, rather assiduously, develops skills and credentials that provide the right passport for upward mobility. This age is greatly enhanced by the mentor's introductions and coaching... and having reached a point of "social validity" in the mid-20s, and given hard and smart work and continued pressure to participate in the right social events a lifetime as a successful socialite is on-line (if not assured).

As he/she becomes accomplished at the **social game** (and not merely a player or pretender) during the 30s and 40s, the fruitless hours of dancing and missed connections, drab repartee at cocktail parties and unproductive social sorties, are largely a thing of the past. In this **fourth age**, the socialite has reached a point of grace, where exposure and experience and just enough subtlety, have created a competent-and-competitive human being, values and standards in order, and no sign of selling-out on the horizon.

The **trophy hunter** represents the **fifth age** in a socialite's development. Numbers of balls and galas chaired, amount of money raised, awards from gleeful non-profit organizations, peer recognition and prominent memberships are the focus of life, the more plentiful the more socially sophisticated the person. Society is now international with a strong base and constituency in Palm Beach or Newport, New York, Monaco or London. This is, perhaps the socialite's **golden age** (during the years 45-65); one of supreme social skills and power, robust economic and personal health — the best of times, all that he/she has sought since childhood. It is also the beginning of the finale.

In the **sixth age**, the socialite assumes the role of **sage**, advocating the ways/means of social ascension, serving as welcome critic to the communal structuring of others; not quite so vigorous, not quite able to dance the night away nor handle all those gleaming tulips of Perignon. Yet, wise and magnanimous, and very willing to be part of (versus leading).

The **seventh** and **final age** brings elysian memories; of tales and triumphs, tears of joy, glossy nights at the French Embassy, the stunning dinner party for visiting royalty at the White House, soft music and silver skies, yes, even the feeling of being in love, with someone, and with life; the exquisite gifts and the honest laughter, those smiling eyes and daffodils prayers that are answered, promises that are kept, honor that is real, friends that last a lifetime. Camelot.

86. HOW IS A CHARITY BALL "CHAIRMAN" BEST DESCRIBED?

(Anyone who has ever been an event chairman knows the rigors and pressures of the job; it is unrelenting hard work. Yet, each Chairman fantasizes a wonderful role, script, performance and resounding applause; and a **lifestyle and worship as presented in this fantasy version** of a Chairman.)

"The distinguished air, the regal hair, the unique flair. She's the Lady in search of excellence, never blames subordinates for mistakes, never bullies, always prefers the pursuit of the best to the pursuit of the latest. Has 100 gowns and a cellular phone. She's a Washington Queen. **A Chairman.**

She calls Her driver by his first name; knows all the hoteliers intimately, uses a jacuzzi for instant gratification. Thinks $200 for a private makeover by Olivier Echaudemaison is right on the money. Is surrounded by worshipers and totes an alligator briefcase in which crisp $100 bills are stashed for tipping.

Always has something to talk about other than Herself; is positively zealous about Her cause. Spends sleepless nights wondering about Her imperfections, yet gets up each morning expecting to win whatever confrontation might make Her day. Looks great on telly; slides into soft sell on radio like a virtuoso. Doesn't appreciate the bodyguard provided by her beaming husband. Wears provocative perfume and occasionally likes to slum in a leather flying jacket and Polo jeans. Knows that there are no draws in games of power, and that all flatterers are lackeys. Drinks two (but no more) Bombay "silver bullets" a day; then on to the more mundane pourables like champagne. Loves Her Man to appear in an urbane satin-lapelled tux, with cummerbund and self-tied bow tie, boutonniere and silk handkerchief; and adores bringing out the Astaire in this King of Hers. Gives Him gifts of mink sweat suit, jackets, blazers, scarves. Smythson stationery.

Dances till dawn when the cause is good; has the masseuse in every other day. Prefers to write Her thank you notes on Smythson stationery with a Mont Blanc pen. Knows computers like the back of Her elegant hands, and isn't afraid to put those finely-chiseled paws to work on table decorations and touch-ups.

She's turned Her Charity around. This year, over $200,000 gross. Applause. Smiles all around. Could be a corporate tycoon but is too humane. Heads turn when She walks into a room; She knows the jive of party-planners, fund-raisers, banquet managers, caterers. She knows the bottom line, and baloney from a phony when She hears it. She doesn't mince words; they tumble from Her sensual mouth with legislative authority. She's a cover girl; a public relations expert who knows the esoteric of hostile takeovers in the friendliest way. She can tell an off-color joke with the best of the Boys without being offensive, and when protocol requires it, She can speak French and Russian. She's impressed by people but not by titles or positions, and can always come up with a clever toast.

The Chairman loves Her caviar from the Caspian Sea and thinks nothing of spending $1 million to build a greenhouse on Her hilly estate. She believes in the maxim—I may not have as much money as some people, but

I've got as much courage as anybody, and that's the next best thing to money.
(Note: Her courage is neatly and delightfully presented.)

She loves to turn the Boys on with Her luscious ruby red lips and a sleek
hiphugging white Chanel gown. And She loves to go topless... in Her new
XJS, V12 black Jag convertible. Drives it at full-throttle on full-moon nights.
She can always find a way to be useful in an emergency and never hesitate
to speak up if She doesn't understand something. She never talks about Her
considerable fortune and wouldn't dream of asking anyone about finances.
She is a Master of the universe yet handles Her own turf with great dexterity.
Instant, and passing, friendships don't appeal to Her, and in consummating
charitable deals She knows the difference between teasing (She is a No. 10)
and harassment.

Our wondrous Washington Chairman keeps Her promises and never
promises what She can't deliver; She never stoops to gratuitous personal
criticism of associates in their collective goal of making the world better, and
stays in Her own lane. She is a walking think-tank, an advisor to presidents,
a well-placed source for all data vital to the success of Her cause. Her rewards
for jobs well done are 10-day holidays in Her (really His) Gulfstream IV (she
has a Golden Parachute) to Monte Carlo, Kathmandu, Rio. Or a $200,000 19-
inch South Sea pearl necklace (Tiffany). Or buying a dozen suits for Her Man
at H. Huntsman and Sons Ltd. in London (about $1800 per copy). Her florist
bill of $300 a week keeps Her in petals; she does all Her own arrangements
(yes, She has a silver thumb).

She is an expert on the Testosterone Factor and hormonal puissance; will
not tolerate those who engage in bang-the-drum posturing and free-floating
self-anguish. She has never been a wannabee at anything; Her credo, in short,
is "I'm gonna Be." And She is.

Chairman of the Year, may You reign forever. And, in time, when the
question— *Ou sont les neiges d'antan? Where are the snows of yesteryear?*
—comes, may it evoke remembrance of the Brilliant Role You played in the
Great Game of Life." (From an editorial in *Palm Beach Society Magazine* by
James Jennings Sheeran)

87. WHAT ARE A BALL CHAIRMAN'S INNER THOUGHTS?

The first **fundraisers** probably go back to the years 150-200 B.C. when
the likes of Caesar, Cicero, Epicurus, Marcus Aurelius and Petronius staged
any number of special events and debaucheries to entertain the populace and
fleece them of tax money. Through the years, the **esoteric of generating
monies** for good causes has been mastered over and over again, and today
is practiced with consummate skill in Washington.

Taking a little Latin from the Roman days, and combining it with the
thoughts and quiet statements of a **Washington Chairman** (Chair), these
considerations come to mind. . .

* The opening sentence in the Chair's letter to Committee people

"Adeste Fideles"— **O come, all ye faithful.**

* What every Chair seeks in a fundraising performance: "Ne plus ultra" —**Perfection!**

* The motto, invariably, of all Chairs: "Mox nox in rem" —**Let's get on with it.**

* The Chair of her detractors after a successful gala: "Damnant quod non intelligent" —**They condemn what they do not understand.**

* Note from the Chair on being told that Neiman Marcus would not be donating table gifts: "Absit omen"—**May this not be an omen.**

* The Chair knows this must be done occasionally : "Asinus asinum fricat"—**One fool rubs the other's back.**

* An integral part of every Chair's lexicon: "Humanum est errare" — **To err is human.**

* What every Chair knows and appreciates: "Donec eris felix, multos numerabis amicos" —**When you're successful, everybody wants to be your friend.**

* What a Chair may want after a particularly bruising Committee meeting: "Consule Planco"—**The good old days.**

* After a cancelled underwriting, the Chair accepts this homily: "Ignis aurum probat, miseria fortes viros" —**Life is not a bowl of cherries.**

* The philanthropist, according to a Chair, is: "Amicus humani generis" —**A friend of the human race.**

* The greatest need of a Chair: "Amicus usque ad aras"—**A friend to the end.**

* What a Chair is expected to be: "Arbiter elegantiae" —**An authority in matters of taste.**

* In certain situations, only the Chair knows the source of special underwriting; it is the "Arcanum arcanorum"—**Secret of secrets.**

* What a Chair says in developing a new idea: "Audaces fortuna iuvat" —**Fortune favors the bold.**

* What a Chair knows for certain: "Aureo hamo piscari"—**Money talks!**

* The Chair's pact with a recruit to the cause: "Aut bibat aut abeat" — **You're either for us or against us.**

* On hearing about the sell-out of a gala, the Chair can only think: "Gaudeamus igitur"—**Let us therefore rejoice.**

* How a Chair expresses happiness with a collective success: "Non mihi, non tibi, sed nobis"—**Not for you, not for me, but for us.**

* A Chair's perception of gala guests: "Spectatum veniunt, veniunt spectentur ut ipsae" —**They wish as much to be seen as to see.**

* After giving it everything, a Chair can only: "Permitte divis cetera" — **Leave the rest to the Gods.**

* What a Chair says of a new rich and connected Committee leader: "Felicitas habet multos amicos"—**Prosperity has many friends.**

* A Chair understands how things get done: "Argumentum ad crumenam" —**An appeal based on money or the promise of profit.**

* One of the great appreciations of a Chair: "Dis dat qui cito dat" —**He gives twice who gives quickly.**

* A Chair knows motivation: "Bonum vinum laetificat cor hominis"— **Good wine gladdens a person's heart.**

* In joy, a Chair thinks this after a particularly successful benefit: "Annuit coeptis" —**He (God) has favored our undertaking.**

* For those who are indifferent, the Chair notes: "Caeca invidia est"—**Envy is blind.**

* In the matter of contracts, a sage Chair knows: "Beati possidentes"— **Possession is nine points of the law.**

* Only the most egomaniacal of Chairs would utter this: "Exegi monumentum aere perennius" —**I have raised a monument more durable than bronze.**

* What no Chair ever wants to experience: "Ars moriendi"—**The art of dying.**

* Of someone who abandons the Chair's cause, but picks up on another, it is said: "Coelum non animum mutant qui trans mare currunt"—**Those who cross the sea change the sky, not their spirits.**

* The Chair's understanding with staffers: "Summa sedes non capit duos"— **There's only room for one at the top.**

* What every Chair hopes for: "Magnum opus"—**One's crowning achievement.**

* Yet, what every Chair is ready to say (after a losing effort): "Mea culpa"— **I am to blame.**

* Said of a Chair who stared failure down, took the hits, did it graciously, and did it her way: "Fluctuat nec megiture"—**She is unsinkable.**

* The Chair knows the reality of life, and knows when it's time: "Nunc est bibendum"—**Break out the champagne.**

FINALLY, the Chair respects the three great maxims by which we live:

* "Extinctus amabitur ideam"—**How quickly they forget.**

* "Fugaces labuntur anni"—**You wake up one morning and find you are old.**

* "Dei gratia"—**By the grace of God, go I.**

88. HOW MUCH DOES THE AVERAGE WASHINGTONIAN DONATE TO CHARITIES EACH YEAR?

Approximately $2,850 per household. This compares to $1,343 per household in the South, $829 in the Midwest and $826 in the East. In Palm Beach, the average is $8,850 per household.

89. WHAT ARE THE MOST PRESTIGIOUS CHARITIES IN WASHINGTON?

American Cancer Society, American Heart Association, Hospice Guild of Washington, International Red Cross, Juvenile Diabetes Foundation, Children's Hospital, Vincent Lombardi Cancer Research Center at Georgetown University, Project Hope, Multiple Sclerosis, Kennedy Center Honors, CARE, Capital Children's Museum, The Phillips Collection and Folger Shakespeare Library.

0. HOW EFFICIENT ARE CHARITY EVENTS IN RAISING MONEY?

As in most towns across the country, there is a tightening of funds for major philanthropies and volunteers labor more vigorously to generate significant monies; while smaller, newer charities are finding less expensive and more creative formats for funding. Here are a few recent examples of how effective organizations are in sustaining themselves based on a CEQ (Charity Efficiency Quotient) with 10 as tops:

Event	#Guests	Gross/Net Income	CEQ
Weizman Founders Gala	300	$92,000/$83,000	9.1
Kennedy Center Honors Gala	1,800	$2,093,000/$1,610,000	7.7
Arts for Aging Gala	340	$45,699/$35,300	7.7
Project HOPE Ball	850	$246,400/$161,400	6.6
Kidney Foundation Ball	530	$218,400/$132,400	6.1
Red Cross New Year's Eve Ball	500	$130,000/$58,600	4.5

Because of bad press about excessive spending and misallocation of funds (most notably in the case of United Way), donors are questioning their contribution more closely, and a young element (formerly serving as Junior Committee members) has moved in and developed new and more exciting ways to support their philanthropies. Good examples would be the recent Multiple Sclerosis Movers & Shakers Mardi Gras Ball (CEQ of 7.0) and th Junior Beethoven Society Ball (6.0).

91. HOW MUCH DOES IT COST TO ATTEND MAJOR FUNCTIONS?

Prices vary but a night doing good work and having fun makes cost minor consideration:

St. Francis Center Benefit	$ 125*
Weizmann Founders Gala	$1,500
Multiple Sclerosis Society Ball	$ 250
Kennedy Center Honors Gala	$1,000
Arts for the Aging Gala	$ 175
Children's National Medical Center Ball	$ 500
HOPE Ball	$ 250
American Cancer Society Luncheon	$ 150
National Symphony Orchestra Ball	$ 350
American Diabetes Association Gala	$ 150
Service Guild of Washington Gala	$ 350
Wolf Trap Associates Ball	$ 200
American Red Cross New Year's Eve Charity Ball	$ 200

Top fashion show tickets begin at $100 per person
Top luncheon tickets begin at $125 per person
Bidders pay $150 for auction tickets
*All figures are per ticket

92. WHAT ARE THE NEW TRENDS IN FUNDRAISING?

Few people know that the nonprofit sector of our society is by fa America's largest employer—a total of 80 million people work as volunteer in raising monies to help our needy. Each puts in about five hours a wee which equals 10 million full-time jobs; were they paid, even at minimum wages, the payroll would amount to $150 billion or about five percent of ou Gross National Product. And on a relative basis, each volunteer is highl effective. As an example, the Girl Scouts, which employs 730,000 voluntee and only 6,000 paid staff for 3.5 million members, generates more funds tha corporations of comparable size, and is able to keep a greater percentage them. Other highly cost-effective organizations are: Jewish Guild for th Blind, Catholic Relief Service, Legal Aid Society, National Council on th Aging, CARE, Project HOPE, United Cerebral Palsy Associations, Amer can Diabetes Association and the City of Hope.

Part of the success of these organizations is manpower; another part is th creative ways and means by which monies are generated. Since "don fatigue" is a way of life, and more people think twice about giving to a charit (based on tax and other economic considerations), fundraisers are introduc ing novelty as a means of raising interest. It's not uncommon to have a Las Vegas night, celebrity auction, bidding for bachelors night, fashion show, pink elephant sale, auction, murder mystery night or even a bingo night as part of the draw to a particular charity.

Americans, and Washingtonians, are very selective about their donations and the type of charity they embrace. Over 52 percent favor religious causes; 24 percent favor human services; 23 percent prefer health services;18 percent favor youth development causes; education is the favorite of 15 percent of people and the environment of 10 percent. Art, culture and the humanities are favored by eight percent; and public and social benefits, and international causes by the remaining people.

Coming on with enthusiasm are various environmental/conservation groups. International organizations like the African Wildlife Foundation (Washington, DC), Caribbean Conservation Corporation (Gainesville, FL), Cousteau Society (Norfolk, VA), Nature Conservancy (Arlington, VA), Rainforest Alliance (New York, NY) and Sierra Club (San Francisco, CA) have gained momentum in recent years and now receive substantial monies from philanthropic foundations and individuals.

It should be noted that affluent families are giving less and less to charity across the board. According to the Internal Revenue Service, Independent Sector, taxpayers with income over $1 million (per year, adjusted gross income, itemized returns), the average charitable contribution in 1980 was almost $200,000; by '90, it had dropped to $140,000; and in '92 it was only $60,000. Taxpayers with incomes in the $500,000 and up range, gave about $40,000 in '80 and dropped off to $20,000 in '92. Management guru Peter Drucker who advises the top corporations in the country calls the lack of generosity among the affluent "our shame and disgrace."

WHAT WAS THE PRICE OF THE MOST EXPENSIVE BALL GOWN PURCHASED IN WASHINGTON?

One charming newly-arrived Leading Lady paid $16,000 for a red-beaded, fur-trimmed creation by Bob Mackie. The most expensive gown for sale in Washington last season was an elaborate pink ball gown in velvet, taffeta and satin with a sprinkling of beads handmade in Paris. The cost of the gown was $40,000.

The price of gowns at this exalted-price level isn't generally advertised by wearers; people often discern a conspicuous consumption complex in Ladies who parade around in a dress as expensive as the family car. In Palm Beach, for example, where chairmen of galas own as many as 20 expensive gowns, the cost of the threads rarely gets expression; when one development director of a leading charity was told that the chairman would be wearing a $35,000 Galanos gown to the annual ball, she commented: "That's about what we'll make from the ball; she could have just given us the money and we'd be better off."

Although expensive gowns still sell well (Bill Blass generated a co
$500,000 in sales at a recent four-day trunk show at Saks in NYC; and Ral
Lauren trunk-showed his way to $1.2 million at a three-day fall show at h
Madison Avenue store), all is not well in the fashion industry. Bob Mack
closed his NYC designer showroom; the haute house of Christian Lacro
lost $5.5 million in '92 (the sixth consecutive year of losses), retailer Martl
of NYC and Palm Beach went into Chapter 11, and troubled manufactur
Gruppo GFT (which makes Giorgio Armani, Valentino, Emanuel Unga
and Claude Montana) admitted to losing $60 million last year. This is due
part, to fashionable women trading down to more modest expenditures, st
prim and proper and very much with it, but not with quite the san
extravagance.

**94. WHAT IS THE AVERAGE NUMBER OF BALL GOWNS OWNEI
BY A WASHINGTON BALL-GOER?**

Eighteen. An average of **two** are very feminine in the southern trac
tion—off the shoulders or pouf sleeves, fitted bodice with a full billowi
skirt in a semi-stiff material such as silk taffeta or organza, maybe sor
glitter, reminiscent of Scarlett O'Hara and Tara. **One** in flamboyant cok
ings and **four** of traditional color such as black or white, perhaps a bead
two with a flower or velvet bow as accent. **One** "strapless" high decollete
black or red, the fabric conforms to the body contours, cut velvet on chiffc
silk crepe or lame. (For variety one might have a very high neckline and lo
sleeves.) **Four** are "short" (something new to wear to the lesser balls
dinner dances). Lace, organza, satin and silk are desired fabrics. Necklir
vary from strapless to jeweled with long sleeves, maybe one with a hi
neckline and a very low back (the teaser). **One** must be in a fashional
designer pattern perhaps edged with sequins, rhinestones or gold braid.
least **one** beaded (top) dress is a must for the most elegant affair, some pre
one shade of beads while others select a beaded pattern in multi-colo
Something in velvet is very festive for the holidays and early January. T
remaining gowns are old favorites and have been proven over the years
floating chiffons that were "in" then "out" and once again "in." **One** mi
even be a pleated Mary McFadden romantic creation that always seems to
au courant, or a glamorous Stavropoulos chiffon. Average price per go
$2,000.

Colorwise, black and red, and traditional colors are always acceptable.
the last few years, more flamboyant gowns have been introduced, howev
with brocade, cut velvet, gold lame, and rhinestone among the more "glit
costuming. As Washington is growing younger, the formal dress is refl
tive; it has a bit more "dynamics" built in, and a greater percentage of
human body is presented (more provocatively). Long gowns take the lead
the more elegant affairs, such as the Red Cross, Heart and Cancer Balls,
younger Washington women opt for shorter lengths about half the time

other galas.

Leading men usually have three tuxedos. A very formal, elegant unit (by Brioni, Armani or Versace at $2,200) for the more playful parties; an orthodox-cut garment (probably by After-Six) for the prosaic evening affairs, and a combination presentation (maybe a double-breasted black velvet jacket, trousers with gray and black stripes) for those "point-of-difference" galas. The orthodox cut unit is the most actively worn.

Men usually have one white tie and tails (or access to same) for supremely formal occasions—state dinners, the Swan Ball in Nashville, opening night at the San Francisco Opera, the Al Smith Dinner at the Waldorf in NYC, or for special weddings.

Somewhat facetiously, fashion editors in various feature stories have indicated the high cost of being impeccably dressed, and the even higher cost of making the right connections and appearing at the right events, balls and functions, so as to be a candidate for the International Best Dressed List (see Chapter I). Some of the costs are (figures provided by the late *Connoisseur* Magazine):

Evening clothes
* 7 short couture dresses @ $10,000 and up;
* 2 long couture dresses @ $7,000 to $25,000 (and up) for the most formal affairs;
* 3 pairs of black shoes or sandals ($1,200);
* 3 pairs of metallic sandals ($1,400);
* 1 or 2 gold jeweled small metallic bags (Judith Leiber, $3,300).

Restaurant, cocktail parties, more informal dining
* 6 short evening dresses with the emphasis on pretty tops. For this season, at least one will be in chiffon; two will be bare with jackets or boleros to go over them. One of the jackets should be beaded and perhaps do double duty with other dresses ($30,000).

Dining at home
* 2 long hostess dresses for very glamorous nights ($5,400).

Cover-ups
* 1 long sable coat ($125,000);
* 1 long-haired fur coat (fox or chinchilla), to wear on really bad days or nights, cut so as to double for the country ($250,000);
* 1 long opera-cloak wrap, fur trimmed and in a rich color like red or burgundy so that it will go over every outfit ($9,500);
* 1 fur-lined raincoat ($8,000).

Daytime wear
* 6 suits—2 Chanel (one black-and-white, the other tweed); 1 dressmaker

suit with peplum or other detail; 1 strictly tailored Yves Saint Laurent chi
1 suit of the season (for fall, it would be in unmatched fabrics); 1 pants su
($32,000);

    * 5 silk dresses, some with matching jackets. If she likes prints she shou
stay with classics (dots, stripes and plaids)—that is the designer messa
($18,000).

    Accessories (this includes only the important pieces)
    * 2 strands 13-mm pearls (up to $200,000);
    * 1 jeweled compact, real ($1,500-$90,000) or Isabel Canovas ($350)
    * 3 black alligator handbags of different sizes, one having a metallic cla
to show it is of jewel quality ($15,000);
    20 pairs of handmade shoes ($20,000);
    3 pairs of earrings—1 pearl, 1 black and gold, 1 gold and diamoi
($35,000 for the lot);
    * 1 gold cuff for day or evening ($8,500);
    * 1 jeweled Indian maharani necklace to wear for informal evenin
($15,000-$20,000);
    * 3 long, long dangling pairs of earrings for evening ($75,000 and up f
the lot);
    * 6 pairs of leather gloves in different colors—to hold if she can't
bothered putting them on ($4,500).

    Based on one's motivation, needs/wants, desperation level, the cost of t
couture life can easily be in the **high six-figure** category each and every yea
For some of the more magnificent and munificent Ladies, a **cool million p
annum** is just another household and lifestyle budget consideration.

95. HOW IMPORTANT IS THE DRESS CODE IN TOWN?

    One of the capital's most sophisticated and gracious socialites, a deca
younger than her peers on the gala committee, showed her style by attendi
a very prestigious ball wearing elegant black silk pants, a white blouse a
gray dinner jacket. She was more than ravishing, and caught the eye of eve
attendee as she addressed the assembly on behalf of the cause. The eveni
proceeded with **deferent nods and salutations** to the fashionable wom
with zero comments about her untraditional approach to gala dressing. T
next morning her phone pulsed constantly—the media was on her case
daring to wear pants to a formal gala, perhaps the first time in history a chan
official had been that audacious. Over the next few days, there was hyped
verbiage about her dress code and enough headlines to get major public
for the event/cause (and a few more donations and followers). In that rega
the event was successful; for the panted-one, however, there was extrei
isolation and her ranking on party lists dropped to C. Her fashions may ha
escalated consciousness of the event, but de-escalated her social desirabili

Just a matter of fashion protocol in a conservative community where propriety is sacred.

In a given lifetime, most people have gone through some of the psychological exercises of the era—**Zen, Iridology, Numerology, Hydrotherapy, Hypnosis, Psychoanalysis, EST, Psychic Readings, Regression Therapy** and the like. Many do it because of peer-pressure; many because of real need, many for the hell of it. These forms of therapy are to the mind what fashion is to the body. If engaging in intellectual revelation of this type raises eyebrows in Washington, so do highly designed fashions. Balenciaga need never worry; he's safely tucked away in history and his gowns still fill the closets of Cave Dwellers. His fashions will live forever despite the fact that they aren't fashionable in the obsessed-with-newness '90s.

Having gone the route of formal pants at a ball (the act was never repeated), the next leap forward would have to be miniskirts for evening wear or formal hot pants or some other **dazzling concoction** from the likes of Mackie, Scaasi or Karan. But such a display of flesh won't hack it in Washington, where the north side of breasts can occasionally be seen, but also, where low-cut is defined as skin showing beneath the Adam's apple. Quiet elegance continues to be the keynote of fashion in Town.

An **arriviste from LA or NY** may show up at a committee meeting in a leather mini and high heels and not cause a noticeable ripple; but her assignment will be modest and enthusiasm for her output limited. Her pizzazz may be too much for semi-Victorian associates and she may be taken for a Player—not really in it for the cause, but for self-aggrandizement. Being a genuine team member requires dressing down to a somewhat indistinguishable level, nonetheless being well turned out. It's not a contradiction—a Lady can be glamourously plebeian.

Much of the Washington dress code revolves around **public-versus-private galas**, parties and outings. At a major fundraising event where the cause requires seriousness, supporters tend to relate to the circumstance. Bland, twilight zone creations fill the ballroom. Women in hard working, dependable styles; no concern with power colors or cuts, just a blend of conformity. At a private party, glimpses of body-hugging designer dresses, arrogantly high heels, jeweled zebra pins and chic whateverhaveyous keep male eyes focused. Although the dialogue may be less than charity grave, it is not necessarily charitable, nor is it totally frivolous. Private party communication deals with universal subjects—the kids or grandchildren, golf, the market, new manager of the club and Republican politics. A few matronly types will always be present (as stabilizers and chaperones) but the general feeling is—glamour is allowable, enjoyable and should be pulled off sans guilt or explanation. Conversely, at a ball, too much glamour is often mistaken for vanity; and vanity has no place in fundraising, the apex of altruism. In short, those who are too aesthetically pleasing are hardly ever perceived as loyalists to the cause.

Unlike other cities—New York or Los Angeles —where women hav' most of the power, **Washington is patriarchal**; men control the socia leverage and are the visible prime movers for most of the Town's action. Th men dress Brooks Brothers and traditional black-tie, and manage quit separate lives, often on the phone, fax or in their library offices. They ar supportive of their wives' work on charities, and willing enough to under write many activities, even high-priced (but not high-powered) gowns an gala accessories. An exotic bird as a wife works no better for her husban than she does for the cause. That ubiquitous tendency for understatemer pervades lifestyle on all fronts.

Sensual, playful people are generally not drawn to fundraising as a outlet; helping generate research megabucks for a debilitating illness ha none of the panache of getting backers for a Broadway play or feature fil starring Burt, Barbra and Liz. Yet, if they are so-drawn, by whateve circumstance, people assume a lesser-dazzling persona; they transfer wha might be physical beauty to a more cerebral style, which simply translates t more work on behalf of the cause, less talk and party-party. Winnin suddenly becomes the only thing in your life, and whereas outside even dictated a life path before, now there's a higher calling which determine everything, even the number of martinis one enjoys each day. So, too, wi the Gala Chairman, who dedicates a portion of her life to the serious busines of running an event and being responsible for generating $$$. The playfe and frivolous is out; replacing the frolic is commitment.

Cartier Chairman Ralph Destino and miracle worker Dina Merrill (Mrs. Ted Hartley).

6. WHAT HAS BEEN THE TREND IN WOMEN'S BALL JEWELRY DURING PAST DECADES?

Precious stones (diamonds, emeralds, rubies and sapphires) have been and will always be "in"—there have, however, been "trendy" stones in recent years. In the '60s Persian turquoise and angel skin coral ensembles (earrings, necklace, bracelet and matching ring) peaked in popularity. These stones were naturally set in platinum mountings; the emphasis was on color. In the '70s black onyx set with diamonds were in vogue. The '80s brought a return to basics—more precious stones, less semi-precious gems; gold settings were preferred to platinum. Pearls, which had not been too popular in the '60s and '70s, made a comeback—with a new twist; the single strand of pearls was out in favor of multi-strands trimmed with a gold and diamond motif. Novelty jewels in the past decade include the popular diamond "tennis" bracelet worn with a Rolex, gold and diamond barrettes and "bow" clip pins set with diamonds. For the ultimate ball-goer this year, Van Cleef & Arpels has a diamond and sapphire necklace or another version with emeralds for $1,700,000; for a red gown, a neck bangle with rubies and diamonds is available for $1,876,000 or if you're a purist, a diamond choker can be had for a mere $1,777,000.

Outside the "ballrooms" unusual jewel designs with touches of "whimsy" are strong in Washington; Cartier's animals (tigers and panthers) fit this category and for only $160,000 the tiger version can be had in bracelet form. Pave settings are also "in." Many Townies are practical in their choice of necklaces—preferring those that can be transformed into a bracelet with matching earrings. Always a "standby" are the traditionally plain gold choker, bracelet, earrings and rings and antique pieces handed down from past generations. A new status symbol of late among the "younger set" is a strand of very fine pearls worn with blue jeans.

Elizabeth Locke (Middleburg) designs many of the jewel fashions worn by local partygoers; semi-precious stones, pearls from the South Seas, burnished gold are the foundations for her works. Of course, *faux* jewelry is always acceptible if not desirable; Barbara Bush gave fake jewels a credibility welcomed by many CapCity Ladies.

7. WHAT ARE THE MOST POPULAR MODES OF TRANSPORTATION TO CHARITY BALLS?

Arriving in a chauffeured limousine is regaining its former popularity; some 20 percent of ball-goers choose this means of transportation. Rolls are at a minimum—about two per ball, self-driven. Mercedes, Jaguars follow in popularity with the ever present American status cars (Cadillac, Lincoln, Chrysler) well represented.

In the suburban areas, depending on the horsepower of the arriving guests, helicopters are quite acceptable; and on waterways, an 80-foot Bertram MasterClass siding up to the dock always commands attention.

98. WHAT ARE THE MOST FREQUENTLY REQUESTED SONGS AT A PARTY?

* **New York, New York** (to get the adrenalin flowing).

* **Tie a Yellow Ribbon Round the Old Oak Tree** (when this song firs became popular, a Washington couple initially met at a party while this son was being played. The couple eventually married and in honor of the son the gent presented his future wife with a "yellow-ribbon pin" custo designed by Van Cleef & Arpels. The $150,000 pin was in the shape of ribbon over 18 kt. yellow gold and trimmed with precious stones).

* **Big Bad Leroy Brown** (usually played after the dinner entree givin party-goers an opportunity to "exercise" before indulging in a fattenin dessert).

***The Best of Times** (theme song from *La Cage Aux Folles*).

* **Memories**

* **Mack the Knife**

***As Time Goes By** (you can just see Bogart and Bergman—a romanti way to conclude a successful party).

In the last season two new songs became very popular; "Wind Beneat My Wings" (theme from the movie *Beaches*) and "All I Ask of You" fro *The Phantom of the Opera*.

At formal affairs, John Philip Sousa music is welcome, and the Marin Corps Band plays whatever it wants at other highly-disciplined events.

99. WHICH ORCHESTRAS ARE MOST FREQUENTLY RETAINED FOR WASHINGTON PARTIES?

The true measure of a party's success is often how much locomotion it ha how many people made their statement by dancing.

Being a social Town, CapCity has its share of society music. **Gene Dona** is probably the area's foremost orchestra leader, having 30 years of exper ence with every type of group and 150 musicians under contract. Born in D and a grad of Catholic University, Donati has played at 24,000 affai including 4,000 weddings (and every inaugural ball since JFK).

"Doc" Scantlin and his Imperial Palms Orchestra claims to be the area premier "big band" and is the only musical group with a "Cotton Club" ty show; he plays at balls, private parties, fundraisers and an occasion concert.

Three other top bands—**Center Stage** (led by Robert Judson), **Odysse** (Bob Jenets) and **Floating Opera** (Glen Pearson) fill the night with mus and have their share of the society action. **The Miles Stiebel Grou** **Howard Devron Orchestra**, **Sidney's Orchestra** and **Mike Carney** sha their sounds with many audiences as do old favorites (on special occasion like **Lester Lanin**, **Miles Davis** and **Peter Duchin**.

0. WHAT ARE BALL-GOERS MOST FREQUENTLY SERVED FOR DINNER?

According to the catering department at The Watergate and The Ritz-Carlton, most commonly served entrees are rack of lamb and veal chops. This is in contrast to the opinion of several veteran ball-goers who remember numerous plates of sliced roast beef and stuffed Cornish gamehens. Catering to today's more calorie-conscious guests, the Watergate has created a new popular dessert, called Coupe Clinton which consists of a chocolate cabbage leaf filled with fresh raspberries and covered with a champagne sabayon sauce. Another favorite is fresh berries with ice cream.

The average cost (of food) at charity luncheons ranges from $28 to $40 per person; at balls, dinner ranges from $80 to $150 per person. Caviar, which is served at 10 percent of balls (and 25 percent of private parties) adds to the cost, but is considered essential.

1. WHEN WAS THE FIRST "OFFICIAL" PARTY FOR A DEBUTANTE IN WASHINGTON?

In 1936, Marjorie Merriweather Post held one of the highlights of that year's social season—a party for her niece, Louise Clisby Wise, who had just made her debut in Wilmington. Washington deb balls then became serious business and ranked with the best—the Passavant Cotillion in Chicago, the Harvest Ball in Atlanta, the Idlewild Ball in Dallas and the Junior Assemblies in NYC.

2. WHAT IS THE AVERAGE COST OF "COMING OUT" FOR A DEB?

About $5,000 per copy; the maximum can come to $25,000, largely based on the extensiveness of a deb's individual party, the lavishness of her gown and the number of people involved. Most gowns run about $500 but a $5,000 tab is not out for big-spending Daddies who want to make it up to their lovely daughters (or are looking for some kind of tax write-off).

3. WHAT WERE SOME OF THE A-LIST PARTIES HELD RECENTLY IN TOWN?

At any given party in the Capital, the usual stereotypes can be found—handsome young girls with sweet souls; a few of the nonverbal, limpid eye types; some social hamsters on their wheels; a few guys who set world records for their hubris; a sprinkling of ladies with sassy attitudes and men with fixed Lothario glares; a cheerleader or two, some benign Brahmins, several diplomats with visceral enthusiasm for everything; the usual quota of narcissists, chauvinists, megalomaniacs, paranoids, and a general smattering of those who love public self-flagellation. It's all part of the screwy machinery of life.

Yet, at most Capital parties, the air is clean, conversation zippy, demean-

ors are in order and constructive dialogue is softly but vigorously decreed. Tha
what took place at these recent outings:

As for **Inauguration** parties, a big winner was the ITT Corporation private je
at the Sheraton Carlton; top company officials greeted politicos, media people ai
assorted local hot shots. Among guests were Rand Araskog, Linda Lou Moor
Harry Truman Moore, Steven and Herman Chanen, Charles Duell, Nan
Thurmond, Mr. and Mrs. Paul Kirk, Shirley MacLaine, former Kentucky Gove
nor John Y. Brown; Michael Kinsly, Bob Bowman, Shelby Soloman, Ell
Goldstein, Robert Harvey, Cathleen Black, Senator Strom Thurmond, To
Harvey, John Kapioltas, Cab Woodward, Bob Bowman, *Washingtonian* Asso
ate Publisher Eleanor Merrill, Esther Coopersmith, Dobli and Sheila Srinivasa
Kitty Kelly and John Zuker.

Buffy Cafritz also staged a lush inaugural party at the Jockey Club where t
Who's Who of political and foreign service life sang and danced and celebrat
the night away with a Hollywood contingent (Barbra Streisand, Warren Beat
Robert DeNiro, Jack Nicholson, Goldie Hawn, Shirley MacLaine) and other VI
like Senator John Warner, Barbara Walters and Joan Rivers; the soiree was t
focus of features in the *New York Times, USA Today* and the *London Daily Ne*
and served as a primer for social aspirants in the fine art of entertaining a
networking.

PETA (People for the Ethical Treatment of Animals) celebrated its 1(
anniversary with the Humanitarian Awards Gala at the Inter-Continental Willa
Hotel; good-looking males in black-tie and women wrapped in Mackie and Sca.
roamed the room enjoying a formal vegetarian dinner. Attendees were Ing
Newkirk, Sabrina LeBeauf, Alex Pacheco, Jane Wiedlin, River Phoenix, Winc
Ryder, Rose Marie Bogley, Carolina Cuono, Elliot Gould, Bill Ginnetti, Ar
Popovich, Kevin Nealon, Chrissy Hynde and David Cohen.

When fabled **Pam Harriman** was officially appointed Ambassador to Fran
John Whitehead and wife Nancy Dickerson tossed a tony shindig at the Ha
Adams Hotel; a few nights later British Ambassador Robert Renwick gave
dinner in Lady Pam's honor at his embassy. New Yorkers Jayne Wrightsman a
Brooke Astor flew in to visit the Ambassadors, as did Barbara Walters, a
Renwick houseguests Robin Leigh Pemberton (Governor of the Bank of Englai
and Norman Lamont (Chancellor of the Exchequer) mingled with other amial
VIPs.

Folger Library's Venetian Masked Ball brought out Townies en masse, a
all enjoyed the intrigue of figuring out who was who. The witching hour for m
Washington parties is 11 p.m., but this event sped on to the l a.m. curfew. Amc
revelers were: Oatsie Charles, Anne Coif Chambers, Tipper Gore, Donna K
McLarty, Katharine Graham, Deborah and Forrest Mars, and Justice Sandra D
O'Connor. Most original mask went to architect Hugh Jacobsen, who wore a tw
story model house on his head, a subtle means of plugging his various enterpris

One of the areas's most celebrated events was the **American Ne**
Women's Club's roast of senior White House correspondent Helen Th

mas; held at the Four Seasons Hotel, some 500 chums joined hands and hearts to pay due respect to the fabled journalist.

Andrea Mitchell, NBC White House correspondent, started things off by saying: "We all have our own ways of getting stories at the White House. Helen brings milk and cookies to George Stephanopoulos, communications director, and is thinking of adopting him."

Columnist Carl Rowan called Thomas, a legend who has covered presidents for 50 years, a martinet hiding behind lipstick and a hairdo, and said she eats politicians for breakfast.

Others roasting Thomas were longtime Congresswoman from Louisiana Lindy Boggs, Abigail van Buren, Sam Donaldson, Sarah McClendon, Jody Powell, who was press secretary to Jimmy Carter; and Dee Dee Myers, the Clinton press secretary.

Congratulatory letters from Presidents Gerald Ford, Ronald Reagan and Jimmy Carter were read, with Carter saying, "Helen is an energizer killer rabbit!" When Thomas took the podium, she said: "I have just come from the White House... Let us pray."

Another smash hit was **Ford's Theater's** 25th Anniversary celebration; satirist Mark Russell was MC at the gala dinner which officially honored producing director Frankie Hewitt. Partyers were Treasury Secretary and Mrs. Lloyd Bentsen, Anne Compton, Dr. Bill Hugher, John O'Neil, Terry Garr, Mrs. Alan Simpson, Peatsy Hollings, Fred Rappoport, Larry Gatlin, Michelle Lee, Harry Hamlin, Janet Langhart, Ken Burns, Sarah Burns and James Earl Jones.

The premier fashion event of the season was the **Seventh Annual International Collection Luncheon and Fashion Show** to benefit the American Cancer Society (at the Sheraton Washington); the event celebrated fashion by bringing the new collection of Emanuel Ungaro to CapCity following its debut in Paris. Alexine Jackson was Chairman; Aliki Bryant, Vice Chairman, and Estelle Gelman, Founder. The luncheon is always one of the Town's best/brightest get-togethers and generally raises about $100,000 for ACS. The International Collection was presented by Saks Fifth Avenue and the Honorary Chairman was His Excellency the Ambassador of France and Mrs. Jacques Andreani. Among committee members were: Ms. Tanya Potter Adler; Dr. Mokhless Al-Hariri; Ms. Audrey Berlinsky; Mrs. Gerald Birnbach; Mrs. Lawrence Brandt; Mrs. Ronald H. Brown; Mrs. William L. Bryant; Ms. Shawny Burns; Mrs. John F.J. Clark; Mrs. Savanna M. Clark; Mrs. Cherie Cushenberry; Mrs. Howard Davis; Mrs. Ralph Deckelbaum; Mrs. Morris Fischer; Mrs. Jeffrey C. Fuge; Mrs. Edward Gilbert; Ms. Vera J. Goodfriend, Ms. Linda Greene; Ms. Barbara Herwood; Mrs. Ralph Hicks; Mrs. Suzanne D. Hillman; Ms. Emily Jackson; Mrs. Edna Jones; Ms. Karyn Keenan; Ms. Kathleen A. Kemper; Mrs. Bernard R. Kolker; Mrs. Sidney Lansburgh; Mrs. Marc Lefkowitz; Mrs. Albert G. McCarthy, III; Ms. Randi-Lynn Meisel; Mrs. Gary Merrill Miller; Mrs.

William Miller; Mrs. Barry Minkoff; Mrs. James Nobil; Ms. Juliet Jackson Othman; Mrs. Nicholas Paleologos; Ms. Reva Pataki; Gwendolyn Russell Ms. Celia Jackson Sarter; Ms. Raleigh Schhein; Dr. Marianne Schuelein Mrs. Robert Snyder; Ms. Arden Staroba; Ms. Janet Steinberg; Mrs. Patricı Suissa; Mrs. Louis Sullivan; Mrs. Barry Taff; Mrs. Joel Taubin; Ms. Shane Uberman; Mr. Don Uselmann; Mrs. Giorgio G. Via; Mr. Robert Waldron Mrs. Robert B. Washington and Ms. Nasreen S. Wills.

Officers of the American Cancer Society, District of Columbia Division Inc. are President Estelle S. Gelman; President-elect Robert Lee DeWitty, Jr M.D.; Vice Presidents Michael G. Carberry, James A. Dalrymple, Walter F Talbot, Jr., D.D.S.; Secretary Diana D. White; Assistant Secretary Merrill S Shugoll; Treasurer W.E. Tige Savage; Assistant Treasurers Kay Fisher an Diana D. White; Counsel George E. Hamilton, III; Executive Vice Presider Sanford C. Milwit and Deputy Executive Vice President Jevita E. Kilpatrick

ACS Director, Public Relations is Lois N. Callahan.

Over the years, some of the parties with the greatest panache and medi coverage were **The Thatcher Dinner**, November 16, '88 at the White Hous **Amazing Grace Ball** to launch the Princess Grace Foundation, February 18 '84 at the State Department Auditorium (now known as Andrew Mello Hall); **Salute to Congress**, January 31, '85 at Sheraton Washington Bal room; **The Dynasty Duo** (or Dinner with Chuck and Di), November 10, '8 at The British Embassy; **At Home Again** (or Gwen Cafritz's Last Party June 10, '86 at her Foxhall Road home; **Abandon Hype, All Ye Who Ente Here** (or The Cancer Ball Goes to Hell), May 16, '87 at the Washingto Hilton Hotel.

Considered the *creme de la creme* of social events in the 90s are: Corcora Ball, Wolf Trap Gala, Alfalfa Dinner, Race for the Cure, Will Awards, Marc of Dimes Gourmet Gala, Gridiron Dinner, White House Corresponden Dinner, Opera Ball, Meridian International Center Ball, openings at th National Gallery, Symphony Ball, Radio/TV Correspondents Gala, Lombard

The Honorable John Whitehead with Linda McPherson and Leslie Stahl—stately at a State Department Reception.

Photo: J.R. Black

96

Ball, Folger's Founder's Day Ball, Kennedy Center Honors, Children's Defense Fund Dinner and the Helen Hayes Awards Gala. Naturally, any special celebrations being held by the White House or State Department rate top billing, too.

Reportage of these social events in most media today is hard copy-oriented with few adjectives and glittery descriptions. The thrust of the '90s is: tell it like it is, quickly, informatively and get on to the next feature. Since the '70s, Baroness Garnett Stackelberg has been "telling it" via newspaper syndication and magazine features. Here's a recent example (April '93) of her coverage at a luncheon honoring Attorney General Reno, and other events:

Attorney General Reno is guest of honor at MacPherson luncheon

WASHINGTON-Janet Reno, the first female Attorney General in the United States, took time off to be the guest of honor at a luncheon at the Jefferson Hotel last week. The party for 40 distinguished women was hosted by Myra MacPherson, wife of retired Florida Senator Jack Gordon. They divide their time between Washington and Miami. MacPherson is a feature writer for *The Washington Post* as well as the author of *Long Time Passing*, a Vietnam book for which she was nominated for a Pulitzer Prize.

Veteran White House reporter Helen Thomas said of Reno: "She was very serene, took praise in her stride, and seemed to be a very down-to-earth person." Others there were Tipper Gore, *Washington Post* publisher Katharine Graham, Sally Quinn, Judy Woodruff and handgun control proponent Sarah Brady.

Among the Floridians present were Florida Congresswoman Carrie Meek

from the 17th district who was co-honoree; Patricia Ireland, President of the National Organization for Women; Margaret Kempel, political activist; as well as Mary Doyle, dean of the University of Miami Law School.

Though a very serious person, Reno has charmed people in Washington with her good sense of humor. She said: "I'd rather be called Janet than general, and you can even say, 'hey you' if you want to."

Another Washington luncheon was given last week by Graham and Jean Jeffrey in the Willard Inter-Continental Hotel's stately dining room for Immo Stabreit, the Ambassador of the Federal Republic of Germany, and his wife, Barbara. Discussions were going on that day between such prominent men as builder Oliver Carr, Joe Krakora of the National Gallery of Art, and Heinz Diedrichsen, general manager of Luf-thansa, about the much-heralded and somewhat controversial Holocaust Museum open-

ing, which would bring thousands of people to the capital.

The Earl and Countess of Bessborough arrived in Washington from Palm Beach last week where they had come from London to help celebrate the 102nd birthday of Hector O. Munn, the Countess' uncle. Among the many friends they saw in Palm Beach were Nancy Dayton Gough, who is aiding the Bessboroughs in their project to have the Benjamin Franklin House in London made into a museum. She is also chairwoman of the Colonial Dames in London and will be attending their benefit for the Franklin House May 11.

According to Steven Senott, a descendant of Benjamin Franklin, Margaret Thatcher will speak gratis for the benefit of the Franklin House in December at an event to be hosted by Lord Gowrie at Sotheby's. Senott said that Thatcher generally receives 20,000 pounds when she lectures.

Mr. and Mrs. Charles Camalier—
sophisticated dining for the especially deserving.

104. WHO ARE THE TOWN'S FAVORITE PARTY PLANNERS?

Any gathering of people, for whatever reason, can be considered a party weddings, special events, new product launches, anniversaries, birthday embassy soirees, whatever, a party is a party; and there are quite a fe superbly qualified party-professionals to make the event one for the histor books. Among them are:

Washington Inc. was founded about 25 years ago by the formidable tri of **Barbara Boggs, Ellen Proxmire and Gretchen Poston** (now deceased over the years it became the premier company in the destination arriva special events category gathering fees in the $10 million range along th way. Strengthened by the arrival of Harriet Schwartz and further impressiv client work, the company was bought in part by a venture capital group an now has offices in Boston and Philadelphia. It is considered the pioneer i party planning and destination management.

Leslie Hayes, Rose Ann Domenici and **Colleen Nunn** (Hayes, Domeni & Nunn) have been around Town for 20 or more years and formed an allianc several years ago to compete for the growing monies involved in par planning. Their background in communications serves them well in execu ing highly creative concepts at CEO levels. Already a factor with the Clintc Administration (having arranged several inauguration activities), they proje healthy growth in the next few years.

The new firm of **Firestone and Korth, Ltd.** (run by Laurie Fireston Barbara Bush's social sec, and Penne Korth, former Ambassador to Mauritiu has already established a gangbusters advisory council (Esther Coopersmit Nancy Dickerson Whitehead, Barbara Bush, Brent Snowcroft and Bud Chapoton) which should assure them the privilege of presenting their case t almost anybody (the power of an introductory phone call).

Carolyn Peachey (Campbell, Peachey & Associates) serves the spectrum of party activities, most notably the nationally televised *Kennedy Center Honors* and NBC's *Christmas in Washington* plus other "Old Guard" activities and the recent *Jurassic Park* intro party.

105. WHO ARE THE FOREMOST CATERERS IN WASHINGTON?

There's no shortage of professionals who can tempt guests into trying any food concoction; here are some of the best:

Capital Catering; creative food and good service tailored to historic sites.

Catering Company of Washington; small company handles large parties with personalized service.

Design Cuisine; an unblemished reputation, with everything from meat and potatoes to nouvelle cuisine; has unusual presentations, great gifts.

Events Related Industries/Knoppel Catering; gourmet American catering and event planning. (Associated with Sequoia and America restaurants).

Susan Gage Caterer; spectacular presentation of customized menus.

Movable Feast; works closely with clients to complement theme of the occasion.

Occasions Caterers; small enough to give personalized service and create innovative menus.

Ridgewell's; Washington institution since 1928, with a touch of historical flavor.

106. WHAT IS THE AVERAGE COST PER PERSON TO STAGE A LAVISH PRIVATE PARTY?

On an average, the cost of a #10 reception and sit-down dinner for 200 guests at The Ritz-Carlton is in the $30,000 range ($150/person); that same party in a private home, properly catered with parking valets and security, will tote up to about $13,000 (which works out to $65/person).

Since nobody admits to be "average" that figure can easily escalate to $20,000 based on some special imported gourmet delicacies, many nebucadnezzars of Dom Perignon and a pricey band, entertainment or gifts.

One sure thing; the bar must be adequately stocked since potables are the preference of most guests. Here's what is recommended as bar inventory for a party of 200 guests: 12 fifths scotch; 12 fifths vodka; 9 fifths each of bourbon and gin; 3 fifths rum; 3 pints dry vermouth (for martinis); 3 pints sweet vermouth (for Manhattan); 3 cases beer (twenty-four bottles); 3 fifths Dubonnet Red; 3 fifths medium sherry; 3 fifths Seagram's 7; 3 cases white wine (12 bottles); 6 bottles red wine; 18 quarts tonic water; 24 quarts club soda; 18 quarts ginger ale; 19 quarts cola; 9 quarts 7-Up; 9 quarts diet cola or diet 7-Up; 12 quarts Perrier water; 12 quarts orange juice; 3 quarts Bloody Mary mix and 3 quarts sweet-and-sour mix.

107. WHICH RECENT WEDDING WAS THE MOST LAVISH?

Altogether, eight daughters of Presidents have said their vows in the Executive Mansion. The other young women who were married at the White House were Maria Monroe, Eleanor Wilson's sister, Jessie Wilson, Elizabeth Tyler, Ellen Grant and Alice Roosevelt.

For splendor and excitement no White House wedding ever matched that of Alice Roosevelt's marrage to Nicholas Longworth, the balding bachelor Congressman from Ohio in 1906.

The only son of a President ever to say "I do" at the Mansion was John Adams, grandson of Abigail Adams and President John Adams, and the son of John Quincy Adams. He married Mary Hellen of Washington in the East Room in 1828, where his grandmother Abigail is said to have hung the family washing.

Of the three Presidents (John Tyler, Woodrow Wilson and Grover Cleveland), who were married while in office, only Cleveland was married at 1600 Pennsylvania Ave. (in the Blue Room, 1886 when he married Frances Folsom).

Most of the weddings at the Executive Mansion have taken place in the East Room.

(In recent times, Tricia Nixon and Edward Cox and the Lynda Johnson Charles Robb wedding ceremonies were held at the Mansion.)

A cousin of Vice-President Al Gore was recently married at Georgetown' tony Holy Trinity Church and "received" in grand, old-world fashion at the family residence—Marwood—in Potomac, MD. On a spread of almost 200 acres, 500 guests laughed and danced a cool afternoon away as the newly weds Deborah Gore Dean and Richard Pawlik made the rounds chumming with old friends. The bride's mother and aunt, chatelaines Mary Gore Dean and Louise Gore mingled and reminisced about "the way we were." Reputedly costing over $100,000, the affair had all the ingredients of splendor in another era.

For the record, the most expensive private wedding ever was that of Mari Niarchos and Alix Chevassus in Normandy, France. Four stadium sized tents were erected to house 2,000 guests; 12,000 bottles of champagne and one half ton of caviar were consumed. Cost: $1 million plus.

In terms of fantasy, the wedding of Mohammed, son of Shaik Zayid ibn Sa'id al-Makkhtum to Princess Salama in Abu Dhabi ('81) lasted seven days and cost an estimated $33 million including the cost of constructing a stadium for the affair.

Washington, a romantic garden spot by any measurement, attracts an unusual number of weddings each year; whether the private type, or a lavish affair at The Four Seasons, or an intimate family-only vow renewal, the affair is always lovely and lively and costly. Here's how the Town stacks against the rest of the country in wedding-related costs:

	National Average	Washington
Invitations (per 100) and Thank-you cards	$286	$650 (Crane Stock and engraved)
Flowers	$478	$4,900 (one PB couple spent $89,000)
Photographs/videos	$908	$3,000
Music (ceremony/reception)	$882	$4,700
Church/Clergy Donation	$166	$1,200
Limousine (8 hours)	$236	$400 ($50 per hour/car)
Wedding Rings (both)	$1,004	$2,700 (Cartier gold love bands)
Engagement Ring	$2,285	$20,000 ($150-$200,000 top of scale and usually second marriage
Attendants' Gifts	$286	$1,100 (Sterling picture frames)
Rehearsal Dinner	$500	$1,500 (20 @ $75 each)
Bride's Wedding Dress/veil	$1,000	$6,500 (Pat Kerr)
Bridal Attendant Gowns	$745 (5)	$2,500 (5 @ $500 each—Kerr)
Bride's Mother's Gown	$236	$2,100
Groom's Formal Wear	$82	$1,500 (tails)
Groomsmen Attire	$333 (5)	$400 (5 rented @ $80 each)
Honeymoon Attire	$936	$5,100
Wedding Reception	$5,900	$21,000 (150 @ $140 each at The Ritz-Carlton
Honeymoon Costs	$3,200	(Concorde to Europe) - plus "extravagance"
Totals	$16,244	$88,000

* On a **national** basis, the most popular wedding gifts were:
—collectibles such as Lalique or other crystal art
—art deco items
—his and hers monogrammed robes (or anything monogrammed)
—decorative clocks
—silver picture frames
—duvet comforters
—barware such as martini glasses by Baccarat
—California sparkling wines
(Note: on a national basis, one of every three gifts are returned or exchanged.)
Washingtonians preferred:
—clocks
—silver picture frames
—decorative planters
—caviar bowls

—white wicker bed trays

—fine champagnes (cases)

* The favorite patterns of Capital brides are:

Silver—Christofles Aria Gold, silverplate trimmed in gold

(Note: many brides inherit their silver)

China—Festivity by Ceralene or Blue Garland by Herend

Crystal —Montaigen Optic by Baccarat and Lismore by Waterford

* The preferred diamond ring shapes are: brilliant (or round), marquise, emerald, pear and oval. There is considerable variation in choice due to changing trends.

Nationally, the third Saturday in June is the most desired day for a wedding; in '92 some 44,000 couples were married on June 16. The average bride was 24.5 years old; the groom was 26.4.

108. WHAT ARE SOME OF THE WASHINGTON "CHARACTERS"?

The song and dance of the Capital creates a new cast of characters with great regularity; bourbon and bonbons, body-english, fun-worshipping are all part of their ploys as they swim in the Great Goldfish Bowl. Here are some types:

* **AGELAST**—One who never laughs; not much joy and wassail.

* **AMBIDEXTER**—A double-dealer; loves to run fancy patterns.

* **AMBIVERT**—One who is neither an in-or-extrovert.

* **CENTIMILLIONAIRE**—Millionaire with more than $100 million. A one-unit man in Texas.

* **CHASMOPHILE**—A lover of nooks and crannies, mostly in bars and restaurants.

* **COCKALORUM**—A very confident little man; usually with an identity crisis.

* **DEIPNOSOPHIST**—One who is good at dinner-table conversation; loves social steeplechase.

* **FANCYMONGER**—One who deals in tricks of the imagination; often good at theWashington tongue-tango.

* **GNOF**—A curmudgeon, frequently into autolatry (worship of self).

* **GRAMMATICASTER**—A verbal pedant; thinks that misuse of the word "hopefully" threatens Western civilization.

* **LYCHNOBITE**—One who lives by night and sleeps by day; not altogether uncommon in the Capital.

* **MARPLOT**—One who frustrates a plan by his/her officious interference.

* **MINIMIFIDIAN**—One who puts the least possible faith in something; usually hates esoterica like astrology, tarot, the occult.

* **MUMPSIMUS**—A person who refuses to correct an error, habit or practice even though it has been shown to be wrong; often of the pip-pip, stiff upper-lip variety.

* **MYRMIDON**—Someone who carries out commands without hesitation or pity; has lots of life force and no scruples.

* **MYTHOCLAST**—A destroyer of myths; a high stepper who loves standing ovations.

* **ONCER**—One who does something once and never again; has had a terrible experience and "once was enough."

* **OPSIMATH**—One who has learned late in life; has spent too much time in cognac and cogitation.

* **PERPILOCUTIONIST.** One who talks through his top hat; a superficial spieler with too much oom-pah-pah.

* **PHILODOX**—One who loves (and lives by) his/her own opinions.

* **PICKMOTE**—One who habitually points out and dwells on petty faults; a second-rate punkaroo.

* **PYRRHONIST**—An absolute sceptic.

* **SALARIAT**—A person with huge salary (income) and the security to go with it; quite in contrast to a proletariat.

* **SPERMOLOGER**—One who gathers seeds by extension, a triviamonger or gossip; enjoys the people-scape side of life.

* **THAUMATURGIST**—One who works wonders; often the czars of charitable balls who with cool, classic equipoise and a primal passion for perfection create the ultimate "mahvelous pahty dahling" and. . . **the concomitant currency.**

With feelings of benevolence, in vivid color—Leonard and Elaine Silverstein.

**The Honorable and Mrs. Najeeb Elias Halaby—
blue skies and beneficence.**

CHAPTER V

CONSPIRATORS & CAMARADERIE
(Charisma, Class & Civility)

Photo: J.R. Black

Balletic, beautiful, boundless—Mrs. Alexandra de Borchgrave.

109. WHAT ARE THE 10 HOTTEST (TOUGHEST TO GET) INVITES IN TOWN?

To each his own in selecting parties that please; let no man prescribe where and at what functions another must present his credentials. Yet, in the Capital there are a few choice parties that people would either die for or sell portions of their souls. Among them are:

(1) Any invitation to the **White House**; you don't usually go to 1600 Pennsylvania unless The Man and His Wife are there to greet you, so any call to that kind of arms is welcome. (2) A plea from **Pam Harriman** is equivalent to a summons; and guarantees an opportunity to stroke the right stuff; (3) Same for **Kay Graham**, where power exudes and the air is electric with sensible chatter; (4) Box seats at the **Kennedy Center** go for $3,750 so any invite to be a guest for Honors night or an opening is, indeed, an honor and a must-go; (5) A subpoena to check in at the **National Gallery of Art** has plenty of panache and should be carefully observed; (6) A few **embassy parties**, specifically British, French, Italian or Canadian affairs have enough weight to be important, although most embassy functions are sub A-list; (7) Dinner and a feature flick at Jack Valenti's **Motion Picture Association** of America's posh offices/studio make up for plenty of lost bonding—a hodge-podge of celebrity partakes of the fun and frolic; (8) Similarly, sitting next to sports mogul and owner of the Chrysler Building, **Jack Kent Cooke** at his RFK Stadium box is sure to introduce some realities to your mundane life; (9) Opening night at the **National Theater** brings on a little nostalgia since the *ancien regime* mixes with Today Power thereby giving history a better balance, and (10) Any 10th or 30th or **50th anniversary** of anything (the Jockey Club, WETA-TV, the American Red Cross) is a night of stars and memories. When you get invited to the 100th centennial of an organization, you begin to think that some things, definitely and definitively will outlive you!

The **Clinton Administration** has picked up on parties lately with infor-mal dinners at the White House (about 40 guests) for dinner/discussion and a little pumping up by the President. So far, about a dozen such parties have been staged, and among guests there is no shortage of people from the media. Here's a partial list of recent attendees:

Madeleine Albright, US Ambassador to the United Nations; Robert Altman, Deputy Treasury Secretary; Dwayne Andreas, industrialist; R.W Apple, Jr., *New York Times*; Senator Max Baucus, (D-MT); Bob Barnett lawyer; Kathleen Battle, opera singer; Lloyd Bentsen, Treasury Secretary Sidney Blumenthal, *The New Yorker*; Taylor Branch, author; Rita Braver CBS News; Senator John Breaux, (D-LA); Lee Brown, national drug policy director; Warren Buffett, financier; James Burke, Partnership for a Drug Free America; Hodding Carter, political consultant; Warren Christopher Secretary of State; Barbara Cochran, CBS News; John Cochran, NBC News Senator Bill Cohen, (R-ME); John Cook, Disney Channel; Fred Dutton lawyer; James Fallows, *Atlantic Monthly*; Senator Dianne Feinstein, (D-CA); David Geffen, film producer; David Gergen, Counselor to the President; Dan Goodgame, *Time* magazine; Donald Graham, *The Washington Post*; Katharine Graham, The Washington Post Co.; Meg Greenfield, *The Washington Post*; Frank Greer, media consultant; Senator Tom Harkin, (D-IA); John Hechinger, Hechinger Co.; Senator Fritz Hollings (D-SC); Jim Johnson, Fannie Mae; Robert Johnson, Black Entertainment Television; Tom Johnson, Cable News Network; Donna Karan, fashion designer; Mickey Kantor, US Trade Representative; Senator Ted Kennedy, (D-MA); Lane Kirkland, AFL-CIO; Bruce Lindsey, Assistant to the President; Ira Magaziner, Senior Advisor to the President; Paul Marks, Sloan-Kettering Hospital; David McCullough, author; Mary McGrory, *The Washington Post*; Robert Meyerhoff, art collector; Roy Neel, Deputy White House Chief of Staff; Jack Nelson, *Los Angeles Times*; Jessye Norman, opera singer; Tom Oliphant, *Boston Globe*; Federico Pena, Transportation Secretary; Charles Peters, *Washington Monthly*; Colin Powell, Chairman of the Joint Chiefs of Staff; Earl "Rusty" Powell III, National Gallery of Art; Peter Prichard, *USA Today*; Molly Raiser, Chief of Protocol-designate; Janet Reno, Attorney General; Robin Renwick, British Ambassador; Felix Rohatyn, financier; Roger Rosenblatt, *Life* magazine; Representative Dan Rostenkowski (D-IL); David Shribman, *Boston Globe*; John Sculley, Apple Computer; Eli Segal, Office of National Service; Brooke Shearer, White House Fellows Program Director; George Sinner, ex-Governor of North Dakota; Susan Spencer, CBS News; Isaac Stern, violinist; Paul Tagliabue, NFL Commissioner; Amy Tan, author; Evan Thomas, *Newsweek* magazine; Laura D'Andrea Tyson, Council of Economic Affairs; Dick Valeriani, formerly of NBC News; Maggie Williams, Chief of Staff to the First Lady; James D. Wolfensohn, Kennedy Center; Mort Zuckerman, *US News & World Report*.

(Note: contrary to public perception about the Clintons' being untraditional in entertaining—not having a formal state dinner, for example—the couple has hosted some 37,000 guests at 137 events during the first six months of the Administration. The concept is to have more small parties where people can actually talk to one another, and possibly say something meaningful. Guests at smaller parties don't use the State Dining Room; rather they go up to the Yellow Oval Room and onto the Truman Balcony. Dinner is usually in the Blue Room, and about 40 guests mingle in a democratic way.)

110. WHAT ARE THE MOST DESIRABLE SITES FOR PARTIES, RECEPTIONS AND WEDDINGS?

Most of the hotels in Town are superbly outfitted to handle almost any kind of revelry; additionally, there are some very special, lesser-known spots for staging the event of your life:

Arts Club of Washington, 2017 I St. NW. Two connecting 19th century townhouses near George Washington University; **Ella Smith House**, 3rd St.

and Maryland Ave. NE. A private home, two blocks from the Capitol; **Barns of Wolf Trap**, 1635 Trap Rd., Vienna. Two 18th-century log barns, home to the Wolf Trap Opera Company during summer months, are available for wedding ceremonies and receptions the rest of the year; **Historic Car Barn**, 3600 M St. NW. Built as a tobacco warehouse in 1761, this Georgetown landmark was converted in the mid-19th century into a barn for horse-drawn trolley cars; **Le Marie Tranier Gallery**, 3304 M St. This art gallery comes complete with an old propeller plane swooping down from the ceiling; **National Museum of Women in the Arts**, 1250 New York Ave. NW. A grand art-filled setting dedicated to promoting work by women artists; **H.H. Leonard's Mansion**, 2020 O St. NW. The five-story structure is brimming with art and antiques, all for sale; *Lady Anna*, Annapolis Bay Charters, 7310 Edgewood Rd., Annapolis. Classic yacht can accommodate 40 for a cruise and a conference on its aft-deck and its salon; **Meridian House**, 1630 Crescent Pl. NW. Antique furniture and lighting fixtures, a Flemish tapestry, Chinese vases, and Waterford torcheres help create a striking setting; **Old Cafritz House**, 5001 16th St. NW. In keeping with its Mediterranean design, this house has white stucco walls, Spanish-tile floors and wrought-iron decorations; **St. Albans School**, Massachusetts and Wisconsin Aves. NW. Gothic architecture distinguishes the buildings of this school, located next to the Washington National Cathedral; **Washington International School**, 3100 Macomb St. NW. The mansion, once the home of Marjorie Merriweather Post and her husband Ambassador Joseph Davies, has two paneled chambers, one with French doors leading to a large covered terrace overlooking woodlands; **Woodrow Wilson House**, 2340 S St. NW. This is the house where the former President entertained royalty and prime ministers.

Also desirable for entertainment or the rites of matrimony are the OAS Headquarters, Andrew Mellon Hall, Textile Museum and the Anderson House, F Street Club, Metropolitan Club, Mt. Vernon, Prospect House and Tudor Place in Georgetown, the Chapel at GU and the Steam Boat in Old Town (Alexandria).

111. WHAT ARE THE LINES OF PROTOCOL AT A COMMAND PERFORMANCE?

When invited to the White House for an evening of illumination, guests must carry on in ways and manners quite appropriate to the history of the brick and mortar of 1600 Pennsylvania Ave. Here's the tracking:

The anointed enter the White House by the South Portico (or at the new security facility at the East Gate where credentials/bags are checked), present their admittance cards, check their coats, and pause (to adjust heartbeat) in either the China or Vermeil Rooms or the Library; next, up the stairs, through the North Entrance Hall into the East Room for the receiving line. Then, down the Cross Hall, past the Green, Blue and Red Rooms, to the **State Dining Room** (which can seat 130 guests at a massive table resplendent with President Monroe's 13 1/2 ft. bronze centerpiece),where, voila, the democratic process, in all its elegance, prevails!

12. WHAT IS THE OFFICIAL/UNOFFICIAL RANKING OF GOVERNMENT OFFICIALS?

The President of the US
The Vice-President of the US
The Speaker of the House of Representatives
The Chief Justice of the US
Former Presidents of the US
The Secretary of State
The Secretary General of the UN
Ambassadors of Foreign Powers
Widows of Former Presidents of the US
Associate Justices of the Supreme Court of the US
The Cabinet
The Secretary of the Treasury
The Secretary of Defense
The Attorney General
The Secretary of the Interior
The Secretary of Agriculture
The Secretary of Commerce
The Secretary of Labor
The Secretary of Health, Education, and Welfare
The Secretary of Housing and Urban Development
The Secretary of Transportat!on
The Secretary of Energy
The US Representative to the UN
Director, Office of Management and Budget
Chairman, Council of Economic Advisers
Special Representative for Trade Negotiations
The Senate
Governors of States
Former Vice-Presidents of the US
The House of Representatives
Assistants to the President
Charges d'Affaires of Foreign Powers
The Under Secretaries of the Executive Departments and the Deputy
Secretaries
Administrator, Agency for International Development
Director, US Arms Control and Disarmament Agency
Secretaries of the Army, the Navy, and the Air Force
Chairman, Board of Governors of the Federal Reserve System
Chairman, Council on Environmental Quality

Chairman, Joint Chiefs of Staff
Chiefs of Staff of the Army, the Navy, and the Air Force (ranke
according to date of appointment)
Commandant of the Marine Corps
(5 Star) Generals of the Army and Fleet Admirals
The Secretary General, Organization of American States
Representatives to the Organization of American States
Director of Central Intelligence
Administrator, General Services Administration
Director, US Information Agency
Administrator, National Aeronautics and Space Administration
Chairman, Civil Service Commission
Director, Defense Research and Engineering
Director of ACTION
Administrator, Environmental Protection Agency
Deputy Under Secretary of State
Commandant of the Coast Guard
Assistant Secretaries of the Executive Departments
Chief of Protocol
Members of the Council of Economic Advisors
Active or Designate US Ambassadors and Ministers (Career rank, whe
in the US)
The Mayor of the District of Columbia
Under Secretaries of the Army, the Navy, and the Air Force
(4 Star) Generals and Admirals
Assistant Secretaries of the Army, the Navy, and the Air Force
(3 Star) Lieutenant Generals and Vice Admirals
Former US Ambassadors and Ministers to Foreign Countries
Ministers of Foreign Powers (Serving in Embassies, not accredited)
Deputy Assistant Secretaries of the Executive Departments
Deputy Chief of Protocol
Counselors of Embassies or Legations of Foreign Powers
(2 Star) Major Generals and Rear Admirals
(1 Star) Brigadier Generals and Commodores
Assistant Chiefs of Protocol

113. WHAT IS THE SEATING PRECEDENCE AT STATE DINNERS?

The Green Book of Washington (see Chapter I) has a Table of Prec
dence which definitively outlines who sits where and why at any given Sta
function; the Table has never been given an imprimatur by the White Hous
nor has it ever been challenged, thus it remains sovereign to this da
assigning seating with authority, giving status to those with seniorit
presuming an almightiness that mystifies even those who have been in t
protocol or diplomatic corps. Nonetheless, here's the procedure.

In the preference list, the President is #1; the Speaker of the House and select Cabinet members are #s 2-7; Ambassadors fill #8 with special rankings therein; members of the Armed Forces and Congress have designations in the #9 category and then on and on with UN delegates, the Organization of American States, sub-Cabinet officers, etc., etc., etc. In all, there are 61 categories.

For the uninitiated, matters of protocol are neatly delineated in *Protocol: The Handbook of Diplomatic, Official and Social Usage* by Jane McCaffree and Pauline Innis (Devon Books); Mrs. Innis has also penned a book re military manners called *Attention! A Quick Guide to the Armed Services* (Devon Books).

14. HOW IS THE PRESIDENT "SALUTED" AT STATE CEREMONIES?

A 21-gun salute on arrival and departure, with four ruffles and flourishes, is rendered to the President of the US, to an ex-President and to a President-elect. The national anthem or *Hail to the Chief,* as appropriate, is played for the President and the national anthem for the others. A 21-gun salute on arrival and departure, with four ruffles and flourishes, also is rendered to the sovereign or chief of state of a foreign country or a member of a reigning royal family; the national anthem of his or her country is played.

Rank	Salute— Arrive–Leave		Ruffles, flour- ishes	Music
Vice-President of US	19		4	Hail Columbia
Speaker of the House	19		4	March
American or foreign Ambassador	19		4	Nat. anthem of official
Premier or Prime Minister	19		4	Nat. anthem of official
Secretary of Defense, Army, Navy or Air Force	19	19	4	Honors March
Other Cabinet members, Senate President pro tempore, Governor, or Chief Justice of US	19		4	Honors March
Chairman, Joint Chiefs of Staff	19	19	4	
Army Chief of Staff, Chief of Naval Operations, Air Force Chief of Staff, Marine Commandant	19	19	4	General's or Admiral's March
General of the Army, General of the Air Force, Fleet Admiral	19	19	4	
Generals, Admirals	17	17	4	
Assistant Secretaries of Defense, Army, Navy or Air Force	17	17	4	Honors March
Chairman of a committee of Congress	17		4	Honors March

Other salutes (on arrival only) include 15 guns for US envoys or ministers and foreign envoys or ministers accredited to the US; 15 guns for a Lieutenant General or Vice Admiral; 13 guns for a Major General or Rear Admiral (upper half); 13 guns for US ministers resident and ministers resident accredited to the US; 11 guns for a Brigadier General or Rear Admiral (lower half); 11 guns for US Charges d'Affaires and like officials accredited to US; and 11 guns for Consuls General accredited to US.

115. WHAT ARE SOME DIPLOMATIC WAVE-OFFS?

You're at an embassy anniversary party, dressed to the nines, a tulip c Dom in your hand, your attitude very up and your tongue more than ready t commence firing. You approach one of the town's finest and foremos couples and initiate smart-but-small cocktail talk, hoping to be anthropologi cally proper, and accepted.

You expect a rejoinder, but you get a **Disinterest Signal**, a definit reduction in the intensity of the expected friendly reaction, an aversion of th eyes and Mr. Finest actually turns his head away from you. If society wan to show its contempt or basic indifference to you, it first **ignores** you, the **laughs** or **snickers** at you, finally it **attacks** you. A good player picks up o the mood in the first 20 seconds and moves in-or-on accordingly.

The **Cut**, or cutting someone dead is simply done by ignoring a proffere handshake or throwing off **Boredom Signals** (mock yawn, deep-sighing, glazed far-away look or repeated examination of a wristwatch). None c these gestures suggest gentility, but they are all part of any social interactio (however sophisticated or exalted) since such functions are nothing mo than human beings setting up a pecking order with one another.

A **Superiority Signal** really hurts; it's a special act which makes a insulter appear pompous or superior by simply tilting the head back a bi combined with half-closed eyes, which gives rise to a "looked down upo gesture. In reality, people with proper carriage often have their heads he high and are basically always looking down on someone because their nos are always up.

Let's say you're at the premier charity cocktail party of the seaso you're enjoying a pleasant conversation about the decorations with charming couple, when two wannabes sidle up and intro themselves. T charming couple knows them from some other life and makes it know they're not quite comfortable; it's done with a **Deformed Complime Signal**, which is simply distorting a compliment. Example: a friend response is modified to make it unpleasant by using the **Tight Smile** (whe you purse your lips while mouth-corners are pulled back in an ordina smile), or the **Cheek Crease** (a pulling back of the mouth-corner). These a not fun smiles in that the recipient sees only a portion of a smile given glad and fully to others.

Only in the more mundane social settings does one see real **Rejectic Signals**, in which the insulter makes a gesture of mild rejection, like t **Thumb Jerk** (a get-lost signal) or the **Insect Flick**, where the flat hand flap flicks or pushes away the rejected person without touching him. More th a few drinks often bring on this type of behavior.

A form of insult can also take place at a performance where the talent given a **Super-Slow Hand Clap**, a form of applause that is really negativ In Spanish-speaking countries, applause by tapping the back of one thum nail against the other is an act of derision. There are endless ways to sho one's superiority (or one's ignorance).

Since Washington parties are so numerous and can go on for too many hours, you often see **Impatience Signals**—small movements that indicate an urge to get away from the present situation; strumming with the fingers, tapping the feet, a mild, but repeated slapping of the hand against the body, false-smiles and glances toward the door.

It's said that the speed of the impatience signal (how fast the fingers strum) roughly equals the speed with which one could exit, given the chance.

There are plenty of gestures which signal an **appreciation** of a woman or man via the use of hands (with no insult intended). The Greeks were always great at the **Cheek Stroke**, in which the forefinger and thumb of one hand are placed on the gesturer's cheekbones and then stroked gently down to the chin—symbolic of the smooth roundness of the face of a beautiful person.

The **Breast Curve** (and the **Waist Curve**) is simply a gesture where a man's hand describes the forward curve of female breasts or the exaggerated female trunk outline emphasizing a narrow waist and wide hips. What boulevardier has not used these gestures at least a million times in his robust and wicked lifetime?

The **Eye Touch**—where a person places a straight forefinger against the lower eyelid and may even pull it slightly downwards—signals that someone is an "eyeful." And the **Two-Handed Telescope**, where hands are curled and placed in front of the eyes like a telescope, suggests a closer look is in order.

The **Hand-On-Heart**—guy places his right hand over his heart—indicates the girl is so beautiful, she makes his heart beat too fast; we don't see much of this posturing in town. It's a Brazilian manifestation.

The Capital is a proper setting for the **Fingertip Kiss**, where the guy kisses his fingertips and fans them toward the girl; the **Air Kiss** is also popular—a person simply makes a kissing movement with the lips in the direction of another person. It's a quick and effective way to bestow a subtle blessing on someone without getting rouged up from a delicate cheek or abraded by a beard.

At the International Red Cross Ball, it's not unusual to see the **Cheek Screw**, where a straight forefinger is pressed into the middle of the cheek and rotated, to indicate the dimpling of a beautiful girl's cheek.

Naturally, it has to be done deftly by an Ambassador from a Latin country, and the object of his affection should be a 19-year-old waitress.

So much for propriety!

116. WHAT IS THE INTRIGUE OF BEING IN THE FOREIGN SERVICE?

The usual benefits of world travel are obvious as is the spirit and importance of representing the US to foreign lands. Most of our diplomats go through a rigorous training period in college (often at Georgetown

University, School of Foreign Service), are assigned junior staff positions in Washington or abroad, work their way up the ladder (based on superior performance and consistently good reports by their superiors) and, usually, over a 15-year period get to the "starting gate" for an ambassadorship. Between the ages of 35 and 50 these junior officers build toward their ultimate goal of being an ambassador or senior foreign official, which with luck will begin at around age 50 and last through retirement.

The motive for hanging in so long with such repetitious assignments, is threefold: the **prestige** of being in the foreign service, the **aristocracy** that comes with any serious assignment in the service, and a formidable **retirement program** (often assuring $60,000 or more per year based on a formula—80 percent of most recent salary which is usually in the $85,000 to $90,000 per year range, thereby providing a substantial retirement income until death, and further income for spouses and surviving dependents). The biggest payoff, however, is simply in being an official in the Foreign Service of the US, thereby having the opportunity to share cocktails and anecdotes with the world's elite—Ministers, Presidents, the Harrimans and Lodges of the world, even Kings and Queens.

Photo: J.R. Black

**Do-gooder Ina Ginsburg with Minnie
in support of the American Film Institute.**

117. **WHAT IS THE MOTTO OF MOST FOREIGN SERVICE OFFICERS?**

"Never Leave the City Where the Good Bars Are," which simply translates to—cement yourself via whatever device to important posts. Paris, Rome, Tokyo, London (where the US Embassy has a staff of almost 700 people, 60 of whom are US Information Agency members) Buenos Aires and Rio de Janeiro are AAA assignments.

118. **ASSUMING DIPLOMATIC EXCELLENCE, HOW ELSE DO MILITARY OFFICERS ATTAIN RANK?**

Much of a professional military officer's success is based on his performance during a war, actually being in combat. But in long periods of peace, an officer (who hopefully, graduated from West Point, the Air Force Academy or Annapolis and thereby started his "career" at age 18, can move up the ladder by (a) attending the Command and General Staff College at Fort Leavenworth, (KS), (b) putting in some hard time at the Pentagon (especially at the Office of the Secretary of Defense) or the National Security Council (where Alexander Haig and Colin Powell made excellence impressions and contacts), (c) going on to higher education (Master's or Doctor's degrees) at a civilian university—most senior officers in the military today have one or more degrees), (d) attending Defense Information School at Fort Benjamin Harrison, (IN) where "media deportment" is taught (and where Norman Schwarzkopf, Colin Powell and Thomas Kelly polished TV performances before the Gulf War), and finally, (e) attending the National Defense University at Fort McNair in SW Washington, where global strategy and national security are the focus.

Officers in the military are graded by their seniors via OERs—Officer Efficiency Reports—which, in theory, reflect the overall performance of an officer. Top rating is a score of 200 and enough "outstanding" and "superior" comments by various grading officers through the years, can position a subordinate for the ultimate ranking of General or Admiral. In peacetime, however, the process is long and debilitating, and if it happens, may take more years (from college to the first star).

The military is not a high-paying profession; for example, a Brigadier General with 16 years of service is paid $5836.50/month as base salary; a Lieutenant General with 20 years makes $7280.40/month; and a four-star General with 26 years of service takes in $8842.20/month. Pay for all branches of service is comparable.

119. **WHO WERE THE FOREMOST "HOSTESSES" OF ALL TIME IN WASHINGTON?**

The art of brilliant hostessing was unknown in Washington (outside of parties given by the White House) until the early '50s; then, in a peacetime economy, the Capital was a natural habitat for progressive lobbyists and ladies who figured "influence" was the newest and most lucrative of service industries.

Accordingly, a number of unchallenged and unrelenting (and untitled) ladies set up shop. Among them were: **Perle Mesta** (Ike was a favorite, as were scientist Werner von Braun, Adlai and LBJ, which friendships got her the Ambassadorship in Luxembourg in '49); **Marjorie Post**, with her Hillwood mansion, yacht, multiple interests and moods; **Gwen Cafritz**, with her real estate millions and a proclivity for international VIPs; **Mrs. Robert Woods Bliss** who attracted the refined/cultured types to her flowered Dumbarton Oaks manse; **Mrs. Truxtun Beale,** empress of historic Decatur House on Bedrayette Square, who coddled the mighty of the Hill; **Mrs. Robert Low Bacon**, who courted power peddlers in her F Street dwelling; **Mrs. J. Borden Harriman, Alice Longworth** and a few others who had the tenacity to meet/greet consistently and convincingly, often without any tangible result.

In typical pecking order fashion, **Mesta** and **Cafritz**, who were definitely not Cave Dwellers, were quietly dismissed by authentic old-line Washington society (they were "obvious, vulgar, egregiously self-seeking"). The expressions NQOC ("Not quite our class") and NOCD ("Not our class, dear") were originated during the reign of the two formidable outsiders.

Lorraine Cooper was often named "queen" of society during the halcyon days of Washington society; she ran a "safe" house (no resultant publicity from any shenanigans), dignified yet exciting, intelligent and clever. **Liz Stevens** (wife of AFI's George Stevens) was also on the top of the heap as a socializer; for a while the late **Steve Martindale**, lawyer and cosmopolite, ran things his way with the social crowd but, as always, ennui and bad press set in and made powering a memory.

Polly Fritchey, Joe Alsop, Jayne Ikard, Evangeline Bruce, Muffie Brandon, Susan Mary Alsop, Jennifer Phillips (wife of Laughlin Phillips, director of the Phillips Collection), over the years, are also considered grande by any measurement.

Photo: J.R. Black

Polly Fritchy and Oatsie Charles—social legends, with legions of followers.

0. HOW DOES AN ARISTOCRAT RELATE TO THE CAPITAL?

The Aristocrat is that rare, pedigreed breed, a product of several generations that avoid flashy customs, but has its share of divorce, scandal and headlines, is conservative and tight with money, owns plenty of land (especially in the country), seems to do things effortlessly, avoids the vulgarity of politics and congregates around the clock in select places like Saratoga, Newport, Southampton and Palm Beach.

A highly visible **Aristocrat (Ari)** is an oxymoron because like most people of genteel breeding, **privacy** is cherished. If seen at all, those of nobility make appearances at their clubs, fox hunts, an occasional polo game and at any affair that has to do with **horses**. For whatever reason, horses are the favorite hobby of the privileged class and the Kentucky Derby or Belmont Stakes usually attracts a roster of the high-and-mighty (who often breed top thoroughbreds).

When asked crass questions like—how much are you worth? an **Ari** will mutter "Enough." Or what do you do? will get a reply —"I do a little investing" (is President of the NY Stock Exchange). Understatement is the keystone of dialog, and old cars, clothing, furnishings, books, homes are a give-away credential of an **Ari**.

Douglas MacArthur, the General **Ari** of the old school, is said to have had his new uniforms tailored from the material of old uniforms so the new ones would be *old in appearance*. Worn tweeds, faded Brooks Brothers shirts, handmade shoes polished over a 10-year period, modest jewelry (even wedding rings) are the **Ari** ways to impress peers (as if that's important).

The landed gentry has roots deep into **land**, usually a **home** in the country. Granted, apartments in several world capitals, and a house in the Hamptons, McLean or Newport are all part of the package—but it is vital for **Ari** to have a **country home**, usually on several hundred acres with paddocks, fields, a river and mountains, maybe an adjoining vineyard, and, of course, horses. Middleburg, Montana, Santa Fe, New York State all have the right feel, and are places of distinction because of the **Ari** influence. In a small society like Palm Beach, an **Ari** can't easily hide, thus private parties and clubs are a way of life versus public dining/drinking spots.

Politics in general are odious to an **Ari**; yet a number of them end up in government, usually as appointed under-secretaries or advisors for the powers-that-be or members of the CIA (where privacy/secrecy is the modus operandi). Franklin Roosevelt was accused of being a traitor to his class by giving up his Hudson Valley squireship to become a politician and a president; Averell Harriman was confidant to presidents and a Governor of New York before going back to raising cattle. Others—the Dillons, Rockefellers, Warburgs, Mellons, Morgans—all disdained politics but were "drafted" to serve their country via appointed offices; and each served with distinction because they had the right connections to get their jobs done.

Actually, an **Aristocrat** (from the Greek **aristos**—the best, and

krateein—to rule), by definition, was born to leadership, but tends to dow
play that role because it, too, is **public**. Since there is no genetic basis
prove that an **Ari** has any particular intellectual superiority, it's qu
possible that an **Ari** avoids publicness—because he isn't very competiti
doesn't want his pedigree challenged and fears failure and the resultant l
of lineage lustre. Most of Teddy Roosevelt's Oyster Bay friends thought
behaved like a buffoon as president and were indifferent to his return
society. In effect, he had besmirched the name of all good **Aristocrats.**

In the eyes of an **Ari**, sailing is quite acceptable while yachting isr
bridge is an upper-class game, poker is not; squash rates well while golf a
tennis are declasse; a martini is the drink of a gentleman, bourbon and sco
are middle-class libations; label clothing like Gucci, Ferragamo, Blass is
for an Ari nor are "hot" cars like Mercedes or Rolls (an Ari car on the avera
is 8 years old.) When forced to buy, an **Ari** will buy American (GE, Mayt
Sears vs. Sony, Sanyo etc.) and not always new merchandise (many a Th
Shop owes its bottom line to the gentry). Television isn't addictive to an A
news and the public broadcast station are favorites, and a night of theatr
historical play) is one of the acceptable outings. Movies are not on the In
for an **Ari** (although video cassettes are becoming popular, they can be s
in private) and attending a baseball or football game with thousands of ot
people is absolutely intolerable.

By whatever vicissitude, an **Ari** is quite tolerant of **misbehavior,**
own, that of his children, even his peers. In families of prime heritage (m
such families have multiple offspring) there is almost always a designa
"Black Sheep" who gets the press coverage and makes public all that
hoped would always be private. But the disgrace goes as quickly as it con
and no one acknowledges it much (except the media, who work feveris
to make more of an incident than there could possibly be, thereby to
more papers or magazines or to keep tube ratings high); it's just a part of
like **Ari** kids flunking out of Harvard or Princeton, being nailed for d
dealing or impregnating the gardener's daughter.

The **Aristocrat** is an important part of Americana, and in subtle
clever ways is always there, somewhere, at the controls of society, add
to the agenda of life, and guiding everyone to higher pleasures and ide
Here's to **Ari**!

121. WHO WAS THE MOST ROYAL OF ROYALS EVER TO VISIT TOWN?

Queen Helen of Romania, the slender and charming daughter of K
Constantine of Greece was also the granddaughter of Emperor Frederick
of Germany and George I of Greece, the great-granddaughter of Qu
Victoria, Emperor Wilhelm of Germany, and King Christian IX of D
mark, a descendant of Catherine the Great of Russia and James I of Engla
the wife of King Carol of Romania, the mother of King Michael, the si

of three kings of Greece—George II, Alexander, and the then King Paul—and a cousin of the kings of Denmark, Norway, and Sweden and Queen Elizabeth of Britain. She was, in short, betitled and entitled!

22. WHERE WAS THE ORIGINAL "EMBASSY ROW"?

Back in the early '80s, Embassy Row was a home—The Decatur House on Lafayette Square, now a property of the National Trust for Historic Preservation. It was owned by Admiral Stephen Decatur until his death in a duel—his widow rented rooms to many foreigners representing their countries. At that time, the house was a Berlitz instructor's dream with as many as 30 different languages being spoken.

Photo: J.R. Black

Hani Masri and the Honorable Lloyd Norton Cutler—peerless in their cigar-smoking prowess.

23 WHAT DOES THE WORD "EMBASSY" MEAN?

Originally, the word "ambassy" or "embassie" meant an envoy's affairs, plans, missions or the staff that carried them out, not the building that housed diplomats.

24. WHAT IS THE ORIGIN OF EMBASSIES AND AMBASSADORS?

The rules of diplomatic precedence were first manifest at the 1815 congress in Vienna; the rules still stand in Catholic countries; Papal Nuncios generally represent various diplomatic delegations when a single authority is needed; in other countries the dean of the corps is the Ambassador of most seniority (in Town, a DP-1 license plate signifies Number One ranking).

The pecking order for diplomats is—Ambassador Extraordinary and Plenipotentiary, Legate or Nuncio, Envoy or Minister, Charge d'Affaires.

119

125. WHEN WAS THE FIRST EMBASSY ESTABLISHED IN THE USA?

France's envoy **Conrad Alexander Gerad** was appointed "Ministe Plenipotentiary" in 1778 and sent to the US; France was the first nation t recognize the independence of the 13 colonies even though the Revolutionar War was still being waged.

126. WHO WAS THE FIRST WOMAN ENVOY TO THE USA?

In '53, **Madame Vijaya Lakshmi Pandit** arrived in the USA as Amba sador from India; she was sister to the then Prime Minister Jawaharlal Nehr (At her intro party, then-President Johnson dropped in, decided to stay f dinner and created havoc—which everybody loved!)

127. WHEN DID THE "EXECUTIVE PROTECTIVE SERVICE" COM INTO EXISTENCE?

The uniformed arm of Secret Service began patrolling diplomatic buil ings in '70; basically, guards were stationed around embassies to preve public demonstrations and to defuse protestors.

128. WHAT IS THE INFLUENCE OF DIPLOMATS IN THE CAPITAL NOW?

It is estimated that some 50,000 foreign diplomats, representatives a families live in the Washington area; 155 foreign missions and 23 intern tional organizations own 375 buildings around the city. The value of the re estate is upward of $20 billion.

129. WHAT IS THE MAIN BUSINESS OF AN EMBASSY?

There is occasional high-level diplomacy carried on by foreign dignita ies, but mainly embassies work in assisting their nationals, issuing visa dispensing business and travel information, representing their countries parties, receptions, trade fairs and exhibitions, and conducting themselv in a way that reflects favorably on their peers and their country.

The *raison d'etre* for an Ambassador is contact with foreign powers by h country, thereby maintaining a place in the international community.

130. WHAT ARE THE BEST-ATTENDED EMBASSY SPECIAL EVENTS?

There are a handful of truly special embassy soirees: Holland's Tul Festival, Sweden's Santa Lucia Christmas repast, French Bastille Day, Ital Columbus Day, toasts and all hail at the British Embassy on the occasion the Queen's birthday, Ireland's St. Patrick's Day, Independence Day festi ties at whatever embassy has been liberated, and, *creme de la creme*—t annual White House reception, glamorized by the JFKs.

Photo: J.R. Black

Celebrating the Russian New Year—Prince David Chavchavadze, Regina and Vlademir Babashvili.

131. HOW DID CHARITY BECOME PART OF AN EMBASSY PARTY?

In the early '40s, the British Embassy staged a do that requested guests to bring a "Bundle for Britain"—people did! The French then decided to charge visitors a small entrance fee to sightsee their embassy; the fee went to the French Red Cross. Now, most embassies are part of the charity circuit.

132. HOW DID ADLAI STEVENSON DEFINE DIPLOMACY?

Quick of tongue and wit, Stevenson suggested: "A diplomat's life is made up of three ingredients: protocol, Geritol, and alcohol."

133. WHAT WAS A TYPICAL EMBASSY PARTY DESCRIPTION IN THE EARLY SOCIETY PAGES?

Even 15 years ago, embassy parties were covered routinely—an opening paragraph outlining the time, place and nature of the affair, followed by a guest list, and the fashions worn by each (male and female, no discrimination here!) Copy was all on the upside, and nobody was publicly ostracized by *The Diplomat*, a newspaper that reported exclusively on the festivities of foreign ministers from 1941-'66. Based in the Capital, the publication reflected the "gentility" of people moving about the world. A "Who's Who" and "Who's-Coming" feature acted as a current "Celebrity Service" and the rich and famous were tucked into print between ads for Cadillacs and sables and sparkling necklaces from Van Cleef & Arpels and columns like "Confessions of a Grand Duke" and "Celebrities at Play."

For a time, the *Washington Times-Herald* and the *Washington News* assigned an editor to cover society; currently only the *Washington Times* has a regular weekly society feature.

134. WHAT WAS THE FIRST EMBASSY COUNTRY TO CHOOSE MASSACHUSETTS AVENUE FOR ITS EMBASSY?

Great Britain first recognized MassAve as a prime location for it sprawling mansion/embassy as far back as 1922; at that time, there were few homes in the area and the Brits had more than enough privacy; Brazil was th second MassAve embassy inhabitant (1934).

135. WHAT DOES KALORAMA MEAN? WHAT EMBASSIES ARE THERE?

The word Kalorama means "view from on high" and the neighborhood c Kalorama, off Massachusetts Ave. near Florida Ave., is as grand as *terr firma* gets; the residence of the Ambassador of France is at 2221 Connecticu Ave., a 34-room, three-story mansion with one of Washington's most spec tacular views of Rock Creek Park and the Taft Bridge.

Eight embassies are located in Kalorama; Ireland, Burma, UAR (in th former Taft home), Royal Thai, Mali, USSR (Annex), Japan and France.

136. WHAT EMBASSY HAS THE LARGEST STAFF?

The residence of the Ambassador of The Russian Republic has a 50(member diplomatic staff, who at one time were forbidden to mix with th population; they lived secretive, humble lives, probably frustrating, bt serving in the US brightened career possibilities. The Embassy is still at th old Pullman House, 1125 16th St. NW, but the fate of diplomats, and th country itself, is undetermined. (The Russians also have a huge Embass building on Tilden St. with a small staff.)

137. WHO WAS THE MOST SWASHBUCKLING OF AMBASSADORS IN RECENT HISTORY?

Iranian Ambassador **Ardeshir Zahedi**, with his dark good looks, per chant for extravagance, mega-life force, and perspicacious eye for womer splashed around town for almost a decade, falling in love with Elizabet Taylor (just prior to her marriage to Senator John Warner), entertaining th likes of Liza Minnelli, Polly Bergen, senators, megamillionaires, the reg: of society and just about anybody who was anything, holds the title of Err(Flynn of Embassy Row. His charm, persuasiveness and zeal for the good lift at one time or another, touched most of Washington's *creme de la creme* an made Iran (then an ally) far more important in Town than it really was. Ye in the normal evolution of fame, Zahedi was cycled out, forgotten and eve renounced by many of his once-ardent friends.

138. WHAT GOVERNMENT PAID THE MOST FOR ITS EMBASSY?

In '76, the Government of Italy bought the 59-room mansion (Vill Firenze) at 2800 Albemarle St. NW for the staggering price of $4,335,00 from the Robert Guggenheims, noted party-givers and CapCity VIPs (at one time Guggenheim was Ambassador to Portugal); the property had the sixth-highest tax assessment in the District at the time ($145,000). The embassy has the largest dining room of any private home in the city; the Mexican and Belgian Embassies also have massive dining rooms.

39. WHAT EMBASSY HAS CARP SWIMMING ABOUT IN GARDENS, PONDS AND WATERFALLS?

Before the Japanese Embassy moved to its present location (4000 Nebraska Ave. NW), its former mansion had an impressive garden and **ippakutei**, (teahouse) standing in the middle of a pond with a waterfall only yards away. The pond served as a skating rink for staffers in winter (when the weather was accommodating) and a cool escape in summer. The new Embassy also has a pond, teahouse and fish!

40. WHAT EMBASSY SERVED AS A NURSERY SCHOOL FOR THE KENNEDY CHILDREN?

When Sir David Ormsby Gore was the British Ambassador in the early '60s, he and the JFKs became close friends; on occasion he would pick up the Kennedy children and bring them to the Embassy Library where he gave them the history of their ancestry.

41. WHO ARE SOME OF THE LEADING EMBASSY ARCHITECTS AND DESIGNERS?

John Russel Pope (Embassy of Brazil), **Arthur Erickson** (Canada), **Jules Henri de Sibour** (Colombia), **Vilhelm Lauritzen** (Denmark), **Henry Anderson** (Indonesia), **Masao Kinoshita** (Japan), **Jack Samperton** (Korea), **Fossen Schwab** (Kuwait), **Bruce Price** (Luxembourg), **Nathan Wyeth** (Mexico, Russia), **Wilmer Bolling** (Netherlands), **John J. Whelan** (Norway, South Africa), **Arthur Heaton** (Sweden), **George Oakley Totten** (Turkey), **Sir Edward Lutyens** (United Kingdom) and **Frank Vernon Murphy** (Vatican).

42. WHAT IS THE "LAMBCHOP PRINCIPLE"?

Coined by Perle Mesta (or journalist Joseph Alsop) the term refers to the esoteric of feeding friends and fellow-diplomats hearty food and drink despite world conditions and state animosities. Through the years, it has proved to be apt philosophy and a sure-fire way to get a party going, regardless of motive and guest list.

43. WHAT ARE SOME KEY DESIGNATIONS IN THE DIPLOMAT'S DICTIONARY?

• BEYOND THE BELTWAY—the rest of the country outside of Washington, DC (origin: the Capital Beltway, Highway 495, which circles th city).

• PEORIA—a small city in the state of Illinois. Stands for the voters wh may not view political developments in the same light as people in Washing ton (they are also the ones who must elect the President and members Congress); e.g., "How will it play in Peoria?"

• THE FOURTH ESTATE—the members of the press, recognized having a significant political function in society (origin: in European feud history, the main "estates" or social classes were seen as being the clergy, t nobility, and the bourgeoisie).

• SPIN—the skillful interpretation or "spin" that is put on events b members of a particular camp in talking with news reporters or columnis to put the best face on damaging situations or to offer one's own views of event (origin: a way of hitting a tennis ball with a racquet).

• POTOMAC FEVER—the condition of being infatuated with particip tion in Washington decision-making and politicking, this "illness" makes difficult for many to leave the capital to resume life in other parts of t country (origin: the Potomac River, which runs by Washington).

• SPOOKS—spies, infiltrators, the unwanted.

144. HOW EXTENSIVE IS THE WHITE HOUSE STAFF?

When 6,000 people come to visit each day (1.5 million/year) and anoth 50,000/year for dinners and receptions, the property had better be we maintained. Thus, the showcase of America—1600 Pennsylvania, the Wh House, Casa Blanca, the Executive Mansion—is massaged each of the yea 365 days by a staff of 76 professionals.

Forty staff members deal with mundane requirements such as plumbin engineering, gardening, painting, carpentering, adjusting and fine-tuni and whathaveyou. Four members work the soil, arranging 36 flower bc quets to be enjoyed on three floors of the mansion plus selective offices the East and West Wings; if there's a reception, 60 bouquets are required pl 14 centerpieces and all kinds of little flourishes.

The domestic staff of 36 professionals include the President's val First Lady's personal maid, five butlers, four doormen, eight cooks, people who clean up and maintain *status quo*.

Status quo is 18 acres of lawns and gardens, 132 rooms, 412 doors (w brass knobs), 32 bathrooms, 40 chandeliers, 78 sculptures, 492 paintin 468 prints or drawings, 1,121 lighting fixtures, 3,303 pieces of furniture a 13,092 knives, forks and spoons. On the second floor (3,000 sq. ft.), there 18 bedrooms, 20 bathrooms, 29 fireplaces and 147 windows. Operating residence (not including the East or West Wings) costs about $9 millic year. In the West Wing, the President's Oval Office employs some 4 workers (and uses 3,000 more from other agencies) with an annual budget $36 million. The size of the entire complex is estimated at 92,000 sq. ft.

The White House, Executive Mansion, *Casa Blanca*—oldest and
most formidable building in the Capital.

party nights, 25 extra waiters are added to the staff plus a head usher with
three assistants and several extras to shore up defenses wherever needed. In
a way, a State Dinner at the White House is a major stage play with dozens
of actors, lighting experts, stage managers and supernumeraries.

Of all the presidents since '60, only Jimmy Carter didn't use the mandated
(by Congress, way back when) White House staff, nor did he fulfill his
diplomatic role as President of the US. His unorthodox procedures (having
his daughter Amy attend state dinners and sit at his table) and manners
(kissing the Queen Mother on her lips) were always out of sync with proper
Washington, but, for the most part, only the press and a few students of
protocol complained.

The Cabinet, however, did note Carter's expense account discretions; as
CEO he had a $50,000 per year entertainment allowance and could pocket
what he didn't spend. The first year he spent $1,372, the second year only
$12,500. During the third year, Congress mandated that all unspent funds be
returned to the Treasury, so Carter accelerated his sociability but still fell
short of the allocation.

Over the years, members of the staff have seen, and participated in,
various upgrades in the structure of the White House. Home improvements
at the Mansion started in 1801 when **Thomas Jefferson** installed the first
toilets, and dumbwaiters in the dining room so that servants would not hear
top-secret conversations; **Andrew Jackson** put running water in the mansion in 1829; **Andrew Johnson**, the first telegraph in 1865; **Rutherford
Hayes**, the first telephone and typewriter in 1877; **James Garfield** installed
an elevator in 1881 and in 1889 **Benjamin Harrison** turned on the first
electric lights; **William Taft** with his 54" waist had to install oversized

bathtubs in 1909; **Franklin Roosevelt** put in the first swimming pool in 193
and **Harry Truman** the first television in 1945; from '61-'63, **Kenned**
reworked almost all aspects of the Mansion and made it into a showplace; **Ike**
Nixon and **Reagan** served their terms in the Mansion by maintaining th
status quo, with minor upgrades; **Carter** put in solar collectors to heat wate
in '77 and **Bush** furthered one of his forms of relaxation by putting in
horseshoe pit in '89. **Clinton** promises to make the Mansion a model o
environmental excellence.

As a sign of the times, President Clinton will be the most-protected CEC
in history with some 150 aides and Secret Service agents on his flanks, a flee
of jets, helicopters, armored limos and chase cars to tour him about and
budget somewhere in the $5 million range for travel/protection (the offic
has an annual budget of $923,000 for travel; the overages are charged to th
military).

145. WHAT HAS BEEN ONE OF THE MOST DISAPPOINTING PARTIES IN RECENT MEMORY?

Outgoing Merrill Lynch chairman William A. Schreyer recently hoste
the **President's Dinner**, a "Salute to Republican Presidents," a CapCit
fundraiser for GOP members of Congress with ducats going at $1,500 eacl
Idea was to have Republican Presidents attend and orate about the comin
political years. Nixon, Ford, Reagan and Bush were expected to attend—nc
one showed up!

Couples who paid $3,000 each were less than delighted with th
proceedings and a few even demanded their money back (all monies wer
to the Republican National Committee; the dinner was successful as
fundraiser). Cary Koops, communications director of the National Republi
can Senatorial Committee, admits to a mistake: "The invitation stated all for
former presidents were 'invited' versus 'expected.'"

146. ON WHAT OCCASION WAS THE WHITE HOUSE HELD UNDEI "VIGIL" BY THE WIVES OF FOREIGN AMBASSADORS?

In the summer of '82, Casa Blanca witnessed a first; a vigil by some 12
wives of foreign ambassadors, dressed in black, holding candles, forming
half-moon around the White House, night-by-night in protest of Israel
invasion of Lebanon. Chatelaines of the embassies of Lebanon, Sau
Arabia, Qatar, Tunisia, Syria, Sudan, Oman and others from Jordan, Kuwai
United Arab Emirates and many former Peace Corps volunteers stood the
ground in protest not only of the invasion, but of President Reagan
welcome of Israeli Prime Minister Menachem Begin. The vigil was a firs
but what followed was dramatic, too; Secretary of State Al Haig resigne
because of his affirmative stand on the Begin visit, and the Reagan adviso
troika—Jim Baker, Ed Meese and Mike Deaver were besieged by the pre
(and the circumstance) for several weeks.

147. **WHO IS AMERICA'S MOST CELEBRATED CHIEF OF PROTOCOL?**

Based on dollar-valuation projections, **Shirley Temple** earned more than $14 million in the movies by the time she was 10 years old.

A $10 check in 1932 was her first income. Despite her curly-haired cuteness, her flair, dancing, singing and acting abilities, she didn't get immediate recognition—she even "flunked" her first film test, for the part in an *Our Gang* comedy.

But by the time Miss Temple was six she had won a special Oscar, and at seven was riding on top of the box office chart. She remained there for three years making three times as much as the President of the US.

When Temple was 19 and her career almost at an end, she played opposite Ronald Reagan and made her last film. She has been married for over 30 years to Charles Black, and served with distinction as Chief of Protocol for Presidents Nixon and Ford.

The miniature Shirley Temple cottage built on the lot at 20th Century-Fox with its enclosed white fenced garden still stands, but it is used for offices, by necessity, for very short executives.

148. **WHAT ARE WASHINGTON'S "LADIES WHO LUNCH"?**

One of the best ways to get into the columns today is to have a **name-designer** on your guest list; having the likes of Scaasi, Mackie or de la Renta turn up at your very special and very own charity function is sure to get ink in the media. Up until about '60, members of the designer-fraternity were taboo—they were only seen in white frocks with pins in their mouths; but

Gloria Haft and Tanya Potter—
Ladies who lunch for only the best causes.

Photo: J.R. Black

when Jackie O (then First lady) started hanging around with Oleg Cassini and Halston designed her famous pillbox hat for the inauguration, designer emerged from salons and took their dutiful positions in all the finest places They dined with their client-Ladies at La Grenouille, Jockey Club and L Cirque, explored fine art at the National Gallery and the Met Museum danced the night away at whatever disco was in at the moment, and **lunche** for heavy discussions about hemlines, flared pants and the state-of-the-ar Today, class-acts like Chessy Rayner won't be seen without Bill Blas Ivana makes headlines with costume jewelry mogul Kenny Lane, an Barbara Bush put Arnold Scaasi on her AAA invite list. If image is vital, th image-maker is king.

Through the years, **clothes** have been a symbol of **identity**. In the 19 century, the WASP **old rich**—those that would not acknowledge a Gould Fisk or Kennedy, were either abundantly fancy dressers or so fearful of bein ostentatious that their clothes were threadbare. Since clothes often were a **insignia** of leisure, most mega-rich dressed down in public so the masse wouldn't be alienated, but dressed up in private moments. In the '90 fashionable clothes intimate success and respect-for-self and a forwar position in the pecking order. Finely rendered dresses and jackets and slack are a mark of the Lady and the perfect **locus** for showcasing them is, of a places, the **Lunch**.

There are several categories of women engaged in the rituals luncheons. Ladies who **do lunch** are a special breed; usually on a diet, slin lean, meaning well but mean, devoid of interest in anything that has calori or fat content or the potential of creating adipose tissue. Yet, they gather La Colline, Duke Zeibert's or Lion D'Or to show their fastidious manners ar the latest from the collections of Yves or Geoffrey or Calvin. It's a wonderf world. All the while conducting serious business.

These **do-lunch** Ladies are fearsome, ferocious performers who mu do something to justify their lovely lives; they are beaverish in plottin executing, analyzing, conspiring and organizing charitable and busine affairs, if not empires. They can be seen in two-three-and-foursomes talkir with animation, nodding agreement almost always and being very discre about scanning the room. They are immaculately turned out and do prese an image of assertive perfection.

Ladies **who lunch** are a different breed; they are more internalize purely social and motiveless in their acceptance of food. They reign, ha reigned or will reign (through marriage, inheritance, circumstance, chronc ogy, anything but work) and are all atwitter, usually about larger issues—the families, grandchildren, the rain forest, weather or how noisy jets still are.

Another category of diner is Ladies who **meet for lunch**. Quite we presented, proper, but a little overweight and tacky, these wholesome bein accept an occasional date as a means of getting away from domestic duties ai seeing how the rest of this admirable world is getting on. There are mod constraints on the amount of money and time being spent on the outing and the degree to which one must listen to the endless problems (or the passionate affairs) another member has. Feminism plays a big role in these discussions. The clothes are from Loehmann's, a glass of house wine is the beverage, Cobb Salad is the entree and desserts are allowed. There is much bill-scrutinizing and doling out of dollars and quarters to pay Caesar for what he has rendered. Tips are **invisible** according to waiters who wonder why meet-for-lunch Ladies aren't at Sizzler's.

As to **availability**, Ladies **who lunch** usually have their dance-card-of-life filled (at least temporarily); they flash their security via Van Cleef and Winston, Chanel and Galanos, and it's automatically assumed that their "man" is powerful, more than affluent, part of the Old Boys network, and thereby, possibly even dangerous. **Do-lunch** women prefer quick but elegant outings, with arrangements made by secretaries (even down to the mineral water being consumed). They are wrapped in a power-dress (having just come from an hour of inspired aerobics), are clear-eyed, quick-witted and desirous of getting the matter resolved. They invariably attract males, and as a courtesy do a little eye-flirting; it's likely that their names and vitals will be requested from the maitre d' after their departure by some husky hormonal gent. **Meet-for-lunch** women scrutinize the men in the room as closely as the bill, but their circumstance in life usually disallows any serious dalliance. They enjoy major desserts, take their time in ordering, don't turn anybody on and use the occasion as the "dream of an everyday housewife." For them, it's showtime—escape from realty.

Since **clothing** signifies rank and breeding, it's natural that women can be pre-classified as they enter a restaurant. Owners and managers can discern a **do-luncher** from a **lunch meeter** or **lunch haver** in seconds, and know just how to handle each species. They fear most, long-term, the **have-lunch** type who can spoil things permanently if they're not pleased with the service, level of deference and presentation of the lunch; although subtle and unassuming, Ladies who **have lunch** expect perfection, and anything less can bring forth unexpected wrath. The **lunch meeters** accept mediocre performance without much ado; they're living out an illusion and don't notice untidy things. In between is the **do-lunch** Lady who demands a top performance, enjoys it, comments on it, and becomes a press agent for the restaurant if satisfied; anything too mundane will rate a rebuke but usually not disenfranchisement. Being in a power-restaurant is often more important than the food.

In short, **you are where you eat!**

Jasmine Aga Khan Jeffries and Arnold Scaasi—
fundraising the high-fashion way.

CHAPTER VI

PRECOCIOUS PERSONALITIES, THE PROFESSIONALS
(Pundits, Practitioners & Promoters)

Photo: J.R. Black

Irene and Abe Pollin—stars of the spirit, and of sports.

149. WHY IS WASHINGTON OFTEN CALLED THE "LAND OF MAKE-BELIEVE"?

Nothing seems to result from the constancy of bureaucrats conferring, presidents proclaiming and Congress legislating; the tangible results from the massive amounts of verbal movements are so minimal as to create an atmosphere of "make-believe" in which everybody presumes forward movement, when there is none!

Washington is a Town of lip-service, high-calorie verbiage and plenty of derring-do. Contradictions abound—the city is the world's biggest spender, but its residents reflect only a middle-class lifestyle; it eats and sleeps politics but has fewer political rights than other Americans; it creates lifelong memories for officials who serve only a few years on a job. And, the power elite are almost all from other cities; only five percent of any given administration's hierarchy is from Washington!

The capital is indeed a magnet for the ambitious who want a make-believe sequence in their lives.

150. WHAT, TECHNICALLY, IS A LOBBYIST?

As prescribed by the Federal Lobbying Act, a "lobbyist is one who solicits, collects, or receives contributions where one of the main purposes is to influence the passage or defeat of congressional legislation and the intended method of accomplishing the purpose is through conversation with members of Congress."

In Washington today, there are about 100,000 "lobbyists" although only about 7,500 are registered as such under federal law. Further, many lobbyists are after-the-fact-government-service lobbyists, having served in some crucial role for the government. At latest count, 81 former congressmen are working as Washington lobbyists.

The most effective lobbyists are "ex-officials"—ex-congressmen, ex-White House staffers, ex-cabinet officers, ex-assistant secretaries, ex-generals or admirals, ex-press secretaries and the like. Most grow accustomed to Washington and the power structure, and rather than return to a mundane life in Des Moines, many once highly-appointed people turn to lobbying. In that role, they can frequent the Metropolitan Club, all the status-oriented watering holes and private clubs, share bagels with the current high-and-mighty and generally keep pace with government.

A prime example of lobbying endurance is **Jack Valenti**, president of the Motion Picture Association of America (he was once an aide to Lyndon Johnson, shares the same Texan drawl and was put in the job as a favor by Johnson) who has been on the job for almost 30 years. He is a major player in Town, charms legislators with private screenings and sumptuous buffets in his lavish Washington headquarters, spends freely on causes and cases that affect the film business, and receives about $500,000/annum for his efforts. His celebrity reaches far beyond the Capital; he is well-known throughout the world, at least in those countries where movies and entertainment are part of the normal lifestyle.

151. WHO ARE THE CAPITAL'S MOST POWERFUL LOBBYISTS?

One thing is as certain as sunrise; all lobbyists are charter members of Handshakers Supreme. Most are brilliant raconteurs whose maniacal energy eventually turns listeners into numb and listless respondents. They deal in pure persuasion.

Lobbyists either work for an Association or corporation, or are "hired guns," individuals or small groups who act as sales agents for a given company or cause. Philip Morris, for example, has some 25 people on Capitol Hill conning and cajoling in favor of the cigarette industry; Pepsi, Coke, General Mills, Ford and General Motors, the airlines and cruiselines, and practically every category of consumer goods spend small fortunes in maintaining a pipeline to legislators who have authority over issues which might affect sales, profits, futures. In many ways, the lobbyists' game is social—right clubs, connections, conduits; in many ways it is cerebral— developing strategies to combat negatively-impacting legislation. Whatever, there is a pecking order of lobbyists in the Capital; here's how the players stack up:

The heaviest hitter is **Tommy Boggs**, a lawyer and offspring of parents who were both respected members of Congress; over the years, Boggs has pitched for Chrysler, GM, the late and great BCCI and other billion dollar

Photo: J.R. Black

Positive thinking practitioners—Barbara, Tom, Lindy and Stuart Boggs.

133

corporations. His firm—Patton, Boggs & Blow—reputedly has fees in the $5 million range, and the ebullient, cigar-smoking Mr. Boggs plays his game in the fashion of the rich and famous. ABC political analyst Cokie Roberts is his sister.

Patrick Griffin and **David Johnson** (Griffin, Johnson & Associates) are right up there with insurance, tobacco and drug (Merck) clients. Fairly new on the block, but very impressive credentials and connections. Take in several million in fees annually.

Owned by an international advertising complex (WPP Group in London) **Timmons & Company** courts for such clients as Union Pacific, Amoco, Anheuser-Busch and G.D. Searle. Principals Tom Korologos and Bill Timmons date back to the Nixon days and are relishing roles as seniors in the business. Their income is folded into WPP Group financial statements.

Akin, Gump, Strauss, Hauer & Feld has superlawyer Robert Strauss on its payroll and is credited with being buffer in Matsushita Corporation's acquisition of MCA. Top gun in the shop is Joel Jankowsky, and several million in fees is reported. The firm also has formidable litigator Mike Madigan on staff.

Stuart Eizenstat of **Powell, Goldstein, Frazer & Murphy** has major credits and a solid track-record; he was Jimmy Carter's chief domestic-policy adviser, and after serving his country, his country served him via alliances with Proctor & Gamble, Hitachi and the resultant seven-figure fees. He is ubiquitous in the Capital, highly respected and a crusader for better relations with Israel.

Other firms in the major lobbyist leagues are: **Wilmer, Cutler & Pickering**; giant p.r. firm **Hill & Knowlton**; **Williams & Jensen**; **The Wexler Group** (Powerlady Anne Wexler is a Clinton confidante); **R. Dully Wall & Associates**; and unusually named **Walker/Free Associates** (headed by Charis Walker) where nothing is free!

152. WHAT ARE WASHINGTON'S MOST INFLUENTIAL BANKS?

Despite some harrowing years (starting in 1990) and the demise of some assumedly impregnable financial institutions (like the District's oldest bank—**National Bank of Washington**, and other favorites—**Madison National** and **Perpetual Savings Banks**) the flow of money to the area continues at an impressive level, and banks generally are healthy. Based on assets, the principal measure of bank size, and as reported in a filing made by Sheshunoff Information Services, Inc. (which analyses info provided by institutions to federal regulators), banks rank as follows (in millions of dollars):

Riggs NB of Washington	District	$4,414
NationsBank of MD NA	Bethesda	4,096
American Security Bk NA	District	3,731
First Virginia Bk	Falls Church	3,079

For the record, the biggest bank by assets in the DC/VA/MD area is NationsBank of VA NA, Richmond, at $11,893(millions); the largest commercial bank in the US is Citicorp (NY) at $216,922 (millions) followed by Chemical Banking Corp. at $138,930 (millions) and BankAmerica Corp. (San Francisco) at $115,509 (millions). The richest bank in the world is the Hong Kong & Shanghai Bank (Hong Kong) with a staggering $3 billion in profits, more than any other bank in history. It owns the Marine Midland Bank in the US.

53. WHAT AREA COMPANIES ARE NOTED AS SOME OF AMERICA'S "MOST ADMIRED COMPANIES"?

Peer approval comes in many ways. *Fortune Magazine* conducts an annual survey to determine what companies are performing well enough to be "most admired." In the local area, **Bell Atlantic** (which operates C&P Telephone) got the most kudos. **Black & Decker, Fannie Mae, Gannett, Mobil, NationsBank, MCA, Martin Marietta, Marriott, CSX** and **May Department Stores** (Hecht Company and Lord & Taylor) all scored impressively. **Sears** and **Hartmarx** occupied the lowest end of the scale while companies like **Giant Food**, the **Washington Post Company, GEICO** and **PEPCO** weren't big enough to be surveyed. Each has a productive market niche and continues to serve residents well.

54. WHAT FINANCIAL GROUP IS ONE OF WASHINGTON'S QUIETEST, YET MOST POWERFUL?

With top players like Jim Baker, Frank Carlucci, Colin Powell, Bill Conway, Richard Darman, Stephen Norris, Dan D'Aniello, and David Rubenstein, the **Carlyle Group** has become the darling of the take-over game in recent years.

Launched in '86 by Rubenstein with financial support from the Richard King Mellon Family, and attracting high-priced executives from Marriott, MCI plus a few from the federal government (notably former Secretary of State Jim Baker, and Defense Secretary Frank Carlucci), the group scored quickly with a major acquisition of the aerospace division of Ford Motor Company in a monumental shoot-out that had half of Wall Street and a half-dozen major corporations involved. Other deals followed: Baker & Taylor, the nation's largest book distributor; Vinnell Corporation, a defense contractor and the aircraft division of LTV Corporation, Caterair International, Four Seasons Communications, the Electronic Division of General Dynamics (GDE), CB Commercial (formerly Coldwell Banker Commercial Real Estate) and The Reilly Group (formerly Oakite Products). The Group's most recent acquisition is Magnavox Electronics Systems Co., a unit of Dutch consumer giant Phillips Electronics NV.

Carlyle now owns eight companies with gross sales of about $4.1 billion; each of the partners can easily afford a fleet of cars and a $3 million estate, but each pushes forward without ostentation, suggesting the **deal** is more important than the glitz.

Members of the Carlyle Group's management team sit on the boards of many prominent companies; among them are Ashland Oil, Bell Atlantic, Connecticut Mutual Life Insurance, General Dynamics, Northern Telecom, Quaker Oats, Upjohn, Vought Aircraft and Westinghouse Electric.

155. WHAT ARE THE BIGGEST BANKRUPTCIES IN THE AREA LATELY?

Since a 1978 revision in the federal bankruptcy law, corporations (and individuals) now find the easy-way-out is simply to file for Chapter 13 and let the courts decide what the financial direction of a down-and-out company or situation should be. In 1992, *bankruptcy filings* totaled 971,517, up 178 percent from 10 years earlier. The 900,874 **personal bankruptcies** accounted for most and cost creditors $21.5 billion.

It's hard to out-bankruptcy giants like TWA, Continental Airlines, Bally, Johns Manville Corp., A.H. Robins (maker of the infamous Dalkon Shield), Leslie Fay Cos., Columbia Gas Systems and Texaco, but a few locals went into Chapter 13 with real gusto.

Most celebrated of the local bankruptcies was that of parking lot impresario **Dominic Antonelli** who at one point had a real estate empire worth several billion dollars. Bad times encroached on his territory, his fortune has been tagged and what was once one of the Town's biggest fortunes now is being fragmented by the courts in an effort to pay off some 3,000 creditors.

Antonelli's Potomac mansion is for sale at $12.7 million as is the property his enterprises own under International Square (estimated at $100 million). He has given up his 103-foot yacht and his stake in Virginia' Natural Bridge, a popular tourist attraction (once owned by Thomas Jefferson). Yet, based on projections for a happy ending, the courts allowed him to keep $5 million in assets and creditors are paying him $400,000/year. All this despite the fact that in '91 when he filed for bankruptcy, debts were $250 million and assets only $120 million.

Other locals who got assigned the unlucky #13 are **Dart Drugs**, big real estate developers **Conrad Cafritz, Mohammad Hadid, Gary and Ann Grimm, Joey Kempfer, Reed Wills, Garfinckel's** and **NBW**.

For the record, **Harry Truman** went bust as a Kansas City haberdasher (but paid all of his debts back in time), and the late mogul/politico **John Connally** of Texas was in the midst of re-emerging from Chapter 13 when he died.

As a sign of the times, some of the normally odds-on-favorites for bankruptcy like shopping malls, hotels and office buildings are becoming healthier as our economy edges forward; and the slogan of tax litigators—"Forgive Us Our Debts"— is becoming somewhat academic.

156. WHAT ARE THE TOP LEGAL FIRMS IN TOWN?

The oldest and biggest law firm in the area was **Covington & Burling**, by any measurement the premier firm in the Capital. It has recently been eclipsed by **Arnold & Porter** in the biggest category.

And by no means does the firm sleep easily at night; dozens of other practitioners of jurisprudence move forward relentlessly with powerful connections, high-velocity strategies and friendships at all levels of the legal system. About 35,000 lawyers are members of the DC Bar Association and they handle the **range of law**: criminal, personal injury, worker's compensation, divorce and family, landlord and tenant, wills-trusts-estate planning-probate, real estate, business-commercial, taxation, bankruptcy, contract, immigration, sports and entertainment, consumer rights and protection, international, juvenile, labor, patent-trademark-copyright and libel.

Skadden Arps, Slate, Meagher & Flom handle monster cases—Clark Clifford, Cap Weinberger—in an orderly, one-upmanship style. Famous in NYC, too, the firm has longevity and track-record on its side.

Arnold & Porter take on clients like Stanford University vs. the federal government (a matter of research grants) or Holiday Spas in a racial discrimination suit. Well-staffed, rich in lore and perceived as superbly intelligent in handling cases, the firm charges high fees and gets high marks in performance.

Wilmer, Cutler & Pickering works the side of the street that focuses on insider trading and stock and securities fraud, and has very successfully defended clients. With several staffers formerly with the SEC it has a trove of knowledge about procedures and practices.

Hogan & Hartson, third biggest firm in the city, represents school boards and educational facilities and serves its clients by getting proper funding for institutions who have been constitutionally deprived.

Akin, Gump, Hauer & Feld gets into litigation about tax evasion, gambling (Pete Rose), savings-and-loans irregularities; the firm still represents major league baseball's commissioner and other mortal immortals.

Other lawyers/legal firms fit specifications: for divorces leading barristers are **Rita Bank** and **Marna S. Tucker** (Feldesman, Tucker, Leifer, Fideil & Bank), **Gwen Lewis** (Lewis, Dack, Paradisso, O'Conner & Good); **Armin Kuder** and **John Long** (Kuder, Smollar & Friedman); **Hal Witt** (Nolan and Bindeman), **Mark Sandground** (Sandground, Barondess & West); **Peter Sherman** (Sherman, Meehan & Curtin). Other top "Terminators" are: **Beverly Anne Groner** (Groner & Groner) and **Bruce Goldberg** (Tietz & Goldberg). **Jack H. Olender** (Olender, Inc.) is a specialist in medical malpractice suits; **Richard Wiley** (Wiley, Rein & Fielding) handles FCC or communication matters; **Brendan Sullivan** (Williams & Connolly) excels at high-profile murder and character assassination cases; **Lloyd Leva Plaine** (Sutherland, Asbill & Brennan) works taxation cases; and **Williams & Connolly** serves many legal masters.

Prestigious Milbank, Tweed, Hadley & McCloy takes on mega-cases in DC and NYC, usually with winning results (**Judge William Webster**, former Director of the CIA and FBI, recently joined the firm): **Whayne Quin** is considered a master at legal zoning matters; and **David Berger** of Philadelphia-based Berger & Montague handles many class action suits in CapCity.

The Capital's biggest firm—**Arnold & Porter** has 370 lawyers and over 1,000 employees, fees in the several hundred million range, offices in NYC, Denver, LA and Tokyo, and each of its 148 partners takes home about $400,000/year.

Other high profits/partner firms are:

Covington & Burling	$435,000	salary/partner
Wilmer, Cutler & Pickering	$425,000	
Akin, Gump, Hauer & Feld	$380,000	
Hogan & Hartson	$365,000	
Steptoe & Johnson	$320,000	
Sutherland, Asbill & Brennan	$300,000	
Arent, Fox, Kintner, Plotkin & Kahn	$215,000	

For the record, the highest-grossing law firms in the country are ($ million in '92):

Firm (City)	Gross	Profits	#Lawyers	#Partners
Baker & McKenzie (Chicago)	$503.5	$ 415,000	1,604	470
Skadden Arps (NY)	440.0	885,000	920	215
Jones Day (Cleveland)	394.5	310,000	1,170	409
Gibson, Dunn & Crutcher (LA)	291.0	505,000	612	210
Weil, Gotshal & Manges (NY)	287.5	725,000	605	143
Shearman & Sterling (NY)	270.0	680,000	548	134
Sullivan & Cromwell (NY)	270.0	1,080,000	361	102
Davis Polk & Wardell (NY)	267.0	1,020,000	400	96
Cleary Gottlieb (NY)	255.0	880,000	436	117
Sidley & Austin (Chicago)	244.0	410,000	646	167
O'Melveny & Myers (LA)	239.5	605,000	537	178
Latham & Watkins (LA)	236.6	455,000	519	216
Morgan, Lewis & Bocklus (Philadelphia)	229.0	365,000	638	243
Mayer, Brown & Platt (Chicago)	217.0	330,000	533	241
Pillsbury Madison & Sutro (San Francisco)	216.0	345,000	592	197
Fried Frank (NY)	215.5	905,000	292	104
Fulbright & Jaworski (Houston)	213.5	355,000	580	262
Cravath, Swaine & Moore (NY)	209.0	1,385,000	308	73
Simpson Thatcher & Bartlett (NY)	207.0	960,000	403	99
Morrison & Foerster (San Francisco)	200.0	235,000	572	230

Source: The American Lawyer

157. WHAT IS THE BUSINESS CLIMATE IN WASHINGTON?

Money is printed at the Bureau of Printing and Engraving, and created at the Federal Reserve Board, but it is still as invisible, perishable and difficult to amass as it is in any other world capital.

Unlike New York or Chicago, Washington is not a city of big business; only five percent of Townies work in manufacturing, with about 35 percent in service industries and the rest in government or government-oriented jobs.

As a matter of fact, only 18 percent of all Washingtonians work for the government per se. The biggest company in the area is the **Marriott** Corporation with some $6 billion in revenues; but **Mobil**, in Fairfax County, with its massive staff and facilities is vying for supremacy. Champions, also, in size are **USAir Group, MCI Communications, Giant Foods** and **Intel**. Printing and publishing is the biggest single industry in the area with tourism, computer graphics and trade associations (about 3,200 associations lobby for soft drinks, movies, tennis shoes, gun control, ozone layer education, etc.) not far behind. Although not based in DC, **IBM** has a massive presence in the area with some 12,000 people on various payrolls.

"Beltway Bandits" like **Martin Marietta** ($5 billion in sales) do government work, but do not work for the government; it does have massive revenues from the Department of Defense, but it is not considered a "captive" company of the bureaucracy.

The average local family makes 40 percent more than the typical American household, about $47,000/year (vs. $33,000 for the US as an average); two-thirds of Washington women have jobs (one-third of them in professional posts). One local family in three makes more than $50,000/year. Washington is a middle-class city in income, with the usual extremes of incredible wealth and dire poverty.

**Bill Seidman—financing
and funding favorite.**

158. HOW POWERFUL IS THE MEDIA IN GOVERNMENT?

Awesomely so. Press secretaries, information officers, communication experts and assorted other functionaries in the world of getting the word out have high placement in the pecking order of any given official. For example, last year, these government offices had this number of employees on the payroll in the service of "communications" (advertising, public relations, media management, etc.):

Agriculture	513
Health and Human Services	266
Treasury	212
Interior	155
Tennessee Valley Authority	135
NASA	116
EPA	91
Energy	89
Transportation	74
Justice	60
Commerce	59
State	59
Veterans' Affairs	56
Labor	54

Further, there are about 800 Press Secretaries on Capitol Hill and over 1,600 media managers at the Pentagon. In each case, the designated "Press Secretary" is, in fact, a media celebrity, often appearing on national television (especially during a crisis that affects a particular department) several times a day. Although salaries for Press Secretaries are not high (but can reach $100,000 per year) the perks are superb; and when a tour of duty is completed, the Secretary generally moves on to a very high paying job at a network or major new media complex.

159. WHAT ARE THE LEADING MEDIA COMPANIES IN THE AREA?

About 12,000 journalists cover the local scene for publications far and wide, but the biggest staffs are located in Town to serve the needs of the big four:

The Washington Post Company (*The Washington Post, Newsweek* magazine, and broadcasting properties); **Gannett Company** (*USA Today* and broadcast outlets); **United Press International** (editorial services to hundreds of print and broadcast outlets); and **National Geographic Society** (magazine of same name plus maps and specialty publications).

160. WHO ARE THE TOWN'S MOST INFLUENTIAL MEDIA PEOPLE?

In a Town where most journalists have learned to sit with dignity on the razor's edge, there are so many stand-outs it's difficult to be selective, but here's a go at it:

For those who have bled the blood, sweated the sweat and lost the money in gaining their doctorate as sages with staying-power, **David Brinkley** (ABC), **Elizabeth Drew** (free-lancer and pundit), **Paul Duke** (WETA-TV), **Jack Germond** (*Baltimore Sun*), **Walter Mears** (AP), **Helen Thomas** (the forever-girl of UPI) and **Bob Woodward** (*Wash Post*) are the masters of the chase.

Others who have considerable clout are **Sam Donaldson** (ABC), **David Broder** (*Washington Post*), **Maureen Dodd** (*NY Times*), **Johnny Apple** (*NY Times*), **Walter Fineman** (*Newsweek*), **Paul Gigot** (WSJ), **Meg Greenfield** (*Wash Post*), **Brit Hume** (ABC), **Al Hunt** (WSJ), **Larry King** (CNN), **Michael Kinsley** (CNN), **Ted Koppel** (ABC), **Jim Lehrer** (PBS), **John McLaughlin** (Indie), **Doyle McManus** (*LA Times*), **Andrea Mitchell** (NBC), **Jack Nelson** (*LA Times*), **Robert Novak** (Indie), **Peter Richard** (*USA Today*), **Cokie Roberts** (ABC), **Tim Russert** (NBC), *New Republic* deputy editor **Jacob Weisberg** and editor **Andrew Sullivan, William Safire** (*NY Times*), **Bob Schieffer** (CBS), **Bernard Shaw** (CNN), **Susan Watters** (WWD), **Mark Shields** (PBS), **Evan Thomas** (*Newsweek*), **Nina Totenberg** (NPR), **George Will** (ABC), **Judy Woodruff** (CNN), **Sidney Blumenthal** (*New Yorker*), **Wolf Blitzer** (CNN), **Hal Bruno** (ABC), **Mort Zuckerman** (*USNews*), plus a few long-ball hitters from the *Washington Times, Cox, Newhouse, NY Post, Roll Call, Time* and all those bureaus in the National Press Building, 1331 or 2000 Pennsylvania Ave., and 1627 Eye St. and **Rather, Jennings** and **Brokaw** (network anchors).

Legends like **Ben Bradlee** and **Walter Cronkite**, although wanting no more trenchwork, remain powerful voices in the media, and can get an audience at the drop of a syllable.

161. HOW MUCH DOES A TYPICAL WASHINGTON JOURNALIST MAKE?

Based on luck, timing, **hubris** and influential sources, the sky's the limit in income potential for a young writer; one major break can launch a career with the same velocity as a rocket, but the average scribe gets in line for his weekly paycheck just like anybody else.

The minimum salary at the *NY Times* is $1,000/week; the average newsroom salary at the *Washington Post* is $55,000/year; a *Newsweek* senior editor can earn up to $100,000 and feature writers usually take in a six-figure salary. Same for top local broadcast journalists (some local TV favorites easily make $500,000) and newsreaders.

In a league quite beyond reach are latter day **Walter Cronkites** in the form of **Peter Jennings, Dan Rather, Tom Brokaw** who have contracts calling for several million/year (or more – Rather has a $36 million contract for 10 years and his is the least rated of the nightly network newscasts), and columnists like **George Will** (who also authors books), anchor **Bernard Shaw** and commentator **Barbara Walters** rake in largesse too significant to mention (but it's in the millions).

Most of these "communicators" have good credentials; 93 percent have college degrees, 50 percent have attended grad school and 33 percent have advanced degrees including Ph.Ds. Only about 20 percent of adults country wide have college degrees, so the Washington counterpart is elitist by comparison.

Via alliances with book publishers and movie folk, a journalist can make several million on one project alone – *All The President's Men, Absence of Malice, The Killing Fields* and *Network* were works by local journalist which scored big in Hollywood. **Carl Bernstein** and **Bob Woodward** became international celebrities (and earned millions) with their Watergate expose and author of best-sellers **Tom Clancy** now gets a cool $5-10 million advance for his works.

Talk shows, special appearances, lectures and seminars are also income channels for media people, and it's not unusual for someone making $100,000 in salary to pull down another $150,000 via these functional outings.

162. WHO WAS THE DEAN OF THE PRESS ESTABLISHMENT?

Bureau Chief of the *NY Times*, **Arthur Krock** was a long-term Fourth Estater on the Washington scene, a confidante to Presidents, an insider with Congress and a man-about-Town.

His ilk (**Drew Pearson, Kenneth Crawford, Walter Lippmann** often considered the ultimate journalistic insider, he had no qualms calling a President in the middle of the night for confirmation on a story—**Pete Lisagore, Stewart Alsop, Walter Trohan** and **Doris Fleeson**) are long gone and are, basically, irreplaceable; same for publications like *Look*, the *Saturday Evening Post, Newark News, Washington's Dossier* and *Regardie, Evening Star* and *Daily News, Chicago Daily News, Philadelphia Bulletin* and *New York Herald Tribune*, which served well but couldn't master awesome competition.

The **first** newspaper in Town was the *National Intelligencer*; it was also the first national newspaper in the country. The **last** tabloid in the Capital was the *Washington Daily News* which went out of business in '72; its owner Scripps-Howard sold the late Ernie Pyle's desk (he of WWII fame, especially Guadalcanal) for $35,000, and an era ended when the wrecking ball destroyed the offices at 1013 13th St. NW.

The *Washington Star*, owned by Time-Life Inc. folded in 1981 after 128-years of publication. A new daily, the *Washington Times*, owned by the Rev. Sun Myung Moon's controversial Unification Church, started up in '8 to pick up some of the slack, and continues to perform creditably.

Throughout the years, most journalists (including the most famous chronicler of early Washington society – Margaret Bayard Smith) were members of the **National Press Club** or the **Gridiron Club**, where they compared adjectives with peers. Today, the Press Club is a hang-out for intermediates – news, advertising and lobbying professionals, while the Gridiron Club (once the exclusive domain of 50 white scribes) is less than animated and fully democratic with TV journalists and media hypes in the meeting rooms. It still has an annual event and several roasts that attract the muckymucks of Town (and in '92 elected UPI's Helen Thomas as its first woman president).

63. WHO ARE THE MOST INFLUENTIAL EDITORS IN TOWN?

Son of a Boston stockbroker, fourth-generation Harvard graduate, Naval officer in WWII and police reporter for the *Washington Post* in 1948, **Ben Bradlee** is hands-down best editor in the US, or was. He recently ended his monarchy at the *Post* and went into some kind of semi-retirement.

Bradlee became Editor of the *Post* in '69 (after serving as a press attache at the US Embassy in Paris and a foreign correspondent for *Newsweek*) and under his tutelage the newspaper won 23 Pulitzer Prizes, circulation zoomed up to 850,000, the news budget rose from $30 to $60 million and the newsroom staff from 300 to 600 (by comparison, the NY Times has 900 staffers in the newsroom with an operating budget of over $100 million and a circulation of 1.2 million). His third wife is **Sally Quinn**, a formidable novelist and Style-section writer for the *Post* and (after many years in Georgetown), the twosome now lives in a Virginia estate, where his only link to the profession is a room full of computers and tickertapes.

Working day-to-day in Town and flexing their muscles are a number of women who as editors/correspondents are shaping their views in provocative ways, Among them are: **Maureen Dodd**, White House correspondent, **Linda Greenhouse**, Supreme Court and **Robin Toner**, political – all correspondents for the *NY Times*; **Michelle McQueen** of the *Wall Street Journal*, **Ellen Warren**, *Knight-Ridder* and **Ann Devroy** of the *Washington Post*.

64. WHAT IS KNOWN AS THE "HERNIA PACK" OF WASHINGTON?

At 1,184 pages (and 61 ounces in weight), George Shultz's memoirs – *Turmoil and Triumph: My Years as Secretary of State* – is the longest book dealing with the administration in recent history. Shultz devotes an average of 182 pages to each of his six and a half years as Secretary (vs. 66 pages/year for Cap Weinberger at Defense in his book and 748 pages total for Ronald Reagan to chart his way through eight years in the White House). On the short-and-sweet side, Hubert Humphrey enunciated his views – *The Educa-*

tion of a Public Man – in an average of eight pages per year for 60 years.

The former SecState added to his laurels recently when given a honorary doctorate from Hebrew University in Jerusalem; Mayor Tedd Kollek also gave Shultz honorary citizenship in Jerusalem (which nov makes him an honorary citizen of 78 cities/countries).

165. WHAT IS WASHINGTON'S MOST ENDURING MEDIA MOGUL BRAWL?

For years, *USA Today* founder and Gannett President **Al Neuharth** ha been lambasting former *Post* Editor **Ben Bradlee** about the mediocrity of th newspaper's reporting; insults have been returned with some enthusiasm. recent exchange: from Neuharth – Bradlee is a "pluperfect jackass." Fror Bradlee — "If what he's doing is journalism, I don't know what I've bee practicing all these years."

Both publications have enormous leverages: the *Washington Po.* reaches almost 850,000 readers daily with in-depth coverage; *USA Toda* has over 1.3 million readers and features terse editorials on several hundre subjects.

Designer Bob Waldron with Sally Quinn (Mrs. Ben Bradlee)— power and skill via the quill.

Another bloody and public battle took place in '91 when USIA Director **Bruce Gelb** (who had formerly been in the million dollar/annum range as chairman of Bristol Myers Squibb took on his underling **Richard Carlson** (former TV anchor and affluent enough, too), chief of the Voice of America. The VOA produced memorable work under Carlson, including the prediction that Hussein would invade Kuwait, but two headstrong executives invariably cross blades. After months of front-page wrangling, the matter was settled by Mr. Bush with appointments for both men as ambassadors — Gelb to Belgium, and Carlson to the Seychelles (92 nondescript islands in the Indian Ocean).

At the time **Henry Catto** was named CEO of USIA; he had served Mr. Bush as Ambassador to the United Kingdom, was Nixon's representative to the Organization of American States and Ambassador to El Salvador, as well as President Ford's chief of protocol. He also had a long and joyful marriage to journalist Jessica Oveta Hobby (whose mother Oveta Culp Hobby was first US Secretary of Health, Education, and Welfare, the widow of former Texas Governor William Hobby and owner of the *Houston Post* until it was sold in '83 for about $130 million, giving the family a fortune of some $800 million).

In his stint as protocol chief, Catto had the honor of squiring the late Emperor Hirohito of Japan around the country. During a tour of Disneyland, Mickey Mouse pranced about the Emperor bowing and and saluting; a dazed Emperor returned the bow which kept running for 15 minutes until an aware assistant turned to Mickey and said "Piss off, mouse." Just a matter of protocol.

Although residents of Colorado, the Cattos still maintain a sprawling house on 30 acres along the Potomac in McLean.

**Wynona and Naomi Judd with
perennial man-of-the-year—Bob Hope.**

Still ongoing is the **Dart Family** imbroglio; 72-year-old Herbert Haft, family patriarch and 57 percent owner of **Dart Group Corp.** (Crown Books Corp. and Trak Auto Corp.) has fired his son, tossed him off various Dart boards and even removed his wife from any official company duties. The battle began with ever-mounting pressure from 40-year-old son Robert Haft (who founded Crown Books and built it into a $241 million enterprise, the third largest book distributor in the country) to become CEO of the group, thereby having more command than his father. After initial agreement on a time to change the guard, the senior Haft turned 180 degrees, denounced the plan and fired his son and some of his trusted lieutenants. Those who know the Hafts are saddened by the family squabble, but understand — there are no guarantees. (Recently, Haft named his 34-year old son, Ronald, to be Dart CEO and a director of the holding company; at the same time, he was being sued for divorce by his wife of 45 years, who is seeking her share of company stock and by ousted son Robert.)

166. WHAT IS THE COST OF KEEPING UP WITH THE NEWS?

The well-informed allocate several thousands dollars per year for keeping up with the news. Here's how it breaks out:

Newspapers (one year subscription)	Cost
New York Times	$260
Washington Post	119
Washington Times	78
USA Today	107
Wall Street Journal	139

Magazines	
Newsweek	42
Time	62
US News/World Report	40
Forbes	52
Business Week	45
Esquire	16
People	80
Vanity Fair	15
Washingtonian	22
New Republic	70
New Yorker	32

Most expensive of the "reports" is the *Daily Report for Executives* (365 issues) at $4,809; the least costly periodical is *Spy Magazine* (12 issues) at $14.95. (For the record, the largest-selling magazine in the country is *Modern Maturity* with 22.4 million readers, followed by *Reader's Digest* at 16.3 million, *TV Guide* at 15.3 million and *National Geographic* at 9.9 million.)

167. HOW DOES WASHINGTON HANDLE GOSSIP?

Gossip was called the bane and disgrace of society by George Eliot and "intellectual chewing gum" by some anonymous Cave Dweller. Admittedly, it can be harmful, unjust, awesome in implication, false and malicious, but it also can be astute, incisive, instructive and truthful.

As in any society-driven community, Washington is not without **gossip**—it is a daily routine at golf games, club outings and nocturnal pursuits. While gossip may not always be truth, it is at least openly suspect; and while it may not be fair, everyone has access to it, there are no limitations on its availability. It is simply part of our lives—part of the daily 5,000 words each person uses. Much like eye contact, a nod of the head, a wink or pat on the shoulder, gossip is a verbal means of communicating **something special**.

Anthropologists say that gossip is a "given," a universal component of human nature; condemning or ignoring it is futile, and unwise for anybody dealing with other humans as the means to an end. Unlike computer-oriented societies, CapCity deals with charities, funding and power, each predicated on the performance of a person, a group, a committee, **people**. Thus, the imperative of using gossip to its best advantage.

In **Washington**, "Dear Abby" or the *Enquirer* or some nebulous grapevine is not significant, but verifiable gossip—known as "insider information," distilled gossip which equals "informed speculation" and the infamous "leak" which is really a directed flow of gossip—is vital.

Gossip can help move **life forward** in many ways. As an **Equalizer**, the **G-word** softens the myth of the mega-rich; all the intimidating talk about how wealthy he is, or how extensive her properties are, or what company is next on the agenda for acquisition, can be put into better perspective when there's small talk about the peculiarities of the person in question. After the verbal genuflection publicly given to Megaman, small talk can be used to cut big talk down to size and as an antidote to pomposity and authority. Gossip is the Great Leveler when used to talk about the sad relationship the Queen of Society has with her children, or the terrible golf game the King pushes on his peers, or the dismal lack of happiness in the Royal Family.

As a **Morale Booster**, gossip keeps the committee members who work the dull side of an event upbeat and functional; nothing can be more deadly than hour-after-hour addressing of envelopes, and nothing offers a better opportunity for some affirmative rumor-spread. In this case, gossip can be used to politic, socialize and reinforce someone's performance. Gossip implies a negative; but can be very **positive**. By the Chairman simply stating that the assembled group has addressed more envelopes in less time than in any previous effort, the word is out. Winners all!

While gossip is normally chosen by those who want to **slander** others without exposing themselves to cross-examination, facts invariably surface, usually discrediting the slanderer in the process. Thus, as a **Lie Detector**, gossip identifies those whose information **can't** be trusted, and conversely,

those who **can**. Gossip is, in this instance, an ongoing credibility tes
everybody takes, with or without knowing it.

It's said that **hell is a place where everybody is condemned to min**
his own business—there is no hotline in the inferno, no flak, no town crier
It's surprising how **quickly** gossip gets passed from party-to-party; memo
and formal communication may take weeks to reach an audience; gossij
usually leapfrogs from **source-to-subject** in minutes. A Chairman, migh
for example, want to shake up the raffle committee by quietly passing th
word to staff members that raffle sales are slipping, or the raffle prize is no
exciting enough, or whatever. Not surprisingly, that word will flow with th
speed of light, and in all probability, remedial action will be taken.

Gossip is a great medium of **P.R.**; the Chairman can casually sugges
she's heard (from an undisclosed source) that her leadership is too rough o
co-workers (when in fact, she is very patient with the less-fortunate). He
friends will instantly rally-round her with allegiance and praise, all of whicl
simply gives her more momentum in being a bit overbearing (if that's wha
it takes). "Undisclosed sources" have incredible credibility when use
effectively; by being good at what you do and dropping a few lines about th
acceptance of your performance, generally more **favorable** response i
generated.

Very importantly, gossip serves as a **Guidebook** to the prevailing rules
latitudes or morals of a given circumstance; what is considered harsh
obscene or out-of-touch is quickly put into the pipeline of words after a fev
meetings person-to-person. Gossip is mostly nuance in these situations, bu
clearly delineates what the **real** values, ethics and realities are. Rumor ma
have it that the chair's husband loves his cups and is a source of grea
embarrassment for his wife; thus, she is always harried, unsure and indeci
sive. The gossip may be right on the money, and if so, committee people ca
adjust accordingly or confront the issue. Nobody likes to fool around wit
Mother Nature, or a Chairman, but for the well-being of the party, action ma
be required.

Although hype has its place in the world, extended hype or **untrutl**
however circulated, usually is emasculated by truth. In a way, gossi
expedites the process—it exposes the fraudulent, reveals the inept, se
players and pretenders up for failure. It may begin casually, but with eac
messenger, different layers of revelation (and danger) accumulate. Th
finale of a particular rumor may be accommodation, disaster or triumph, bu
each of the **carriers**-of-the-world is exposed for what he truly is, too.

168. WHO ARE THE TOWN'S MOST CELEBRATED AUTHORS?

Except for New York, the Capital probably produces more origina
books via its denizen/authors than any other American city. That's becaus
of the plenitude of info available in the 500 libraries in Town, and th
constant sense of intrigue and excitement that pervades every party an

Walter Cronkite and Maureen Stapleton—noble, notable, nonpareil.

political doing in Town. Here are some written-word winners:

NOVELS

Tom Clancy (*Patriot Games, Red Storm Rising, The Cardinal of the Kremlin, Without Remorse*, etc.); **James Michener** (*Alaska*, and tons of other great stuff); **Larry McMurtry** (prolific author – *Last Picture Show, Electric Horseman,* and owner of Georgetown bookstore); **Betty Beale** (*Power at Play*); **Barbara Raskin** (*The A List); ***Letitia Baldrige** (*Of Diamonds and Diplomats*); **Rachel Carson** (*The Sea Around Us* and *Silent Spring*); **Louis Halle** (*Spring in Washington*); **Christopher Buckley** (*The White House Mess*); **Arnaud de Borchgrave** (*Monimbo*); **Douglas Kiker** (*Death at the Cut*); **Larry L. King** (*Because of Lozo Brown* and a dozen other fine works); **Charles McCarry** (*The Bride of the Wilderness* and many others); **Phyllis Reynolds Naylor** (*Unexpected Pleasures*); **Sally Quinn** (*Regrets Only*); **Sam Shepard** (*Chicago & Other Plays*); **Susan Richards Shreve** (*A Country of Strangers*); **Judith Viorst** (*Necessary Losses*); **Herman Wouk** (*War and Remembrance* and many of the great novels of our time); **Patrick Anderson** (*The Pleasure Business*); **Alan Cheuse** (*The Grandmother's Club*); **Marita Golden** (*Long Distance Life*); **Stephen Goodwin** (*Blood of Paradise*); **Jim Grady** (*Steeltown*); **Martha Grimes** (*The Five Bells & Bladebone*).

HUMOR

Russell Baker (*The Good Times*); **Art Buchwald** (*I Think I Do*
Remember); **Herblock** (*Herblock at Large*); **Jeff MacNelly** (*Shoe Goes*
Wrigley Field); **Judith Martin** (*Common Courtesy*); **Diana McClell**
(*Ear On Washington*); **Michelle Slung** (*The Only Child Book*).

NONFICTION

Scott Armstrong (*The Brethren: Inside the Supreme Court*); **Sidr**
Blumenthal (*Our Long National Daydream*); **Daniel Boorstin** (*Hidc*
History); **Tom Boswell** (*the Heart of the Order*); **Benjamin Brad**
(*Conversations with Kennedy*); **David Brinkley** (*Washington Goes*
War); **David Broder** (*Behind the Front Page*); **Patrick J. Buchanan** (*Ri*
from the Beginning); **Sam Donaldson** (*Hold On, Mr. President!*); **Jan**
Fallows (*Human Capital*); **Jon Franklin** (*Molecules of the Mind*); **Seymo**
M. Hersh ("*The Target is Destroyed*"); **Gary Hart** (*The Good Fight*); **B**
Hume (*Inside Story*); **Kitty Kelley** (*Nancy Reagan*); **Tom Kelly** (*l*
Imperial Post: The Meyers, The Grahams); **Frank Mankiewicz** (*Televis*
& The Manipulation of American Life); **Eugene McCarthy** (*A Decade*
Political Wit & Wisdom); **David McCullough** (*Mornings On Horsebac*
Daniel P. Moynihan (*Loyalties*); **Joseph Persico** (*Biography of Willi*
Casey); **Carl T. Rowan** (*You Can't Get There From Here*); **William Saf**
(*Take My Word For It*); **Letitia Baldrige** (*Guide to Executive Manne*
Neil Sheehan (*A Bright Shining Lie*); **Jack Valenti** (*Speak with Confiden*
Protect & Defend); **Ben J. Wattenberg** (*The Birth Dearth*); **George F. V**
(*Men At Work*); **Bob Woodward** (*Veil: The Secret Wars of the Cl*
Lawrence Leamer (*As Time Goes By*).

The most celebrated husband/wife writing teams in Town are **Jim a**
Kate Lehrer, who have 10 works (independently or collectively) under tl
belts (*Man in the Moon, Blue Hearts*, etc.), and **John Naisbitt** and v
Patricia Aburden, who made *Megatrends* part of the language. Other w
known team novelists are **Colin and Kathryn Harrison, Joan Didion a**
John Gregory Dunne, Stephen and Tabitha King and **Louise Erdrich a**
Michael Dorris.

The most enduring journalist in the area is **Eric Friedheim**, Editor of
well-respected weekly magazine—*Travel Agent*. For some 40 ye
Friedheim has authored a weekly editorial on the impact of travel
tourism on the world economy; in that period he has produced over 2,
editorials which qualifies him for the *Guinness Book of World Record*
"Longest running weekly magazine columnist." His latest book—*Tr*
Agents, from Caravans and Clippers to the Concorde ($23, Universal Me
is in distribution, and his multiple philanthropies—funding the Friedh
Library at the National Press Club, the Eric Friedheim Journalism Center
electronic newroom) and the Friedheim Quadrangle at American Univer:
plus the annual Friedheim Competition for Orchestral and Chamber M

by American Composers at Kennedy Center are a reflection of his appreciation of journalism and the arts.

69. WHO ARE WASHINGTON'S TOP LITERARY AGENTS?

Although Washington isn't quite as formidable a literary market as New York, there is plenty of celebrity and a plethora of top-grade books coming from the area. A good book is often the function of a good agent, who puts the property in the right publishing hands, where in turn it is put in the right channels of distribution. Thus, the best seller. Here are the Town's top book deal negotiators:

Robert B. Barnett, Adult nonfiction and fiction titles, Williams & Connolly; **David Cutler & Associates,** Adult nonfiction and fiction titles; **Anne Edelstein Literary Agency,** Adult nonfiction and fiction titles; **Evelyn Freyman,** Adult nonfiction and fiction titles; **Ronald Goldfarb,** Adult nonfiction and fiction titles; feature films/plays/television shows. Public relations services and lecture bookings for authors (Newsmakers, Inc.); **Larry Kaltman Literary Agency,** Adult nonfiction and fiction titles; **Literary Agency of Washington,** Adult and juvenile nonfiction and fiction titles, short stories, magazine fiction, articles for national magazines; **Muriel Nellis,** Feature films/plays/television shows; adult nonfiction and fiction titles; The **Sagalyn Literary Agency,** Adult nonfiction and fiction titles; **Ann Tobias,** Children's and juvenile nonfiction and fiction titles; **Audrey Adler Wolf,** Adult nonfiction and fiction titles, feature films/plays/television shows.

The *enfant terrible* of Town now is **Bob Barnett** who charges his star-clients as much as $400 for conferences on their upcoming projects. He has negotiated some of the biggest deals in the Capital, and according to his peers, he doesn't have impeccable manners, but his performance is always outstanding. On his current roster are:

Chris Wallace, Willard Scott, Katie Couric, Andrea Mitchell, Susan Spencer, Phil Jones, Bernard Shaw, Wolf Blitzer, Cokie Roberts, Judy Woodruff, John Palmer, and such local TV personalities as **Paul Getty, Kathleen Matthews, Wendy Rieger, Cindy DiBiasi, Sue Palka,** and **Lark McCarthy.**

70. WHAT IS THE AREA'S MOST SUCCESSFUL AD AGENCY?

The nation's 21st-largest (and only one of six big shops outside of NYC) is **Earle Palmer Brown** (EPB) of Bethesda, with billings of about $500 million, a staff of 600 employees and clients like Marriott, USAir, Weight-Watchers, ChemLawn and Domino's.

With offices in NYC, Philadelphia, Richmond, Atlanta, Norfolk, Tampa, Nashville and Kalamazoo (plus headquarters in Bethesda), the agency competes against giants like Omnicom, Leo Burnett, J. Walter Thompson, Foote, Cone & Belding, (all in the $2-5 billion billing range), and succeeds often based on its superior knowledge of a local area or product.

EPB is run by Jeb Brown, son of founder Earle Palmer Brown who starte the agency in 1952; in the last 10 years, the agency has grown dramatically, ar is far-and-away the biggest and best equipped agency in Town.

171. WHO IS THE TOWN'S TOP ADMAN?

Recently, **Edward N. Ney** was elected to the Board of Directors Power Financial Corporation (group of companies holding substanti interests in the financial services industry in Canada and the USA; in Euro the company also has equity in companies in communications, industrial ar energy sectors) after a long and fruitful career as Chairman and CEO of gia NYC-based agency Young & Rubicon, Inc. He was Ambassador to Cana from '89-'92 and now serves as Chairman of the Board of Advisors Burston-Marsteller of NYC and DC. He is a member of the Advisory Boa of the Center for Strategic and International Studies, the Executive Comm tee of the Foreign Policy Association, the Council on Foreign Relations, t Advertising Hall of Fame and a Trustee Emeritus of Amherst College.

During his tenure in various jobs, Mr. Ney used "marketing" as t medium to build acceptance for products and services; and as Ambassad to Canada was instrumental in putting the groundwork in place for the Nor American Free Trade Agreement.

172. WHO ARE THE CAPITAL'S TOP PHYSICIANS?

There's a plenitude of medical help in Town; here are leaders (listed office location and hospitals at which they perform their wonders):

Dr. Shelby H. Josephs, Bethesda. Hospitals: Children's National Me cal Center, Georgetown, Holy Cross;

Dr. Robert T. Scanlon, Bethesda. Hospitals: Georgetown, Sha Grove;

Dr. LaSalle Leffall, DC. Hospitals: Georgetown, Sibley, Harvard;

Dr. George Bren, downtown DC. Hospitals: Georgetown, Geor Washington, Washington Hospital Center;

Dr. John V. Russo, Northwest DC. Hospitals: Georgetown, Sibl Washington Hospital Center;

Dr. Marc Lippman, Georgetown University;

Dr. Robert J. Carnathan, downtown DC. Hospitals: Georgetov Sibley, Suburban;

Dr. Richard J. Castiello, Bethesda, Northwest DC. Hospita Georgetown, Sibley, Suburban;

Dr. Douglas N. Robins, downtown DC., Silver Spring. Hospit George Washington, Holy Cross, Sibley, Washington Hospital Center;

Dr. James N. Ramey, downtown DC. Hospitals: Georgetown, Geor Washington, Washington Hospital Center;

Dr. Neil D. Ravin, Chevy Chase. Hospitals: Georgetown, George Washington, Sibley;

Dr. Katherine L. Alley, offices in downtown DC.; hospital privileges at Columbia Hospital for Women, George Washington, Sibley;

Dr. J. Richard Thistlethwaite, Bethesda. Hospitals: Holy Cross, Shady Grove, Suburban;

Dr. Charles R. Boice, Bethesda. Hospitals: Columbia for Women, Holy Cross, Shady Grove, Washington Hospital Center;

Dr. Kenneth Goldstein, Chevy Chase, downtown DC. Hospitals: George Washington, Sibley, Washington Hospital Center;

Dr. Stanley A. Schwartz, Chevy Chase, Silver Spring, Washington Hospital Center; privileges also at Georgetown, Holy Cross, Sibley, Suburban;

Dr. Carol Salzman, Chevy Chase. Hospitals: Georgetown, George Washington, Sibley;

Dr. Mark I. Cinnamon, downtown DC. Hospitals: Columbia for Women, George Washington, Washington Hospital Center;

Dr. Bruce N. Garrett, downtown DC. Hospitals: George Washington, Washington Hospital Center;

Dr. Stephen G. Goldberger, Alexandria, Clinton. Hospitals: Greater Southeast, Mt. Vernon, Southern Maryland, Washington Hospital Center;

Dr. John W. Cochran, Alexandria, Annandale, Reston. Hospitals: Alexandria, National Orthopaedics and Rehabilitation, Jefferson Memorial.

Dr. Craig A. Dickman, Rockville, Silver Spring. Hospitals: Holy Cross, Shady Grove, Washington Hospital Center;

Dr. Gustavo A. Rossi, Arlington, Reston. Hospital: Arlington;

Dr. H. Jane Blackman, Northwest DC. Hospitals: Georgetown, Sibley, Washington Hospital Center;

Dr. David Plotsky, downtown and Northwest DC. Hospitals: Children's, Columbia for Women, Howard County General, Washington Hospital Center;

Dr. Stephen S. Haas, Chevy Chase, downtown DC. Hospitals: Georgetown, George Washington, Sibley;

Dr. Edward C. Rabbitt, Alexandria, Clinton, downtown DC., Waldorf. Hospitals: Georgetown, Mt. Vernon, Southern Maryland;

Dr. Norman Lee Barr, Jr., downtown DC., McLean. Hospitals: George Washington, Sibley;

Dr. Daniel D. Rooney, Fairfax, Vienna. Hospitals: Fairfax, Fair Oaks, Reston;

Dr. Allan B. Coleman, downtown DC., Rockville. Hospitals: Holy Cross, Shady Grove, Sibley;

Dr. Robert L. McDowell, Jr., Northwest DC. Hospitals: Children's, Georgetown, George Washington;

Dr. Steven D. Lerner, Chevy Chase, downtown DC. Hospitals: George

Washington, Sibley, Washington Hospital Center;

Dr. Susan E. Otero, downtown DC. Hospitals: Providence, Sibley Washington Hospital Center;

Dr. Robert J. Wilensky, Chevy Chase, downtown DC. Hospitals Columbia for Women, Sibley, Suburban;

Dr. Howard I. Levine, Bethesda, Rockville. Hospitals: Shady Grove Suburban;

Dr. Patience White, Children's Hospital, George Washington;

Dr. Barry L. Levin, Bethesda, Northwest DC., Rockville. Hospitals Holy Cross, Shady Grove, Suburban;

Dr. Nicholas L. Constantinople, downtown and Northwest DC. Hospitals: Georgetown, Sibley, Washington Hospital Center;

Dr. Michael H. Phillips, Chevy Chase, downtown DC. Hospitals Sibley, Washington Hospital Center;

Dr. Hugh H. Trout, Bethesda, downtown DC. Hospitals: Holy Cross George Washington, Sibley, Suburban.

173. **WHO ARE THE BEST-RATED DENTISTS IN THE CAPITAL?**

Based on a survey by *Washington Consumer's Checkbook Magazine* these professionals led their field:

Dr. George Baxter, 1234 19th St. NW

Dr. Chester Seil Selig, 4327 Nebraska Ave. NW

Dr. Everett Cobb, 4400 Jenifer St. NW

Dr. J. William Donaldson, 5225 Wisconsin Ave. NW

Dr. John Drumm, 2124 Tunlaw Rd. NW

Dr. Joseph Eanet, 916 19th St. NW

Dr. Gary Elder, 17121 St. NW

Dr. A. Patrick Flynn, 1111 19th St. NW

Dr. Vincent Greco, 1712 I. St. NW

Dr. Fred Greenspon, 1145 19th St. NW

Dr. Robert Hood, 499 South Capitol St. SW

Dr. Bernard Kirshbaum, 2506 Virginia Ave. NW

Dr. Robert G. Lange, 3409 Wisconsin Ave. NW

Dr. Larry J. Peterson, 1234 19th St. NW

Dr. Jon Presley, 1145 19th St. NW

Dr. Richard Robinson, 5406 Connecticut Ave. NW

Dr. Richard Rogers, 1234 19th St. NW

Dr. Salvatore Selvaggio, 3601 Connecticut Ave. NW

Dr. Richard Thomas, 1919 Pennsylvania Ave. NW

Dr. Lloyd Vakay, 2440 M St. NW

Dr. Bernard Yanowitz, 4900 Massachusetts Ave. NW

Dr. Edwin Zimmet, K St. NW

Dr. Pasqual Tijani, 2021 K St. NW

74. WHY IS WASHINGTON THE EPICENTER OF RHODES SCHOLARS?

Cecil John Rhodes set up his Oxford scholarship with the millions he made in gold and diamonds from his South African mines; he wanted his followers to be soldiers in the "world's fight" and to spread the gospel of western civilization all over the world.

Today, candidates for the scholarship are culled from each state; two per state gain entry into a regional shoot-out and finally meet with the masters to determine who will be one of the 32 Rhodes Scholars from the US (incidentally, when President Clinton was a Scholar in 1968 only men were eligible – this year 15 of the 32 Rhodes Scholars attending Oxford will be women). Scholars have two years in England, not unduly pressured to perform (eight weeks of school, six weeks of vacation, eight more school weeks and six more "vac" weeks, three months of vacation and travel and learning how the pundits handle life – it's a reprieve that requires lots of self-ignition). Students report to tutors and basically discover knowledge on their own, so only the strong-of-heart-and-discipline make their mark.

More Rhodes Scholars per capita live in Washington than in any other city in the US; at last count, 225 members of that elite group call the Capital home. They do their jobs as lawyers, senators, journalists, educators, "egg-heads," military or intelligence officers or administrators.

Seven Rhodes Scholars are currently on Capitol Hill: Senators **Sarbanes** of MD, **Bradley** of NJ, **Boren** of OK, **Lugar** of IN, **Pressler** of SD and Representatives **McMillen** of MD and **Cooper** of TN. Justices **Byron White** and **David Souter** are scholars as are **James Billington** (Librarian of Congress), retired Senator **J. William Fulbright**, **James Fallows** of *The Atlantic*, **Howard K. Smith**, **Jacob Weisberg** of *The New Republic*, columnist **Michael Kinsley**, retired **Admiral Stansfield Turner**, a slew of Clinton aides (**Stephanopoulos, Magaziner, Reed** and **Reich**) and educators (three scholars each at Georgetown and U. Maryland, for example). Most live in NW Washington and via whatever device have six-figure incomes.

Washington is a magnet for Rhodes Scholars in that government and international law are key subjects studied by scholars, and the old boy network has its greatest strength in the Capital.

75. HOW MANY ASSOCIATIONS HQ IN WASHINGTON?

Of the leading 100 "Associations" in the US almost 40 of them call the Washington area home; they range broadly in size and scope, national vs. provincial interest, age categories and historical orientation.

The biggest group is the **American Automobile Association** (Falls Church) with 28 million members; next is the **American Association of Retired Persons** (DC) with 25 million stalwarts; followed by the **National Right-to-Life Committee** (DC) at 12 million members, the **National Geographic Society** (DC) with 10 million geography-lovers and the **4-H Program** (DC) with 5 million members.

The National Geographic Society is a media empire with print and broadca channels to members plus direct mail, seminars, workshops, even a nation "Geographic Bee" (contest to determine most knowledgeable geographe Members in 200 countries are reached through the monthly publication (*Nation Geographic*) with a readership of 44 million people. Second only to BBC is t society's TV production arm which makes dozens of documentaries each ye the book division produces about 20 books/year and via an affiliation wi National Public Radio, a broadcast "Unheard World" is carried on 450 rad stations. With annual fees of $21/member, the society generates some $2 million annually.

176. WHY IS WASHINGTON OFTEN CONSIDERED A "WOMAN'S BEST FRIEND"?

Only about four percent of private foundation money goes to program that support women and girls, yet this audience makes up to 75 percent of t poverty-stricken and is the fastest growing segment of the homeless. T Capital has a number of nonprofit organizations that serve women's nee and is therefore a "friend" in need. Some organizations are:

National Coalition Against Domestic Violence
National Coalition Against Sexual Abuse
National Institute for Women of Color
National Displaced Homemakers' Network
National Committee on Pay Equity
Women's Legal Defense Fund
National Women's Law Center

177. WHO IS "FONZ" IN WASHINGTON?

City dwellers who want a place to contemplate life can join FON (Friends of the National Zoo) and spend pleasant hours working in educ tion, conservation or research, all projects which open doors to field tri community festivals, lab volunteers, zoo keeper aides and any number zoo-related activities. Socially, events like the ZooNight, ZooFari a ZooBilee keep everybody happy and in the right mood to talk to the anima

178. WHAT IS WASHINGTON NARCISSISM?

"I never said—I want to be alone," noted Greta Garbo, "I only said I wa to be **left** alone." The fabled actress was so notorious in her search f anonymity that she qualified as a masterful **Narcissist** for she needed cont over her life (to avoid criticism) and demanded-but-repudiated adulation a way that kept her prominently in the press. Never has a person used t media so adroitly; in her absence she was constantly present, and feeding h ego without exposing it. **Image-makers** through the years have prais Garbo for her Machiavellian use of the media and her frequency of messag

Whatever imperfections she might have had never came to light on the front page of *The National Enquirer*, a feat unto itself in this era of visible, electronic self-adulation. Typifying the narcissism of the '80s (and now the '90s) was Warren Beatty's evaluation of Madonna: "She doesn't want to live off-camera."

Narcissism comes from success, hard-won or ill-gained. An 18-year-old model or actress who suddenly is cover girl to all the world gains entrance to **mates, money, respect** almost too easily and too quickly. After a while it's difficult to separate her need for personal acceptance from the requisites of her profession; she's in the limelight whenever in public and soon becomes the petulant personality expected of her. If her image-program goes well, she'll soon be the darling of the press for her **conspicuous self-indulgence** (a la Streisand and the late MM); whatever her public aberrations, they will add to her perception as a star, and feed her **narcissistic** needs, too.

A particularly disturbing aspect of narcissism can be the great divide between a warm, overindulgent **childhood** and **a real world** that never can match expectations—result is a tentative adult who searches for love indiscriminately, never finding it because to get love, one has to be capable of returning it. This is especially true when adulation is based on inherited physical beauty or wealth, and the **inheritor** feels that praise for her is false in that looks or money were bestowed on her and were not from personal accomplishments. Look to Barbara Hutton, Gloria Vanderbilt, Doris Duke (even Leona Helmsley who presumed infallibility) for proof of this vulnerability.

What makes **narcissism** of the '90s even worse is the love of **publication**; all the world reveres a winner, and many people model their lives after a great public figure, a hero, icon, manipulator of the media. In contemporary America, there is nothing **worse** than **not** being talked about. Today's **narcissist** has little trouble getting adulation—he/she can spread the word about bouts with alcohol, AIDS, family mayhem, drugs, any perversity by talking to **Oprah**, or **Sally** or **Phil**; the messiest divorces and legal hassles are on display in *Divorce Court*; and if Kitty Dukakis won't talk to the *Boston Globe*, she will tell **Barbara Walters** and millions of viewers about her booze addiction. **George Bernard Shaw** observed decades ago that "An American has no sense of privacy. He does not know what it means. There is no such thing in the country." By most standards, we enjoyed great privacy when that statement was made; today, privacy suggests isolation from the press, and thereby a kind of loser attitude. To be a winner = being the object of the media—exposed, examined, accepted or rejected.

Once upon a time there were honor and discretion in the **mass media**; when **FDR** was sworn in as President, the majority of his fellow Americans were unaware he was crippled; the drinking bouts of **William Holden** and **Spencer Tracy** were carefully guarded by Hollywood moguls (who controlled the lives of stars with uncanny success); **Joan Crawford** was the

perfect mommy for several decades; and **JFK** was portrayed as the quinte
sential family man. The modus operandi of the press in that era wasn
motivated as much by the bottom line, but with more competition and a ne
rash of mergers/acquisitions, media companies had to dig deeper to come
with more provocative headlines and more exposure of members of t
sacred society on TV. When a pair of junior reporters brought down t
Nixon administration via Watergate, all barriers vanished, everybody w
fair game for young journalists who found it easier to make their reputati
by devastating an icon than by thoroughly investigating a story. With gravi
on their side, totaling a person, company, or institution was relatively eas

Nobody craves **negative publicity**, but plenty of society types wa
media coverage. No wonder high-powered social publicists can get fees
to $100,000 to launch a social career or hype a particular benefit. The Ladi
who Lunch, chefs, restaurateurs, florists, designers, models, artists a
writers all seek the media limelight as a way to enhance careers and add
their portfolios. For these mobile-and-visible media seekers, **privacy
death**; they are the antithesis of Howard Hughes who became so reclusi
that upon his demise it was said: "It's a shame Hughes had to die to prove
was alive."

The media in Washington, and the need for coverage, is more subtle th
in other capitals; Scott Fitzgerald's line about the rich being different appli
perfectly. Most dwellers here have had their fling with the press, felt
ecstasy of winning (and the agony of losing), have worn honors comfortab
and then placed them on the mantel. Like J.P. Morgan who so detest
publicity that he never attended a public meeting or made a speech, m
Washingtonians treasure privacy and the internalized life. There are c
tainly occasions when publicity of self-and-cause is welcomed—Chairin
Ball, for example, but once the function is over and the money is in the ba
a retiring but very self-assured personality reemerges and carries on with t
quotidian routines of life.

Invading privacy is big-buck stuff for the tabloids; a really inside st
of the personal tragedy or perversity of a celebrated one can earn a repor
$50,000; and a tip about insider-trading and the attendant arrest of t
offender, all live, on camera, in the trader's office, can make a TV journa
an overnight star, and launch him (and his hair spray) into the big tin
Nothing is too mundane, nothing is sacred, there are no boundaries, a
ethics-be-damned in the quest for hot copy. Wanting to be left alone alm
guarantees that someone will come after you.

Even a **Narcissist** knows the danger of talking too much, revealing
much history, or being too chummy with the press. The loyalty of a repor
is to the story; **human interest** is the operative word; **human being is j**
a means by which the story end is justified.

Hermen and Monica Greenberg—dashing, daring, distinguished.

Mrs. Wilhelmina Holladay—purposeful and provocative.

Photo: J.R. Black

Aliki and Bill Bryant—tasteful, talented and terrific.

Grace Bender—captivating, classy, charismatic.

The Honorable and Mrs. Sidney Dillon Ripley, II—masterly and matchless.

Photo: J.R. Black

Barbara Franceaux—always there, always loveable.

**Sarah and Jim Brady with Frank Resnick and Will Rogers, Jr.—
tall tales from respective titans.**

**Ed, Mark and Kim Hoffman with Kyle Samperton (r)—
partners in the Great Game, wherever!**

166

Photo: J.R. Black

**Father Leo J. Donovan, President, Georgetown University—
gratified by a little help from friends.**

167

**N.S.O. supporters Noel Levine and Audrey Mars,
in the planning process.**

**Marlene Malek, Jane Neal, designer Adolfo and Donna Marriott—
an Affair of the Heart.**

Martin Marietta CEO Norman Augustine and wife Meg at "Achievement Rewards" benefit.

Photo: J.R. Black

Alice and Tom Blair—youthful, kinetic and result-oriented.

Photo: J.R. Black

Coca-Cola Chairman Roberto Goizueta gets warm international
embrace from China's Zheng Wenjin.

172

Photo: Palm Beach Society Magazine

Author Aline, Countess of Romanones with the inimitable Marylou Whitney.

Dr. and Mrs. Clyde Litton with Jane Stern—celebrating the cause.

Photo: J.R. Black

**Morty Bender reveling in a Casino Night Fundraiser;
the price of generosity.**

175

Reprieve. Middleburg and the steeplechase pre-race parade.

The Trustees of the National Gallery of Art
on behalf of
Republic National Bank of New York
request the pleasure of your company
at a reception and viewing of
Giambologna's Cesarini Venus
and the Permanent Collection
on the occasion of the
Annual Meetings of the
International Monetary Fund–World Bank
on Tuesday, the twenty-eighth of September
Nineteen hundred and ninety-three
from six-thirty until midnight
National Gallery of Art
Washington

Valet Parking   Constitution Avenue Entrance
Please reply by enclosed card   West Building

Under the Honorary Patronage
of
The President and Mrs. Clinton
You are cordially invited
to attend the
15th Annual

Ambassadors Ball

in honor of
The Diplomatic Corps of Washington

Wednesday, the twenty-second of September
Nineteen hundred and ninety-three
The Independence Ballroom
The Grand Hyatt Washington
1000 H Street, NW
Washington, District of Columbia

to benefit
The National Multiple Sclerosis Society

Black Tie or   *Reception 7:00 p.m.*
National Attire   *Dinner 8:00 p.m.*

Esther Coopersmith—living, lively legend.

179

Baroness Garnett Stackelberg—singularly sensational; one-of-a-kind!

Michael Winston—the optimum man, audacious and admirable.

Sally Chapoton—knock-out socialite and servant of the needy.

Pat Dixson—gracious and gregarious; the Golden Girl of real estate.

Designer Carol Lascaris—evolutionary and exhilarating.

Photo: J.R. Black

Giselle Theberge—gorgeously alive, born to be appreciated.

Elizabeth Taylor—by whatever name, still, always, one of the greats.

Photo: J.R. Black

Virginia Mars and Robin Phillips—compatriots in another exalted event.

Cheryl O'Donnell—perfect portrayal of the "Ritz."

Photo: J.R. Black

Judy and Dr. Ahmad Esfandiary—up to speed on matters of mankind.

The Honorable William McSweeney giving former
Marine Commandant General P.X. Kelley new civilian headgear.

Photo: J.R. Black

The Honorable and Mrs. Charles A. Camalier, Jr.—
celebrated and veddy civilized Cave Dwellers.

Librarian of Congress James Billington and the
Honorable Lindy Boggs—luminaries.

Photo: J.R. Black

Mr. and Mrs. Charles E. Long—great human beings and friends of the
Vincent T. Lombardi Cancer Research Center.

Liz and Dick Dubin—lots of life force and affirmative action.

**Young Friend of the Red Cross Davis Camalier gives
new meaning to effervescence.**

**Janice and Gilbert Wolf—smiles-all-around,
affable and effective samaritans.**

Photo: J.R. Black

Richard O. Haase—
on a light-hearted, happy-go-lucky outing.

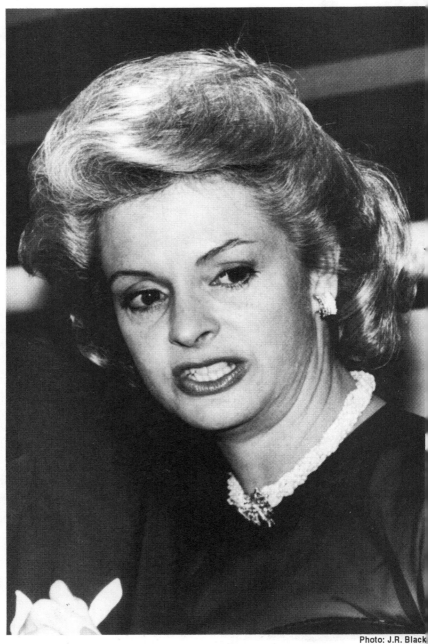

The Honorable Penne Percy Korth—forever, and triumphantly, heading into tomorrow.

Mrs. Lynda Webster, J. Carter Brown, the Honorable William William Hedgcock Webster and Ambassador of Spain H.E. Jaime De Ojeda—collective power, taste and gentility.

Albert J. Beveridge, Peggy and Kenneth McCorkle Crosby and Madzy Beveridge—liberated and lovely, at play.

Photo: J.R. Black

Wilma and Stuart Bernstein, the Honorable and Mrs. Jack Kemp—universally admired and emulated.

201

Photo: J.R. Black

Joe and Barbara Allbritton—magnificent, masterful, matchless.

Mrs. Catherine Filene Shouse—queenly and vibrant Lady of Wolf Trap, with Carol Hartford.

Deborah Dingell, Marie Carr and Mrs. Jacques Andreani—the fashionables at the American Cancer Society/International Collection Luncheon.

Jim Akers, Mayor Sharon Pratt Kelly and Dorothy McSweeney—with 5,000-watt smiles in support of the Washington Ballet.

Photo: J.R. Black

205

Aniko Gaal Schott, Charlton Heston and Dominique Kuhlman—a jazzy, joyous and jaunty trio.

Senator Howard Metzenbaum, Adrienne Arsht Feldman and Senator Fritz Hollings—
panache, persuasion and passion to do anything!

Mary Frances and the Honorable Marion H. Smoak with Toni and Wilson Lucom—

Patricia and William F. Buckley Jr., Count and Countess Frederic Chandon—
oracular, orderly and outstanding, by any measurement.

Mrs. Gerda McGrath, the Honorable True Davis and Denise McGrath—vibrant and vivid, wonderful and wise.

Yardley and John A. Manfuso—provocative and poised.

Mr. and Mrs. Bernard Samuel (Sarah) Gewirz—aristocratic, amiable and admirable.

Gabi Steers and Marilyn Quayle—well-designed, designing and dynamic Ladies.

213

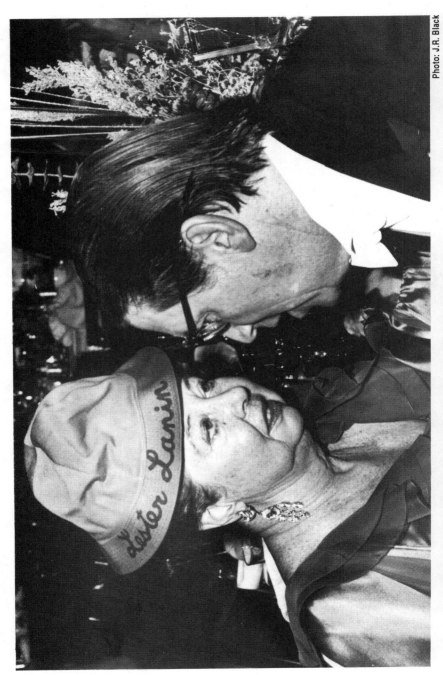

The Honorable Jayne Brumley Ikard and R. Francis Saul

214

Mary Louise "Gogo" and Austin Huntington Kiplinger—who could ask for anything more?

Photo: J.R. Black

His Excellency the former Ambassador of the Federal Republic of Germany and Mrs. Jeurgen Ruhfus —gifted and giving.

216

Senator Alan K. Simpson and (retired) Associate Supreme Court Justice Byron Raymond "Whizzer" White—passing time, tales and secrets.

Associate Justice of the Supreme Court and Mrs. Antonin Scalia—

Senator Daniel Patrick Moynihan (c) with Loraine and Charles Percy—mannered, marvelous and meritorious.

Photo: Showcase Magazine

Mrs. Mariana Grove and Nash Whitney Schott—enjoying the infinite variety of human/charitable pleasures.

ACS International Collection Luncheon founder Estelle S. Gelman (l) with event chairman
Alexine C. Jackson (r) and vice-chair Aliki Bryant.

Secretary of Commerce Ron Brown and Senator Ted Kennedy—political power and performance.

Former U.N. Ambassador Jeane and Mr. Evron Kirkpatrick—as sure and as stunning as sunrise.

Secretary of Defense Les Aspin and journalist Arnaud de Borchgrave—cracking the code with leveraged style.

Society authority Mrs. James McSherry "Maggie" Wimsatt with renaissance man Victor Shargai.

Photo: J.R. Black

Maximum-fashion designer Bill Blass with the best testimonial to high-style—Rose Marie Bogley.

226

Vernon E. Jordan—master of the quantum jump.

Actor Walter Matthau and Martin Feinstein—lots of top spin and spirit.

Photo: J.R. Black

Joy and John Safer—individual, informed, inspiring.

The Honorable Gilbert Gude—onward/upward, charmingly.

230

Photo: J.R. Black

Tanya and Dr. John Francis Potter—zip, zest and walking tall.

Photo: J.R. Black

Barbara Dana and husband Dr. Charles Infosino—admixture of science and society.

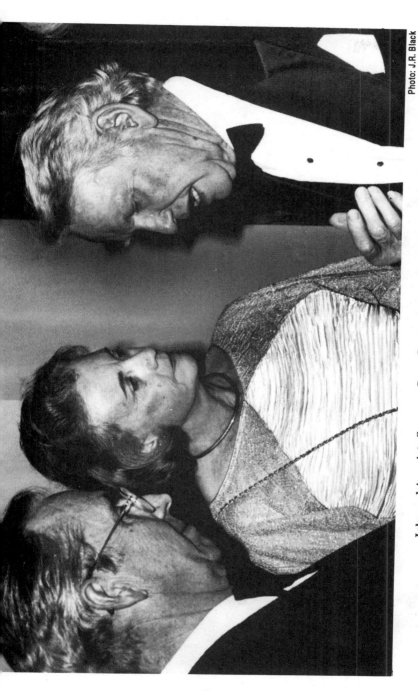

John and Associate Supreme Court Justice Sandra Day O'Connor with Commander John Conway Hunt—jurisprudence and *joie de vivre.*

Ted and Lea, Wanda and Jim Pedas—command and commendation through cinema.

Photo: J.R. Black

The One and Only—Catherine Deneuve, a Washington favorite.

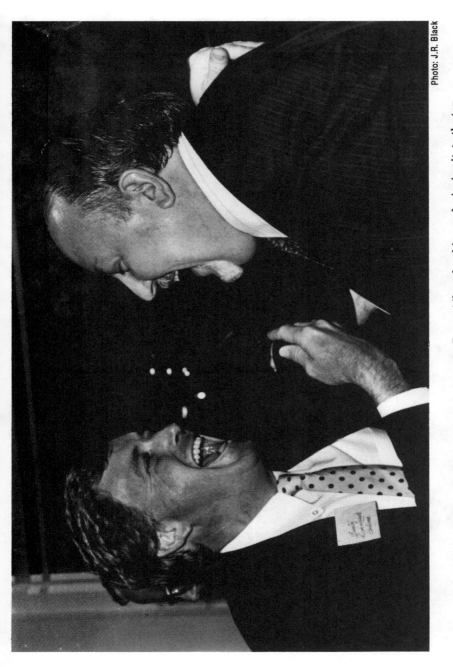

Photo: J.R. Black

The Honorable J. Danforth Quayle and strategist Roger Ailes—laughing and winging it, to the top.

Mollie and the Honorable John Ottina—good news and goodness.

Hunt country—the other Washington world.

CHAPTER VII

CONSPICUOUS/INCONSPICUOUS CONSUMPTION
(Possessions, Passions & Pageants)

Photo: J.R. Black

**Lady of all ladies Katharine Graham,
with man-for-all-seasons A. Alfred Taubman.**

179. WHAT IS THE OFFICIAL FLOWER OF THE DISTRICT?

The 69-square-mile District of Columbia, whose motto is "Justiti omnibus" - Justice for all, has as its official flower, the **American Beaut Rose**; the District's official tree is the **Scarlet Oak** and the official bird is th **Wood Thrush**.

180. WHAT ARE THE TOWN'S MOST UNUSUAL GARDENS?

In the spring, few towns in American can match the flowery beauty c the Nation's Capital; every street is lined with carpets of colorful flowei making it a pastoral fairyland. Some of the best sight-seeing is:

The US Botanical Garden, along the Mall, is filled with a cornucopi of varied and historic blossoms—most noteworthy is the orchid collectioi from which several hundred bloom weekly. The **German-American Friend ship Garden** at 16th St. and Constitution Ave. was designed by the note Washington landscape firm of Oehme van Sweden & Associates; nativ plants and grasses tell the horticultural history of the two nations. **Feder; Reserve Board Garden**, located between 18th and 20th Sts. at Virgini Ave. pioneered the use of ornamental grasses in contemporary garde design. Georgetown's **Dumbarton Oaks** is a 10-acre parcel which exempl fies the role of the elegant private garden, combining both the formal an informal varieties. Areas of the garden like the Orangery, featuring a 14(year-old fig tree, were designed originally to meet the owner's entertainin needs. Noteworthy in May and June are the 1,000-plant Rose Garden and tl late-blooming azaleas and lilacs. The gardens surrounding the **Hillwoo Museum**, the former home of cereal heiress Marjorie Merriweather Pos overlook Rock Creek Park; the garden path near the Adirondack-style cabi where the surrounding beds feature native trillium and ferns, is matchles a few steps away, a Japanese water garden descends the hillside, effective miniaturizing a Japanese mountainside; also of note are the pink "Quee Elizabeths" rose garden and the greenhouses in which orchids, Post favorite flower, are raised. The **National Arboretum** offers 444 acres botanical diversity; in the Lee Garden many late-blooming Japanese varie ies illuminate the east slope of Mount Hamilton; the exquisite Japane; Bonsai and Chinese Penjing collections are popular (the oldest specimen a 350-year-old Japanese white pine): the specialty herb gardens across tl road are explorations into the cultural, medicinal and industrial uses plants; and one of the most pastoral settings in the city is Dogwood Circ where native and Asian varieties adorn a sloping lawn near the Anacost River. The **Kenilworth Aquatic Gardens** feature 44 natural and six ceme ponds of wetland and aquatic plants from around the world, many of whi start blooming in June; although the gardens were once a commerci enterprise, they were donated to the federal government in 1938 (a visit is n complete without seeing local fauna that includes frogs, snakes, beavei muskrats, turtles, wading birds and the occasional fox). In Suburban Mar

240

land, **Brookside Gardens** is famous for azaleas and the two conservatories which display impatiens, fuchsias, caladiums and tropicals set against a towering bird of paradise tree; natural and paved paths lead out to the newer aquatic and butterfly gardens and the tasteful Japanese tea house.

As an international center, Washington also draws foreigners who carry with them memories of the gardens in their native lands. The formal gardens behind the headquarters of the **Organization of American States** are as Latin as a samba.

And few cities display a broader collection of period gardens: the Victorian **Haupt Garden** behind the Smithsonian Castle, the **Federal** gardens of **Tudor Place**, the medieval gardens of the **Franciscan Monastery**.

Rounding out this unique mix of gardens from various periods and countries are the landscapes of trees and flowers maintained by the US government. The National Arboretum, and the grounds of the US Capitol headline the list. (Each year in mid-April, the White House headlines its "Spring Garden," with an opening for tourists.)

Photo courtesy of the Washington, DC Convention and Visitors Association

A view of the Washington Monument from the Tidal Basin, with cherry trees blooming.

181. WHAT ARE WASHINGTON'S MOST EXOTIC FLOWERS?

At the **Kenilworth Aquatic Gardens,** over 100,000 of the rarest water lilies and lotus make for a Monet landscape.

The **Franciscan Monastery of Mount Saint Sepulchre** rises on a wooded hillside in northeast Washington. Replicas of principal shrines and chapels found in the Holy Land dominate the 40-acre site. A lavish assortment of flowers, trees, and shrubs add color and texture. In the spring, thousands of daffodils dance on hillsides while tulips and Easter lilies nod beneath blossoming cherry and dogwood trees. During warm months the tropical perennials are moved from the greenhouse to outdoors: hibiscus, lantanas, tiger lilies, and palm and banana trees.

Every June, 600 rosebushes burst into bloom. A spectacle credited both to loving care by the monastery brothers and to their use of the most up-to-date methods for developing hybrids.

At least 250 native shrubs and trees line 300 miles of city streets, march in dense columns along Potomac River banks, and flourish in the woods of Rock Creek Park. Although many of the city's thousands of trees are native, more exotics grow in CapCity than in any other American city. Over 1,800 varieties of flowers bloom, and 300 species of birds flutter across the sky. Within the boundaries of the Capital lives a scampering, squeaking, chirping, warbling, hooting population. Bald eagles nest. Immigrating Canadian geese and ducks stop to rest. Wild turkeys, bobcats, and white-tailed deer roam in bordering forests. Raccoons and squirrels forage along city streets.

This abundance of wildlife is due primarily to the fact that the edges of four different geographical zones extend over the District and its environs. Thus, Washington is host to varieties and species that are native to both the North and the South. In addition, due to government expeditions and gifts of foreign delegations, Washington boasts trees and flowers from around the world. (*The Washington Post Guide to Washington*)

182. HOW MANY TULIPS ARE PLANTED EACH YEAR BY THE PARK SERVICE?

According to the Park Service, there are 171,300 tulips planted around the mall and on federal properties downtown each year. Of these, 103,750 are red. Other colors: 27,400 yellow; 24,200 white flamed with red; 7,200 pink; 5,5950 white; and 2,800 orange. About 18,000 are planted inside the White House grounds.

183. WHO OFFICIALLY RECOGNIZES THE FIRST FLOWERS OF SPRING?

A botanist with the Smithsonian Institution, **Stanwyn Shetler,** (and his wife Elaine) search for the first flowers of spring each year by traipsing along the C&O Canal or the grounds of IRS headquarters on Constitution Ave., or the edges of neighboring gardens, even the flagstone areas of sidewalks.

The Shetlers have been searching for, and recording, the first spring flowers for years, and in his Smithsonian office, a book—*First Dates of Flowering*—is left for peers and flower-comrades to record the first dates of the appearance of various blossoms. In the course of their exploration, fellow botanists discover unique flowers like the trillium, erigenia, hepatica (with its liver-shaped leaves), bluebells, Quaker ladies, even dandelions!

Henry Mitchell, *Post* columnist, is also an expert on the early arrival of flowers.

184. WHAT ARE THE MOST FAMOUS TREES IN WASHINGTON?

The most famous of the trees is the Washington elm in front of the Senate entrance, believed to have shaded our first President when he laid the Capitol cornerstone. Some of the oldest trees are two English elms and a spreading American elm. The American elm, known as the Cameron elm, stands near the southwest corner of the House wing. The tree is named in honor of Senator Simon Cameron, who, in 1875, saw workers about to uproot it to put in a sidewalk; he hurried to the Senate floor, and pleaded that the tree be saved. His efforts were successful: instead of demolishing the tree, the workers laid the sidewalk around it.

Few people realize that when they visit the Capitol building, they walk through one of the finest arboretums in the world. Over 3,000 trees from 33 states, Europe, and Asia grow on the Capitol grounds. In addition to one of the most varied collections of trees in the country, the 155-acre grounds also boast 100 species of wooded plants.

The Japanese cherry trees in the Tidal Basin area are also world-class and give joy to nature lovers. The early-April Cherry Blossom Festival showcases the 6,000 cherry trees each year and provides the format for an annual parade and much merry-making.

Photo: J.R. Black

Senator Harry and Mrs. Byrd with Mrs. Lloyd Bentsen (center)—espousing the preservation of nature.

185. **WHAT ARE THE TOWN'S TOP-RATED GARDEN CENTER/ NURSERIES?**

Some of the garden centers rated highest for quality and service are American Plant Food, Bethesda; 301/656-3311; Bennett's Nursery, Vienna 703/938-6925; Campbell & Ferrara Nurseries, Alexandria, 703/354-6724 Cox Farms, Vienna, 703/281-0165; Green Giant Nursery, Lorton, 703/690 1231; Merrifield Garden Center, Fairfax; 703/968-9600.

186. **WHO OWNS THE AREA'S MOST EXPENSIVE CAR COLLECTION?**

With a handful of Ferraris as the keystone to his collection, **J. Willard Marriott, Jr.** is big boss of local car collectors; his 30-car stable is valued at $12 million and includes such rich and rare machines as a 500 TRC Ferrari 300 hp, $140,000 Testarossa which breezes along at 140 mph, a vintage Duesenberg, a 1927 Rolls (once owned by Sir Henry Royce himself), two T-Birds from the '50s, 1937 Jaguar SS-100, 1929 Packard, a rare Mercedes gul wing roadster, several classic Porsches and an Alfa Romeo and Maserati.

Michael Winston (Carey Winston Co.) and A.C. Rosner, Jr. also keep a dozen or so special cars handy for showcasing and pleasure.

187. **WHAT ARE THE MOST POPULAR AUTOMOBILES IN WASHINGTON?**

Mercedes-Benz has the lead—the 500SL and convertible are very much in demand (the convertible is the favorite of women). There are also a few Rolls Royces, black or white versions, seen only on special occasions (weddings, anniversaries). Jaguars are increasing in popularity. The recently introduced Turbo Bentley is showing up often too. Of the American luxury cars, the Lincoln Town Car is leader, with Cadillac and Lexus close behind The younger set has embraced the Range Rover as its status vehicle. (BMWs are also very popular.)

188. **WHAT ARE THE FIVE MOST WANTED AUTOMOBILES BY WASHINGTONIANS (IN THEIR FANTASY)?**

1. **Ferrari Daytona Spyder**—red of course, clocking in at $650,000 (only 125 such convertibles built between '69 and '73).

2. **Rolls Royce Corniche**—convertible; favorite colors are black and white. (Only 100 shipped to the US from Britain with a price tag of $190,000—among the most expensive imports anyone can buy).

3. **Lamborghini Countach**—Red, 180 miles per hour is top speed; car is bold, loud, fast and expensive at $187,000. It is the widest and lowest auto ever built — referred to as a "sexy, space car."

4. **Mercedes AMG Hammer**—color red, top speed of 186 miles per hour. Price tag at $167,000.

244

Photo: Palm Beach Society Magazine

Magnificent, motorized mobility.

5. **Aston-Martin Volante** convertible in black, made famous by James Bond, attaining speeds of 168 miles per hour—only $167,000.

For the record, the most expensive car in the world is a recently sold 59-year-old Bugatti Royale (made in Italy in 1931; cost then was $22,300)—selling price was $14 million to a group of Japanese businessmen. It was one of only six models made. Another recent top seller was a '63 Ferrari GTO that fetched $13 million.

Last spring, Sotheby's held a vintage and classic car auction; 25 cars from the collection of Rick Carroll were put on sale. Included in the group were eight classic Rolls-Royces, seven restored Duesenbergs, a 1902 Mercedes and a McLaren race car used by Johnny Rutherford to win the Indy 500 in '74.

Several hundred Townies attended the auction and put in appropriate bids for their favorite car; over $21 million was paid by car collectors from England, Switzerland and the US.

9. WHAT ARE THE FAVORITE SPORTS OF WASHINGTONIANS?

Not surprisingly, **walking** is the favorite sport of our denizens; 50 percent of our residents actively walk as a physical outlet. Swimming is next (favored by 32 percent of Washingtonians) followed by tennis (24 percent), cycling (21 percent), golf (20 percent), jogging (12 percent), dancing (11 percent), boating and fishing (11 percent) and gymnastics/aerobics (10 percent). Croquet and playing polo are pursued by a small but select number of residents, as is skiing off-season, and fox hunting.

190. WHAT DANCES DO WASHINGTONIANS LIKE (AND DO) MOST?

The most popular is the **Fox Trot**, danced to a "society tempo." Abo 60 percent of music played at various balls is the Fox Trot, followed by Tango and the Rumba, and a variety of modern day dances. The Waltz i perennial favorite.

In early Washington, dances like the Jazz Ramble (1917), the Chica Toddle and Hello Pal (1920s), the Charleston, Black Bottom and St. Lo Hoop (1930s) and the French Tango and Valencia (1940s) came and went always proved popular to socialites. As far back as the turn of the century Cake Walk (originated by employees of the Willard Hotel who did animated two-step as they served cakes and other food to guests) was novelty of the times.

Through the years, Washingtonians kept up with the tempo and rock'n roll (in the late' 50s, influenced by swiveling hipster Elvis Presle the twist in the '60s (with the gyrations of Chubby Checker and the hullygu and the boogaloo); and even the hustle and the bump (spurred by the succ of *Saturday Night Live*). The '90s have seen a return to sanity with ballro dancing, cheek-to-cheek movements, and even a touch of dirty dancing

191. WHAT IS THE MOST POPULAR PET IN WASHINGTON?

Dogs still have the honor of being the most popular of the little creatu but cats are not far behind. The most common small dog is the Poodle; am large dog fanciers the Black Labrador and Golden Retriever are m desired. The most common cat in Town is the Alley Cat. In the US there 50 million dogs; 58 million cats.

192. WHAT IS CURRENTLY THE MOST "IN" DOG IN WASHINGTON?

Although there are many Labrador Retrievers, Poodles and Coc Spaniels in the Capital, the Chinese Shar-pei is the current favorite. species was brought from mainland China 11 years ago. Fully grown SI peis weigh about 60 pounds; they do not worry about their wrinkles (as many residents), in fact, the more wrinkles the better the dog. The dogs highly intelligent, lovable and expensive which may be the reason they considered so "in."

According to the American Kennel Club, across the US the most pop dog is the Cocker Spaniel followed by the Labrador, Poodle, Gol Retriever, German Shepherd, Chow, Rottweiler, Beagle, Dachshund Miniature Schnauzer. The Poodle holds the all-time record for being " dog" for the longest period of time (a 25-year span from '59-84 when Cocker became supreme).

Through the years, dogs have been popular with Washingtonians with Presidents: Franklin Roosevelt had a Scottie; Coolidge, a White Col

Kennedy, an assortment—Beagle, German Shepherd, Cocker Spaniel, Welsh Terrier, Irish Wolfhound and Russian Puppy; Nixon, an Irish Setter; Ford, a Golden Retriever; Reagan, a Bouvier des Flandres. The First Dog in the Bush administration was an English Springer named "Ranger."

Dumbarton Oaks is official meeting place for top dogs in Town (along with their masters/mistresses).

3. WHAT IS THE MOST EXPENSIVE DOG IN TOWN TODAY?

A **Komodor** valued at approximately $10,000. Not surprisingly, the owner of the Komodor prefers not to be identified; although "animal" snatching is hardly big business in Washington, it is a continuing threat. A pedigreed dog is something of value—not only emotionally, but, quite importantly, economically.

4. WHAT ARE THE MOST EXPENSIVE BIRDS OWNED BY WASHINGTONIANS?

Exotic South American Parrots and Love Birds valued at up to $10,000. There are also several Yellow Crested Cockatoos valued at $5,000. The Robert Fomons (of Palm Beach and the Capital) have parrots—Amazon and African Gray.

5. WHO IS "FIRST CAT" OF THE NATION?

Although "Socks" who lives at 1600 Pennsylvania Avenue with the Clintons, hasn't really had "15 minutes" of fame yet, he will become the darling of cat-lovers across the world soon. Recently, he served as Honorary Chaircat of the Bark Ball, an affair which benefits the Washington Humane Society.

6. WHAT PUBLICATIONS ARE MOST COMMONLY READ BY WASHINGTONIANS?

Outside of several local publications (*Washington Post, USA Today, New York Times*), residents favor (by ranking): *National Geographic, Time, Better Homes & Gardens, People, Reader's Digest, Town & Country, Newsweek, The Wall Street Journal, Business Week* and *US. News & World Report*. Although magazines like *Gourmet, Food & Wine, Bazaar, Vogue* and *Vanity Fair* and *W* have a strong following in Town, they are not in the most commonly read category. *The Washingtonian* is the best-read local magazine (with a circulation of 166,900 vs. *Newsweek* with 89,000 readers, *People* (70,512), *US News* (56,200) and *Vogue* (32,500).

7. WHAT TELEVISION PROGRAMS ARE OF MOST INTEREST TO WASHINGTONIANS?

For network news, preferences are: *Dan Rather/CBS; Peter Jennings/*

ABC; *Tom Brokaw*/NBC; *Nightline*/ABC; *MacNeil-Lehrer*/WETA. F[
public affairs programs, leaders are: *60 Minutes*/CBS; *McLaughlin Grou[
WRC; *Inside Washington*/WUSA; *Meet the Press*/NBC; *David Brinkle[
ABC; *Face the Nation*/CBS; *Washington Week*/WETA. Local news favo[
ites (at 6 p.m.) are: WUSA/9; WRC/4; WJLA/7; (at 11 p.m.): WRC/[
WTTG/5; WUSA/9; WJLA/7.

198. WHAT ARE SOME WASHINGTON/USA EQUIVALENTS?

Traveling from CapCity to the City of Angels or the Big App[
introduces many new people, places and things, but they're all basical[
"equivalents" – same game, different name. Here's the scorecard:

WASHINGTON	PALM BEACH	BEVERLY HILLS	NEW YORK CIT[
Kalorama	South Ocean Area	Bel Air	Upper Fifth Avenu[
Willard	The Breakers	Beverly Wilshire	Waldorf-Astoria
Kennedy Center	Royal Poinciana Playhouse	Dorothy Chandler Playhouse	Lincoln Center Pavilion
Connecticut Avenue	Worth Avenue	Rodeo Drive	Fifth Avenue
Adams Morgan	Phipps Park	Venice Boardwalk	Coney Island
495	I-95	San Diego Freeway	Long Is. Expressw[
National Gallery	Society of The Four Arts	Museum of Contemporary Art	Whitney Museum American Art
Jockey Club	Cafe L'Europe	Chasen's	The "21" Club
Billy Martin's	Dempsey's	Fatburger	P.J. Clarke's
Rehoboth Beach	Bahamas	Palm Springs	The Hamptons
Washington Life	*Palm Beach Society*	*Los Angeles Magazine*	*Avenue*
202	407	213	212
Palm	Nando's	Musso & Frank	Sardi's
Black tie	Black tie	Sportscoat	Tails
Diplomacy	Sociability	Envy	Anger
Ritz-Carlton	The Chesterfield	Beverly Hills Hotel	Carlyle Hotel
Sutton Place	C'est Si Bon	Vincente Foods	Zabar's
Blackie's	Rio Bar	Polo Lounge	Laurent
Limo	Rolls	Bentley	Mercedes
Frankie Hewitt	Barbara Gault	Barbra Streisand	Barbara Walters
Park	Beach	Valley	Bridge and Tunne[
Washington Harbor	Australian Docks	Santa Monica Pier	South Street Seap[
Georgetown Park	Esplanade	Century City	Trump Tower Atrium
Cosmos Club	Club Colette	Pacific Club	Lotus Club

199. WHAT ARE THE TOWN'S MOST FREQUENTLY PRESCRIBED DRUGS?

For antibiotics–it's Keflex and Amoxil; Stomach ulcers–Zantac a[
Tagamet; Blood pressure–Dyazide; Heart rate control–Inderal; Skin–Re[
A; Pain–Tylenol with codeine; Tranquilizer–Valium and Xanax and Proza[
Hormone–Premarin; Asthma–Ventolin; Sleeping–Halcion, Xanax. M[
popular sunning lotion is Bain de Soleil (followed by Coppertone a[
Hawaiian Tropic); older people prefer lotions with sunblock while t[
younger set goes for deep tanning juices. Most popular cold remedy [
Sudafed (tied with Contac); Robitussin DM is most popular cough syr[

Advil is most popular pain killer; Centrum most popular vitamin. As for mouth washes, it's Scope and Listerine; Crest is most popular toothpaste, and Plax is the most wanted plaque control; Alka Seltzer wins it for antacids; and Vaseline Intensive Care is the most popular lotion.

200. WHAT IS THE FAVORITE PEN?

Bic and Flair share the honors as Washington's most "popular pen" (Bic is also the largest manufacturer of over-the-counter pens in the US). The most popular "status" pen is the Cross, with Montblanc gaining in popularity. In the past five years, fountain pens have become increasingly popular with last year's consumer purchases totaling more then $126 million vs. $1.4 billion spent for ballpoint pens.

Washingtonians also prefer Montblanc and Cross desk sets. The most expensive fountain pen in Washington can be purchased at Cartier for $775. The most expensive new pen in the world is a solid gold Montblanc Diplomat retailing for $7600.

General Manager of The Ritz-Carlton, Cheryl O'Donnell uses an expensive Pelikan while Mayor Sharon Kelly prefers a Mitsubishi; and inveterate document signers like Henry Kissinger, Margaret Thatcher and Helmut Kohn depend on Montblanc to give their John Hancocks more panache.

Buffy Cafritz uses a number of different pens with her varied stationery—bought from Tiffany, Cartier and Mrs. John Strong Stationers in NYC.

On a note of miscellany, according to statistics, when writing love letters, 42 percent of the public prefer fountain pens, 24 percent ballpoints and one percent word processors.

201. WHAT ARE THE FAVORITE AIRLINE CLUBS?

Since we're a town of active travelers, airline clubs are important. Here's how they rank: (1) American/Admirals Club–in 25 airports; (2) Delta/Crown Room–in 34 airports; (3) TWA/Ambassador Club–in 28 airports; (4) United/Red Carpet Club–in 27 airports.

202. THE PREFERRED CREDIT CARD?

The Visa Card is used by 70 percent of Washingtonians, followed by MasterCard (58 percent) and American Express (43 percent); 69 percent carry department store credit cards, and only six percent of Washingtonians have no credit cards at all. The cards are most actively used for purchases in the entertainment, travel, photographic equipment, accessories and sportswear categories.

203. HOW DO WASHINGTON HAIR STYLING PRICES RANK?

In scissors-to-scissors combat with other markets where vanity and a perfect personal presentation are keys to success, Washington fits the mold rather well; prices for various beauty treatments are a shade below those of two other status-conscious metro areas–New York and Beverly Hills.

Here's how we rate (based on average figures at a leading salon, women only):

Item	DC	BH	NY
Comb-out	$ 15	$ 25	$ 20
Shampoo/Dry	$ 30	$ 35	$ 30
Shampoo/Cut/Dry	$ 55	$ 75	$ 65
Permanent	$ 80	$100	$ 90
Basic Coloring	$ 45	$ 50	$ 45
Highlighting	$ 65	$ 80	$ 70
Facial	$ 55	$ 70	$ 60
Make-Up	$ 30	$ 40	$ 35
Manicure	$ 12	$ 20	$ 15
Pedicure	$ 25	$ 35	$ 30

Washington salons have not declared war on each other as leading hair gurus in other cities have; in New York, for example, when a salon employee reaches an income level of $100,000/year, he usually takes his Rolodex rents posh space and hires his friends away to work on his new clientele. The most notable of these entrepreneurs was **Mr. Kenneth**, 62-year-old grand eminence of the salon business, who left Lilly Dache in '63 to set up shop in an elegant East 54th St. townhouse. Currently, in Manhattan, leading salons like The Spot, Vartali, Parallel and Thomas Morrissey are all owned and operated by former employees of well-known beauty emporiums. In Los Angeles, **Jose Eber** is a legend in his own time with a product line and a list of "Who's Who" clients; he worked for $150/week at the shampoo sink just 15 years ago. And now, there is **Cristophe**!

204. WHAT IS THE FAVORITE HAIR COLOR OF WASHINGTON WOMEN?

Blond is still the predominant hair color among women; golden tresses shimmer in the soft light at the various galas, and a lighting technician from on high sees only a sea of Rapunzels and Goldilocks as he scans the assemblage. Yet, Washington blonds of the '90s are more natural, with myriad blond streaks and highlights versus the "platinum" shading of years ago (according to leading hairdresser Ned Sezer who fine-tunes the locks of Tipper Gore and mother-in-law Pauline Gore). Companies like L'Oreal Revlon and Clairol find the Capital a most unusual and attractive target market with per capita consumption of their tints, dyes and various hair coloring products almost as high as that in Las Vegas and Hollywood.

For the record, according to a survey by *Allure*:

–16% of women have brown, black or auburn hair; and 1% are redheads
–27% of Mensa's 18,000 female members are blond.
–33% of Miss America contestants in '90 were blond.

-58% of *Playboy's* '90 centerfolds were blond.

-64% of female anchors on network shows are blond; Faith Daniels, Judy Woodruff, Joan Lunden, Diane Sawyer, Lesley Stahl, Barbara Walters and Paula Zahn.

-91% of blonds consider themselves popular with men; 74% of brunettes think the same as do 64% of redheads.

5. HOW MANY WASHINGTONIANS HAVE HAD COSMETIC SURGERY?

Approximately 99 percent of American women would change something about their looks if they could; approximately 38 percent of Washingtonians over 40 do so through cosmetic surgery of some kind (including collagen injections and liposuction). The number is growing and includes many patients under 40. Last year, nationally, approximately 395,000 people had cosmetic surgery compared to 300,000 in '88 (these figures were based on procedures performed by surgeons certified for cosmetic procedures by the American Society of Plastic and Reconstructive Surgeons; including cases done by non-certified physicians, 1.5 million people would be a more realistic figure) and next year it is projected that 1.7 million people will have cosmetic surgery. Last year, 13 percent of plastic surgery patients were men; the top four procedures were rhinoplasty (nose), blepharoplasty (eyelids), liposuction and abdominoplasty (tummy tuck). The top four cosmetic procedures for females were liposuction (the fastest growing), facelift, collegen injections and blepharoplasty.

According to **Dr. Clyde Litton** (DC) and **Dr. Fredric M. Barr** (Palm Beach), although the occasional "obvious" results seen from some cosmetic surgeries are unfortunately visible, the majority of good results for most patients are noted as "pleasingly subtle changes." Locally, eyelid surgery followed by face and neck lift (rhytidectomy) procedures remain the most popular for both male and female patients. The cost varies for each procedure depending on the surgeon's fee, facility charge, and type of anesthesia utilized. The goal of such "restorative" surgery is to provide a "well rested, refreshed look." For the majority of patients who have undergone successful cosmetic procedures, only they and their plastic surgeons will note the change since the visual effects will be subtle.

It's interesting to note that the District has the highest ratio of ASPRS Members (MD's dealing with cosmetic surgery) to population in the US— 1:30,345 meaning one doctor for each 30,345 people; Florida has the next best ratio at 1:40,558. Yet, only about 10 percent of CapCity's population has undergone cosmetic procedures.

Social surgeon Dr. Harvey Austin (McLean), often considered the nation's busiest "mouth man," notes that more cosmetic work is being done on droopy and grim lips, a function of people wanting a cheerful look and instant smile.

206. WHAT IS THE SURGEON'S FEE FOR THE MOST POPULAR COSMETIC PROCEDURES?

Liposuction: $750 - $4,000 (81 percent increase in the number procedures performed in the past seven years.)

Breast Enlargement: $2,000 - $4,000
Eyelid Tucks: $1,500 - $4,000
Nose Reshape: $2,000 - $6,000
Facelifts: $2,000 - $10,000

207. WHAT HAVE BEEN THE ALL-TIME FAVORITE FRAGRANCE OF WASHINGTONIANS?

Over the years, Washingtonians have tried every conceivable ne frangrance as a means of winning friends and impressing peers. Mc marketers favor Washington as a point of product introduction because of tl substantial influence a typical Resident has over family, friends and otl potential fragrance users. Here's the scorecard since the 1920s.

1920s–Chanel No. 5 by Chanel (1923); Shalimar by Guerlain (192: Arpege by Lanvin (1925); L'Aimant by Coty (1928); No. 22 by Chanel (192

1930s–Joy by Jean Patou (1930); Taby by Dana Perfumes (1932); Reviens by Parfumes Worth (1932); White Shoulders by Evyan (1939)

1940s–Chantilly by Houbigant (1941); Miss Dior by Christian Di (1947); L'Air du Temps by Nina Ricci (1948)

1950s–Youth Dew by Estee Lauder (1953); L'Interdot by Givencl (1957); Le De Givenchy

1960s–Calandre by Paco Rabanne (1969); Azuree by Estee Laud (1969); Charmade by Guerlain

1970s–Givenchy 111 by Hubert De Givenchy (1970); Aliage by Est Lauder (1972); Private Collection by Estee Lauder (1973); Chloe by K Lagerfeld (1975); Opium by Yves Saint Laurent (1977); Oscar de la Ren by Oscar de la Renta (1977); Cinnabar by Estee Lauder (1978); White Lin by Estee Lauder (1978); No. 19 by Chanel (1970)

1980s–Passion by Annick Coutal (Elizabeth Taylor) (1980); Armani l Giorgio Armani (1982); KL by Karl Lagerfeld (1983); Jardins de Bagate] by Guerlain (1983); Diva by Emanuel Ungaro (1984); Ysatis by Hubert I Givenchy (1985); Fendi by Fendi; Poison by Christian Dior (1985); Obse sion by Calvin Klein (1985); Beautiful by Estee Lauder (1985); Musk Cartier by Cartier (1981); Coco by Chanel (1985); Red by Giorgio (198! Knowing by Estee Lauder (1988); Tiffany by Tiffany (1989); Eternity l Calvin Klein (1988); Carolina Herrera by Carolina Herrera (1988); Panth by Cartier (1989); Misha by Baryshnikov (1989); Montana by Monta (1989); Alfred Sung by Alfred Sung (1989).

In '89, the most popular fragrances among Washingtonians we Carolina Herrera by Carolina Herrera; Bijan by Bijan; Tiffany by Tiffan Coco by Chanel; Musk de Cartier by Cartier; Panther by Cartier; Misha l

252

Baryshnikov (Saks exclusive); Alfred Sun by Alfred Sun (Bonwit exclusive); Eternity by Calvin Klein; Red by Giorgio; Fendi by Fendi; Montana by Montana.

1990s–Leading fragrances included scents making personal unique statements that seized upon current popular trends. La Prairie introduced "One Perfect Rose"–world's costliest scent at $1,500 per ounce packed in Boehm porcelain and decorated with 24-karat gold leaf. Of all the newest fragrances the favorites included Bill Blass' Black Magic, Nude and Hot, Cassini by Oleg Cassini, Escada's Escada Beaute, Romeo Gigli, Realities, Safari, Lacroix's C'est la Vie, Byzance by Rochas, Lagerfeld's Photo, Sung's Encore and Nina Ricci's Ricci-Club; enduring favorites include Boucheron, Coco, Gale Hayman's Beverly Hills and 273. Carolina Herrera, Obsession, Opium, Guerlain's Samsara, Lauders Knowing and White Linen, and Klein's Eternity, Gio by Armani, Catalyst by Halston Borghese, Wings by Giorgio of Beverly Hills, Crazy Krizia by Krizia and Gems by VCA.

Washingtonians wishing to commission their own scent can go to fragrance analyst Don Stephen, who, for a mere $100,000 will create individual floral masterpieces.

It's interesting to note that in '73 only 17 new fragrances were introduced; in '92, 60 new fragrances were brought to market; the trend is eternally upward. Today there are approximately 800 fragrances on the market (almost every other major designer has a signed fragrance); one-third are for men. Further, despite all the competition, **Chanel No. 5, Shalimar** and **Joy** remain the most popular classic fragrances of all time.

For the gentlemen, the most popular colognes last year were: Bijan by Bijan; Fahrenheit by Christian Dior; Polo by Ralph Lauren; Armani by Armani; Aramis by Estee Lauder; Obsession by Calvin Klein; Hugo Boss by Hugo Boss; Jazz by Yves Saint Laurent; Imperiale by Guerlain; Lagerfeld by Karl Lagerfeld; Santos by Cartier. At the recent Fragrance Foundation Recognitions Awards gala in New York, Elizabeth Arden won three "Fifis" (top award) and Leonard Lauder was inducted into the Foundation's Hall of Fame.

Photo: Palm Beach Society Magazine

High-spirited, high-styled original Lady—Mrs. Aniko Gaal Schott.

253

Ronald Lauder with cosmetic legend Estee Lauder and public relations master Bob Gray.

208. WHAT ARE THE FAVORITE APHRODISIACS?

Caviar–In addition to being nutritious (30 percent protein), caviar has been considered an aphrodisiac because of its obvious place in the reproductive process. All fish and their by-products have been linked to the myth of Aphrodite, the goddess of love who was born from the foam of the sea. Supposedly, anything that came from the sea would partake of Aphrodite's power. Supreme at **Jean-Louis**, Watergate.

Garlic–Both Eastern and Western cultures have long regarded garlic as an aphrodisiac. The Greeks and Romans sang its praises and oriental lovers claimed to be towers of strength because of eating it. **Caffe Italiano** gives great garlic!

Honey–Honey is highly nutritious and rich in minerals, amino acids, enzymes, and B-complex vitamins. Galen, Ovid and Sheikh Nefzawi, author of *The Perfumed Garden*, believed that honey has outstanding aphrodisiac powers. Try **The Front Page** for a honey of a time.

Lobster–The lobster has been described as an amatory excitant by many writers, including Henry Fielding in *Tom Jones*. In addition, it shares the Aphrodite-derived power attributed to all seafood. Always, **The Palm**.

Oysters–Oysters are one of the most renowned aphrodisiac foods; like other seafoods, they are rich in phosphorus. Although they are not a high source of energy, oysters are easily digestible. Among the eminent lovers who have vouched for oysters was Casanova, who called them "spur to the spirit and to love." **At the Blue Point Grill** in Alexandria.

Peaches–(For those who enjoy their champagne decorated with a slice of fresh peaches)– "Venus owns this tree... the fruit provokes lust..." wrote Herbalist Nicholas Culpepper. The Chinese considered the fruit's sweet juices symbolic of the effluvia of the vagina, and both the Chinese and Arabs regard its deep fur-edged cleft as symbolic of the female genitalia. A "peach house" was once a common English slang term for a house of prostitution, and the term "peach" has been used almost universally to describe a pretty or sexually appealing girl. Now at the new **Vidalia**.

Truffles–Used by Washington gourmets, these expensive underground fungi are similar to oysters in that they are composed mostly of water and rich in protein, and have similar effects on the indulgent. Perfect at **Palladin** by Jean-Louis.

Asparagus–A vegetable rich in potassium, phosphorus, and calcium, all necessary for maintenance of a high energy level. Kingly at **Kinkead's**.

Some of the newer aphrodisiacs like Welbutrin (a cure-all for a reduced sexual drive), Yohimbine (for men with psychogenic impotence) and Papaverine (enhances the sexual appetite) are reaching the market in successful ways; most require a prescription and use-supervision. On the other hand, not enough can be said about the aphrodisiacs of MONEY and POWER and YOUTH and SUCCESS and GOOD LOOKS... all of these play especially important roles in the Washington lifestyle. Suffice it to say, that an individual possessing any two of those aphrodisiacs is already well-place[d] on the social pyramid.

209. WHAT ARE THE FAVORITE BEAUTY FOODS?

The ideal way for Ladies to get skin, nails and hair quite in order is not t[o] overdo one nutrient and thereby undo the rest, but to have a balanced guide t[o] foods. Here's what Washingtonians consume as a matter of looking goo[d]: **watermelon** (plenty of water to flush toxins from the system); **olive oil** (lots o[f] vitamin E to slow the skin's aging process); **mangos** (vitamin A, an importan[t] skin-nurturer; helps regulate sebaceous glands); **yogurt** (a generous supplier o[f] calcium to help skin glow and strengthen bones and teeth); **lobster** (yields plent[y] of zinc, a great mineral for bolstering skin, hair, nails and eyes); **red peppe[r]** (stocked with vitamin C; helps to maintain skin-plumping collagen); **pasta** (a[n] American favorite for everything–contains selenium to keep the immune syste[m] in order); **salmon** (plenty of body building vitamin D for better grooming an[d] posture); **nuts** (peanuts, pecans, walnuts, almonds–the B family of vitamins f[or] increased energy); **beefsteak** (has the iron needed to form hemoglobin, t[he] oxygen-carrying portion of red blood cells); and the most fundamental source [of] great nutrition–**apples** and **papaya**.

There's been a modest preoccupation lately with the consumption (eatin[g] that is) of flowers. Some safe and delectable flowers-as-food are: **geraniums**–f[or] tea and other beverages; **chrysanthemum**–quite edible and tasty; **fuchsia**–ta[rt] but tasteful; **honeysuckle**–sweet and bracing; **marigolds**–peppery and poten[t;] **carnations**–look great on cakes and have a pleasant after-taste; and **chamomil[e]** bitter, but good in tea.

Bob and Arlette Gordon—disciples of distinguished wining and dining.

210. WHAT ARE THE GOURMET FOOD SOCIETIES IN THE CAPITAL?

Chevalier du Tastevin–an international fraternity dedicated to fine dining and the wines of Burgundy. Le Grand Senechal of the Washington Chapter hosts dinner for 35 people in various restaurants and clubs in Town. A Tastevin is a small silver saucer that is used for wine tasting; often hung around the neck of a wine steward as a sign of authority. It is also the Society's symbol.

Confrerie de la Chaine des Rotisseurs–a group dealing with the esoteric of food, wine and spirits. Bailli Norman Larsen heads the Bailliage de Washington with Vice Conseiller Gastronomique Henry Greenwald; and hosts a group of about 100 members and guests 8-10 times/year. The group is known for top entertainment and highly creative food preparation and presentation. The annual induction dinner is the season highlight; last year it was held at The Mayflower under the direction of Chef Tino Bruggio (of the hotel). Lately, the group has enjoyed "amicals"—informal get-togethers which match good food and conversation.

In '93, **Robert Gordon**, bailli of the Palm Beach chapter, was named "Bailli of the Year" at the annual convention of the Chaine held in Manalapan, FL at the Ritz-Carlton Hotel. Doyle Rogers, bailli of the United States for the Chaine, called Gordon "Mr. Hospitality" and presented him with a crystal trophy; he was selected from among 145 baillis in the country.

International Wine and Food Society–also dedicated to the fine art of dining; group caters to about 50 members and guests at each outing.

Each of the societies holds about four dinners per year (half of them in major hotels); up to $150 per person is spent on the dinner and accompanying wines and amenities.

211. WHAT ARE THE LATEST GOURMET DELICACIES WASHINGTONIANS CRAVE?

Caviar—$340-$544 per pound; Fresh foie gras—$100 per pound; Extra virgin olive oil—$15.95 for 10 ounces; Truffles—$700-$1,000 per pound; Balsamic vinegar—$65 for 10 ounces; Dolman chevre—$11.70 per pound; Imported chocolates—$23-$32 per pound; Smoked Queen Trout (Finland)—$22 per pound; Goose Foie Gras with Truffles—$108 per 14.8 oz. serving, and Etoile (chocolate truffle cake)—$108 per 14.8 oz. serving.

212. WHAT ARE THE ALL-TIME FAVORITE COCKTAILS OF WASHINGTONIANS?

Cocktails and gimmick drinks come and go, and each year aggressive liquor marketers induce further consumption with novelty spirits, new recipes and very socially "in" concoctions. But the favorites remain through the years and have long been sources of refreshment for Washingtonians via these creations.

Brandy Alexander. The perfect cocktail for an afternoon rendezvous—cognac and dark creme de cacao with some heavy creme. Always a favorite at the Mayflower's Town and Country.

Rob Roy. Scotch and sweet vermouth, perfect for the serious drinker. Goes down so easily at the River Club.

Sidecar. Brandy or armagnac, Triple-Sec and lemon juice; created by a WWI officer who traveled to his favorite Paris bistro in the sidecar of his motorcycle. A legendary drink at Clyde's.

Stinger. An ounce and a half of any spirit (usually brandy) and either white creme de menthe or peppermint schnapps served on the rocks, in an old-fashioned glass. Popular at Dominique's.

Cuba Libre. The El Morocco Special in NYC; a hit at Garett's. Coke and Bacardi (or Mount Gay) Rum. Hemingway loved the drink in his Havana days; Castro tried to ban it.

Old-fashioned. The ultimate whiskey cocktail; sugar cube, good whiskey, dash of bitters, soda and lemon peel. Then and now, a favorite at the Monocle.

Martini. Gin or Vodka with a touch of vermouth, either up or on the rocks. The gentleman's libation. Veddy civilized if done expertly. Perfect at the Jockey Club.

Incidentally, recent surveys have indicated that between the ages of 18-24, men like rum and coke, women prefer Screwdrivers; between ages 25-44, men like gin and tonic, women Margaritas; from ages 45-54, it's martinis for the guys, Bloody Marys for the ladies. Some surveys show up to 80 percent of people order a cocktail before dinner (when eating out).

213. WHAT ARE THE PREFERRED BEERS IN TOWN?

Beer dates back more than 8,000 years; it was a favorite of the Babylonians, Greeks, Chinese and Romans. Reputedly, it was even on Noah's Ark. The Pilgrims brought it to the US; it was brewed by the English Colonists and the Dutch at New Amsterdam. William Penn was one of the early brewers in his Quaker settlement in Pennsylvania; Samuel Adams, George Washington and Thomas Jefferson were also pioneers in the beer business. Today, 500 brands of beer are available in this country, many of them at Brickskeller, 1523 22nd St. NW; about half of them are imported. Here's how they rank with Washingtonians: the favorite domestic beers are Budweiser, Miller Lite, Bud Lite, Coors Light, Busch, Miller High Life and Michelob; tops among imports are Heineken (Netherlands), Corona (Mexico), Molson (Canada), Beck's (West Germany), Labatt (Canada) and Amstel Light (Netherlands). Non-alcoholic favorite beers are Moussey, O'Doul's and Sharps. For the record, Americans quaffed 192 million barrels of beer last year; on a per capita basis, that's about three-quarters of a barrel per person!

214. WHAT FAMOUS MUSICAL INSTRUMENTS CAN BE SEEN IN TOWN?

The **Hall of Musical Instruments** (in the National Museum of American History, on the Mall), delights the ear and eye. The finest stringed instruments, antique harpsichords, chamber organs, and grand pianos can be seen and heard. For their chamber music programs, the staff moves choice instruments into a 180-seat theater, where quartets, trios, and larger groups perform.

The **Violin Treasures** exhibit shows the work of four of the finest craftsmen of string instruments: Gaspero da Sallo de Brescia, Nicolo Amati, Gluseppe Guarneri, and Antonio Stradivari.

Taking the spotlight are two violins, a viola, and violoncello made by Stradivari between 1687 and 1709. Producing beautiful sounds was just part of the master violin-maker's skill. Stradivari also ornamented his pieces with ivory inlays in the form of grapevines, cupids, and arrows. For contrast, he inlaid ebony sawdust in the cutout portions, with dark and light ornamentations against the rich wood.

The highest price ever paid for a violin was almost $300,000 for one of the "Hubermann" from Kreisler Stradivari (dated 1773) at Sotheby's, London in '79. (Some 700 of the 1,116 violins by Stradivarius are still around the world.) About $290,000 was shelled out at the same Sotheby's auction for a violoncello by Stradivarius.

Recently, a new exhibit opened in the Hall of Musical Instruments. Highlights included a forte-piano made in Salzburg in 1788 by Schmidt, a 1761 Parisian harpsichord by Stehlin, various 18th-century wind and brass instruments, stringed instruments by the great Tyrolean maker Stainer, and a pair of kettle drums. A new touch-screen-activated sound system offers the opportunity to hear works by Mozart played on museum instruments by members of the Smithsonian's staff.

The museum's **History of Jazz Collection**, which shows some of the 200,000 music manuscripts, photographs, and art in the Duke Ellington archive, is very popular. The jazz collection also includes trumpets of Dizzy Gillespie, Harry James, and Charlie Shavers; Hymie Scherter's saxophone; Buddy Rich's drum set, and even the "famous door" of the Famous Door nightclub in New York City.

The museum pioneered the development and publication of critically based record sets interpreting the history of jazz. More than 20 important important albums, including The Smithsonian Collection of Classic Jazz and Big Band Jazz are available. (*The Washington Post Guide to Washington*)

215. WHAT ARE THE MOST EXCLUSIVE COUNTRY CLUBS IN THE AREA?

Ever since there was a pecking order, there were country clubs, because there is no better place to be all-important and pompous than in a private

259

club, amid social brahmins, generational families and those with stiff upper lips.

The first club of record was the **Country Club of Brookline (MA)**, founded in 1882 by members of the Boston-based Somerset Club. In New York, members of the Union Club developed the Tuxedo Club in Hudson Valley, and in 1892, some assertive and proper gents from the Capital's Metropolitan Club formed their very own **Washington Golf & Country Club** in Arlington. There are now about 5,000 country clubs in the US.

That club still stands, proudly and imperiously. An eight-year waiting list prevails at the Washington G&CC with a hearty initiation fee of $30,000 and annual dues in the $3,600 range. About 300 members vie for tee-off time.

At **Columbia Country Club** in Chevy Chase, members can play 36 holes of golf on a world-class course only after paying their $25,000 initiation fee and spending five years in the waiting game.

Burning Tree Country Club near the Beltway in Bethesda is the ultimate hang-out for top government officials and the corollary lobbyists. World-famous because of its affiliation with US Presidents (Truman, Ike, JFK – who was sponsored for membership by then VP Nixon, Johnson, Ford, Reagan and Clinton have all played the course; only Carter declined) and cabinet members, it is the choice of most Washingtonians. There are no tennis courts, swimming pool, or women! And it isn't very social (12 dinners per year) except on the links. Entry fee is about $50,000; dues $3,000; 300 members. It's the definitive place for "People Like Us."

Congressional Country Club, Bethesda, was founded by then-Secretary of Commerce Herbert Hoover, who conned his buddies Astor, Armour, Vanderbilt, Firestone and Chrysler into funding it, for their collective pleasure. It went under during the Depression, but came back as a paratrooper school (WWII) then re-emerging as one of the area's best clubs, catering to suburban professions. It has 500 members, initiation fee of $20,000, annual dues of $2,500 and is considered a good place for people on the move. It is not as WASPy as the other clubs and has a good mixture of Irish and Italians.

For world-class WASPiness, the **Chevy Chase Country Club** takes honors. It is one of the oldest, most sophisticated, most discerning (re new members) and quietest clubs in the area. Fees are high, waiting list is long, facilities are good but not great, and very much in keeping with an anglo-orientation; CCCC is private, low-key, unassuming, rich and right on!

Located in Rockville, **Woodmont CC** was the creation of an assembly of Jews in 1913; rather than be rejected by their Cave Dwelling associates, the group simply formed its own very posh club (has the most luxurious clubhouse of any), set high standards, ($65,000 entry fee, $5,000 yearly dues, 10-year waiting list), and played out their roles. No WASPs welcome, although young Ms. Chelsea Clinton has been hitting the sandtraps as she learns the game; she's a guest of any number of friends to Clinton, among

Arts for the Aging advocate Lolo Sarnoff (top right) with some bright, new Sarnoff Fellows.

them Duke Ziebert and Martin Agronsky.

Belle Haven CC (Alexandria), **Kenwood G & CC** (Bethesda) and **Tantallon CC** (Tantallon, MD) each has its own panache and caters to snobbish, clubbish types of differing dimensions and delights.

The most exclusive club in the country is said to be **Palm Beach Country Club**, in Palm Beach; 200 members, $100,000 initiation fee, $10,000 yearly dues, totally restricted (no gentiles), regular assessments of $10,000 or $15,000, and a typical Saturday night tab of $200 a couple – dinner, drinks and dancing.

216. WHAT ARE THE MOST PRESTIGIOUS PRIVATE CLUBS IN TOWN?

Although there are several dozen assorted social, professional, country and trade clubs in Town, all considered "private," there are only a handful of superb A-list clubs where the intelligentsia of Town meet with power-brokers and congressional might in privacy. Each has its own code(limited publicity is a basic tenet) and its own coterie. Here's a list:

One of Washington's oldest fraternities is the **Alfalfa Club** housed in the offices of the National Geographic Society. High-powered and exclusive, its annual dinner draws the mightiest-of-the-mighty and is dedicated to panning all those superior senators and industrialists and real estate tycoons who are all members. The annual roast at the Capital Hilton is the only formal meeting of the year—smaller groups meet at will in the club offices. Membership is $5,000 with dues at $500/month.

Members of Congress, Supreme Court justices and business notables make up the membership of the **Alibi Club**, located in a townhouse on I Street. The club was formed by disgruntled members of the Metropolitan Club who felt it was too liberal in its admittance policies. It is the most secretive of any club (only 1,000 members) in Town and has a new member entry fee of $5,000, dues at $4,500 yearly.

The **Cosmos Club** is a private social club "for individuals of distinction, character and sociability"; it was formed in 1878 by men active in science, literature and the arts (1,988 women were accepted as members). The club is located at 2121 Massachusetts Ave. and offers many facilities including sleeping rooms and a full educational agenda. There is a fixed ceiling of 2,500 members with a modest $1,500 initiation fee and yearly dues of $1,000 (JFK was passed over for membership in the Cosmos Club when his proposer, Ambassador to India John Galbraith, resigned from the Club in a protest over its admittance policies).

Housed at 1700 H St., the **Metropolitan Club** is a mix of younger aspirants and upwardly-mobiles who have it all (or most of it); with 3,000 members and modest fees it is one of the less difficult clubs to gain access to. Largely business-oriented, it does have women as members (about 10 percent, and growing).

The **International Club** (1800 K St.) was founded in '64 when the Cosmos Club denied membership to black journalist Carl Rowan; it still has a healthy black member roster as well as a number of foreign statesmen. Noted for dealing with far-flung issues in a social setting, the 2,000 member club ($3,500 initiations; $3,500 dues) is gaining in prestige and popularity.

The **Sulgrave Club** at 1801 Massachusetts Ave. is "For Ladies Only." It is housed in a mansion named after George Washington's ancestral home in England, and absolutely shuns publicity. It will not divulge its members' names and fees are unknown. Those in the inner sanctum can be censured for telling the outside world too much; the club activities and goals are known only to the 750 women that make up the membership.

Used as a hangout (and founded) by Korean influence-peddler Tongsun Park in the mid-'70s, the **Georgetown Club** on Wisconsin Ave. (Suter's Tavern) is a superior club with enough horsepower and star-quality to be desirable. Membered mostly by younger attorneys and professionals, it serves as a convenient home away from home.

Other gathering spots like the **University Club, Capitol Hill Club, City Tavern Club, Pisces II, Federal City Club, National Press Club, 1925 F St. Club** and **Washington Club** have their objectives and body-politic in order and round out the selection of meeting places in Town. As in any other city, clubs are a personal matter and often are handy instruments for gaining the privilege of thin-air atmosphere.

Private clubs have long been associated with seduction, of the mind or of the flesh. By any source of historical evidence, some of the first **mating grounds** were the hunting lodges and fishing camps maintained by royalty back in the days of the Crusades. Properly married royals may have projected a blissful image to the public but liaisons of many varieties occupied the private sanctuaries of their kingdoms. Who can forget the greatest of all love triangles and how it was played out—King Arthur, his spectacular wife Guenevere and his top knight Sir Lancelot? Lance and Ginny were simply doing what had been done for centuries; enjoying the simple pleasures of being non-throne for a while, and expressing passion in its most primitive way.

From the secretiveness of a hunting camp as a **locus for seduction** came the formation of more public but also more subtle enclaves to serve personal purposes. The **private club.** In his 18th century dictionary, Samuel Johnson defined a club as "an assembly of good fellows, meeting under certain circumstances." Assuming that definition, the first club in America was the **Fish House** in Philadelphia, founded in 1732, four years before White's was established in London (although the latter had been functioning for years without formal rules and a constitution). The club allowed the **men** of a family—businessmen or statesman or bachelors to have a place to go, without question and need for elaboration. "I'm going to my club" was the complete declarative, rarely challenged.

Actually, the first formal club was the **Union Club** (1836)—it fit the specs in that it was a "home away from home." Rather than being a place to conduct business, the club was a refuge from the deals and hazards of commerce, and its members used the facility for good food, congenial conversation and entertainment. No women were allowed in the **Union Club**, or the many similar organizations that followed in the 1850-1900 era: the **Somerset Club** in Boston, **Philadelphia Club, Union Pacific Club** in San Francisco, **Knickerbocker Club** (NYC) and the grandest of all—the **Metropolitan Club**, which was founded by J.P. Morgan when one of his friends was blackballed by the Union League. Half-a-century later the country flourished with clubs—the **Century** and **Player's Clubs** in NYC, **St. Botolph's** in Boston, the **Cosmos** in Washington, the **Cactus Club** in Denver and the famed **Bohemian Club** in San Francisco. All the clubs continued to be for **men only**; they served as a quasi-family for singles and a hideout for married men who were ill-equipped to deal with the propriety of an upper-class mid-Victorian home. Most of all clubs functioned as a place where men could talk openly about their **extramarital affairs**, or their social aberrations or whatever business or human conquest would draw the interest of their peers. Importantly, the club served as a sound excuse for the **infidelities** of members, for the statement—"I'm going to my club" remained inviolate and covered many a dubious activity.

William B. Astor II, for example, belonged to several private clubs and often sought refuge in them as a means of expressing a love-void for his wife. During the Gilded Age, when Mrs. Astor was delighting society with her annual "400" Ball, Astor was consorting with the lowest level of streetwalker. Between his clubs and his tarts, he led a perfectly neurotic life, but it was better than facing the imperious Mrs. Astor (who didn't mind, her passion for William was very modest). Astor's proclivity for mundane women had a precedent—the **Duke of York's** penchant for ugly, questionable ladies led friends to agree that "he chose his mistresses as a form of penance."

William Randolph Hearst used the Union Pacific Club in San Francisco as his hideout from a drab 15-year marriage to Millicent Willson; it was also the place from which he launched a 33-year love affair with actress **Marion Davies**, and faced the daily ridicule that accompanies romance with a woman 30 years his junior and hardly star-quality (by the standards of the fabled Hearst Organization, the most powerful media force in the country). Davies and Hearst never were able to marry legally, although their affair had all the conveniences of marriage; yet Hearst was a man's man, and spent most of his "faithful" hours between his offices and private clubs.

Another serious club member was **James Fisk, Jr.** who with Wall Street legend Jay Gould, took control of the Erie Railway from Commodore Whitney. After a long marriage, Fisk took to a young gold digger named **Josie Mansfield** and set up housekeeping with her under the guise of hanging out at the Union Club. Mansfield tired of his hypocritical ways and got involved with another man, who was financially ruined by Fisk and later got his revenge by killing the tycoon. Club members paid proper respect to their fallen leader by lifting a glass.

It's been said that the Knickerbocker Club was the place where Florida megamillionaire **Henry M. Flagler** finally decided to have his second wife—Ida—committed to a mental institution (she claimed the Czar of Russia, whom she had never met, was in love with her), thereby setting up his marriage to Mary Lily Kenan, 39 years younger, from a wealthy southern family. Mary Lily made the last 12 years of Flagler's life happy and complete **without clubs.** At death, he willed her his vast fortune; she later married Robert Worth Bingham of the Louisville newspaper clan and died suddenly less than a year later. Bingham was willed $5 million. But Flagler, clubby gent that he was, never abandoned his psychotic wife Ida; when she died at age 82 (in 1930) she left an estate of $15 million. Today, **The Breakers in**

Palm Beach is the most visible symbol of the fruits of the Flagler-Kenan alliance.

217. WHAT IS THE MOST EXPENSIVE YACHT IN THE AREA?

Many spectacular yachts make their way to the Annapolis Harbor as a social port of call, or simply to refuel and recharge. With each arrival/ departure there is plenty of partying and exchanges of summer or foreign addresses, so that hope prevails until "we meet again."

At this time, the most expensive yacht in the Harbor (Chesapeake Marina) is the *Britannia*, a high-tech, high-speed, 111-115 ft. long Broward yacht with a price tag of around $10 million. Owned by Dr. Loren Simkowitzk the powerboat (three 1,500 hp engines) can skim across the water at 51 mph (44 knots).

Jack Miller of Miller and Long owns the 90-ft. *Seabird*, probably the largest and most expensive yacht ($3.5 million) in dock at Annapolis Harbor; it can be leased for a week at $60,000, ($100,000 for the *Britannia*).

Through the years the Vanderbilts' *Alva*, Solomon Guggenheim's *Frientze*, Horace Dodge's *Delfine*, and J.P. Morgan's *Corsair* (all ranging in length from 150 to 300 ft.) were the biggest yachts to dock in the Washington area; each carried a crew of 25 men. Actual costs for these ships topped at $2 million.

Presently several world-class yachts cruise the Potomac:

The *Maid Marion* owned by Mrs. C.H. Bliss is a 100-ft. all wood boat built in the 1930s. Because of the maintenance required on a wooden boat, this old classic requires a crew of six to eight. Building the *Marion* today would run up to $5 million.

The 90-ft. *Whitefin* (a copy of the *Ticonderoga*) built in Maine by Gody Stevens, was owned by Mr. Tom Zetkoff (now deceased). Built in '84 she is considered the most luxurious sailboat—sleeping 10 and carrying a crew of six. The most unusual feature aboard is a bathtub made entirely of wood.

Two of the most expensive ($5 million range) and luxurious boats for their size are the *Grindstone* and the *Buckpasser*, both carrying crews of five-six men. *Grindstone* owned by Eugene Dixon, Jr. is a 98-ft. aluminum Burger designed by Jack Hargrave; Ogden Phipps' *Buckpasser*, also all aluminum, was designed by Jack Hargrave and built in Japan.

The *Octopussy*, owned by Abe Gosman is considered a mega-yacht by any measurement; in addition to being a state-of-the-art craft, it can speed up to 65 mph, whch makes it among the swiftest vessels in the country (it is powered by three 3,500 horsepower, three-stage turbocharged MTU engines). It was featured in the James Bond movie—*Octopussy*.

There was a time when Washington docks were the winter home of some of the great names in the world. For example, these yachts/owners made the pilgrimage to the Capital: *Colmena*, Jules S. Bache; *Eagle Point*, Bernard M. Baruch; *Little Nourmahal*, Vincent Astor; *Onika*, Edsel B. Ford, *Sea Urchin*,

The Octopussy—extraordinary megayacht,
frequent Potomac River visitor.

Henry F. duPont; *Sonia*, Henry Carnegie Phipps. The 353-ft. *Sea Cloud* (Marjorie Merriweather Post's wedding present from E.F. Hutton) was frequently in residence; at that time it was the largest sailing yacht ever built. Mrs. Post eventually sold the four-masted barque to Rafael Trujillo, dictator of the Dominican Republic, who made it a warship. The *Sea Cloud* is now a charter vessel in the Caribbean.

The late Malcolm Forbes staged many parties in DC on his luxurious yacht *The Highlander*—proving that capitalism has its advantages.

218. WHAT ARE THE PREFERRED BOARDING SCHOOLS FOR WASHINGTONIANS?

Private boarding schools, like private clubs, have a particular chemistry that either does or doesn't meet the needs/wants of students. But, based on facilities, curriculum and cost, here are the favorites of Capital dwellers (Costs given are for yearly boarding students):

St. Albans, DC ($15,750)
Episcopal High School, Alexandria ($15,650)
Foxcroft School, Middleburg ($18,600)
Madeira School, McLean ($18,325)
Garrison Forest School, Owings Mill ($18,260)
Gunston School, Centreville ($17,000)
Oldsfields, Glencoe ($18,500)
St. Timothy's School, Stevenson ($17,800)

Some boarding schools have unique attractions for students with unique interests: **Garrison Forest** has the only all-girl high school polo team in the country; **Madeira** offers part-time internships at the Smithsonian and National Public Radio; **St. Albans** provides a course in communications for quick-starts in the media world, and most of the schools have "total immersion" sessions for students falling behind in their studies.

219. WHERE DO YOUNG WASHINGTONIANS LEARN THE ESOTERIC OF BALLROOM DANCING?

A course in **"Etiquette and Ballroom Dancing"** is offered by the super-exclusive studio of Mrs. Edmund Gordon Simpson to young people from the fourth-through-ninth grades; 10 lessons, 1 1/2 hours each at $150 (from 6:30-8 p.m. at 5521 Landy Ln. in Bethesda). Young people are taught all the dance steps as well as proprieties of the up-and-coming upper class; deportment is critical and students are selected very carefully, thereby assuring compatibility of interest, desire and background. Mrs. Simpson has been an enduring factor in etiquette and dancing instructions for 20 years and assumed the mantle from the legendary Mrs. Shippen (who dominated the junior Cave Dweller category for 50 years). Lately, questions about discrimination and ethnic balance of her students have been raised, with no resolution.

The **Washington Assembly**, another dancing/etiquette school favors FFVs (first family Virginians) as students; and the **Woodley School**, sponsored by the Wellesley Club of Washington, brings youngsters up to snuff on manners and movements, too.

220. IN WHAT CHURCH CAN YOU SEE THE SUN SET ON A ROSE?

At the Cathedral of **St. Peter and St. Paul** (on Mount St. Alban), artist Rowan LeCompte's west rose window is brilliantly illuminated by the fading sun; it is a majestic, transcendent sight.

221. WHERE IS "LITTLE ROME"?

The neighborhood surrounding **Catholic University** is so-named because of the multitude of Catholic institutions in the area: **Trinity College** and its Chapel of Notre Dame (Michigan Ave. at Harewood Rd.); the **Franciscan Monastery** (1400 Quincy Rd.) with many facsimiles of Holy Land shrines and the University itself with numerous chapels.

222. WHAT IS KNOWN AS THE "STREET OF CHURCHES"?

One of the city's most distinguished thoroughfares, 16th St. is the *locus* of many churches: **St. John's** (H St.), itself called "Church of the Presidents" because of frequent visitations by the Head of State (a brass plaque identifies Pew 54 as the Presidents' pew); **The Third Church of Christ** (I St.); **Swedenborgian Church of the Holy City** (Corcoran St.); **First Baptist** (O St.); **Unification** (Harvard St.); **All Souls Unitarian** (Columbia Rd.); **National Baptist Memorial** (F St.) and the **Shrine of the Sacred Heart** (Park Rd.).

223. WHAT CHURCH DISPLAYS A MASSIVE COPPER DOME?

St. Matthew's Cathedral (1725 Rhode Island) with its impressive red-brick exterior is surmounted by a great copper dome, which creates a stirring visual at sunrise/set.

224. WHAT CHURCH SERVED WASHINGTON AND LEE?

President George Washington and General Robert E. Lee were reverent participants in religious ceremonies at **Christ Episcopal Church** in Alexandria; a Georgian classic, the church has been in continuous operation since 1773.

225. WHAT IS SOME OTHER CHURCH LORE?

The **Washington Hebrew** Congregation (DuPont Circle) has the city's oldest and largest Reform congregation; the **Islamic Mosque and Center** (Macomb Street) has the only minaret in the city; Greek Orthodox **Saint Sophia Cathedral** (36th St.) has a presidential touch – Eisenhower laid the cornerstone in '56; the **Third Church of Christ Scientist** (16th and I) is the only city church designed by I.M. Pei; and the **First Baptist Church** (16th and O) was Jimmy Carter's Sunday morning drop-in.

226. WHERE IN THE CITY IS A "RETURN TO NATURE"?

Theodore Roosevelt is credited with protecting the four-mile parcel of wilderness that bisects the District and is known as Rock Creek Park. Over 15 miles of hiking, biking and riding trails are deliciously served up, with 70 groves for picnics, a 180-year-old gristmill (Pierce Mill),world-class zoo (National Zoo) and even a 2.4 kilometer exercise course that begins near Calvert St. and Connecticut Ave. and runs toward Beach Dr. For nature at its best, Rock Creek Park is every man's return!

Other natural havens are:

Dumbarton Oaks with its Renaissance Gardens and potential for romance or solitude. Dumbarton hosted world leaders in 1944 who were laying the groundwork for the United Nations Chapter. The 10-acres of gardens were welcomed by the officials and specific areas like the Pebble Garden, Urn Terrace, Rose Garden, Camellia Circle, Crabapple Hill, Lover's Lane Pool and the fountains were a delightful reprieve. The estate is now a research center owned by Harvard; collections of Byzantine and Pre-Columbian art, plus tapestries and fine furniture are on display;

The Franciscan Monastery with 40 acres of gardens and woodlands and replicas of Holy Land shrines;

Potomac Park and Hains Point, a 700-acre expanse along the flowing Potomac, great for picnics and undergoing an "Awakening";

The National Arboretum, with its myriad plants and trees, some 450 acres of nature at its best;

Kenilworth Aquatic Garden, ponds and a tidal marsh, water plants, 50 acres of water wonderland;

Washington National Cathedral, the royal edifice of Town – gardens, plants, hills, herbs, glorious sights, even GOD!

Georgetown's **Tudor Place, Oak Hill Cemetery, Montrose Park** and **Mackall Square** also deliver solace and a sensitive environment for "communing."

Maestro "Slava" Rostropovich—
orchestrating in a new medium at Corcoran Art School.

Mrs. Jean McDuffie Nowack and Wallace Holladay—bringing their special harmony to the Hope Ball.

CHAPTER VIII

MEMORABLE MILESTONES & MAXIMA
(Properties, Pinnacles & Panoramas)

Photo: J.R. Black

**Ms. Kristin Bryant and Mrs. Dianne Kay—celebrating the
rites of life, munificently.**

227. WHERE DO MOST CAVE DWELLERS AND ASSORTED BRAHMINS LIVE?

The heaviest concentration of those born to the manner is **Chevy Chase** a quiet, tree-lined, lane twisting, country-clubbish neighborhood just north of the District line (although the official mailing address is Washington). It's the DC version of the Main Line in Philadelphia and a haven for blue bloods with Green Book status.

Chevy Chase is bordered by Western Ave. on the north, extends east to Rock Creek Park, jogs around Albemarle St. on the south, and roams around Fessenden and Harrison Sts. on the west. The 560-acre area was founded by Colonel Joseph Belt and registered in 1725 as "Cheivy Chace" (after the Cheviat Chays Forest in Northumberland, the boundary between England and Scotland). In the early 1800s, former Nevada Senator Francis Griffith Newlands set up the Chevy Chase Land Company and began developing the area. Today, there is a Chevy Chase in DC and an incorporated town of Chevy Chase in Maryland (it extends from Chevy Chase Village to Chevy Chase Circle to Bradley Ln. in Maryland and is bordered by Kirkside Dr. and Grove, Montgomery and Hesketh Sts.); it is the oldest Chevy Chase neighborhood and considered the most prestigious. Longtime residents think of it as the only "real" Chevy Chase.

Names like **Appleby, Armstrong, Charles, Herndon, Mallory, Ourisman, Ragan, Stirling, Trudeau, Tweedy, Withers, Wimsatt, Wooten, Worrell** and **Young** are typical of Chevy Chase residents.

McLean, VA also has many heavy-hitters (Senators Alan K. Simpson, Edward M. Kennedy and Charles S. Robb; Frank Carlucci, Fred Malek, Elliot Richardson, Reza Pahlavi, Shah of Iran-presumptive, News World Communication Inc.'s Bo Hi Pak; Prince Bandar bin Sultan, Saudi Arabia Ambassador). **Potomac, MD** has a very pricey crowd (Mary Gore Dean, Senator John Glenn, businessman J. Willard Marriott, Jr., developers Mark Vogel and Tony Natelli and Sugar Ray Leonard, who recently bought a home in LA for a reported $7 million). **Albemarle County, VA** mixes acreage with lineage (White House physician Burton Lee, conglomerateur Edgar Bronfman, artist Peter Max, financier John Kluge, actresses Kate Jackson and Sissy Spacek, philanthropist-divorcee Patricia Kluge). Sportsman Jack Kent Cooke seems to parachute in at many different homes, but one standout is his $ million pad in **Massachusetts Heights** where his neighbors—Haft, Rales, Bender, Pearl, Brandt and Benton—play out the good life.

228. HOW MUCH DOES IT COST TO STAFF A WASHINGTON MANSION TODAY, VERSUS 15 YEARS AGO?

Assuming the mansion is endowed as follows — located on several acres of hilly property, 20 or more rooms, two heated swimming pools (one indoor), greenhouse, tennis court, five automobiles, a total staff of 17 full time members (including six who live-in)—the monthly tab would be:

| ITEM | PER MONTH | |
	TODAY	15 YEARS AGO
Head Gardener	$2,400	$1,000
Five Gardeners ($10 hr.)	6,400	2,500
Butler	2,600	1,000
Butler	3,200+	—
Personal Maid	2,500	900
Parlor Maid	2,000	800
Chef	3,600 +	1,500
Housekeepers	2,000	1,200
Laundress	2,000	1,000
Chauffeur	2,400	1,200
Masseur (daily)	900	300
French Tutor	1,000	500
Social Secretary	2,600	1,200
TOTAL	$33,600	$13,100

The current trend in staffing is **the couple**, live-in husband/wife team who do "double duty"; he's the inside man (butler/houseman/chauffeur), she is cook/housekeeper/personal maid. Their monthly salary totals approximately $4,500 including benefits (insurance, room, board, auto, etc.). In most cases, additional staff is added to the household as needed. The average Washington mansion has a live-in staff of three people; about 25 local mansions maintain staffs of 12 or more.

EXTRA	NOW	THEN
Food	$15,000	$ 5,000
Liquor	2,000	800
Misc./repairs	2,500	1,000
Subtotal	19,500	6,800
GRAND TOTAL	$53,100	$19,900

Not included in these calculations are such things as taxes, club memberships, out-of-home entertainment, charitable contributions, maintenance of plane or boat and assorted other toys of the rich. These costs could easily add another $20,000 to today's monthly ledger (and $10,000 to costs 15 years ago). The bottom line of all this social meandering/machination is that one's income (either via trust or a trusty family-owned corporation or sheer brilliance) must check in at a staggering level. Rich = responsibility and responsibility is extremely costly; so much so that many monied Washingtonians are shedding homes, cars, commitments and superficial expenses in order to better afford a simple-yet-winning lifestyle.

229. HOW DO WASHINGTON PRICES RANK WITH THOSE OF NEW YORK CITY?

For the most part, there is parity in pricing for select products and services in the two cities; since the Big Apple is larger than the Capital, there is bound to be more variety in product/service selection there, but Washington more than makes up for extensive inventory through its gentility and shopping convenience. Some items of comparison are: (A) Housing costs for four—estimate NYC costs for a three-bedroom condo at $750,000 to $2.5 million; similar DC condo would cost $250,000 to $1.5 million. (B) Commuting time—from a suburb to NYC, about 65 minutes and $6.50 on a train; 20 minutes of driving to the center DC of at a petrol cost of $1.50. (C) Health Club membership — from $500 to $2,000/year in NYC; about $900 at the Watergate Health Club. (D) Monthly parking costs in NYC about $350; $75 in DC. (E) Baby sitting charges/hr.—$10 in NYC (if you're lucky); $3-$5 in DC. (F) Initial visit to Internist—$80 in NYC; $50 in DC. (G) Dry Bombay Gin martini at a leading bar — $6 in the Big Apple; $5 in DC. (H) A tennis lesson—$60/hr in NYC; $50/hr in DC. (I) Fifth-grade tuition—$10,500 at Trinity in NYC; $6,760 in DC. (J) Night on the town—upwards of $200 for a NYC couple tapping all the right sources; in the $150 range for two in DC at Dominique's. (K) Lady's hairstyle, shampoo and set—$65 in NYC; $55 in DC. For the men, about $30 and $20 respectively for a haircut. (L) Taxes on a three-bedroom unit—about $7500 in NYC; $4500 in DC.

230. WHO ARE SOME FAMOUS WASHINGTON ARCHITECTS THROUGH THE YEARS?

Being an American city, 200 years old, many creative influences are vividly manifested in the architecture of Washington; with a major immigrant population in the early years, the texture of the city reflects the mores and idiosyncracies of many lands and cultures. Some unforgettable architects and works are:

Daniel Burnham of Chicago (Union Station); **Adolph Cluss** and **Paul Schulz** (Arts and Industries Bldg.,1880); **Hornblower** and **Marshall Natuinlal** (Museum of Natural History); **Charles A. Platt** (Freer Gallery of

Art); **John Russell Pope** (National Gallery of Art, 1941); **McKim, Mead and White** (National Museum of American History,'64); **Gordon Bunshaft** of Skidmore, Owings and Merrill (Hirshhorn Museum,'74); **Gyo Obata** of Hellmuth, Ohata and Kassabaum (National Air and Space Museum,'76); **W. J. Edbrooke's** (Old Post Office,1900); **Mitchell Giurgola** (J.W. Marriott Hotel and National Place Complex,'67); **Hartman-Cox** (Beaux Arts Revival Building,'68 and the Sears World Trade Office,'69); **Arthur Erickson** (Canadian Embassy, '89) and **Arthur Cotton Moore Associates** (Washington Harbour, '86). At the top of the profession also are architects Robert Bell, David Swartz, Richard Williams and George Stavrapolos.

Some newer designers on the scene are: **KressCox Associates**, DC (traditional homes); **Fabry Associates Architects**, DC (artsy, contemporary homes); **McCartney Lewis Architects**, DC (classic stone homes); **O'Neil & Manion Architects**, Bethesda (replications of old homes); **Robert Schwartz Associates**, DC (building conversions) and master creators **George Stavropoulas and Associates** (DC).

Of interest: the **American Institute of Architects** voted the quality of architecture in Washington as fifth-best in the US (Chicago, New York City, San Francisco and Boston were leaders) and selected The Dulles International Airport Terminal by Eero Saarinen and I.M. Pei's National Gallery of Art's East Building as two of the greatest (of 10) American structures ever built. Additionally, Washington had four buildings in the top 25 (best built since '80)—the Vietnam Veterans Memorial, Union Station Restoration, National Cathedral and Metrorail.

231. WHAT ARE THE FOREMOST NEIGHBORHOODS IN THE CAPITAL?

The District is a community of 95 recognized neighborhoods covering 63 square miles; 20 neighborhoods have qualified as historic districts because of their city history and architecture.

Leading neighborhoods are: **DuPont Circle, Georgetown, Old Anacostia, Adams-Morgan, Kalorama Heights, Foggy Bottom, Woodley Park, Cleveland Park, Capitol Hill, Massachusetts Heights, Shaw** (one of the communities abandoned by middle-class residents in the '60s, now making a major comeback as a desirable place to live), **Uptown** and **Downtown** Washington.

Note: the Capital (and its many neighborhoods) lies in what the Department of Agriculture calls Zone 7, which means that in normal years the temperature never falls to zero, thus the area is warmer than New York but colder than Norfolk or the Carolinas.

As for getting around the Capital, some 9,000 taxicabs make life easy; rates are low, the conversation is good, and traffic jams (New York City "gridlock") are rare.

Cabs know how to navigate the Town's 34 circles—some of which

"Boxwood"—a Chevy Chase landmark, available for $3.2 million, includes '87 Rolls Silver Spur.

function for traffic channelization, some for intersections and some to designate a particular landmark (Sheridan, DuPont, etc.), but driving visitor are urged to maneuver slowly into traffic, especially near circles.

In the District proper, only eight service stations fill consumers' needs they are located at: 9th and H St. NW; 13th and N St. NW; New Hampshire Ave. and M St., NW; Southwest Mall area 10th and D Sts. SW; Foggy Bottom—Watergate area, NW; Virginia Ave. at 27th Ave. NW; Pennsylvania Ave. and 26th Ave. NW; 18th and Columbia Rd. NW.

232. HOW HIGH CAN BUILDINGS BE IN THE DISTRICT?

Historians cite that building codes dating back 200 years limited buildings to a height no greater than that of the Capitol Building (the top of the Statue of Freedom atop the dome is 287 ft. high), which translates to 10 stories or 200 ft. high. Skyscrapers, however, surround the Town in Maryland and Virginia, and loom on the horizon as encroaching monoliths to the rustic tranquility of the Nation's Capital.

233. WHAT IS WASHINGTON'S WORST RESIDENTIAL AREA?

The media has hyped the poverty and violence of neighborhood southeast of the Anacostia River as some of the worst in the country; welfare dependency, drug dealing and crime still characterize the areas which have one-third of residents unemployed. During local political campaigns, the dire plight of the neighborhoods becomes an issue and sordid scenes are played out in endless TV commercials, only exacerbating the situation.

4. WHAT ARE THE MOST PROGRESSIVE OF WASHINGTON'S SUBURBS?

In the last decade, the Washington area has been transformed into 14 emerging small cities; each is a self-contained, high-rise, free-enterprise mecca for jobs, shopping, good housing and a peaceful lifestyle. Each of the 14 cities is bigger than Richmond, VA (the state Capital).

The biggest of the smaller cities is **Rockville/Gaithersburg** along Interstate 270; **Tysons** is the largest city (bigger than Miami) in Virginia or Maryland and its buildings are higher than anything in DC. Other emerging cities are **Bethesda/Chevy Chase/Friendship Heights. Arlington** now has an abundance of Vietnamese shops on Wilson Ave. which is aptly called "Ho Chi Minh Trail"; **Rosslyn/Ballston, Reston, Adams County** (Gettysburg, 80 miles west of DC), "commuter" cities; **Montgomery** (bigger than San Francisco) and **Prince George's Counties** in MD and **Fairfax County**, VA, house some 200 major corporations and institutions that serve manufacturing and service industries in the Capital.

5. WHAT SUBURB IS AN OLD TOBACCO PORT?

Founded in 1749 by Scottish merchants, **Alexandria** was a sleepy tobacco port; today having survived the Revolutionary and Civil Wars, it has emerged as a prosperous contemporary town with a historical past. Covering 16 square miles, with a population of 120,000, its West End is called Condo Canyon because of the dozens of high-rise apartments; the town is 80 percent government-oriented and a number of "yuppies" and "upwardly mobile" couples have townhouses or apartments, preferring the 20-minute commute to living in the District.

Master of all he surveys— Jack Kent Cooke.

Photo: J. R. Black

277

Located five miles south of Georgetown in nearby Virginia, past N
tional Airport on the George Washington Memorial Parkway, Alexandr
with its class "Old Town" (16 blocks that contain 2,000 historic homes a
buildings) has been called the "northernmost Southern town"—it was on
the home of George Washington and Robert E. Lee, and still offers just t
right blend of southern gentility and '90s progressiveness.

Homes (Old Town) range in price from $750,000 to $2.5 million a
celebrated names like **Sullivan, Camalier, Rollins, Stock, Stahl, Bu**
Carter (Hodding), and **Schott** call Old Town home.

236. HOW ABOUT GEORGETOWN LORE?

* The first non-Indian visitor to Georgetown was the legendary Capt.
John Smith who sailed up the Potomac to Little Falls in 1608.

*Originally (1752), Georgetown was a "city" of 60 acres from 30th
to Georgetown University and from N St. to the river; the area was purchas
from two farmers for 280 pounds.

* The first Roman Catholic Bishop in the US—John Carroll—found
"Georgetown Academy" in 1789; a bronze statue of him sits inside t
entrance to the university at what is now Georgetown University.

*Two ancient cannon sit just behind Bishop Carroll; they were brou
to the US by the *Ark* and the *Dove* in 1633 (the same ships brought the fi
Catholic settlers to the new world); although there has been much disp
about the target of the fixed-position cannon (the Capitol), the subject is de
with more in jest than in seriousness.

*The 29th President of Georgetown University—**Father Patrick**
Healy—is also known as its "Second Founder" because of the major w
he did in expanding the curriculum (new medical and law facilities, grea
liberal arts studies, foreign service school). He was educated at Holy Cr
College, became President in 1873, and is remembered by the **The He**
Building, landmark of the University with its massive tower (completed
1879). Father Healy was Black (under the law of Georgia he was born a sla
to an Irish father and a former slave mother) and the first to hold a Ph.D
America, as well as the first Black President of a major university.

*Georgetown University athletic teams are called "Hoyas" probabl
derivation of the Greek "Oi saxa" or "On these rocks."

*The original manuscript of Mark Twain's *Tom Sawyer* is one of
university's most prized possessions; it was donated by Mrs. Nicholas Bra
(whose husband was a book collector) and because of her largesse, she w
awarded an honorary Doctor of Laws degree, the first woman to receiv
degree from the then all-male university.

237. HOW MIGHT GEORGETOWN BECOME AMERICA'S FIRST "UNIVERSITY" POWER COMPANY?

Georgetown University has long insisted that it needs to build a po plant on campus to accommodate its own growing needs; together with Dominion Energy, a Virginia-based power company, plans are underway for the merger of energy and scholarship in what would be the first such venture (city officials have given their initial stamp of approval).

Secret financial reports indicate that the new power plant could be a bonanza for the university to the tune of $1 million a month from the sale of excess power to commercial users; a federal law enacted in '78 requires local energy unit **Pepco** to purchase the unit's excess power.

At this writing, the deal is not yet done; but the Hoyas are planning on new energy levels on campus.

8. WHAT CELEBRATED PERSONAGES DWELL IN GEORGETOWN?

The community is a bastion for the high-and-mighty; dozens of leaders in every classification of government or industry call Georgetown home. Some are: **Jack Sharer**, Editor of the *Washington City Paper*; attorney **Maureen Brennan**; UN's **Ann Hollick; Pat Dixson**, real estate expert; Phillips Collection Director **Jennifer Phillips**; writer **Susan Mary Alsop**; Ambassador **Pamela Harriman**; art aficionado **J. Carter Brown; Senator and Mrs. Claiborne Pell** (RI); **Kitty Kelley**, author; **Paul and Bunny Mellon**, National Gallery arts patron; **William Colby**, former CIA Director; **George Stevens**, former CEO, American Film Institute; **Lucky Roosevelt**, former Protocol Chief; **Oatsie Charles**, grande dame; **Bob Bass**, Texas financier; **Katharine Graham**, *Washington Post*; former Senator **Eugene J. McCarthy; Bob Woodward**, author; Senator **Max Baucus** (D-MT); **Clayton and Polly Fritchey**, journalism/society; the **Livingston Biddles**, arts patrons; **Senator Malcolm Wallop** (R-WY); **Sander Vanocur**, ABC News; **Theresa Heinz**, widow of PA Senator; **Rowland Evans**, political columnist (Evans and Novak); **Marvin and Dolly Kay**, cosmetics; Former Senator **Charles Percy; Cord Meyer**, journalist; **Evangeline Bruce**, grande dame; **Madeleine Albright**, UN Ambassador; **Harold Brown**, former Defense Secretary; **Marianne Means and Warren Weaver**, journalists; **Joe Califano**, Carter's HEW Secretary; **Joan Bingham**, newspaper heiress; **Huntington and Amy Block**, Cave Dwellers; **Smith Bagley**, Reynolds Tobacco heir; **R.W. Apple**, *New York Times*; photographer **Richard Avedon**; former FDIC head **William Seidman**; lawyer **Boyden Gray**; politico **Harvey Sloane;** and the **Hazeltines**.

9. WHAT'S GOING ON COMMERCIALLY IN GEORGETOWN?

There are more important things in life than a little money and one of them is a lot of money! That's the credo of many enterprises along Wisconsin Ave., and there are many enterprises: 22 art galleries; 20 boutiques, 18 shoe stores; 17 hair salons; 14 antique shops; 13 bookstores; 12 dry cleaners; 12 tailors; seven T-shirt shops; seven jewelers; seven record stores; six real

estate offices; six ice cream shops; six athletic stores; five grocery stores; fiv
photo shops; five gift shops; four shoe repair shops; four liquor stores; fou
pizza joints; two video stores; two florists; two poster shops; two toy store
two surf shops; two bike shops; two palm readers; one tobacco shop; on
tanning salon.

240. WHAT ARE THE LATEST REAL ESTATE TRENDS?

Almost invariably, over the long haul, real estate prices escalate; it ma
take several decades in a typical neighborhood evolution (desirable-date
demolished-restored-resurrected) to return significant monies to an owne
but it's a reality that real estate values **affirm** themselves time and time agai

In Washington, for example, if you had purchased a house in '85 and he
onto it, today's value would be about 60 percent greater than your purcha
price. Here's a breakdown of property appreciation over the '85-'93 perio

Neighborhood	'85 Purchase Price	'93 Value	% Change
Mass. Heights	$811,000	$1,398,000	+72
Kalorama	426,000	662,000	+55
Georgetown	301,000	503,000	+67
Chevy Chase	176,000	343,000	+95
Foxhall	151,000	277,000	+83
Capitol Hill	148,000	231,000	+56

In outlying areas, values rose even more significantly:

Potomac	199,000	469,000	+136
Bethesda	166,000	338,000	+104
Gaithersburg	102,000	226,000	+122
Silver Spring	107,000	177,000	+65
McLean	232,000	443,000	+91
Vienna	153,000	267,000	+75
Reston	121,000	211,000	+74
Alexandria (Old Town)	115,000	197,000	+71

241. WHAT ARE THE HIGHLIGHTS OF WASHINGTON REAL ESTATE TODAY?

Some 3,500 real estate agents sell the brick and mortar that mak
Washington such a desirable place to live; they represent over 100 register
real estate firms and sell, collectively, about $1 billion/year (residential

* The **most expensive home** on the market now is the residence of
late CEO of GEICO, David Lloyd Kreeger; the 30-room mansion on Foxh
Rd. is listed at $15 million. (The Brady mansion on Foxhill Rd. was recen
listed at $27 million; for the record, until '91 the most expensive home so
in the area was the Phillips mansion at $9 million; it was resold the next ye
at $14 million to the Prime Minister of Lebanon.)

* The **most expensive apartment** in Town is owned by the Stu

Bernsteins in Georgetown's Washington Harbour; it has panoramic views of the Potomac River, 5,423 sq. ft. of living space, three bedrooms, exercise room with jacuzzi, library and glass walls (in certain rooms); listed at $5.2 million.

* The best addresses (and streets) on which to live are:
  Georgetown, at 31st and R St.
  Cleveland Park, on Highland Pl.
  Massachusetts Avenue Heights, on Woodland Dr. and 32nd St.
  Kent Spring Valley, Glenbrook Rd. or Rockwood Parkway
  Chain Bridge Rd., University Terr. or Palisade Ln.
  Chevy Chase
  Dupont Circle, on R St.
  Kalorama, at Tracy Pl. and Kalorama Rd.
  Wesley Heights
  Forest Hills

* **Watergate South and West** are considered temporary homes for the rich and famous; next to the Kennedy Center, they are convenient to everything, have room service and maids and access to office services, restaurants and the National Airport; rents range from $2,500 to $5,000/ month.

* More townhouses are being built; row houses ranging from $100,000 in **Petworth** to $2.9 million in **Georgetown** are an ideal answer to busy, professional couples.

* New developments like **Hillandale** (across from Georgetown University Hospital) with tennis courts, swimming pool and security are also desirable—prices from $500,000 to $1.6 million; **Sutton Place** near American University offers townhouses in the $300,000 range for administration newcomers; and **Foxhall Crescents** provides a community environment for homes with tennis and swimming facilities and some privacy—about $1 million.

* The top real estate broker in Town in '92 was **Susan A. Safer** of Pardoe Real Estate with $15.7 in transactions; **Thomas P. Murphy** of Prudential Preferred Properties was first in number of transactions with 66 closings. Some 277 realtors qualified as "Top Producers Club" members ($4 million in sales or 30 transactions) or the "Multi-Million Dollar Club" ($2 million in sales or 15 transactions).

Leading (top producing) owner-brokers in the area are: **Pat Dixson** and **Jean Smith** (of Pat Dixson Inc.) and **Virginia Chew** and **Kathy Kennety** of Arnold, Bradley, Sargent, Davy and Chew, Inc.; each generates some $12-20 million in real estate sales each year.

Swimming pools adjoining homes are at a premium in CapCity; only about three percent of homes have pools. The largest indoor pool is at the

11,000 sq. ft. contemporary home designed by Chloethiel Woodard Smith a Rock Creek Park in Forest Hills. The pool room area is 2,604 sq. ft. with tw dressing rooms and a two-level balcony overlooking the heated pool. An other home with a planned swimming pool is Wetzell Farmstead (443 Reservoir Rd.), designed by Robert Bell Architects to preserve an old lo cabin (built by Lazarus Wetzell in 1847) on the property; the residenc preserves the cabin and rural character of the setting and remains adjacent t 400 acres of National Park land, Archbold Glover Park.

For the record, the **largest private house** in the world is the 250-roor Biltmore House in Asheville, NC. It is owned by George and William Ceci grandsons of George Washington Vanderbilt II (1862-1914). The house wa built between 1890 and 1895 on an estate of 119,000 acres, at a cost of $4. million, and is now valued at $55 million with 12,000 acres.

The **most expensive private house** ever built is the Hearst Ranch at Sa Simeon, CA. It was built 1922-1939 for William Randolph Hearst (1863 1951), at a total cost of more than $30 million. It has more than 100 room a 104-ft.-long heated swimming pool, an 83-ft.-long assembly hall and garage for 25 limousines. The house requires 60 servants to maintain it.

The **highest asking price** for any private house in the US is $30. million for the late Conrad Hilton's Casa Encantada built in 1938 in an 1/2-acre estate in Bel-Air. It has 64 rooms and 26 bathrooms and 23,000 s ft. of living space. The Hilton attorney reportedly discouraged viewing b anyone less than a centi-millionaire. (The former Beverly Hills estate c silent screen star Harold Lloyd recently was sold for $20 million by Sotheby International Realty.)

The residence of the late king of Saudi Arabia in London, Kenstead Hal with the adjoining property, was put on the market a few years ago at $2 million.

The **most expensive apartment** is the $15 million quoted for th penthouse of the Trump Tower, 68 stories above Fifth Ave. at 56th St., NYC The Trump penthouse surpasses the four story penthouse at the top c Galleria International on East 57th St., NYC. With four main bedrooms, 22-ft. swimming pool, library, sauna and several solariums, the Galleri apartment was on the market for just over $5 million.

Further, Washington is **not** trending toward buying a mansion an demolishing it to make way for a contemporary home—the new "teardown trend in Los Angeles where it is not uncommon to buy a $4 million home, raz it, and build a $20 million mansion. This is especially true in the Platinur Triangle (Beverly Hills, Bel-Air and Holmby Hills) where, for example, T mogul Aaron Spelling bought the former home of Bing Crosby for $1 million, demolished it and replaced it with a 56,500 sq. ft. mansion worth $5 million. Today, however, remodeling a home is still more popular tha demolishing and rebuilding.

42. WHERE IS THE MOST EXPENSIVE "TEMPORARY" HOME IN THE AREA?

Ambassador to the US, **Prince Bandar bin Sultan** of Saudi Arabia, recently dropped $4.7 million for a four-story, 26-room Queen Anne-style mansion on Chain Bridge Rd. in McLean, VA as a place to hang out until his $8.7 million palace next door is completed.

Via the negotiation, the Prince now has 12 acres valued at $15.3 in county tax records. His current home overlooking the Potomac, called McLean House, is a 15-year-old brick residence, two-story living room, 15 bedrooms and a 30-by-50 ft. swimming pool. The mansion is located along an exclusive stretch of Chain Bridge Rd. that already has Senators Ted Kennedy and Chuck Robb as neighbors as well as developer Alan I. Kay and moguls Frank Carlucci and Fred Malek.

The 45-year-old nephew of King Faud, Bandar is an Embassy Row regular, a high-flyer (jet fighter pilot), falconer and raconteur; he is one of the Town's most fastidious dressers and social martinets and promises to pay his taxes on time, a true Mideast ally.

Prince Bandar bin Sultan— irresistible, irrepressible, irreplaceable.

Photo: J. R. Black

43. WHAT ARE CONSIDERED THE CAPITAL'S MOST ELABORATE MANSIONS?

The hilltop **Evermay Estate** (1823 28th St. NW) in Georgetown is about 100 years old and had changed hands seven times since its construction by real estate tycoon Stuart Davidson (the mansion has been in the Belin family

283

Louise Sullivan, Bob Mosbacher and Marlene Malek—consummate and
confident, civic-minded citizens.

for 60 years). It is a two-story brick residence, with formal gardens, a soli
imperious look, and a history to match same.

The **Vanderbilt Mansion** (2929 Massachusetts Ave. NW) boasts
massive ballroom (28 by 60 ft.), 40 rooms, meeting and committee chambe
and an illustrious heritage. The late Philippine President Ferdinand Marc
once owned it and intended to lease it to foreign governments but never g
around to it. The property is now owned by real estate mogul Robert Kogc

Ishpiming (Chevy Chase Circle) became a student dormitory in the '7
after serving a Senator (Nevada's Senator Francis Newlands, founder
Chevy Chase) and Treasury Secretary Lyman Gage. Its 30-ft.-high Gre
Hall was the *locus* of many great parties during the '30s and '40s, but up
the death of then-owner Mrs. William Corby, the mansion was given
National Cathedral School for Girls. It was used by students at the Universi
of Maryland for a while, and finally purchased by developer Bob Blitz (
$850,000) who renovated the 26-room property.

The Lindens (2401 Kalorama Rd. NW) is one of the oldest bri
buildings in the Capital (it was moved brick-by-brick to Washington fro
Danvers, MA in 1934 by Mrs. George Morris) and remains a classic with
lofty setting and three-story gracefulness. The home is now owned
executive Norman Bernstein, and is being renovated

Located atop Georgetown Bluff, **Prospect House** (3708 Prospect
NW) was built in 1788 by Revolutionary War patriot General James Linga
at one point it was owned by James Forrestal, Secretary of Navy und
Truman and later first Secretary of the Defense Department in 1947. T
property (unique in Town with its undergound tunnel to the Potomac) we

Amiable master of motion— Mandell Ourisman.

Photo: J. R. Black

to Representative Thurmond Chatham (NC), to Louise Ansberry, a Pennsylvania coal heiress, to attorney David Shapiro (in '77 at $435,000) and finally to a foreign government.

In the mansion class are the **Robert Todd Lincoln House** (owned by the Ben Bradlees), the "Victorian" home on R St. (owned by Oatsie Charles) and the **Boyden Gray** manse on 28th St.

Although the value of these homes has varied greatly, they are still what is today a "mansion" by any measurement.

4. WHAT RECENT EVENT WAS BILLED AS "THE LARGEST SINGLE CITY AUCTION IN THE WORLD"?

Over 70 properties from the greater Washington area (plus Baltimore, Richmond and Tidewater) with a value of $350 million were recently offered by the DeCaro/Carey Winston Companies as the "largest single city auction in the world." According to the prospectus: "This is the astute buyer's opportunity to purchase desirable commercial properties in the number one commercial real estate market in the country." The auction didn't quite make it, although about $240 million in properties was sold.

5. WHAT FAMOUS AVENUE IS NOW CALLED "AVENUE OF THE RESIDENTS"?

The newest power label in Town is at Pennsylvania Ave. and 6th St. NW—**Pennsylvania Plaza**, a major complex of 942 apartments, health club, market square, theater, sidewalk cafes and posh jewelry and fashion stores. Rents range from $1,500 to $4,000 for studios up to three-bedroom apartments facing the avenue that is normally saved for Presidents on inauguration day (in fact, there have been no full-time residents on PennAve for over 30

years). Apartment dwellers can look out on the Capitol or the Mall and str
over to most of the federal buildings from their "city center" dwelling.

246. WHAT FANCY WASHINGTON CONDO SITS ATOP THE POTOMAC?

At 3030 K St. NW, a new living/shopping/office complex call
Washington Harbour assures socially-ambitious people of the right a
dress; with units going at anywhere from $250,000 up and amenities li
gold-plated hardware, the Harbour offers a little of everything for resident
There's a stone courtyard with a shooting fountain and rotating sculpture
plus a boardwalk where magnificent views of the Watergate Hotel, Roosev
Island and Kennedy Center can be enjoyed. Shopping, dining, health co
ditioning, office facilities, parking and the good life are available at a
elevator-served floor. (There is also the Bernstein penthouse at $5.2 millior

247. WHAT REAL ESTATE DEVELOPMENT FEATURES EIGHT DISTINCTIVE AND DIFFERENT NEIGHBORHOODS?

In one of the most expensive developments in recent history, **Avenel**
Potomac, MD combined the energies of many major track-record develo
ers to create a complete living/lifestyle community that appeals to suburb
sophisticates with roughly $500,000 to spend.

Patterned after such places as Hilton Head and Pebble Beach, Avenel
a planned community for the work hard/play hard set. Besides the Tourn
ment Plays Club at Avenel, as the golf course is known, the developme
boasts miles of biking and hiking paths, bridle trails, 50 acres of wood
parkland, and a future 30-acre public park, equipped with tennis cour
soccer fields, baseball diamonds and an Equestrian Center for jumpin
dressage and western rings, lessons, and boarding facilities. Avenel featur
eight distinct and distinctive neighborhoods. Traditional styling unifies t
community; all homes are brick and roofed with cedar or slate. Buyers ha
many choices. Golf enthusiasts can live in one of the 200 homes borderi
the course. Recluses can hide out in the custom manses high up on Eag
Ridge. Avenel also introduces a new kind of housing to the area: yard hom
which gather a few detached houses with small lots around a shared cent
courtyard. The denser communities, as well as the 50 moderate dwelling un
are the center of Avenel, and the houses with larger lots circle the perimet

Developers of **Avenel** (and price of units) are:

Chartwell (Martians-Edward Development Co.) $700,000
Eagle Ridge (G.B. Builders and Developers Inc.) $1.1 million
The Gates (Rocky Gorge Properties) $545,000
Oaklyn Woods (Saddlebrook Development Inc.) $650,000
Player's Turning (C-I Mitchell & Best Co.) $700,000
Player's Crossing (C-I Mitchell & Best Co.) $650,000

Chris Dana and William du Pont—land-lovers and lords of the manor.

Prescott (Samuel P. Pardoe Inc.) $600,000
Willowgate at Avenel (Porten Sullivan) $580,000

48. WHAT IS THE CURRENT SIGNIFICANCE OF THE "MARWOOD" ESTATE?

The **Marwood Estate** in Potomac is a 33-room replication of **Malmaison**, the chateau Napoleon built for Josephine near Paris; it sits regally overlooking the winding Potomac River on some 190 acres and is estimated to be worth $13 million. Currently occupied by Mary Gore Dean and Louise Dean, it has been the domicile through the years of the Pulitzers and the Joseph Kennedys; FDR used it as a summer house when he wasn't tooling off to Hyde Park.

Colonel H. Gore was a real estate investor from Tennessee who bought Marwood in 1941; he had come to Town in the early 1930s and built a fortune during the Depression buying foreclosed properties at a nickel on the dollar. On his death, he left Marwood to his four children. Daughter Mary Gore Dean (whose husband—Gordon Dean was Truman's first chief of the Atomic Energy Commission and a prosecutor at the Nuremberg Trials—was killed in a plane crash in '54) became chatelaine of the property and still entertains elaborately there, recently staging a majestic wedding for her daughter Deborah.

Louise Gore, another daughter of the late Colonel Gore, also lives at Marwood; she was a two-time Maryland gubernatorial candidate and manager of the family-held Fairfax Hotel (now the Ritz-Carlton) on Massachusetts Ave. Young Albert Gore (now Vice-President) was raised at the Fairfax, where he would trot off to St. Albans School each morning while his father Albert Gore, Sr. would head off to the Senate.

In the usual evolution of real estate holdings, Marwood is being sub-

287

divided; the family will keep 19 of the 190 acres and two developments wi
fill the remaining land.

249. WHAT ARE THE MOST POPULAR AWAY-FROM-HOME AREAS FOR WASHINGTONIANS?

Washingtonians head for the hills of nearby Pennsylvania or Virgini
the horses in McLean or Middleburg or all manner of beaches along tl
Chesapeake Bay and Atlantic Ocean. With historical possibilities lil
Gettysburg and Fredericksburg, social enclaves like Middleburg, Potoma
and Reston, and formidable (WASPy) beaches with appellations like Fenwic
Island, South Bethany, Middlesex Beach and Slaughter Beach, and tl
premier sun-worshiping point of eastern Delaware—Rehoboth Beach, the
is ample space for Cave Dwellers and assorted friends to break bread a
break with tradition.

For years, Rehoboth Beach was considered the Nation's Summer Cap
tol; with its sister coastal resort towns along the Delmarva Peninsula and
myriad of sports activities, music festivals, tournaments and special even
the expansive resort area was an easy and restful holiday for harrie
Washingtonians. Even today, Town leaders like the Clem Congers and Har
Farrs still retreat to their homes on the beach with pleasure.

The majority of the Washington affluent head for the shore but mai
prefer horse country. The 9,000-acre home—Albemarle Farms—near Cha
lottesville, VA of billionaire **John Kluge** has an 18-hole golf course, priva
shoot, swimming and tennis facilities, stables, cars galore, a collection
fine coaches, several natural ponds, 900 head of cattle, over 50 horses anc
200-year-old lodge with 25 rooms filled with priceless antiques. Somewhe
in the $25 million range, the country estate pleases its CEO and guests almc
every weekend.

Charlottesville (Albemarle County) itself is a magnet for many of tl
power-elite. Just 110 miles southwest of CapCity, the quaint community
about 40,000 residents blends plateaus, rivers and farm acreage with tl
University of Virginia, several well-known companies (State Farm Insu
ance, Central Telephone) and historic attractions to a perfect degree. Re:
dents include **Lawrence Eagleburger**, Bush's Secretary of State, newspap
owner **Edward W. Scripps**, *James Bond* novel author **John Gardne**
writer/lawyer **John Grisham** (who just bought the 188-acre Oakwood Far
for $1.1 million), actors **Sissy Spacek, Sam Shepard, Jessica Lange, Ka
Jackson** and **Tim Reed**, liquor potentate **Edgar Bronfman** (Seagrams) a
Frank Hardy, international realtor (only handles $5 million and up estate

Washington in-and-outer **Walter Annenberg** (whose wife Lee w
Chief of Protocol for the Reagan Administration) keeps a place at Waterga
but prefers the comforts of his Palm Springs, CA estate—Sunnylands
which houses his vast collection of art (Renoir, Cezanne, Seurat, Van Gog
Gauguin, Bonnard, Manet, Picasso, Rodin and on and on), has 30 rooms

200-acre golf course, about 35,000 sq. ft. and luxury galore. Many Townies have visited the manse and put it in the category of "Unequalled."

The **Douglas Coopers** and **Mandell Ourismans** have showplace homes in Jamaica; as does **Margaret Hodges**. Other Townies go to Martha's Vineyard, Aspen, Nantucket or Palm Beach (January-April).

250. **WHERE IS THE CAPITAL'S MOST LUXURIOUS SHOPPING?**

The international flavor and the fashion-plated quality of store "legends" (Cartier, Burberry's, Louis Vuitton, Bally of Switzerland, Ralph Lauren, Jaeger, Hugo Boss, The Gap, The Limited, Victoria's Secret and others) make **Connecticut Ave.** the equivalent of Fifth Ave., Rodeo Dr., Worth Ave. or other world-class shopping meccas. Chic couture designs, bedazzling jewels, finely-tooled handbags and luggage, elegant formalwear for men, noteworthy stationery and silverware and more please shoppers and challenge merchants to provide even more, and more and more. (Note: **Wisconsin Ave. in Chevy Chase** has snob appeal and all the right cachet, too; the stores are simply farther away from city center and less concentrated.)

Merchants on Connecticut Avenue understand the economics of serving the carriage trade; store rental space may be in the high-ticket category, but is not outlandish.

Here's how the Avenue compares with other international shopping districts: (costs are per sq. ft.):

Ginza District, Tokyo	$675
Nathan Rd., Hong Kong	$575
East 57th St., New York	$550
Fifth Ave., New York	$500
Worth Ave., Palm Beach	$450
Madison Ave., New York	$400
Rodeo Dr., Beverly Hills	$275
Connecticut Ave., DC	$250
Bond St., London	$200
Rue du Faubourg-St. Honore, Paris	$175
Via Condotti, Rome	$175

Leslie Wexner's **Limited,** and **Victoria's Secret** are national stores with Connecticut Avenue locations—they are considered the richest "specialty" stores in the country—the enterprise is valued at $3.2 billion.

Cartier is undoubtedly the highest-ticket jewelry retailer on the Avenue—it's no secret that you can invest $5,000 in a 10-minute period at the outlet or collect one of the famed "Love Bracelets."

For women's wear and big bucks, **Hermes, Neiman-Marcus, Fendi, Gucci** *et al* (on Connecticut or Wisconsin Avenues) fill the needs; clientele is *creme de la creme* society, international players, people with USP (unique selling propositions), the best-of-the-best and world-class players. The staff is equally sophisticated.

289

251. WHAT ARE THE BIGGEST/BEST SHOPPING MALLS IN THE AREA?

The cosmopolitan character of Washington is mirrored in the myriad shopping facilities available. Here are the heroes:

Mall/Address	# of Stores	Leaders
Mazza Gallerie 5300 Wisconsin Ave. NW	52	Neiman Marcus, Jaeger, Saks, Gucci
Union Station	120	The Limited, Ann Taylor
Georgetown Park 3222 M St. NW	100	J. Crew, F.A.O. Schwarz, Sharper Image
The Fashion Centre at Pentagon City, Arlington	150	Macy's, Nordstrom
The Galleria at Tysons II, McLean	120	Fendi, Hermes, Gucci Tiffany, Cartier
Tysons Corner Center, McLean	230	Nordstrom, Hecht's, Lord & Taylor, Woodward & Lothrop, Bloomingdale's
Montgomery Mall 7101 Democracy Blvd.	160	Hecht's, Woodward and Lothrop, Bloomingdale's, Sears and Nordstrom

252. WHAT IS AMERICA'S OLDEST JEWELRY HOUSE?

Established in 1802 by silversmith and watchmaker James Galt, **Galt & Bro., Inc.** (607 15th St. NW) is the Town's oldest continuing business and the oldest jewelry house in the US. Over the years, clients have included President Lincoln, Alexander Graham Bell and J. Edgar Hoover.

253. WHAT IS THE TIFFANY CONNECTION ON CONNECTICUT AVENUE?

For over a century **Pampillonia Jewelers** (1213 Connecticut Ave.) has served Washingtonians with fine jewelry, some of which carries the Tiffany & Co. indicia.

254. WHAT STORE IS KNOWN AS "LUGGAGIER" TO PRESIDENTS?

Former Presidents Johnson, Nixon and Reagan dropped in to **T. Anthony, Ltd.** (1201 Connecticut Ave.) when they were looking for wallets, briefcases, handbags or luggage to give to foreign dignitaries and friends. A longtime fixture on Park Avenue in NYC, T. Anthony monograms most of its items.

Camalier & Buckley (1141 Connecticut Ave.) also serves the carriage trade and lofty officials; it has three locations in the area.

255. HOW DOES WASHINGTON SERVE THE ANTIQUER?

CapCity is loaded with objects of history, the most imaginative inventory in Georgetown, where an antiquer can fulfill any and all dreams of finding just the right artifact. Some 20 dealers in medium-to-high-price antiques plus nine antiquarian bookshops and a dozen galleries offering vintage paintings and sculpture are clustered in Georgetown. Among the leaders are:

GUARISCO GALLERY (2828 Pennsylvania Ave.)—English and Continental paintings (1875 to1920) with prices, in the $5,000 to $150,000 range. Laura Guarisco obtains provenances or origins of pieces as a service.

G.K.S. BUSH (2828 Pennsylvania Ave.)—top-quality American furniture on the pricey side (example: Maryland Federal-period dining table at $14,500); plenty of selections provided by Guy Bush.

JUSTINE MEHLMAN ANTIQUES (2824 Pennsylvania Ave.)—Art Deco/Nouveau silver and costume jewelry with great imagination.

JANIS ALDRIDGE INC. (2900 M St.)—highly decorative antique prints with prices in the $2,000 to $40,000 range.

ASHBURNER-BEARGIE ANTIQUES (2920 M St.)—wide range of French and Italian tabletop pieces and furniture at $300 to $3,000.

THE PROUD AMERICAN (1529 Wisconsin Ave.)—broad selection of high-quality silver as well as American, French and Italian furniture; run by Deborah Gore Pawlik, cousin of the Veep.

Other antique shops—**William Donohue's Antiques of Georgetown, the Cherub Gallery, David Friedman's Susquehanna Antique Co., Ann Gallop Ltd., Michael Getz Antiques, the Old Print Gallery, Rooms With A View, the Georgetown Gallery of Art, Frank Milwee Antiques, International Furniture Galleries, Blair House, Julie Walters** and **Rosebud Antiques** offer a full panoply of crafts and antiques.

256. WHAT ARE THE TOWN'S TOP FOUNDATIONS?

At a time when most foundations are troubled due to a general malaise in the economy, the Capital's two major foundations—**The Cafritz Foundation** (assets of $184.5 million) and **The Philip L. Graham Fund** (assets of $162.3 million) continue to dole out monies to worthy causes but with slightly less vigor. Both foundations have cut back about 15 percent over the last three years largely because of real estate investments which have not yielded at a high level.

257. HOW WELL ENDOWED ARE WASHINGTON UNIVERSITIES?

By most standards, the Town's institutions fare very well:

Georgetown University	$296 million
George Washington University	$279 million
Howard University	$ 86 million
Catholic Univeristy	$ 60 million
Gallaudet University	$ 28 million
American University	$ 23 million
University of DC	$ 12 million
Marymount University	$ 9 million
Trinity College	$ 4 million

In no way does this affluence compare to the Big Boys who have staggering commitments:

Harvard University	$4.7 billion
University of Texas	$3.4 billion
Princeton University	$2.6 billion
Yale University	$2.6 billion
Stanford University	$2.0 billion

By way of comparison, cultural institutions stand at this level:

Smithsonian Institution	$314 million
National Gallery of Art	$186 million
Folger Shakespeare Library	$ 52 million
Kennedy Center	$ 39 million
Corcoran Gallery of Art	$ 13 million

(For the record, the individuals who shepherd and manage endowments are highly rewarded: Dave Mittleman got $1,237,874 for handling Harvard's endowment needs; Laurance Hoagland received $576,343 for his efforts at Stanford; Yale paid David Swensen about $200,000 for his professionalism; and Princeton rewarded Randall A. Hack with $208,000.)

CHAPTER IX

PLUTOCRATS IN PARADISE
(Pleasures, Perfections & Phenomena)

Photo: J. R. Black

Senator John Warner and Nancy Dickerson Whitehead—preparing the feast, another act of good fellowship.

258. HOW HAS PRESIDENTIAL STYLE CHANGED THROUGH THE YEARS?

For most of the decades, our Presidents have been precise images of conservative, small-town businessmen; their off-the-rack suits have been blue or grey, not well tailored, and often ill-fitting. The image of Presidents entering staff meetings with baggy suit jackets and trousers, or deplaning in the latest rumpled look, is a fixture in our perception of the country's leading man.

Enter **JFK**. With his good looks, two-button suits and Ivy League style, a swashbuckler personality topped with an all-American smile, a whole new format was created.

As President, styles are set worldwide based on the type and cut of clothes worn, and the propriety each demands. **Johnson** took a step backward; **Ford** took one step forward with a style that had no faults, but no magic either; **Carter** clipped along merrily if not impressively; **Nixon** introduced a severe Wall Street conservatism that was a bit daunting ("no fun" said the fashion elite); **Reagan**, with his broad shoulders and expansive handsomeness made clothes look good, and he handled dark blue (and dark brown) well enough to come off as something of a clothes guru. **Bush** epitomized the Mr. Natural WASP Look, with the natural shoulder, natural droop, natural normalness that bored anybody with a sense of aesthetics. The tally on **Clinton** isn't in yet, but most clothes horses are betting on him to handle his quite healthy body with the right cuts, suits and jackets.

At this point, probably the most compelling mind photo people have of Clinton is him as a jogger (not terribly attractive) or in casual sweats chug-a-lugging Big Macs with truck driver visored cap and all. A believer in blues and grays (almost every President wears a dark blue or gray suit with red tie for those informal "Hail to the Chief" sessions), Clinton is tall and wears his weight well; but various designers recommend wider shoulders to balance his large head and longer shirt collars with a generous spread, to offset his full face. French-cuffs would be more stately, too. Even double-breasted suits are suggested; if well tailored, they might reduce his ample chest and stomach.

Whatever. In time, Mr. Nibs will make his mark; now, only some faddy sweats have become big-sellers in retail stores. The Brooks Brothers' bomber jacket given to him by Mrs. Clinton is catching on as an administration fad, but, as yet, no one has perceived him as Christopher Reeve with that *Superman* look (a look, which, surprisingly, is linked to Al Gore).

259. WHAT WASHINGTON BUILDING IS DESIGNATED WITH BOB HOPE'S NAME?

The USO is an organization chartered by Congress to help members of the armed forces in their travels. The Capital has two such facilities, both very able to assist in tour planning, entertainment, lodging and recreation. One is the **Bob Hope USO Building** at 601 Indiana Ave. NW. For years,

Hope has been entertaining troops all over the world at Christmas and his name is synonymous with USO; thus the building in his honor.

260. WHY IS HANS CHRISTIAN ANDERSEN DEAR TO WASHINGTON?

The Library of Congress houses the most extensive collection of books and manuscripts of **Hans Christian Andersen** outside of his native Denmark. The imposing works were donated by actor Jean Hersholt and his wife "as a small token of the gratitude and love" they felt for the US.

Similarly, **Harry Houdini**, world-famous magician, donated his vast collection of books on psychic phenomena, spiritualism, magic, witchcraft, demonology and evil spirits to the Library of Congress on his death in 1926. It is still the ultimate source on the occult.

261. WHAT IS THE MIDDLEBURG CONNECTION TO THE CAPITAL?

Only an hour's drive west of the Capital is the lazy little town of **Middleburg**, VA (550 residents, 272 houses and farms) where a combination of Washington power-wealth and rural-wealth happily meet to create some excitement during any given period of time.

Names like **Mimi Mills, Abel Smith, Josh Muss, Senator John Warner, Pamela Harriman** (and her 6-acre Willow Oaks estate), **Elizabeth Worrall, Marion Smoak, the Paul Mellons, Lorraine and Dickie Smothers, Phil Thomas, Mary Farland, Reuters Roose, Pam Brown, Rose Marie Bogley, Burt Firestone, Bettina Belmont Ward, Dr. James Gable, Jack Kent Cooke** (**Kent Field** is one of the octogenarian's many acquisitions), **Roy Ash** and **John Pettibone** are mainstays in the social meanderings of Middleburg. Polo, thoroughbred racing, equestrian activities of all sorts are the backbone of entertainment in the horsey, affluent expanse of nature. **Jackie Onassis** pops in for the hunt occasionally.

The village of Middleburg is two blocks wide and eight long, filled with antique stores, pubs, gift shops and real estate firms. Acreage in the area is pricey (about $30,000/acre) and farms such as **Atoka** (owned by Senator John Warner), **Rokeby, Oak Spring** and **Far Acres** sell for $2.5 to $7.5 million. Each year, the Virginia Gold Cup (which is the Kentucky Derby of steeplechasing) comes to Town, and visitors get a chance to mingle with the horsey rich-and-famous and to see the chandelier in the local Safeway. Robert E. Smith (of Charles E. Smith Co. Construction Inc.) is the biggest developer in the area and therefore a saint or sinner, based on viewpoint.

262. HOW MANY ART GALLERIES DOES WASHINGTON HAVE?

Any way it's measured, the Capital has an abundance of choices for the art lover.

Concentrated within downtown Washington and Georgetown are 12 major art museums; add 10 smaller but elite museums and some 80 private galleries, and a universe of over 100 fine art exhibitions are available during the year.

International favorites like the **National Gallery, Corcoran, Phillips Collection, Freer** and the like are world-class collections of art. Here are some AAA commercial art galleries, lesser-known but equally rewarding:

Adams Davidson Gallery (3233 P St. NW), 19th and early 20th century American art in a rarefied atmosphere;

Franz Bader Gallery (1500 K St. NW), the city's oldest gallery;

Baumgartner Gallery (2016 R St. NW), home of Hundertwasser, the Viennese magic realist;

Kathleen Ewing Gallery (1609 Connecticut Ave. NW), vintage and master photography;

Govinda Gallery (1227 34th St. NW), photography, pop culture and celebrity iconography;

Barbara Kornblatt Gallery (406 Seventh St. NW), important names (Rauschenberg, Noland) in a cool space;

Le Marie Tranier Gallery (3304 M St. NW), contemporary figurative European art;

Marsha Mateyka Gallery (2012 R St. NW), academic presentations of respected modern artists like Robert Motherwell;

Osuna Gallery (1919 Q St. NW), Old Masters and contemporary local artists;

Tartt Gallery (2017 Q St. NW), historic photographs and outsider folk art;

Zenith Gallery (413 Seventh St. NW), humor, kitsch, and neon (usually with erotic undercurrents).

263. WHO ARE WASHINGTON'S MOST POWERFUL ART WORLD PEOPLE?

In a recent survey by respected *ARTnews Magazine* on "The 50 – The Art World's Most Powerful People," only **J. Carter Brown**, Director Emeritus National Gallery of Art, was listed as a powerhouse in the Washington area. His legend is well-known (see Chapter III) and his interest now lies in the field of cable television and a "Museum" Network.

In '92, three important art offices were filled: **Earl A. Powell, III** was appointed Director of the National Gallery of Art; **Charles Moffett** was named Director of the Phillips Collection; and **Jack Cowart** was named Deputy Director and Chief Curator of the Corcoran Gallery—each of these executives has significant power in the Washington world of art.

Jennifer Laughlin Phillips, the Gilbert Kinney's, Olga Hirshhorn, Carmen Kreeger, Frank Pearl and **Ambassador Nicolas Salgo** (once owner of the Watergate complex) all are influential in the Capital art scene.

Other notables in the "Most Powerful" survey, who are linked to the

Nancy and Richard Marriott—enjoy a special affection for *terra firma*.

Photo: J. R. Black

Capital via business or creative connections are: New York dealer **Leo Castelli**, Curator **Germano Celant** (Solomon R. Guggenheim Museum, New York), Director **Philippe De Montebello** (Metropolitan Museum of New York), dealer **Larry Gagosian** of New York, artists **Jasper Johns, Roy Lichtenstein** and **Robert Rauschenberg**, Board President **Agnes Gund** (Museum of Modern Art, New York), Paris dealer **Daniel Wildenstein** and CEO **Harold Williams** (J. Paul Getty Trust in Santa Monica).

The late **Norton Simon**, California industralist and art collector who founded the Norton Simon Museum of Art in Pasadena, was often in the Capital, as was **Andy Warhol**, the pop art friend of presidents (whose $220 million estate is probably the largest estate left by an American artist); **Lowell Nesbitt**, who recently died at age 59, first began painting as a night watchman at the Corcoran in the '50s—in '80 the US Post Office issued four stamps depicting his flower paintings, and he later served as official artist for the Apollo 9 and Apollo 13 space missions.

264. WHERE IS THE BEST COLLECTION OF ART BY WOMEN IN TOWN?

Founded in '81 by Wilhemina Holladay, the **National Museum of Women in the Arts** (1250 New York Ave. NW) is the single most important collection of art by women in the world (from the Renaissance to present); it draws from diverse cultures and includes paintings and sculptures.

Among exhibited artists are: **Mary Cassatt, Elaine de Kooning, Helen Frankenthaler**; one outstanding visual is a 1937 self-portrait by **Frida Kahlo**, donated by Clare Boothe Luce.

Henri (Henriette Marie Springer) is a highly influential art dealer who has been in Town for 35-years at 21st and P Streets. She exhibits very creative, unorthodox works by known and unknown artists, male or female, and is among the most colorful dealers in the area.

265. TO WHAT DEGREE HAS WASHINGTON ART APPRECIATED OVER THE LAST FEW DECADES?

In the last five years, the art market has been cyclothymic, but in the last few decades it has risen dramatically:

* The art market continues to outstrip the stock market, precious metals and interest rates.

* According to the Sotheby's Art Index, modern paintings showed an annual increase of 37.5 percent.

* Lithographs and serigraphs have consistently gone up in value, whatever their price range.

* A magnificent Original Miro Print worth $895 in '79 could fetch $10,000 in today's market.

* A Chagall lithograph could sell for $960 in '73, while Chagalls on the New York and London markets now sell anywhere from $15,000 to $25,000 US (up to 2500 percent and more).

* Jasper John's Screen Print, *Target* jumped in value 285 percent in just six months.

* Eric Fischl's Print, *Year of the Ground Dog*, issued at $3,000 in '73, now sells anywhere from $26,400 to $41,000.

At the turn of the century, the typical salesroom price of a painting by Vincent van Gogh was the equivalent of $829 in current dollars; however, in '90, the artist's *Portrait du Dr. Gatchet* fetched $82.5 million at auction, setting a new record for the sale of a painting.

Recent prices for classic art have been astronomical; *Irises* by Van Gogh went for $53.9 million; *Pierrette's Wedding* by Picasso sold for $48.9 million; *Yo Picasso* by Picasso at $47.8 million; *Sunflowers* by Van Gogh at $39.9 million and *Acrobat and Young Harlequin* by Picasso at $38.4 million.

Picasso was the most prolific of all painters. During a career that lasted 78 years, it has been estimated that he produced about 13,500 paintings or designs, 100,000 prints or engravings, 34,000 book illustrations and 300 sculptures and ceramics plus drawings and tapestries. His lifetime work has been valued at well over $1.5 billion.

The highest price ever bid in a **public auction** for any painting was $6,400,000 for *Juliet and Her Nurse*, painted by Joseph Mallard William Turner (1775-1851) in Venice in 1836, and sold in '80 at Sotheby Parke Bernet, NYC, to an undisclosed collector. The previous owner was 82-year-old Flora Whitney Miller. The 3 ft. x 4 ft. canvas had been in Mrs. Miller's family since 1901 and had not been on public view until '66.

The highest price ever paid for a painting by a **female artist** is $1,100,000 at Christie's, NYC on May 17, '83, for *Reading Le Figaro* by Mary Cassatt (1844-1926).

As for the most valuable painting of all time, the *Mona Lisa* (La Gioconda) by Leonardo da Vinci (1452-1519) in the Louvre, Paris, was assessed for insurance purposes at the highest figure ever ($100 million) for its move for exhibition in Washington, DC and NYC. It was painted in c. 1503-07 and measures 30.5 x 20.9 in. It is believed to portray Mona (short for Madonna) Lisa Gherardini, the wife of Francesco de Giocondo of Florence. The husband is said to have disliked it and refused to pay for it. Francis I, King of France, in 1517 bought the painting for his bathroom for 4,000 gold florins or 92 oz. of gold.

266. WHO HAS BEEN THE FAVORITE ARTIST OF RECENT PRESIDENTS?

Since '60, artist **Peter Max** has either been Official-or-Unofficial Artist of the White House. JFK thought his work was masterful in its patriotism (flags, doves, harmonious settings and people); Carter was uninspired but wasn't particularly keen on the artwork; Reagan loved the uncharted waters Max would navigate while making his statement, and to Bush, Mr. Max could do no wrong.

Max opened one of his shows on the front lawn of the White House when Bush presided; he then took the exhibition to Leningrad and unveiled a 25-year retrospective which included his canvas of Old Glory – it was cheered wildly. Collectors from all over the world made the Soviet scene to share honors with Max.

Now Max has introduced his newest work – *100 Clintons* – 100-14" x 16" portraits done in the Warhol silk screen style (a la Monroe, Kennedy); administration biggies think it's a grand idea and the President himself is flattered by the work.

267. HOW WELL DOES WASHINGTON SERVE THE BIBLIOPHILE?

It's said that if Washington was a walled city, its walls would be lined with books.

Since the founding of the Capital, **books** have been a mainstay of its culture; Jefferson sold his collection of 6,700 books to the then-fledgling Library of Congress; the collection became the basis of a book respository of some 500 libraries and over 10 billion books. There is a literary work for every conceivable subject; departments of Agriculture, Interior, Transportation have vast libraries dealing with their special interests; there are books of poetry by the hundreds of thousands, sports books, medical books, historical treatments, fiction and non-fiction, comic books, anything and everything.

For the record, each year the Library of Congress Cataloging-in-Publication Division issues card numbers to over 500,000 authors and the universe of books is growing at a rapid clip. All this despite the fact that only five percent of Americans really read books (this small percentage accounts for almost 70 percent of book sales). For bibliophiles a book is precious, and for authors the bibliophile is the *sine qua non* of success.

In the '80s, authors got record advances, chain booksellers began discounting, and reading became more of a national pastime. Some of the best-sellers of the '80s were: *Clear and Present Danger* by Tom Clancy (Putnam), 1.6 million copies; *The Dark Half* by Stephen King (Viking), 1.5 million; *The Mammoth Hunters* by Jean M. Auel (Crown), 1.3 million; *Daddy* by Danielle Steel (Delacorte), 1.3 million; *Texas* by James A. Michener (Random House), 1.2 million copies; and non-fiction *Fatherhood* by Bill Cosby (2.3 million), *Fit for Life* (2 million), *In Search of Excellence* (1.3 million) and *Jane Fonda's Workout Book* (1.2 million).

268. WHAT IS WASHINGTON'S FOCUS ON ORTHOGRAPHY?

Each year, the **National Spelling Bee** is held in the Capital; it pits particularly bright *Wunderkinder* against each other to determine who can outspell the other.

Officially titled the "Annual Scripps-Howard National Spelling Bee," the event draws about 230 spellers from the 48 states plus Mexico, Puerto Rico, Guam and the Virgin Islands. These semi-winners are culled from about nine million students who vie at the local level to reach the finals, and on that basis, the event is considered the premier academic contest in the US (the Bee was originated in 1925 by the Bingham family in Louisville who used it as a promotional gimmick to outploy rival newspapers).

Orthography (the area of language study dealing with systems in spelling) and the event are taken seriously by participants with coaches, special seminars, ungodly amounts of homework, blitzes and immersion courses and a constant barrage of "how do you spell?" Winners are heroes for a few weeks, then go back to their normal lives. What was in 1925 a $500 first prize now scales in at $5,000 and some morning talk show celebrity, but then, the task of making a living at something other than spelling 20-syllable words becomes a reality!

269. WHO ARE THE AREA'S TOP-RATED POLO PLAYERS?

Through the years, legendary polo players like **Winston Guest, Mike Phipps, Harry Payne Whitney, C.V. Whitney, Peter Bostwick, Stewart Iglehart, Raymond Guest, Elbridge T. Gerry, Cecil Smith, Allan Scherer, Mario G. deMendoza III** and **William T. Ylvisacker** have shown their mastery at the Potomac Polo Club and then flaunted it elsewhere, usually at the Palm Beach Polo and Country Club in Wellington , FL, Boca Raton, FL and Santa Barbara, CA.

In the Capital, **Jack Whittemore III, Joseph Muldoon Jr.** (patriarch of a family of polo players and founder of the 700-acre Potomac Polo Club in Poolesville, MD), **Joe Muldoon III** and **Ami Shinitzky** an entrepreneur who made his fortune from polo (starting as an equine dentist, then parlayed his skills into ownership of *Polo Magazine, Equus* and a vast Frederick County spread known as Windsford Farm) are the most active players.

Other high-scoring players are: **Carlos Warren, Frank Stallone, Stephen Seager, Manual Rojas, Octavio Pasten, Alan Nash, Ralph Manaker, Reza Malek, Tom Leonard, Gary Lachman, Jack Burlbaugh, Peter Arundel, Tom Kirlin, Byron Limehouse, Tommy Lee Jones, Francisco Escobar, Julio D'Angelo, Elizabeth Beer, Rick Heald, Vickie Armour, Rick Barrow** and **Roberto Villegas**.

Sponsors for Potomac Polo Club tournaments are: Anheuser Busch, Guarisco Gallery Ltd., Advantage Recognition, Rosemont Estates, *Spur* Magazine, Diamond Associates, Hermes, Langy Landscaping, Makers Mark, Julie's Dixie Pig, Evian Water and British Airways. Some of the **charities** who have had special benefits at the club are: The National Center for Therapeuticc Riding, The Marion DuPont Scott Equine Hospital, The National Rehabilitation Hospital, The Lab School of Washington, Children's

**Here's to the winners—honored guests Phyllis George Brown
and Curt Gowdy salute the Michelob Polo Team.**

Hospice International, American Cancer Society, American Kidney Association, Boy Scouts of America, The National Museum for Women in the Arts, The Orphan Foundation, American Paralysis Association and the YMCA.

One of the highlights of the '93 season was the **International Polo Match** under the patronage of His Excellency The Ambassador of France and Madame Andreani; the tournament was played in the afternoon at the club and a cocktail reception was staged at the residence of the Ambassador (2221 Kalorama Rd.) as a post-polo activity. The events benefited the National Center for Therapeutic Riding, Inc. (Robert D. Douglas is President and Executive Director) and entertained over 300 prominent Washingtonians.

270. **WHAT COMPANIES IN THE AREA SPONSOR POLO TEAMS?**

In addition to those previously mentioned, **Cadillac, Cartier, Revlon, Hermes, Lexus, Rolex, Ralph Lauren, Black, Starr & Frost, BMW, Cellular One, Chanel, Cunard Cruise Lines, LaBatt's Brewing Company, Liz Claiborne, Perrier, Pimm's No. 1 Cup, Watergate Hotel and Woodward & Lothrop** all have major polo involvement. About 10 years ago, polo sponsorship was virtually zip; today companies spend up to $ million for tournament sponsorship over a 12-month period. Ralph Destino (Cartier, Inc. chairman) notes: "Polo is about style, quality, taste, beauty and

302

elegance—the affinity appeals." Although the cost of sponsorship can be as little as $35,000 (for a single tournament), Cartier has spent more than $1 million for matches. Cadillac's role as official car (on the playing field) is very expensive and the Cadillac World Cup Tournament has been so successful that Toyota has also picked up on tourney sponsorship. Rolex has a Gold Cup Tournament that has attracted the likes of Prince Charles. The Ralph Lauren image has benefited greatly by the famous silhouette of a horseman with mallet; and Lauren has participated in a series of polo tournaments to the satisfaction of the sales curve.

On an individual basis, polo playing is very expensive; an enthusiast should be prepared to spend about $15,000 to play polo twice a week for three months; maintaining the three required ponies costs at least $30,000 annually and ground fees can add another $5,000 per year. As a pony stable grows, $5,000 to $10,000 each month is needed for 12-14 horses. Playing to win can easily cost $500,000 to $1 million per year (most costs go towards purchase and upkeep of horses; good horses can cost $40,000; an average polo pony costs $20,000). Personal equipment adds up, too; mallet @ $30 to $70; ball @ $2; helmet @ $60 to $100; jersey @ $20 to $60; pants @ $65; knee guards @ $100; boots @ $200 to $600; spurs @ $50; bridle @ $150 to $300; saddle @ $400 to $1,000. The average replacement of these items for a rider and horse is $2,000 per year.

If someone wants to be the best-of-the-best in polo, a budget of about $1 million is in order. Competition in the 60 countries and 255 clubs where polo is played is tough, and the fans (who have an annual income of at least $100,000 and a net worth of $500,000) are very demanding.

Some top polo players who are also top social figures in the Capital area are **Martin Tarnapol**, Senior Vice President, Bear, Stearns; **Martin Gruss**, CEO, Gruss & Co.; **Geoffrey Kent**, CEO, Abercrombie & Fitch; **Henryk de Kwiatkowski**, international aircraft merchant; **Norman Brinker**, CEO, Chili's; the **Busch** Clan (Adolphus, Billy, Andy, Peter), brewers; **George Haas**, CEO, Haas Financial Corp.; and **Guy de Wildenstein**, owner Wildenstein Galleries.

71. WHO IS KNOWN AS THE "GOODWILL AMBASSADOR OF POLO"?

Helen Boehm has been a polo aficionado over the years, and recently sponsored a major tournament – The Boehm International Open and Handicap Tournament at the Palm Beach Polo & Country Club; it was the first occasion in which Mrs. Boehm funded a purse ($60,000) which was divided by the three winning teams; and it was her way of attracting more people to the sport. This event and other efforts on behalf of the sport have earned her the title "Goodwill Ambassador of Polo." Her official title is "Ambassador to the International Polo Federation" and she is a member of the US Polo Training Foundation committee. She lives between the Capital and Palm Beach.

Helen Boehm—
polo aficionado
and queen of
porcelain.

Photo: Lisa Smith

Mrs. Boehm is Chairman of the Board of Boehm Porcelains and has presented her works to world leaders: Queen Elizabeth, the Prince and Princess of Wales, the late Princess Grace of Monaco, Richard Nixon, present and past Popes.

Most recently, Mrs. Boehm presented Pope John Paul II with the largest Madonna and child ever created in porcelain; the work was put in the Pope's private living quarters. The Vatican honored her by naming a section of the Museum in the Boehm name. Other creations were introduced in Tokyo (a 9-ft. floral centerpiece at the Osaka Exposition, valued at $250,000); and a special *American Bald Eagle* was accepted by Barbara Bush as a tribute to forces in the Persian Gulf.

272. WHAT WASHINGTONIANS HAVE BEEN THE OWNERS OF WINNING THOROUGHBREDS?

Ogden Phipps – his horses have won just about every race except the Kentucky Derby. Recently he retired his famous four-year-old unbeaten filly "Personal Ensign" who set a modern-day record of consistent wins. Recently, Phipps was honored for having the most successful racing year ever experienced by an independent stable; his stable received three prestigious Eclipse Awards; best three-year-old (and up) female racer "Personal Ensign"; best two-year-old "Easy Goer" and outstanding trainer of the year (Shug McGaughey).

Paul Mellon—"Sea Hero" won the Kentucky Derby in '93.

Bert Firestone—"Genuine Risk" is a consistent winner.

Joe Allbritton, John Manfuso (owner of Laurel and Pimlico Race tracks) and **Hermen Greenberg** have all had their share of winnings, and the attendant joys of life on the thoroughbred track.

273. HOW MANY OFFICIAL MARATHONS ARE RUN IN THE CAPITAL?

The **authentic 26-mile outing** is called the **Marine Corps Marathon** and is executed on a course that winds through Arlington to downtown

Washington in front of the monuments and past Arlington Cemetery to finish at the Iwo Jima Memorial. Shorter distance races, the 10-mile **Cherry Blossom** and the **George Washington Parkway Race** are also challenging, as are the **Race for Life** (breast cancer) and the **Look Good/Feel Better** challenges.

274. WHO IS WASHINGTON'S REIGNING COIFFEUR?

The media went ballistic over the Clinton hair episode when Air Force One was held up two hours in LA so the President could be coiffed by **Cristophe**, the Beverly Hills stylist credited with head-unbanding Hillary. Introduced to the Clintons during a fundraiser in the City of Angels in '92, the Brussels-born stylist quickly became a favorite and now has salons in the Capital and the Big Apple; he is expert at unisex cuts (both male and female styles).

For years, **Jean-Paul & Co.** graced the southest corner of Wisconsin Avenue and M Street and satisfied the fancies of Lady Bird, Lee, Deeda, Val, Golda, Indira, Jackie, Zsa-Zsa and a bevy of glamorous women; it was *Numero Uno* for a 25-year period, and still operates from Spring Valley.

A top flight area barber is **Milton Pitts** of the Sheraton-Carlton Hotel, one of the Town's charmers. Pitts has been clipping presidents since '69 when he met President Nixon; many of them have come to him at his shop in the Sheraton-Carlton, and at other times he has tripped to the White House. He has cut Bush's hair for 16 years, as well as the locks of Gerald Ford, Jimmy Carter and Ronald Reagan. His list includes other prominent players— Richard Cheney, Henry Kissinger, Caspar Weinberger, George Schultz and many congressmen and senators.

Among high-scoring beauty salons are:

Bogart, Inc. (1063 Wisconsin Ave. NW); big time, professional group with loyal celeb clients.

Ilo (1637 Wisconsin Ave. NW); hustling, give-the-lady-what-she-wants salon with appeal to juniors and seniors.

Okyo (1519 Wisconsin Ave. NW); one of the best and most-happening places in Town with just the right countenances and curls.

Robin Weir & Co. (2134 P St. NW); favorite of Nancy and presidential ladies through the years; tony, pricey, a touch of glory.

Watergate Salon (Watergate Hotel); top of line, top of social ladder, top prices and performance.

275. WHERE CAN WALTER CRONKITE'S FORMER YACHT BE RENTED?

With all the comforts of home (wood-burning fireplace, two bedrooms, sleeps 10), Cronkite's 46-foot yacht is now in the **Annapolis Sailing Yacht Marina**; it rents for cocktail parties or short overnight jaunts at $500/day.

276. WHERE CAN ONE LEARN THE FINE ART OF COOKING?

A multitude of culinary institutes and cooking classes are available for aspiring chefs (of their own home/restaurant) or emissaries who want to bone up on what bones are best served to the cognoscenti. Among them are:

California Cooking (1710 37th St. NW); foods of the Mediterranean, France, the American Southwest, and Asian countries of the Pacific Rim.

Fete Accomplie (3714 Macomb St. NW); elegant French catering establishment offers weekly evening classes on everything from pizza to chocolate truffles.

Kitchen Coach (Arlington); offers classes including cajun and creole cooking, catch of the day, pasta, and southwestern cuisines.

L'Academie de Cuisine (Bethesda); one of the most prestigious cooking schools in the area, L'Academie sponsors special one-time events and workshops that have included a Bastille Day Dinner and Recipe Writing Seminar. The curriculm includes French, Italian, Asian, American Indian, vegetarian, and low-fat cuisine, as well as wine tasting, baking and food science.

Sutton Place Gourmet (Bethesda); focus on participation under the Peter Gump cooking school formula, baking, roasting in a professional kitchen.

277. WHAT ARE THE TOWN'S TOP-RATED FLORISTS?

Flowers fit every occasion in Washington; they are ambassadors of good-will in many situations, a form of negotiation in tense alliances, a trump card when needed, and a general panacea for most of the troubles of a democracy. Here's where to pick up the best petals:

Blackistone, Inc. (1427 H St. NW), rated tops by most experts (has three other locations);

Greenworks, Inc. (Willard Hotel), great for splashy monumental flower showcases;

Watergate Florist (Watergate Hotel), super-chic and pricey but a guarantor of major results;

Friendship Flower Shop (3236 Wisconsin Ave. NW), inventive, flexible, classy.

278. WHAT IS CONSIDERED THE BEST LIMOUSINE SERVICE IN TOWN?

The most bizarre limo in Town is from **Zuber Limousine Service** – a 35-foot choo-choo (longest in the area) that clocks in at $1,350/eight hours; another in the same fleet is the new 12-passenger burgundy-and-gold chassis that goes at $1,000/12 hours.

For the record, the world's largest car is 104 ft., an ultra-limo in every way with swimming pool, putting green, aquarium and price tag of $3 million—rental at $12,000/day.

Celebrity chefs Lynda and Charles Robb sample
the cooking wizardry of Carol Young.

On the smaller scale, leading limo operators in Town are:

A-1 Quality Limousine (1234 Massachusettes Ave. NW), just what the name says.

Admiral Limousine Service (1234 1st St. SE), lots of stretches.

Classy Chassis (6505 Chillum Pl. NW), antique Rolls and other esoterica.

Diplomat Limousine Service (1511 K St. NW), veddy proper and productive.

279. WHAT ARE THE TOWN'S TOP-RATED BOOKSTORES?

Described as a Bibliophiles-Babylon, the Capital abounds with great bookstores. Among them:

Bridge Street Books (2814 Pennsylvania Ave. NW); specializes in politics, literature, philosophy, Judaica, history and film.

Calliope Bookshop (3424 Connecticut Ave. NW); strong in the humanities—literature, poetry, philosophy, mythology, history, music, fine art and photography.politics, literature, philosophy, Judaica, history and film.

Chapters: A Literary Bookstore (1613 I St. NW); specializes in literature, poetry and criticism, small and university press titles.

Francis Scott Key Bookshop (28th and O St. NW); emphasis on biography, art, travel, English literature, political science and gardening.

Kramerbooks & Afterwords (1517 Connecticut Ave. NW); carries something for everyone; particularly strong in history, biography, literature, art, travel and non-North American fiction.

Olsson's Books & Records (DuPont Circle, Georgetown, Metro Center, Bethesda and Alexandria); large, full-service bookstores offering quality fiction and nonfiction in a broad range of categories. Books-on-tape, calendars and postcards; full line of records, tapes and CDs.

Politics and Prose Bookstore (5010 Connecticut Ave. NW); large sections of fiction, biography, psychology, Penguin Classics, Vintage Contemporaries, health books, cookbooks and children's books. Also stocks greeting cards, bookmarks, wrapping paper and gifts.

Trover Shop (Capitol Hill, Farragut Square, McPherson Square); offers large selections of hardcover bestsellers, travel guides, children's books and cookbooks.

B. Dalton Bookseller (Mazza Gallerie, Shops at National Place, Union Station); full selection of fiction and non-fiction titles in all categories, including large reference section, history, biography, psychology, mystery and romance. Special section for children's books (B. Dalton Junior).

Crown Books (Cleveland Park, Downtown/K Street, Farragut North, Franklin Square, Friendship Heights, Georgetown, Lafayette Square, Van Ness/UDC, West End); best-selling fiction and nonfiction books, many deeply discounted, including reference, health, history, biography, mystery and detective, art and many other titles. Adult and children's books, magazines, newspapers some videocassettes.

Waldenbooks (Georgetown, Spring Valley, Presidential Mall, Pennsylvania Ave.); large variety of fiction and non-fiction titles in many categories, including reference, biography, history, mystery, health, New Age, literature and art, adult and children's books, magazines, tapes, videocassettes, computer books and software.

280. WHERE IS WASHINGTON'S LARGEST NEWSSTAND?

The NewsRoom at 1753 Connecticut Ave. NW has a humongous inventory of newspapers (representing each of the 50 states and 40 foreign countries) plus several thousand magazines plus 240 maps, greeting cards and foreign language periodicals. It is always buzzing with researchers and pleasure-readers catching up on ploys and pranks around the world.

281. WHERE IS THE TOWN'S BEST ICE SKATING?

If Mother Nature deigns, ice will form and despite a chilly draft or two skating is right on the money. Here's where to let your blades show their stuff.

C&O Canal; great scenic outing but never trust thin ice.

Fort DuPont Ice Arena; safe and sure place to meet friends and have some exercise out of the spotlight.

National Sculpture Garden Ice Rink; across from the Hirshhorn and very fit for a pleasant interlude.

Pershing Park; plenty of fresh air and faces in this sporty outdoor rink

Mall Reflecting Pool; probably the most dramatic rink with a skyline hovering over and history surrounding your figure-8.

282. POWER TENNIS, ANYONE?

The Department of Recreation offers 135 tennis courts at 44 different locations in the District; for night play, 61 courts are lit. But quantity doesn't translate to quality in tennis.

The star-quality guys and dolls hit their aces in the power-corridors of tennis, at places like **St. Alban's Tennis Club** (clay courts that befit the likes of Senators Hollings, Kennedy, Warner, Pressler and other high-profilers Carl Rowan, Justice Scalia, Jack Valenti and Al Hunt); the **"Winter Court"** in McLean (indoors, with leading players George Shultz and Kay Graham); **Mt. Vernon College** on Foxhall Rd. (lots of social top spin from players like Art Buchwald, James Baker, Ted Koppel, Maria Shriver, Mike Wallace, Andrea Mitchell and pro Kathy Kemper, #1 instructor and master of all she

Photo: J. R. Black

**Congresswoman Pat Schroeder dancing the tango with
"ANGO" star Juan Carlos Cofees.**

surveys on the courts); the **Hart Senate Office Building**, where only senato
get to test their backhands (and some do, among them Mitchell, Nickles a
Warner). **Aliki and Bill Bryant** welcome powerful friends to their court
home (in McLean), as do **the Ben Bradlees**.

The **White House** has, naturally, the **most exclusive** court in Town, a
the biggest security contingent. Only deputy assistants to the president a
senior rankers can use the court, and even if you lose to the President of t
United States, the memories are great.

283. PLAYFUL GOLF, ANYONE?

Unlike Japan with 1,900 golf courses and a frenzied pace (bookin
three months in advance, regular tee off times at 5 a.m.), the District has thr
challenging courses that are built for pleasure and not a professio
performance. A quick listing:

East Potomac Park Golf Course (900 Ohio Dr. NE); two 18-h
courses, a miniature golf course, and a driving range.

Langston Golf Course (66th St. and Benning Rd. NE); sporty, long a
casual.

Rock Creek Golf Course (16th and Rittenhouse St. NW); perfect hi
and valleys and water talent tests.

284. WHO IS THE TOWN'S BEST TOBACCONIST?

Probably the best known purveyor of the leaf in Town is **Draper**
Curtis Tobacconist, Inc. (640 14th St. NW) who carries a complete line
pipes, cigars and accessories. Dunhill and Montecruz cigars are always
demand by visiting dignitaries and Mr. Curtis is quick to oblige.

285. WHERE IS THE ONLY INDOOR MINIATURE GOLF COURSE IN TOWN?

The little people play their games at **City Golf Washington** (E.
Atrium of the Old Post Office Pavilion) where replicas of district monume
flank the course and add to the excitement of shooting par without the us
agony. The course is one of three miniature indoor courses in the count
"Putt, Putt" in Georgetown also offers small challenges (outdoors).

286. WHERE IS "LOVER'S LANE" IN WASHINGTON?

"Lover's Lane" runs between Massachusetts Ave. and R St. NW, insi
Rock Creek Park; long closed to vehicular traffic and resembling a grave
country lane more than a city street, it is missing on most modern street ma
The northern entrance to Lover's Lane is just west of the Massachusetts A
bridge over Rock Creek Park. It got its official name in 1900, long after it h
gained its reputation as a popular trysting place.

87. WHAT IS KNOWN AS THE "LOVE NEST"?

The former residence of Senator and presidential aspirant **Gary Hart** at 517 6th St. SE is the *locus* where he was spotted by *Miami Herald* reporters with model and actress Donna Rice, who was not his wife. His career went south from that point on.

88. WHERE CAN ONE GET A QUICK PARRY AND THRUST IN TOWN?

Those interested in an improved parry or quicker riposte, use the **DC Fencer's Club**, which meets for practice and competition five nights a week at Deal Junior High School on Fort Rd. and Nebraska Ave.; the club offers individual and group lessons for experienced competitors or for those first picking up the foil, saber or epee.

Photo: J. R. Black

**Fastest man on the Hill—Senator Larry Pressler,
finishing the Marine Corps Marathon.**

"Barefoot in the park"—Senator Richard Lugar
at the Gourmet Gala.

CHAPTER X

THAT'S ENTERTAINMENT
(Bars, Bistros & Bon Vivant)

Photo: Motion Picture Association of America, Inc.

Jack and Mary Margaret Valenti—laudatory, luminous and lasting.

289. WHERE DO THE HIGH-AND-MIGHTY OF WASHINGTON HANG OUT?

In a Town with over 5,000 restaurants, bars, lounges and assorted watering holes, the menu of opportunities is delicious. But, as always, a few places seem to have staying power and raw social power (see and be seen while wolfing down carpaccio with dried root-vegetable chips). Here they are:

Embassy Row Hotel, where Prince Charles pads down when in the Cap

La Colline, La Brasserie and **The Monocle** on Capitol Hill—dining with big time pols;

Gridiron Club, where serious scribes consume whatever;

the **Social Safeway** on Wisconsin Ave.– shopping paradise for the lofty

Jockey Club, a favorite ever since JFK days, the perfect, upbeat, high fashion drop-in; The Ritz-Carlton;

Four Seasons Hotel, a blend of rock stars, international hot dogs wannabees and really-ares, best brunch in Town;

National Airport, especially the NY Shuttle where just about everybody shows up;

The Jefferson, wall-to-wall history and tradition, choice of the intelligentsia;

City Club, ideal for making business propositions and proposals;

Cosmos Club, where only IQ's of 140 plus are admitted;

White House Tennis Court, where special administration aces serve up aces;

Madison Hotel, the trove for info for *Post* writers, also headquarters for sheiks and type-A foreigners;

Watergate Health Club, for jocks of all varieties, sizes and shapes, an ideal mating ground; hotel and restaurants—Jean-Louis and Palladin wall to-wall with celebs, too;

Corcoran Gallery, for the annual ball (April), a season highlight;

Duke Zeibert's, just goes on and on as a social and dining legend;

Chief Ike's Mambo Room, for administrative yuppies and groupies;

Hay-Adams Hotel, where smoothies eavesdrop and braggadocio always have an audience, supremely elegant;

Restaurant Nora, newly anointed Clinton clubhouse - chow and entertainment, with Democratic top spin; and

Cafe Milano, Georgetown's favorite stop-in for the Kleins, Bernstein, Ed Ames, Vicki Bagley, Ruth Noble Groom, Hannae Masri *et al.*

290. WHAT IS THE CAPITAL'S HIGHEST PRICED HOTEL?

When Jordan's King Hussein or Queen Sophia of Spain visit the Cap they expect royal treatment, and are quite willing to handle the tarif Accordingly, several hotels have prices fit-for-royalty:

The **Mayflower's** Presidential Suite checks in at $3,500/night and th

Mayflower Suite at $3,000/night.

The Presidential Suite at the **Willard** Intercontinental Hotel clocks in at $2,500 and includes security for the elegant sixth-floor suite.

The most expensive combination of rooms was offered by **The Ritz-Carlton** during the inauguration; for a mere $23,000 guests got four nights in the Presidential Suite plus a daily massage plus a personal valet and concierge plus a chauffeured Bentley plus any number of free periodicals and hospitality check-ups and little chocolates at night.

The largest hotel in Town is the **Washington Hilton & Towers** with 1,150 rooms. Smallest is **The Mansion** on O St., where two adjoining townhouses provide 10 bedrooms, 21 bathrooms, dining rooms, ballroom, bar and pool; the novel property is also a licensed B&B and allows guests to buy **anything** in the hotel at the moment of departure.

91. WHAT IS THE OLDEST HOTEL IN TOWN?

Named after the famous hostelry of Chaucer's *Canterbury Tales*, the **Tabard Inn** (1739 N St. NW) looks the part as oldest, continuously operating caravansary in the Capital. Resembling an English Inn, it is just unsophisticated enough to conjure up images of Tom Jones and his busty ladies. It has a good restaurant, terrace garden and prices that please (about $60/night).

92. WHAT HOTELS OFFER HIGH TEA?

Those seeking a little hyperventilation or time to ponder their life statement – Blame Nobody, Expect Nothing, Do Something – spend happy hours in these havens:

Henley-Park Hotel, off the beaten-track cheer;

Sheraton-Carlton Hotel, light tea in the Great Hall;

Jefferson Restaurant, tea near a fireplace in the classic tradition;

Grand Hotel, full English tea in the Promenade;

Ritz-Carlton, sipping and people watching in style;

Four Seasons Hotel, sandwiches, tea, people, power;

Hay-Adams Hotel, scones and eclat in the John Hay Room;

Park Hyatt Hotel, "all you can eat" teatime with piano entertainment and a hand reader;

Watergate Hotel, intimate lobby tea in the Potomac Lounge with wonderful views and conversation;

Washington National Cathedral, a most unusual experience following special tours; spiritual perfection.

93. WHAT WASHINGTON HOTEL HAS A COCKTAIL LOUNGE NAMED AFTER A NATIONAL LIFESTYLE MAGAZINE?

Hearst Corporation's *Town & Country* has been the social arbiter in America for over 30 years; it has selected, embellished, targeted and cel-

ebrated the happier days and foolish never-to-be-forgotten moments in socie
with exactitude, and has always shown grace under pressure (especially of la
when ad pages slipped seriously, and futures were not at all assured).

Designated as a Historic Hotel, the grand old Mayflower Hotel (with its 5
miles of millwork for crown moldings, and 46,000 sq. ft. of Italian marble f
bathrooms) has a **Town & Country** lounge where patrons can enjoy de
luncheons, cocktails or light dinners in an English club atmosphere, plus tl
intrigue of seeking many of the Town's most prominent leaders.

294. WHAT HOTEL IS KNOWN AS "THE WHITE HOUSE NORTH"?

Four blocks north of the Executive Mansion is **The Jefferson**, an eight-sto
Beaux-Arts inspired hotel built in 1923 as a residence of Washington society;
1940 it became a hotel for military personnel and was renovated in '86 as a worl
class property. Among its most-prized possessions are original documents (whi
line the walls of the reading room and lounge areas) signed by Thomas Jeffers
during his terms as Secretary of State, Governor of Virginia and President. Tl
lobby is home to a bust of Jefferson, obtained from Monticello.

295. WHAT IS THE CAPITAL'S ONLY FIVE-STAR (MOBIL) RESTAURANT?

Jean-Louis (Watergate Hotel) has always been a gourmet's dream; wi
recessed lighting on mirrored ceilings, silk wall hangings and exotic flowei
the environment smacks of high quality; with artistic presentations ai
perfect garnishments, Jean-Louis looks, and acts and produces as a five-st
restaurant should. Table d'hote dinners run about $85; prix fixe at $4
Specialties are magret duck with dates and honey, Maine lobster with cavi
butter, or stuffed veal and wild mushrooms. Extensive bar, own bakery, val
parking. Perfection!

Three Washington restaurants rate a four-star designation by Mobil: I
Lion D'Or (1150 Connecticut Ave. NW) with its classical French men
Melrose (Park Hyatt Hotel) featuring a reasonable continental menu; and t
Willard Room (Willard Hotel), offering American regional cuisine.

Jean-Louis Palladin, owner of **Jean-Louis** and **Palladin** restaurants
Watergate is a 48-year-old chef wonder-kid who was anointed as Chef of t
Year (along with Larry Forgione of NYC's American Place) by the Jam
Beard Foundation. He is the acquisive-type—in addition to his Waterga
properties, he owns **Pesce**, a DC fish market and storefront cafe (with Robei
Donna, owner of **Galileo**) and is a partner in Richmond at **The Frog and t
Redneck** (with Jimmy Sneed) and in Atlanta at **Resto des Amis** (wi
Guenter Seeger). Jean-Louis has generally been considered (since its ince
tion 15 years ago) one of the leading French restaurants in the US, along wi
Le Bec-Fin in Philadelphia, **Fleur de Lys** in San Francisco and **Lespinas**
in NYC, but Frenchman Palladin doesn't serve exclusively French cuisir
he's an eclectic!

These restaurants are **not** among those who have been the target of irate diners who are unhappy with their waiters to the degree of requesting another waiter. A survey by MasterCard International finds that almost half of diners are displeased with their waiter (because of unfamiliarity with menu, refusal to give separate checks, bad attitude) and are being encouraged to ask for a different waiter. The National Restaurant Association in DC is promoting the concept as a means of upgrading waiter performance.

96. WHAT TWO RESTAURANTS ARE AS FAMOUS AS THEIR PATRONS?

Having a power lunch with **Duke Zeibert** in his restaurant allows you to chum with Bob Haft, Sam Donaldson, former Mayor Marion Berry, billionaire Jack Kent Cooke or king pol "Tip" O'Neil, and lately, the Clintons.

Zeibert started in the early 1940s as a small restaurant located in the then LaSalle Apartment Building (1028 Connecticut Avenue); his partners— broadcast mogul Donald Flamm and Builder Milton Ritzenberg were part owners of the building and brought their friends and other celebs and mediapeople to Duke's. Although they eased out in the mid-'70s, they are still part owners of the new office building which houses the restaurant. Flamm lives in NYC and Palm Beach; Ritzenberg in DC and Middleburg.

Similarly, dining at **Mo Sussman's** (formerly Joe and Mo's, on Connecticut Ave., almost opposite Duke Zeibert's) gets one into the mix of media personalities, showbiz winners and legislators – a potpourri of people like Eddie Murphy, Pierre Salinger, Jack Anderson, David Brinkley, Senators Dodd and Kerry, Kitty Kelley and on and on.

Surprisingly, Duke and Mo, competitors though they may be, are also best friends; they often take to the links at Woodmont and trade anecdotes (both have full inventories) in moments of leisure.

97. WHAT IS THE TOWN'S ONLY FLOATING RESTAURANT?

The **Gangplank Restaurant** (600 Water St. SW), around since '69, has five dining rooms set at different locations on the pier. Rick's Bar and Grill for lighter fare; Patio Cafe for casual luncheons; Tower Lounge for views; the Dining Room for the big stuff and the Gangplank itself for the best of everything. Boat charters, banquets, entertainment are all part of the offerings. (The **Dandy** in Old Town, Alexandria also floats!)

98. AT WHAT RESTAURANT SHOULD ONE TELL "NO LIES"?

Geppetto (Georgetown and Bethesda) serves Italian food (and pizzas) with gusto and verisimilitude; decorations on the walls reflect the Geppetto syndrome with dozens of puppets staring at diners hoping they won't go through the same transformation "Pinocchio" did when shifting the truth around. The restaurant even has a "Delicato" pizza for waist-watchers, suggesting honesty to one's own body.

299. WHAT RESTAURANT IS KNOWN FOR POWER BREAKFASTS?

The *Washington Post* calls the **Hay-Adams Restaurant** (in the hotel of same name) the "location of choice for power breakfasts" and the epitome of what's "in" in Town. The hotel happens to be near the newspaper's headquarters and is a convenient drop in for reporters and editors, so there is reciprocity; power players need the media, media people seek the presence of the powerful! The ideal marriage of convenience!

300. WHERE DOES JURISPRUDENCE HAVE GREAT VISIBILITY?

The **Monocle** on Capitol Hill caters to biggies in the Supreme Court and members of Congress; the kitchen of two adjoining townhouses bedazzle clients with Monocle Crab cakes and seafood pasta and a current of legislation-in-the-making as busy members of the governing profession ply their skills and enjoy their repast.

301. WHERE IS THE BEST-STOCKED BAR IN THE EAST?

At 3150 M St. at Wisconsin Ave., **Nathan's** has a bar with world viewing windows and an inventory of potables that received the Award of Excellence (*Wine Spectator* magazine) for extensiveness and variety of distilled spirits and wines. Several thousand bottles of alcohol at varying proofs and colors await the eager consumer.

302. WHAT RESTAURANT HAS SERVED MOST OF THE PRESIDENTS?

First established as a boarding house, **Old Ebbitt Grill** (675 15th St. NW) came on line in 1856 (the oldest restaurant in Town) and began serving the elite of government – Presidents Grant, Andrew Johnson, Cleveland, Harding and Theodore Roosevelt. Its heritage demands that contemporary Presidents pay an obligatory visit to the grill where celebrities and out-of towners break bread.

303. WHERE IS MAYFEST AND OCTOBERFEST A FEAST?

The old-world German Restaurant – **Old Europe** (2434 Wisconsin Ave. NW) – serves up traditional fare such as Wiener schnitzel and bratwurst, and makes a major celebration of Mayfest and Octoberfest with season specialties and a lot of oom-pah-pah.

304. WHAT IS WASHINGTON'S "21" CLUB?

When Jackie Kennedy ventured into the **Jockey Club** in '61 and had a cocktail, there was a stillness in the air; it was a first for the new club (located in the then-Fairfax, now-Ritz-Carlton Hotel) and for the First Lady. Soon the world followed and the Jockey Club, which has a touch of an English hunt club, became the ultimate power-trading-and-playing club in Town. Even

At the Decorator's Showhouse (Phillips Mansion), designer Michelle Berman and mega-publisher Cathleen Black.

now, habitues like Donald Graham, Deeda Blair, Arnold Scaasi, Lucky Roosevelt, Buffy Cafritz, Oatsie Charles, John McLaughlin, Pauline Trigere, Marlene Malik, Margaret Hodges, Sander Vanocur, Louise Gore, Mary Gore Dean (who was a co-owner of the Fairfax), Kirk Douglas, Robert McNamara and scores of senators, ambassadors and lobbyists have special designated tables. The levels of awareness, emotional ping-pong, and territorial imperatives make the Jockey Club a local version of NYC's fabled "21."

05. WHAT RESTAURANT OFFERS THE BEST VIEW OF TOWN?

In the **Sky Terrace** Lounge and the **Two Continents** Rooftop Restaurant of the Hotel Washington (15th and Pennsylvania Ave. NW), there are brilliant views of the Capital and a chance to regroup and understand which direction is NE and where SW begins and how far SW extends and all sorts of critical information that will keep one from making the invariable statement – "I'm lost!" Best views of the Potomac are from any number of places at the **Watergate Hotel** and the **Roof Terrace Restaurant** (at the Kennedy Center) is a posh way to dine and sight-see pre-performance. (Note: for a view of CapCity from afar, **Windows** in Rosslyn presents a panorama of the city.)

06. WHAT IS THE TOWN'S PRE-EMINENT ETHIOPIAN EATERY?

By any standard, **Meskerem** (2434 18th St. NW) is a standout; *Good Housekeeping, New York Newsday*, the *Washingtonian* and other media critics have given it #10 ratings since '85. For those who relish Ethiopian food, Meskerem is a blessing.

307. WHERE IS THE BEST "SOUTHWEST" FOOD IN THE CAPITAL?

In a peculiar name juxtaposition, **Roxanne** and **Peyote Cafe** (2319 18th S NW) beguile visitors with Tex-mex fare or more traditional southweste cuisine. The restaurant has been praised by the *Washington Post* and most trav guides, and promises a salutary dining experience and just enough residual stir in the throat to be unforgettable. (**Red Sage** is also easy to remember.)

308. WHERE ARE THE BIGGEST LOBSTERS SERVED?

Steak freaks head for **The Palm** (1225 19th St. NW) for the biggest ai juiciest protein in Town; so do lobster-lovers, who can fumble through a fi hour with 4 1/2 lbs. of fresh lobster and assorted garnishments. As a favori in NY, LA and the Capital, The Palm generates a loyal and mighty clientel always ready for the most vigorous of eating sessions.

309. WHAT RESTAURANT IS NOTED FOR ITS VAST COLLECTION OF CELEBRITY PHOTOGRAPHS?

Since its opening in 1906 next to the Willard Hotel, **The Occident Restaurant** has collected and exhibited photos of famous people the wor over. Today, about 1,500 such photos covering the gamut – Thomas Ediso George Patton, Winston Churchill, Buffalo Bill Cody, Tom Clancy, Jes Jackson, Mario Cuomo, Jay Leno and Willard Scott – cover the walls on tv floors. Visitors spend as much time gawking at the photo gallery as they eating. Every President since the turn of the century (except Carter, Reag and Bush) has dined at Occidental and all have their visages propei displayed in the gallery.

310. WHO IS THE RATTLESNAKE KING IN TOWN?

Although many locals qualify for the title, only one accepts it Dominique of **Dominique's Restaurant** (20th St. and Pennsylvania Av NW), a French canteen with specialties in wild and exotic categories as w as seafood. Rattlesnake is put on the menu occasionally to see if people a really surveying all the delicacies available, and to demand a little respect a purveyor of way-out, esoteric fare.

311. WHAT RESTAURANT HAS THE WORLD'S LARGEST SELECTION OF BREWS?

Over 500 American and imported beers are available at **Brickskell** (1523 22nd St. NW) a local down home saloon and dining house opened '57 (then with only 51 brands of beer). Aficionados can sample beer from t Orient, or suds brewed in Belgium by Trappist monks, or Australian a pints of English guinness, whatever. Backgammon, darts and cards make t Brickskeller a formidable place to meet/greet.

312. WHAT IS CHINATOWN'S MOST CELEBRATED RESTAURANT?

Chinatown's oldest (and largest, 450 seats) eating spot is **China Inn** (631 H St. NW) which has served patrons for almost 50 years. It pleases Cantonese diners and thrives on its reputation for drop-dead chop suey.

313. WHAT WAS THE PREDECESSOR OF GO-LO'S RESTAURANT?

The **Surratt House** during the Civil War was a boarding house that once dominated the area. It figured in the plotting of the Lincoln assassination—typically described as "the nest where the egg of treason was hatched"—and Mary Surratt, the woman who ran the boarding house, was hanged as a co-conspirator. The building has been described as a typical example of a pre-Civil War downtown residence and (604 H Street NW) is now Go-Lo's.

314. WHAT IS THE MOST EXCLUSIVE RESTAURANT TO HAVE OPENED AND CLOSED IN 15 MONTHS?

Flamboyant restaurateur Warner LeRoy threw all his wizardry into the **Potomac Restaurant** (Washington Harbour, 3050 K St. NW) in July, '86, spending about $12 million in masterful detail (an electric train running between dinner tables, 23,000 sq. ft. of jewels and crystals, silk and gossamer). Having become a legend in the business via his Maxwell's Plum and Tavern-on-the-Green in Manhattan, LeRoy figured his DC venture was a shoo-in.

Despite serving almost 375,000 meals in the first year, critical reviews, and overwhelming payroll, monstrous debt service and a slack economy forced the extravagant venture to fold in October, '87.

The restaurant is now called **Sequoia**.

315. WHERE IS THE BEST TAKE-OUT STEAK IN TOWN?

Six 12-ounce filet mignons at $100 at **The Palm Pac** (1010 16th St. NW) is considered the best USDA prime beef in the area. Each 12-ounce portion can easily serve two people, thus 24 servings are provided for $100, which amounts to only $5+ per pop. Inexpensive, anywhere, anytime.

316. WHAT WASHINGTON DELI PLEASES EVEN NEW YORKERS?

Maybe the pickles and bread aren't quite right, but most New Yorkers sing the praises of **Carnegie Deli** (Embassy Suites Hotel) where the panoply of food/beverage is complete, and the pastrami or corned beef satisfies the toughest of customers. **Loeb's** also passes muster as does **Toojays!**

317. WHAT IS THE TOWN'S HOT DOG OF CHOICE?

It's hard to beat **Hebrew National** kosher beef frankfurters — they look good, taste good, really are made with quality ingredients, are firm, slightly spiced and cook/grill without losing any magic. They're, by far, "le grande dog hot" of choice.

318. WHAT'S THE FASTEST PIZZA IN TOWN?

Making its reputation on celerity all across the country, **Domino's** is also the speediest pizza in Town; what it lacks in taste appeal is offset by the 15-20 minute delivery time. And the price is right, usually cheaper than most equivalents (averages out to about $6.50/pizza).

319. WHAT ARE THE MOST NOTORIOUS SINGLES BARS AROUND?

The terminally hip can always find a cabaret to visit with the eternal hope of finding the perfect mate in the Great Game of Life. With odds about 1,000 to 1 against finding a four-leaf clover, there is often disillusionment with the process, but given no option, here's where the action is:

Champions (Georgetown); a "best" selection by *Playboy* makes this a hangout for all kinds of players and pretenders, and that occasional "find."

Clyde's (Georgetown); one of the oldest canteens in Town, celebs and locals sing in their beer and talk about the ozone layer.

Third Edition (Georgetown); "ladies night" and Trinity College grads share their spare time with whoever is voluble– good energy and exercise.

Duddington's (319 Pennsylvania Ave. SE); an authentic sportsbar with video games, humongous TV monitors, pinballs and jocks galore – loud spirited, a bit on the unrestrained side.

Rumors (1900 M St. NW); *locus* for young profs, those who have seen their swami, horizontal men and ladies who have let go of their albatross - no CUBO (conduct unbecoming an officer) here.

Sign of the Whale (1825 M St. NW) claims to have the best male/female ratio, does have great burgers, also some very attractive buns (nicely embellished) – a place to start the search for the blue moon.

The River Club (Georgetown); slightly on the senior side (35+) with more civility and less open-challenge than most – not really great for balls of fire.

The **Embassies** of Spain, South Africa and Italy are also superb collect, connect outlets; trick is being proper while on the make, and while diplomatic eyes are focused your way.

320. WHAT ARE THE BEST KNOWN PIANO BARS IN THE CAPITAL?

As a transition from the embattlement of the office and lazy, hazy duties at home, the ideal is to down a cocktail while being chastened (cheerfully) by an inspiring pianist. Try these piano bars:

Allegro (The Sheraton-Carlton Hotel)

The Fairfax Bar (Ritz-Carlton Hotel)
The Bar (The Capital Hilton Hotel)
The Federal Bar (Vista International Hotel)
John Hay Room (The Hay-Adams Hotel)
Old Ebbitt Grill (675 15th St. NW)
The Terrace Room (The Mayflower Hotel).

321. WHERE IS THE CAPITAL'S BEST OUTDOOR DINING?

Spring and summer is time for the great outdoors; and Washington has some great places for dining in the fresh air. Here are some:

Sea Catch Restaurant (on C&O Canal in Georgetown); built in 1842, the brick and stone building has a rich history and a richer future – seafood, jumbo lobsters, barges floating by, breezes blowing and well-wishing all-around make this a superb venue.

Bice (601 Pennsylvania Ave. NW) serves up green umbrellas on the sidewalk cafe and the choicest Italian morsels (famed worldwide, what else?). Bice pulls in the likes of Pavarotti, Sophia Loren and most of the Italian Embassy crowd. *Mange, mange* is the operative word.

Fino (Georgetown) has a bi-level patio enveloped by greenery, marble statues, fountains and magnificent Italian fare (linguini pesto at $14.95 is cosmic).

Perry's (1811 Columbia Rd. NW) is funky fun and very feasible on a low budget. There's a lower level sushi bar and a roof that presents Adams Morgan in all its splendor. New-wave Jap food is the specialty but California pizzas and lobster dumplings also vie for honors.

La Brasserie (239 Massachusetts Ave. NE) is Paris in the spring; elegant, lilting, with refreshing gazpacho, many varieties of mushrooms, shallots and heartbreak *creme brulee*.

Washington Harbour has multiple restaurants that overlook the Potomac and provide good food, fresh air and unlimited star-or-sky gazing.

322. WHAT IS THE ONLY BREWERY IN TOWN?

The **Capital City Brewing Company** (1100 New York Ave. NW) housed in an industrial Deco setting with overhead pipes and catwalks exposed, turns out its own pretty good brew and serves up a storm of burgers and sandwiches which are happily chased by the suds. Pretzels, horseradish mustard sauce, a tour around the plant, checking brewmaster secrets and a young, preppy crowd make the Brewing Company excellent company for an evening.

323. WHAT IS THE IMBIBER'S DICTIONARY?

Festive lunches, the nightly give-and-take of balls or embassy outings and afternoons at polo make the grape or the hop or the spirit (whatever it may be) an important factor; here are some of the terms used by the Town's expert imbibers as they make the social rounds:

Agrafes—the cage that holds a champagne cork in place (a French word, pronounced a-graph).

Barm—the froth on beer; sometimes called fob.

Beeswing—filmy tartar scales that form in some white wines after a long period of storage; so called because they look like the wings of bees.

BIB—short for Bottled in Bond.

Bottle Ticket—a small plaque hung around the neck of a bottle or decanter with the name of the beverage inside; often made of silver.

Bouge—the belly of a cask, the point where the circumference is the greatest.

Brimmer—a glass so full that the liquid touches the brim; although liquid has climbed to the brim, there is a slight depression in the center of the surface.

Bumper—a brimmer to which extra drops have been added to fill the hollow to a bump.

Depart—the final taste of wine in the mouth (French).

Dunder—the dregs left after the distillation of rum; in some rum-making processes, dunder from one rum is added to the next for added flavor.

Fliers—white, fluffy particles that float in white wine; most likely to appear when the wine is transported from a warm to a colder climate.

Hogen-mogen—said of strong booze; an explanation and a description.

Jirble—to pour out a drink unsteadily.

Katzenjammer— a cat's whining; literally, but most often applied to a hangover.

Legs—streaks that run down the side of a glass after wine has been swirled in it; wine with pronounced streaks is said to have "good legs."

Mini-petillances—light sparkle or crackle in a wine.

Muddler—the technical name for a swizzle stick, sometimes called a mosser.

Nebuchadnezzar —the largest champagne bottle (holds 104 glasses); it is larger than the 83-glass Balthazar—the 62-glass Salmanazar—the 41-glass Methuselah—the 31-glass Rehoboam—the 21-glass Jeroboam and the 10-glass Magnum (the standard bottle holds a mere five glasses).

Oenology—the art and science of wine making.

Peated—Scotch taster's term for the degree to which a particular Scotch has a smoky or peaty character (a Scotch may be "well peated," "lightly peated," etc.)

Plonk—cheap ordinary table wine (British slang).

Pomace—the substance remaining after the juice has been extracted from apples, grapes, or whatever; often used as animal food.

Pony—half a jigger; three quarters of a shot, an ounce.

Pricked—wine that has turned to vinegar.

Shive—a circular wooden plug that is hammered into a hole in a cask after it has been filled.

Sling—synonym for cocktail, as in Singapore Sling.

Soda back—current bar talk for soda on the side.

Tastevin —the small silver saucer that is used for wine tasting; often hung around the neck of a wine steward as a symbol of authority.

V.S.O.—initialism associated with cognac for Very Special Old.

Worm—the business end of a corkscrew.

Worn—term for wine that has been too long in the bottle, or spirits too long in the cask.

"When men drink, then they are rich and successful and win lawsuits and are happy and help friends." So said the Greek philosopher Aristophanes some 2,000 years ago.

Photo: J. R. Black

**The great mouthpiece with the king of hospitality—
Larry King and Duke Zeibert.**

324. WHAT IS THE NATION'S ONLY NATIONAL PARK FOR THE PERFORMING ARTS?

Given as a gift from Catherine Filene Shouse (Boston's Filene's Department Store heritage), **Wolf Trap Farm Park** and its amphitheater, the Filene Center, is the nation's only national park for the performing arts. Seating some 3,800 people on the sprawling lawn, musical stars of the caliber of Van Cliburn, Sills, Bernstein and Previn, companies (New York City Opera, National Symphony) and offbeats like Willie Nelson and Bonnie Raitt have kept audiences tuned in and turned on. The Center debuted in '66, the Park in '71; both are the stuff of which legends are made.

325. WHAT LOCAL THEATER PRODUCTION HOLDS THE ALL-TIME HIGH IN TICKET SALES?

Phantom of the Opera holds many records in many cities; in Washington, it is top grosser of all time at Kennedy Center with a run worth $16,250,000 (in NYC, it grossed $34 million). Other big winners are: *Les Miserables* ($14.5 million); *Shear Madness* ($11million); *Search for Signs* ($4.9 million) and *Annie* ($3.2 million).

326. WHAT CAPITAL LOCATIONS HAVE BEEN USED IN MOVIES?

The Capital is a natural for movie settings with its many-splendored buildings and classic architecture. Here's how Hollywood has taken advantage of the city's special star-quality.

The **Union Station** was used by Hitchcock in *Strangers on a Train* ('51); **The Ellipse** had a spaceship land on it in *The Day The Earth Stood Still* ('51); the **Steps** at 35th and Prospect were doomsday in *The Exorcist* ('73); **Key Bridge** was the setting for a scene in *Suspect* ('87); **The National Theater** provided the stage for *This Is The Army* (1943); **Neam's Market** was backdrop for scenes in *Heartburn* ('85); **Vietnam Veterans Memorial** was used as backdrop for *In Country* ('88); **The White House** has been the site for *Birth of a Nation*, (1915); *Fail Safe* ('64), and *Assassination* ('86); The **Supreme Court** was *locus* for *Magnificent Yankee* ('50) and *First Monday in October* ('81); **New York Avenue Presbyterian Church** was used for *A Man Called Peter* ('55); offices of The *Washington Post* served as backdrop for *Chances Are* ('89) and the **US Capitol** has been prominent in many films.

The **oldest** film ever made in Washington was at **Columbus Memorial Fountain**— *Filial Love* (1912). Other films—*No Way Out, Pelican Brief, Garden of Stone, The Happy Hooker Comes to Washington* and the recent Secret Service saga—*In the Line of Fire*—used CapCity as the *locus* or background for sequences,

A '93 feature flick to play against the Capital was *Dave* – the fantasy of a guy who is a dead-ringer for the current President and walks through his day often as an impersonator of the President at golf outings and car dealership openings. In the film, UPI star Helen Thomas plays herself, as do Senators Alan Simpson and Paul Simon, P.R. executive Frank Mankiewicz, members of "The McLaughlin Group" and CNN's Mike Kinsley and Robert Novak.

327. WHAT LOCAL MOVIE THEATER WAS VOTED SECOND BEST IN THE US?

Some 55 years ago, the **Uptown Theater** (3426 Connecticut Ave. NW) was born; it was recently selected by the *Hollywood Reporter* as the second best single screen movie theater in the US; first was Mann Village in Los Angeles. Selections were from among 23,000 silver screens in the country.

An impeccably preserved relic of the movie palaces of yesteryear, the Uptown boasts art deco decor, a huge wraparound screen, a real balcony and the best popcorn in Town.

328. WHY IS THE METRORAIL CONSIDERED "WORLD-CLASS"?

The Metro subway system is the **largest** urban public works project ever undertaken as a single unified design; built at a cost of $7.5 billion, its 90 miles of tracks thread through Virginia, Maryland and the District.

About 500,000 riders take the Metro each day which tallies up to some 17.5 million passengers/year; the system already has chalked up 1.5 billion happy customers. It works in tandem with the Metro Bus System.

About 50,000 work years have been put into the system so far, with more to come (as the remaining 14.5 miles of the 103.4 mile system are made operational); the 70 stations will be increased to 76 and the continued prestige of Metro (it was voted best system in the country in '88 by the American Public Transit Association) is assured by its proud riders (unlike those in NYC, who show their creativity off via grotesque graffiti).

329. WHAT OF WASHINGTON MISERS AND SCROOGES?

Always entertaining and always right on the mark is the story about the rich old guy who asks his young paramour if she'd still love him if he lost all his money. "Oh, I'd still love you," she notes, "and I'd miss you, too!" So much for romance when challenged by money; so much for love when pitted against poverty.

Being without liquid funds is no fun; having the "shorts" is a sure way to social oblivion and generates castigation from all sorts of friends, foes, allies and presumed associates. Maybe that's why so many people, even those in the mega-rich category, work their way through life with parsimony; always coveting small sums in the hopes of never being without huge sums for a grand lifestyle.

There are people in CapCity who never buy soap but simply accumulate dozens of bars at hotels; wash out zip-lock plastic bags for reuse; fee around the cushions of chairs trying to find coins; burn dinner candles down to the last fraction of an inch; eliminate costly telephone bills by calling late hours and speaking too fast for comprehension; buy small dogs or small horses to cut down on feeding bills; travel on airlines wearing several layer of clothes to avoid extra baggage charges; save rubber bands and paper clip and cigarette butts (for one or two more puffs) and all sorts of containers and used oversized envelopes and gift wrappings and tea bags and old socks (fo rags) and on and on. There's even the frugal Lady who drives her Rolls o the inside of road curves thinking that she might save a gallon of petrol o a long trip. Such is the **spirit of the scrooge.**

There are also **extreme cases** of niggardliness: **Benjamin Altman,** th greatest retail merchant, died when he refused to pay the high price of medical specialist in his case of pneumonia; and **William Vanderbilt** wh was worth $194 million in 1883 (and said "I am the richest man in the world I would not walk across the street to make a million dollars.") spent hundred of thousands of dollars rearranging his various homes, but constantl endangered his world-class gardens by limiting the amount of water an electricity gardeners could use.

John Paul Getty knew how to handle his guests with economy; he ha a pay phone installed at Sutton Place, his stately English mansion, so tha guests could chatter on at their own expense. He justified his position b suggesting that most of his friends saved the pins from new shirts, hoarde cocktail napkins from bars, and drank the lowest cost liquors. Getty onc declared: "There are people who have been destroyed, physically an morally, by their wealth. The same people, born poor, would probably hav become alcoholics or thieves." His philosophy was summed up as—"Wast not, want not."

The late comedian **Jack Benny** built a fortune via his showbiz image a a miser, yet he was extremely liberal in supporting charities and the less fortunate. He once peeled off ten $100 bills for a down-and-out fello comedian whose skit talked about rich men who "poor mouth" it through life Benny had compassion; after the donation, the needy comedian neve mentioned Benny again in his routine.

William Randolph Hearst, who was the most powerful media mogu of his era, lavished money on his girlfriend Marion Davies, while scrimpin on such things as razor blades, a toothpaste and toiletries. He'd use blade dozens of times, washing and rewashing his face (with soap lifted from hotel) to hopefully get a clean shave; then splash on an after-shave lotion h concocted from water and leftover lemons or limes. Like the late **Malcolr Forbes, Jr.** he refused to part with a tube of toothpaste until it was decimated Twisting tubes to the point of total emptiness was the habit of many capitalist and was, in fact, capitalized on by Tiffany & Co., who markets sardine can-type sterling silver key ($50) which when engaged with tooth paste tube assures that ingredients are fully expelled.

Washington has its share of **scrooges**. Who hasn't seen those cuties who use the cocktail hour largesse of embassies and bars (comp hors d'oeuvres) to not only accommodate their drinking/dining needs of the day, but provide for breakfast on the morn via a few rolls and leftovers? Or those who bike around Town in the interest of exercise, when, actually, their sportscar has been in the shop for years. Or those who attend funerals and ask for wreaths and assorted flowers after-the-fact as a "memory" of the deceased? Same technique at balls where centerpieces are fought for quite competitively; a superb centerpiece can easily conserve $100 for the household budget.

After finishing a meal, many is the **doggie bag** that accompanies home a couple who abhor pets; and many is the unfinished bottle of Chablis that tends to walk out of a restaurant with its purchaser; napkins, cruets, salt/pepper shakers, envelopes of sugar and other spices have a tendency to vanish after the delights of a dinner. This miserly little larceny is all built into the price, suggest hoteliers and restaurateurs.

And you've seen the **scrooge** at work during a "Dutch treat" meal. He's calculating his share-of-cost throughout the feast, growing a little more paranoid with each course. He settles for his half of the food charges but will rarely pick up the tax portion or the tip. By the time that calculation comes into focus, he's already in the men's room. A scrooge is a scrooge even with best friends.

It's said that **presence** can be misunderstood for **miserliness**; those who walk taller than others simply aren't expected to pay, they're guests wherever they go. The late **Averell Harriman** never paid for a meal, taxi or ticket; he'd simply excuse himself, walk straight out of the circumstance, assuming others would take care of the bill. And they always did!

The patrician who knows the **value of money**, spends it wisely—lavishly when expected, conservatively when required—and always makes it a source of **enjoyment** for you and those who have chosen to walk through the corridors of life with him/her is the *rara avis* of our times!

Photo: J. R. Black

Second Genesis—Dr. Sidney Shankman, with Debbie and Donald Sigmund.

Dauntless, decorous and divine—Elizabeth Bagley.

CHAPTER XI

HIGH ON A WINDY HILL
(Apostles, Adagios & Anthems)

Photo: J. R. Black

Leader of leaders and sovereign Senator—Robert Dole.

330. HOW POWERFUL IS THE PRESIDENT OF THE US?

Scholars generally agree that President Clinton is the smartest president since Nixon, and Nixon was the brightest CEO since Woodrow Wilson. Why then is Clinton's "approval rating" (after four months in office) the lowest of any President in history (Truman had a 92 percent approval; Johnson, 78 percent; Eisenhower, 74 percent; Kennedy, 74 percent; Carter, 64 percent; Nixon and Bush, 62 percent; Reagan, 59 percent, Ford, 42 percent; and Clinton, 36 percent)?

Although the presidency is regarded as the most powerful office in the world, in fact the office is more show-and-tell than direct-and-execute. The President is CEO of government (and on that basis, directly or indirectly influences roughly 23 cents of every dollar spent in the US), Chief of State, Commander-in-Chief of the armed services and titular head of the Democratic party; he heads an enterprise with over four million employees and a budget of several trillion dollars, and his personal staff is comprised of over 3,000 enthusiastic partisans, most of whom the President doesn't know. Some six million letters per year are received from people unknown to the President, but responded to by his staff of 130 community relations managers.

The President, any President, has two audiences that he must befriend — **members of Congress** who control the voting, and thereby implementation of any bill put forth by the Chief of State, and the **media**, who have the power to create an image of the President that either appeals to or displeases the public (who in turn influence their local representatives to vote for/against certain bills). In a way, the job as President is impossible— outside of FDR who had a mandate from the Americans to move the country out of the Depression and win WWII, no modern President has been a consistent winner. Although each has little victories (LBJ, for example, did move the Great Society forward; Reagan did get inflation down) there is always an offset (Vietnam for LBJ; a $2 trillion deficit in federal spending for RR); life in the White House goes on with equanimity and seeming harmony, but always with the potential for disaster just minutes away. And generally without any significant contribution to the country or the world.

Indeed, the powers of the President's office are often illusory; most heads of state feel powerless themselves to affect major changes; **LBJ** admitted that all his extraordinary efforts in Vietnam didn't change anything; **Nixon** was unable to extricate himself from his own Watergate mess; and even **Abraham Lincoln** declared that he didn't control events during his reign, but events controlled him.

Historian Bradley H. Patterson, Jr. suggested that "the incoherencies of pluralism beyond the White House gates" will always prevent a President from truly leading a nation to great reform, or great advance, or great welfare for humankind. And so it seems, and so goes the Office of the President of the US, the most powerful leader of the most powerful country in the world.

For the record, here's how former Presidents have described their jobs:

Woodrow Wilson: "No bath of rosewater."

George Washington: "I feel like a culprit going to the place of my execution."

John Adams: "No man who ever held the office would congratulate a friend on obtaining it."

Grover Cleveland: "A self-inflicted penance for the good of the country."

Warren Harding: "A hell of a job."

James Buchanan: "The Presidency is a distinction far more glorious than the crown of any hereditary monarch in Christendom, but, yet, it is a crown of thorns."

In terms of materialism, the President holds his own; his annual salary of $200,000 taxable plus a $50,000 expense allowance plus $100,000 for travel plus $20,000 for retirement plus many other perks. Upon retirement, a President receives $69,630/year as a lifetime pension, free mailing privileges, free office space and up to $150,000 for office help. (By comparison, a Vice-President gets $160,600/year in salary plus $20,000 in expenses, all taxable.)

331. WHAT IS THE LIFESTYLE OF WHITE HOUSE RESIDENTS?

There's no place quite like the 132-room mansion on Pennsylvania Ave. called the White House or Casa Blanca.

Formal though it may be, and awesomely solemn in its history, the White House is a residence, and thereby, has humanity and amusement and humor as part of its legacy.

Photo: J. R. Black

George and Barbara Bush in a lighter, memorable moment, NSO Dinner.

The official state rooms on the first floor are the *locus* for dignified dinners and entertainment; there heads of state from around the globe exchange pleasantries with administration powers. Formal offices of the President and his staff in the West Wing of the White House are separated from those in the East Wing, of his wife and her assistants. Usually, the West Wing issues orders, East Wingers follow them, but in recent presidencies (Carter, Reagan, Clinton) there has been a lessening of historical lines and both wings work together more actively.

Reagan held press conferences in the East Room, the same room in which Abigail Adams (first of the First Ladies) hung her laundry; Teddy Roosevelt held wrestling matches there, while Susan Ford staged her high school prom there, and Amy Carter roller-skated on the magnificent floors of the East Room.

Over the years, horses have pranced into the White House as a prank, the most celebrated entertainers in the world have performed there, a few liaisons have been played out and all sorts of madcap family squabbles have taken place; and life at large has been conducted by the First Family in the upstairs living quarters, where, as in any household in America, there are no guarantees, and life is an ongoing parade, sometimes even a charade.

332. WHAT HAVE BEEN SOME OF THE LONGEST HONEYMOONS FOR NEWLY ELECTED PRESIDENTS?

Even in the best of times, no future President will ever have a honeymoon longer than the first 100 days; inaction, media fault-finding, indirection, inept imaging and a stubborn Congress will take its toll on any perfection-aspiring head of state.

FDR had about a year of fun-and-games-and-resolute-action based on the desperation of the country. What limited press there was then had only kind words for the President, and even members of the opposition felt obliged to give the man at 1600 Pennsylvania what he wanted. His 100 Days with passage of banking and national relief and homeowner's loan and farm mortgage bills (and 15 other major pieces of legislation) will never again be duplicated.

Truman had a legacy and was given enough latitude to carry it forward without too much harping from Congress; he had about nine months of easy labor before the pain set in; **Ike**, jovial to the end (but always troubled) got by for six months, negotiated a peace treaty in Korea and was evasive enough (to the press) to avoid direct confrontation and the resultant humbling.

JFK had a lifestyle and panache that disoriented sharpshooters, but history records more style than substance; in his final year in office, artillery was incoming from every angle, and his re-election efforts in '64 would not have been easy.

LBJ had a productive sprint for almost a year with bills on federal aid to education, civil rights, Medicare and immigration reform going into the records; but Vietnam was his undoing.

Nixon had no honeymoon, nor any agenda as he entered office; he relied on then Professor Daniel Patrick Moynihan and economist Arthur Burns to run domestic issues while he toured the world, most notably China. When nothing seemed to be happening, Nixon gave the two most famous Germans in recent government — John Erlichman and H.R. Haldeman—the reins of power and Watergate became part of the language.

Ford didn't have enough horsepower to last long, but his pardon of Nixon terminated him quickly. Same for **Carter**, who was such an enigma, that until the Bert Lance affair (conflict of interest) the American public didn't know who their President was; they quickly found out and dispensed with all congeniality.

Reagan won a substantial victory in '80 and had a Republican Congress on his side; then he got shot and public sympathy favored a temporary free ride, and he played out his two terms with enough showbiz to please most folks and mediatypes, so as the 40th President and the only one since FDR to last out two terms successfully, Mr. Reagan was record-setting in his own way.

Bush got into office without a concise plan, was quickly tagged as a wimp and only because of the Gulf War (in which he took decisive action, with no other option) managed to last his four years without being really whip-sawed by the press and a weary constituency.

As for **Clinton**? The honeymoon was too short-lived to be taken into account. He was a victim of media's awesome power to victimize (a fact that mediapowers fully understand and perversely rejoice in) but is still an unknown to the American public. People react to what they see; it is the media who select what they see, therefore, any future President or high-office office-holder will invariably be only as good as the media makes them.

33. WHO WERE THE MOST FAMOUS OF "ALL THE PRESIDENTS' WOMEN"?

On those days when nothing is happening, mediamavens play games fantasizing situations, which with enough fantasy-substance, become real games and thereby are reported as real circumstances. So goes dignified journalism.

Over the decades, there seems to have been "another woman" in the lives of many Presidents. The liaisons may have been nothing more than a lustful look, a harmless peck on the cheek, a gentle grab below the table or a bodies-united dance, but the tabloids can generally manufacture a valid enough story from the event to generate a ripple effect with other media—slowly waving out with a broader pattern and an ever-increasing universe of potential receivers.

Thus, over a century or so, various Presidents have had various encounters with these ladies:

Thomas Jefferson had a love interest in Paris with Mrs. Maria Cosway.

Grover Cleveland had a child born out of wedlock with Mrs. Maria C. Halpin.

Warren Harding was accused of fathering the child of Nan Britton.

Woodrow Wilson had a soulful if not lustful relationship in Bermuda with Mrs. Mary Hulbert Peck.

FDR played games with his live-in secretary Miss Lehand, and Eleanor's social sec Lucy Page Mercer.

Ike had a bigger-than-life but less-than-consummated love affair with his WWII driver Kay Summersby.

JFK had brief trysts, supposedly, with Jayne Mansfield, Judith Campbell Exner, Marilyn Monroe, Angie Dickinson and Balza Starr.

Johnson was sued for $10.5 million in palimony by Madeline Brown and her son.

Hart backed off as possible head of state via an infamous alliance with Donna Rice.

334. WHAT IS BROOKS BROTHERS' ALLIANCE WITH PRESIDENTS?

Hillary Rodham Clinton recently gave her President a $395 jacket from Brooks Brothers, a company that has clothed heads of state (and blue bloods everywhere) since the FDR days; this time the jacket was not a traditional blue blazer with gold buttons, but a chocolate brown suede bomber-jacket reminiscent of the garb worn by airmen in WWII.

The President was so taken with the jacket, it is now a priority item in his wardrobe, worn on military occasions and when semi-slumming, but not really slumming a la the grungy, baggy sweats that he prefers when jogging.

335. WHAT ARE THE FACTS OF LIFE ABOUT THE NEW CLINTON CABINET?

With each new administration, a whole library of new faces, new philosophies and new schemes is put in place in the Capital; each performs according to script for a while, then begins dealing with personal agendas and pleasures. In the current Cabinet (and salaried at $143,800/year) there are:

Six women: **Carol M. Browner**, Administrator, Environmental Protection Agency; **Laura D'Andrea**, Chairman, Council of Economic Advisors; **Hazel R. O'Leary**, Secretary of Energy; **Janet Reno**, Attorney General; **Donna E. Shalala**, Secretary of Health and Human Services; **Madeleine K. Albright**, Ambassador; US Mission to the UN.

Three African Americans: **Ronald H. Brown**, Secretary of Commerce; **Jesse Brown**, Secretary of Veterans Affairs; **Mike Espy**, Secretary of Agriculture.

Two Hispanics: **Henry G. Cisneros**, Secretary of Housing and Urban

Mrs. Edward Derwinski with General Colin and Mrs. Alma Powell—
eminent, enlightened, elite.

Photo: J. R. Black

Development; **Frederico F. Pena**, Secretary of Transportation.

Two Rhodes Scholars: **Robert B. Reich**, Secretary of Labor; **Mickey Kantor**, US Trade Representative.

Seven lawyers: **Bruce Babbitt**, Secretary of Interior; **Warren Christopher**, Secretary of State; **Richard W. Riley**, Secretary of Education; **Les Aspin**, Secretary of Defense; **Robert E. Rubin**, Chairman, National Economic Council; **Lloyd Bentsen**, Secretary of Treasury; and **Janet Reno**, Attorney General.

* **Les Aspin** gets to ride a golf cart around his office—the Pentagon, very large office building.

* **Lloyd Bentsen** has his name on paper money (along with Treasurer of US) and feels guilt with each expenditure.

* **Janet Reno** is tallest Cabinet member at 6'2" and is the first woman Attorney General in history.

* **Robert B. Reich** is shortest member at 4'10".

* **Madeleine K. Albright** got promoted to Cabinet level as UN Ambassador; same for **Robert E. Rubin** whose department was created by Clinton and given Cabinet status.

* **Leon E. Panette**, Director of the Office of Management and Budget has the onerous task of paring $500 billion from fed government over next five years.

* **Jesse Brown** heads biggest fed agency with 220,000 employees administering the welfare of some 30 million vets.

Each adminstration brings a group of scholars to the Capital who

337

represent a brand of thinking unique to a given university. Outside of the Rhodes Scholar influence in the Clinton administration, **MIT** (Massachusetts Institute of Technology) is playing a major role, especially in the formulation of economic policy.

Kennedy and Johnson had their **Harvard** affiliations; Reagan, his honchos from the **University of Chicago.** Clinton will introduce a group — Alan Binder, Lawrence Katz, Laura Tyson, David Cutler and Joseph Stiglitz — from MIT who are technically sophisticated, internationally oriented, Keynesian in approach and highly mathematical. They will assist in the monumental task of lessening government debt without recession, depression, massive unemployment, insurmountable trade deficit and all those little negatives in government.

The Clinton Administration also brings a number of "K-Schoolers" to CapCity; they are graduates of Harvard University's John F. Kennedy School of Government, often considered the nation's leading public-policy school. Some in the Cabinet are: Les Aspin, Ron Brown, Robert Reich, Richard Riley, Donna Shalala and Bruce Babbitt; in other top administration positions are Roy Neel, Joseph Nye, Leon Fuerth, Leo McKay, David Wilhelm, Alice Rivlin and Susan Brophy.

336. WHO ARE THE MEMBERS OF PRESIDENT CLINTON'S INNER SANCTUM?

Like managers of professional sports teams, leaders in various categories of power in the White House tend to be migratory. Only about 50 percent of the players of an incoming administration are in place after four years; the other 50 percent have been sandbagged or rendered inoperable or are too frazzled to function. At this point, these operatives look as if they have staying-power and will perform seriously for the Clintons:

Carol Rasco, White House Domestic Policy Adviser; native Arkansan, imperious personality, FOH (friend of Hillary) and savvy campaigner.

David Wilhelm, Chairman, Democratic National Committee; sound political sense, superb experience as a mouthpiece, young and attractive (38 years of age), capable of coming up with original buzz words and party lines.

Bruce Lindsey, White House Personnel Director; cool, trustworthy, articulate, can make/break White House via selection of top candidates; a good troubleshooter and disciplined hip-shooter.

Gene Sperling, Deputy Assistant for Economic Policy; great experience with heavy-hitters (Mario Cuomo, Michael Dukakis) and sound economic planner. Can jaw with the pols and trade formulae with economists.

Paul Begala, Political Consultant; day-to-day wordsmith for Clinton (along with partner James Carville) charged with creative sales campaigns for admin messages. Will work closely with **Stanley Greenberg** (Presidential Pollster) to bring credibility to programs resulting from public opinion surveys.

Vernon Jordan, Clinton Associate/Advisor; Mr. Get-It-Done in the Capital, will aid and abet the admin in whatever role is appropriate. Good Clinton buddy (also FOH) and ally.

Bernard Nussbaum, White House Counsel; has entree to Casa Blanca, close relationship with President, good understanding of legalities of office.

Ira Magaziner, Senior Advisor; Rhodes scholar, FOB, tight with Mrs. Clinton on health-care reform.

Mark Geran, Deputy Chief of Staff; a law and order man, experienced, priestly with a switchblade, a perfect #2 to McLarty.

Eli Segal, Director, Office of National Service; knows the ropes, is a quiet exorcist, held in high regard, lots of promise.

Margaret "Maggie" Williams, Chief of Staff for First Lady; formerly CommDir for DNC, is experienced and connected, especially persuasive on HRC projects, almost demoniacal in getting results. Will escalate based on her bosses' victories.

Among other (especially young) high-velocity, office-policized staffers on the flying trapeze are: media handler **Dee Dee Myers** (31), domestic policy advisor **Bruce Reed** (32), power-lawyer **Thomas Donilon** (37), researcher **Ricki Seidman** (37) and foreign policy specialist **Nancy Soderberg** (34).

Not so young but highly skilled and motivated, **David Gergen**, general factotum and communication advisor was hired to help shape Clinton's image and help the administration get results from Congress. Only time will tell.

337. WHO IN THE ADMINISTRATION IS OFTEN CALLED "MACK THE NICE"?

Longtime friend of President Clinton, and ace businessman (CEO of Arkla, a Fortune 500 company), **Thomas F. "Mack" McLarty III**, 47, holds the position as White House Chief of Staff, one of the more impossible jobs in Western Civilization.

In his role as "Javelin Catcher" for Clinton, "Mack the Nice" as he is still called, is required to regulate the flow of paper to the President, be the pragmatist about new ideas and options, play top sergeant to staffers who don't toe the party line, take flak directed to the President/administration, be a sounding board for Cabinet members and the President, and when necessary be the fall guy for Mr. Clinton.

338. WHO ARE THE "CLINTON WOMEN"?

According to various press reports, the "Clinton Women" are a group of formidable ladies who don't appreciate verbal ventilation, or cyclothymic personalities, have a feeling for the hot seat and workaholism, fear no man, are independent, direct and enjoy wielding power; and will take a hit without

Mrs. Fritz "Peatsy" Hollings— terribly adroit at altruism.

Photo: J. R. Black

flinching.

Attorney General **Janet Reno** is the showcase example; she doesn' tolerate insubordination or derailment and refuses to be overmatched **Brooke Shearer**, Director of the White House Fellows program knows how to jockey for position with any group; **Christine Varney**, Deputy Assistan for Cabinet Affairs, can extinguish fires with the best of them; and **Dee Dee Myers**, first female White House Press Secretary can be engaging and outgoing and naive, all the while getting even, getting ahead, getting precisely what she wants.

Yet, not everything is power-oriented. For an administration that pro motes family values, there are families: Interior Secretary **Bruce Babbitt** i married to Harriet Babbitt, Ambassador, Organization of American States Senator **Tom Harkin** comes home each night to Ruth Harkin, President Overseas Private Investment Corp; Representative **Robert Matsui's** wife i Dors Matsui, Deputy Assistant to the President; Senator **Jeff Bingaman** i spouse to Anne Bingaman, Assistant Attorney General; and ex-Representa tive **Beryl Anthony** shares life with Sheila Anthony, Assistant Attorney General.

Although the "women" are not outraged by $20,000 Scaasi gowns neither are they clotheshorses. They combine the practicality and propriety of Eleanor Roosevelt with a touch of the '90s (pantsuits, dungarees or weekends); designer labels are not a prerequisite and stores like Macy's and Bloomie's get prior call for people serving an administration where wage are low, and frozen!

Probably the most fashion-oriented of the new women is **Ann Stock** Social Secretary who is a former retail executive and likes Chanel suits and an occasional flourish from Mizrahi. As White House SocSec, Purdu University grad Stock (now age 47) honed her political skills working for VI Walter Mondale and moved on to Bloomingdale's in NYC as Public Rela tions VP. Her current assignment has no "job description" which suggests constant motion for her two assistants and a number of volunteers who assist in entertaining, planning and cajoling the rajahs of the world. Her husband is a DC lawyer, and with a 15-year-old son (Chase) the trio is much-invited and much-ballyhooed around Town.

On a typical Saturday afternoon, the "Clinton Women" if not working, take to Wisconsin Ave. in Georgetown to check out new trends and see how the private-sector goes about glamorizing themselves. But it takes a pretty bizarre presentation to convince these loyalists that change, although necessary for the country, is hardly a commandment for them.

Although many new faces on Capitol Hill or at 1600 Pennsylvania Ave. are FOB in their orientation, many owe their allegiance to Hillary Rodham Clinton, who will be the first First Lady with two offices—the traditional hangout in the East Wing where social doings are done, and the new lair in the West Wing, where Mrs. Clinton will serve as chair of the President's Task Force on National Health Reform. She draws zip for salary from either job and even has to hurry home (upstairs) on occasion to set the table, for her husband and daughter!

39. HOW IS THE NEW ADMINISTRATION DIMINISHING THE ROLE OF "BIG MEDIA"?

Based on then-candidate Clinton's success with the mass media (primarily Larry King on CNN), he, now as President Clinton, is attempting to bypass the print media and their interpretation of what he says by going directly to the American public on the tube.

Ross Perot was a political unknown when he first appealed to the troops on King's show; he got national attention as a result and became a viable option for the '92 presidential election. He used a similar ploy — don't let the news-scavengers take you down with inane and captious queries, make your case to some 60 million viewers at one time and in one philosophical package on national TV.

Big Media, the traditional means by which a story reaches the public, is hardly academic; it's just that the ground rules have changed. Monoliths like the *New York Times, Washington Post, Chicago Tribune, Los Angeles Times, US News & World Report, Time, Business Week,* ABC/CBS/NBC have served the public well through many administrations by sifting and sorting news, slanting it to their liking (despite their continued proclamation of objectivity in presenting news) and availing it to the public via their formats.

Now, **NewNews** is taking over and allowing any significant personage to communicate ideas and ideologies to Oprah, Donahue, Sally Jessy, King, Sunday a.m. talkshows or whathaveyou. Messages can be sent without formal messengers, just by appealing directly to viewers of TV monitors.

The Clinton Administration has less than an impressive scorecard with the command, or manipulation, of the media, so NewNews isn't necessarily

a panacea. But it is a novel opportunity, one that Clintonites are explorin
fully in the hope that the message can be sent without interpretation, and tha
it will be received warmly.

For the record, other presidents have used alternate formats to circum
vent the national press: **FDR** initiated his highly-successful fireside chat
Nixon appeared on *Laugh-In*; **Carter** gave an expansive (and injuriou
interview to *Playboy*; **Reagan** had regular Mutual Broadcast radio show
and **Bush** gave his all on a number of talk shows. Outside of some seriou
pronouncements made on the *Larry King Show* (CNN), not much of th
palaver scored with the public simply because listeners didn't expect an
thing serious to develop from comedy/confession/capricious talkshows.

340. WHO ARE KNOWN AS ADMINISTRATION "STUDS"?

As many as 20 White House staffers— all men — have taken to wearin
earrings (diamond studs) as they putter around in their offices, hopefull
earning their wages as officials of the US government.

Not so at the Department of State, any military force, congression
assistants, Defense and Energy Departments; no studs allowed.

In a democracy, all manner of idiosyncracy must be tolerated, and a
Head Honcho, Clinton can condone whatever he pleases (as long as it
legal). His Assistant for Communications, **David Dreyer** (37 years ol
sports a one-carat diamond earring that demands attention. Maybe that
why Dreyer has so many visitors to his office.

341. WHAT ARE SOME DEMOGRAPHICS OF THE 103rd CONGRESS?

Almost all new Congresses are hailed as a "Reform Congress"—a ti
which hopefully gives thrust to the assemblage that legislates under that tit
The 103rd was considered full of young blood, energy and new ideas. B
so have the last few groups of the lower House.

In fact, the **average age** of its new members is 53, a tad younger than th
previous group. As in other years, **lawyers** are the largest occupational gro
with nearly half (239) of the members; next biggest segment is businessm
and bankers (58).

Roman Catholics are the largest religious factor (141) followed
Methodists (66), Baptists (62), Presbyterians (54) and Episcopalians (5C

Joining 24 female incumbents in the House of Representatives are
new Representatives, making a roster of **48 female legislators.** Among t
firsts—the first Black woman and the first Native American in the Sen
(Carol Moseley Brown of Illinois and Ben Nighthorse Campbell, Colorad
the first all-female Senate delegation (Feinstein and Boxer from Californi
the first Congresswomen from Virginia and Oregon (Leslie Byrne a
Elizabeth Furse), the first Black Congresswomen from Florida (Corin

Brown and Carrie Meek), and the first Puerto Rican Congresswoman from anywhere (Nydia Velazquez of New York).

Like the post-Watergate class of '74, these women talk in terms of reforming the system, ending gridlock, "bringing America back." Standard campaign oratory, perhaps, but with the first unified government in 12 years, it's reasonable to expect that talk will translate into legislative action.

Though each of these women represents a district, not a gender, they intend to work together. The freshman Republican and Democratic women recently held an unprecedented joint press conference to articulate three goals: rapid passage of a Freedom of Choice act to guarantee access to abortion nationwide; a new version of the Family and Medical Leave Act, passed by the last Congress and vetoed by Bush; and full funding for Head Start.

Noteworthy is the fact that three new members of Congress have beards, and 14 have mustaches. **Neil Abercrombie**, Democratic Congressman from Hawaii, has a ponytail and sports brightly colored ties from his island base; new Georgia Congresswoman **Cynthia McKinny** wears signature gold tennis shoes by Stuart Weitzman, loud silk outfits and an oversized Mickey Mouse watch as she makes the Capital rounds.

In terms of **net worth**, the richest of the freshman Congressmen, who has a very attractive wife with an impressive track record (and probably the longest name of any Representative's wife—Arianna Stassinopoulos) is **Michael Huffington**, former businessman (his father's company Roy M. Huffington, Inc. discovered huge reserves of natural gas in Indonesia), man-about-Houston-and-Santa Barbara (plus Montecito, CA where he has a $4 million manse), now in try-out for Casa Blanca. His riches are estimated at $400 million and his life-style gives credence to same.

Mrs. Huffington is formidable in her own right; two decades ago she became prominent in England as the 23-year-old author of *The Female Woman* and dated the likes of Jerry Brown, Mort Zuckerman (*US News & World Report*) and guru Werner Erhard; Greek-born and Harvard educated, she escalated her efforts and wrote *Picasso: Creator and Destroyer* ('88) which portrayed the art genius as a lamentable sadist. She married Huffington (now 45) in '88.

As for the **"Best Buns"** in the fresh Congress, Maureen Dodd (*NY Times*) selected Democrat **Melvin Watt** (NC) and **Walter R. Tucker** (CA).

In terms of **"Biggest Hogs,"** there are many qualifiers. Part of the new Clinton administration and a few hold overs from the past are devotees of Harley-Davidson motorcycles, or "Hogs." Colorado Senator **Ben Nighthorse Campbell**, who won his seat in fall '92, tools around Town on his '93 Harley-Davidson FXSTC with his "103rd Congress" license plate. Congressman **Randy "Duke" Cunningham** of CA, **John Kasich** of OH and **Nick Smith** of MI are big on bikes and are part of the Hill's Angels; and a few former bikers—ID Senator **Larry Craig**, Congressman **Wayne Gilchrest** of MD,

Martin Hoke of OH, **John Linder** of GA and **Charles Wilson** of TX—still put rubber to the road occasionally. Bikes can be parked in the garage under the Capitol.

When everything settles, about 30 percent of Congressional members will settle in on **Capitol Hill** (Capitol City, a rough circle outlined by the Capitol in the west, RFK Stadium in the east, H Street in the north and Eisenhower Freeway in the south). Their neighbors will be climbers—attorneys, lobbyists, aides and federal government groupies.

Based on their frequency of visitation and zeal in learning about life, they, in time, all become "Hill Rats."

342. WHO ARE THE GOVERNING MEMBERS OF THE SENATE?

President, Albert Gore, Vice-President of the US
President Pro Tempore, Robert C. Byrd (D-WV)
Majority Leader, George J. Mitchell (D-ME)
Majority Whip, Wendell Ford (D-KY)
Secretary of Conference, David Pryor (D-AR)
Minority Leader, Robert Dole (R-KS)
Assistant Minority Leader, Alan K. Simpson (R-WY)
Conference Chairman, Thad Cochran (R-MS)
Secretary of the Senate, Walter J. Stewart
Sergeant at Arms, Martha S. Pope
Majority Secretary, C. Abbott Saffold
Minority Secretary, Howard O. Greene, Jr.
Parliamentarian, Alan Frumin
Assistant Secretary, Jeri Thomson
Chaplain, Rev. & Dr. Richard C. Halverson

**Past Senator, present Governor, permanent friends of Capital City—
Gail and Pete Wilson of California.**

344

343. WHO ARE THE SENATE'S MOST VISIBLE MEMBERS?

Senators rate with the media based on a number of characteristics:
Position (on various committees)
Issue/Experience
Personality
Ideology
Reputation
Physical Appearance
Previous Occupation

On that basis, for example, natural leaders would be: Senators **Byrd, Mitchell, Ford** and **Dole** as senior operatives in the Senate; Senator **Nunn** as the expert on military affairs; **Domenici** as most voluble personality; **Helms** as uncompromising ideologue; **Moynihan** as cerebral voice and squeaky-clean reputation; **Simpson**, at 6'7" as physical standout (he is the tallest man ever elected to the Senate); and **Metzenbaum** for self-made millions.

As ideal media subjects (those who make the headlines and are most often interviewed), over the years, Senators Glenn, Dole, Hollings, Kennedy, Helms, Domenici, Moynihan, Dodd, Byrd, Hatch, Nunn, Metzenbaum, Biden and D'Amato have been spokesmen for whatever cause or committee to the point where their recognition-factor is high.

Naturally, being on the right committees is a positive means to media exposure. The most important (and best covered) committees are:
Foreign Relations
Judiciary
Budget
Governmental Affairs
Appropriations
Labor and Human Resources
Joint Economic
Armed Services
Energy and Natural Resources
Finance
Banking, Housing and Urban Affairs
Ethics

The correlation between number of "exposures" in media and amount of press release activity on the part of any given Senator is direct. Senators **Dole, Kennedy, Hollings, Byrd, Helms** and **Moynihan** get the **most** by giving the **most**. Each sends out about 100 releases per year and actively courts the broadcast media for interviews and photo-op coverage.

Other Senators with media clout are: Byrd, Gramm, Dodd, Graham, Nunn, Kassebaum, Mitchell, Kerry, Kerrey, Bradley, Hatfield, Boren, Warner, Robb and Rockefeller.

The Secretary of State and Mrs. Christopher
requests the pleasure of your company
at a reception
on Friday, the thirtieth of April
from six until nine o'clock
The Diplomatic Reception Rooms
Department of State

344. WHO ARE THE WINNERS/LOSERS IN CONGRESS?

Public opinion, private expressions, the "word" of those in power and private conversation with sages at the Jockey Club, Mo Sussman's and The Monocle give these ratings of legislators:

SENATE
Team Captain: Bob Dole (R-KS)
Egghead: Daniel Patrick Moynihan (D-NY)
Rocket Rider: Ted Kennedy (D-MA)
King Among Men: Paul Simon (D-IL)
Matador: Phil Gramm (R-TX)
Highhanded: Bill Bradley (D-NJ)
Camera-Ready: Bob Kerrey (D-NE)
Lothario: Orrin Hatch (R-UT)
Great Box-Office: John Warner (R-VA)
Aphrodisiacal: Chuck Robb (D-VA)
Connoisseur: Jay Rockefeller (D-WV)
Bulldozer: Jesse Helms (R-NC)

HOUSE
Dick Gephardt (D-MO)
Charles Schumer (D-NY)
Ronald Dellums (D-CA)
Lee Hamilton (D-ID)
Ted Weiss (D-NY)
Barney Frank (D-MA)
Joseph Kennedy (D-MA)
Joseph Early (D-MA)
Bob Michel (R-IL)
Pat Schroeder (D-CO)
Vic Fazio (D-CA)
Newt Gingrich (R-GA)

345. WHAT ARE A FEW "PERKS" FOR CONGRESSMEN AND WHITE HOUSE STAFF MEMBERS?

Congressmen are nicely isolated from reality while in the Capital, but face, usually, a fairly fierce audience in their home districts. While Congress is in session, its members enjoy almost unlimited travel (via Congressional Travel Delegations or CODELs to various "troubled" parts of the world, with wives, and other relatives), hideaway offices for "leisure and entertainment," free food/beverages in most places, parking access at National Air-port, indoor tennis and basketball courts at private clubs, free health care (at a cost to the taxpayer of $3,000 per year) plus the free services of Walter Reed Army Medical Center and the Bethesda Naval Medical Institute, video studios where they can make videotapes for political purposes (at a taxpayer cost of $17,000/tape, zip to the member) and on and on. With a substantial salary ($129,500/year) and an expense account of almost $1 million/year (for staff, T&E, constituent relations, etc.), a member of Congress can live handsomely if he/she is the least bit calculating about monies.

White House Staffers enjoy even more privilege, especially if the President is available and comfortable in their presence. Among the fringies: woodburning fireplaces in their offices, reserved parking places and frequent limo service, flights on Air Force One when accompanying the President and the use of Camp David when he's not there, lunch or dinner in the White House mess at a fraction of the normal cost of dining, open access to the White House swimming pool, tennis courts, health club, medical facilities, gym and hair salon, use of the Presidential Box at Kennedy Center, private movie screenings, White House family parties and the like.

346. WHAT ARE THE ANNUAL SALARIES OF FEDERAL OFFICIALS?

President of the US	$200,000
Vice-President of the US	160,600
Cabinet members	138,900
Under Secretaries of executive departments	115,300
Deputy Secretaries of State, Defense, Treasury	125,100
Deputy Attorney General	125,100
Secretaries of the Army, Navy, Air Force	125,100
Senators	101,900
Representatives	125,100
President Pro Tempore of Senate	113,400
Majority and Minority Leader of the Senate	113,400
Majority and Minority Leader of the House	138,900
Speaker of the House	160,600
Chief Justice of the US	160,600
Associate Justices of the Supreme Court	153,600

347. WHAT ARE SOME PROJECTED PENSIONS FOR MEMBERS OF GOVERNMENT?

Ex-Presidents are usually millionaires (as are Presidents of the new era) but the government generously allows them an annual pension of $148,000 plus an office staff (tab usually in the $500,000 range) plus security (bodyguards, not social) plus $150,000 a year in supplemental money from their party, plus whatever they can negotiate from books, revelations, talk show and the chicken-circuit. It's not rare for an ex-chief of state to bank several million a year for as long as he (and someday she) is in the public mainstream.

On the Hill, there's enough swag to keep most people happy, too. Campaign-finance laws, being what they are, have just enough loopholes to allow a vigorous, brainy legislator to plan a future of impressive materialism. Based on some bright maneuvering, here's how a few current lawmakers will spend their waning days (in terms of monetary reward):

Legislator	Age	Estimated Pension
Larry Hopkins (R-KY)	58	$1.6 million
Ed Jenkins (D-GA)	59	$2.4 million
John Hammerschmidt (R-AR)	69	$1.5 million
Walter Jones (D-NC)	78	$770,000
Doug Barnard (D-GA)	70	$945,000
Larry Coughlin (R-PA)	62	$2 million
Bill Lehman (D-FL)	78	$1 million
Don Pease (D-OH)	60	$1.6 million
Ed Roybal (D-CA)	76	$1.1 million
Joseph Gaydos (D-PA)	65	$1.7 million
Andy Ireland (R-FL)	61	$1.4 million
Gus Yatron (D-PA)	64	$1.7 million
Frank Annunzio (D-IL)	77	$920,000
Glenn Anderson (D-CA)	79	$741,000

348. WHO IS THE ADMINISTRATION'S "MS. FIX-IT"?

White House political director **Joan Baggett**, a whiz at telemarketing, is given all the assignments others prefer to ignore; she spends hours schmoozing with state party officials and lesser party dignitaries building a network of support for President Clinton and gathering intelligence. A native of Repton, AL, Baggett grew up the youngest of 10 children on a strawberry farm and got her first "negotiating" experience with her brothers. After graduating from Alabama U, she worked for Senator Jim Allen (D-AL), then honed her skills as political director of the bricklayers' union and chief-of-staff of the Democratic National Committee. On the agenda for 42-year-old super-pol Baggett is passage of the North Atlantic Free Trade Agreement and Clinton's market-based health reform plan, and acceptance of the new Democratic agenda on entitlement cuts and tougher crime laws.

349. WHO IS "RAHMBO"?

Now serving in the communications department, super fundraiser **Rahm Emanuel**, a feisty 34-year-old former ballet dancer, serves as "Rahmbo" for the administration. Somewhat convinced of his supremacy, he's had trouble coddling top party officials but is close to Chief of Staff Thomas "Mack" McLarty (the "Macker" to Emanuel). Rahm's efforts on the West Coast as fundraiser for Clinton during the campaign won him kudos and he is credited with delivering vast amounts of contributions and votes; he was rewarded with his current post, and some vanity-flaunt via a black limo draped with a white banner bearing his name, which actually led the inaugural parade down PennAve. He's a tough guy who doesn't eat quiche and is expected to handle some upcoming assignments where the wit and grit of a "Rahmbo" are in the script.

50. WHAT IS THE ADMINISTRATION "TAG TEAM"?

Fifty something **Richard Gephardt**, 9th term Congressman and Majority Leader from Missouri, and 60-ish **Thomas Foley**, 15th term Speaker of the House from Spokane, WA blend their respective skills—method and intellect—to keep skittish Democrats in line and voting for bills presented by President Clinton. Called the White House "Tag Team," Foley/Gephardt are charged with getting bills passed and setting controls in place to minimize damage to the party and its members (a la the House Post Office scandal and possible vulnerability of House member Dan Rostenkowski). Gephardt, whose district was ravaged by the recent "flood of the century" in the Midwest, suggests his Capital post is similar to experiences at home—"it's the ultimate sandbag operation—filling sandbags at home, filling sandbags here."

51. WHO IS FRIZZEL GRAY/KWEISI MFUME?

A 45-year-old four-term Democratic Congressman from Baltimore, now serving as Chairman of the Congressional Black Caucus, grew up on the streets of Baltimore as **Frizzel Gray**. Through a series of heroic self-development moves, he split from an impoverished, abusive stepfather (after his mother died), worked at numerous jobs while getting a degree at Morgan State University, followed by a stint as a disc jockey and talkshow host in Baltimore, finally moving into politics via the city council, and on to the national level via Congress in '86 (delving into his African heritage caused the name change in '72 to **Kweisi Mfume**—"conquering son of kings"). Pragmatic, studied, intent on success, Mfume has the appeal of the late Martin Luther King Jr. and the respect of President Clinton. His future? Possible head of the Democratic Caucus, member of the Senate, first Black Speaker of the House? Whatever. Upward/onward!

52. WHAT 9 TO 5 WOMAN IS NOW ONE OF THE ADMINISTRATION'S HIGHEST PAID EXECUTIVES?

In the early '70s, **Karen Nussbaum** founded **9 to 5**, the **National Association of Working Women** in Boston; in '77 the organization went national and over the years has grown to representation in 200 cities with almost 250,000 members.

Ms. Nussbaum (married to Ira Arlook, head of Citizen Action, a nationwide grass-roots political group), age 44, is now the 13th Director of

the Woman's Bureau, a small group of activists within the Labor Depar
ment), reporting to Labor Secretary Robert Reich. In command of a
operating budget of $1.3 million, her salary is $115,000/year. (Mr. Reich
salaried at $143,800/annum as is Attorney General Janet Reno.)

Pay equity is a first order for the Bureau but other issues—women
rights under the Pregnancy Discrimination Act, the Civil Rights Act and th
Family and Medical Leave Act, basic fair treatment at work and sexu
harassment—also cry for attention.

Ms. Nussbaum will have a staff of 20 people (not all women) to assist
her efforts—and the considerable clout of the First Lady who, too,
dedicated to equality in the work force for women.

353. WHAT GOES ON IN SENATE ROOM EF-100?

When students of female anatomy like Senators John Warner and Te
Kennedy meet quietly in Room EF-100 of the Capitol, East Front (acro
from the souvenir stand), their agenda is not what is expected.

They gather in this low-visibility chamber to let their angst and frustr
tions take form on canvas; specifically take their pleasures as artists, desig
ing works of art or whathaveyou, self-titillating and satisfying enough
soften the sharp edge and make an otherwise ponderous legislator some-wh
human.

Some 30 lawmakers now retreat to Room EF-100 for therapy an
quietude; and at no time is the privilege of privacy denied or jeopardized

354. WHAT IS CONGRESS'S SECRET DRAWER?

In another arcane manipulation by government, Congresspersons ca
protect each other while keeping constituents in the dark, and pronounce the
positions on various bills in public while ignoring those same positions
private.

The House controls the flow of bills to be voted on via the **Rul
Committee**, which has the authority to sit on bills indefinitely, there
minimizing their potential for enactment. Only a **discharge petition** ca
force issues to the floor, and only then if a majority of members sign th
petition (required number of petitioners is 218) and literally force an issue
be made public, debated, voted on and enacted or dropped. Getting 2
members to sign the petition is close to impossible via a mysterious prohibi
tion imposed in 1931 by then-Speaker John Nance Garner which caus
petitions to be kept in a **"secret drawer"** at the clerk's desk, which can on
be opened at a House session and its contents only seen by signing Membe
of a petition. Thus, a member of Congress has no knowledge about th
position of fellow Members on various issues (their real stand—they ca
make public pronouncements but vote contrarily, or say whatever they wa
in public knowing the bill in question will never reach the floor). It's a
secretive, and in a way sinister in that it disallows passage of important bi

that might positively impact American citizens albeit ruining political careers. (Oklahoma Rep. Jim Inhofe has forced a vote to end "Secret Drawer" rule as of this writing.)

55. WHAT IS WASHINGTON'S "PLUM BOOK"?

The hottest tome on Capitol Hill every four years is *United States Government Policy and Supporting Positions*, a 20-ounce document which lists every job and salary in the executive branch, from presidential appointees to low support staff. Based on the fact that such assignments are "plums" the book has a similar designation.

The "Plum Book" is dreary and tedious for people sans perspective; for those focused on DC, it is a verity, a must-read, a means to an end, the ultimate source for passage, placement and profit.

With each new administration, some 5,684 jobs are available, ranging from Cabinet officers and aides to secretaries; of the high profile jobs, 584 go through Senate confirmation. Salaries can be in/near the six-figure range or at Civil Service levels starting in the low $20 thousands.

Printed by the Government Printing Office (mandated via another questionable maneuver by Congress at a cost of $2 million each year) the book is free to those who get in line and wait out delivery.

56. TO WHAT EXTENT HAVE COKE AND PEPSI PLAYED IMPORTANT POLITICAL ROLES?

With per capita consumption at about 35 gallons per year in the US, soft drink marketers have considerable leverage and persuasion in all the right places, and all the right times.

The Coca-Cola Company and PepsiCo are both in the $10 billion range in gross income, and despite damage from acts of God, recessions, depressions, wars and the utmost general catastrophe, continue to move forward and embellish their positions as part of Americana. Perhaps some of what they do, and how they market their products, is indicated by this outline of their recent generosity to various politicians and political parties:

PARTY	PEPSI	COKE
Republicans (Total)	$567,005	$356,480
Democrats (Total)	188,998	494,487
Republican Incumbents	389,079	285,190
Democratic Incumbents	175,998	394,547
Republican Challengers	67,265	21,080
Democratic Challengers	4,000	47,700
Republican Open Seats	109,461	46,960
Democratic Open Seats	9,000	50,590

Not to be outperformed, the **tobacco industry** makes its statement in anything but clandestine ways with contributions, special expenditures and allocations designed to bring their products to light in a most favorable wa

Legislator	Contribution
Sen. Wendell Ford (D-KY)	$88,473
Rep. Tom Bliley (R-VA)	$86,849
Sen. Terry Sanford (D-NC)	$77,999
Rep. Charlie Rose (D-NC)	$71,050
Sen. Jesse Helms (R-NC)	$68,250
Sen. Bob Kasten (R-WI)	$55,540
Rep. Robert H. Michel (R-IL)	$55,460
Sen. Fritz Hollings (D-SC)	$55,288
Sen. Dan Coats (R-IN)	$53,500
Rep. Rick Boucher (D-VA)	$51,900
Sen. Mitch McConnell (R-KY)	$50,750
Rep. Steve Neal (D-NC)	$50,000
Rep. Bill Hefner (D-NC)	$48,850
Rep. Dick Gephardt (D-MO)	$47,498
Sen. Bob Dole (R-KS)	$47,400

Source: Federal Election Commission. Compiled by Sunshine Press Services.

357. HOW DOES AN ADMINISTRATION BUYOUT EMPLOYEES?

In much the way that major corporations terminate employees by ear
retirement or buyout plans which make their exit feasible and dignified, t
federal government allocates funds to ease bureaucrats into passage with
sense of honor, duty-done and good will.

For example, the President recently signed a bipartisan bill giving t
Central Intelligence Agency authority to pay employees as much as $25,0(
to lay down their sabers this year. The plan is modeled after buyouts bei
offered to some 30,000 Defense Department defenders in order to crea
voluntary vacancies so less senior employees won't be canned.

For the record, Senator John W. Warner (R-VA) and Representati
Dan Glickman (D-KS) sponsored the CIA proposal, Senator David Pryor (I
AR) and Representative William Clay (D-MO) pushed through the origin
Defense buyout package.

The House is expected to approve a plan by Representatives Vic Fazio (I
CA) and James P. Moran Jr. (D-VA) authorizing buyouts to Government Printi
Office, General Accounting Office and Library of Congress workers.

Under the buyouts, which may be extended to other federal agencie
workers can get payments equal to the value of their severance or $25,0(
whichever is less, if they quit, or take regular or early retirement at t
request of their agencies.

The law gives federal agencies, not workers, the option of deciding w
gets an offer. In most cases, workers who are in special-pay jobs that car
a higher salary because they are hard to fill aren't eligible for early retireme
or the buyouts.

358. WHAT IS THE EFFECT OF "BABY BOOMERS" ON WASHINGTON?

Individuals aren't easily assigned sociological or demographic categories in that each is a significant human entity, but "boomers" (people born between 1946 and '64) seem to offer a unique set of qualifications that demand attention.

There are now some 77.1 million boomers in the US and an astonishing half of them are college-educated. On the basis of their smarts, most boomers are personally secure, independent and very affirmative about their careers.

They take themselves seriously, want to make a contribution and are deferent to their parents, often crediting them success for their own attitudes.

The media also fascinates most boomers, and a few of them are obsessed with its power; in large part, boomers are responsible for the explosion of channels on TV, resulting in a program to fit almost any need/want. Since the days of Watergate when two unknown reporters (Woodward and Bernstein) from the *Washington Post* brought a presidency down, young people have taken to the media as a means of earning fame and fortune. In many cases, the media does offer golden possibilities for a fast rise and overnight notoriety; at the *NY Times*, for example, 60 percent of reporters are under 45 years of age.

Boomers are using networking and technological breakthroughs to make them more sophisticated and enable them to deal with complex problems more systematically. Yet, there is no substitute for experience as boomers are finding out, so a certain time in grade is expected as a person moves up the ladder.

At latest count, our population of 228.8 million citizens breaks out this way (millions of people, Source: US Census Bureau):

Generation	# People
Depression/WWII(1925-45)	48.2
Baby-boom ('46-'64)	77.1
Baby-bust ('65-'77)	47.7
Baby-boomlet ('78-'92)	55.8

Most of Clinton's administration is in the boomer category; and the classic battle between Bob Dole, a stereotypical member of the Depression/WWII generation with its discipline and steady-but-unflashy style and boomer Clinton showcases the difference brought about by 35 years of disparate thinking.

Boomers have definitely taken over government but it's too early to tell how successfully. By '95 the votes should be in.

359. WHAT ARE SOME OF WASHINGTON'S POWER-PLOYS?

Since most Capital residents are going for the Holy Grail in whatever format they make a living, there is a constancy of competitiveness, peer pressure (and peer perversion), plays-and-ploys in interpersonal relationships, and general skirmishing for position, rank or privilege. There are probably no business/government environments **free of politics**—one of the major factors in being successful. Here's how people get set up for failure via the many techniques available to a CEO or a Cabinet secretary or a presidential aide or anyone enjoying prominent placement in the pecking order.

* **Disinformation**—giving the wrong word to an associate anticipating word-spread and subsequent credibility diminishment for the spreader.

* **Litmus ploy**—making a bizarre suggestion to get a reaction, which immediately categorizes a peer.

* **Left-out**—purposely not copying an associate on a memo, thereby keeping an adversary out of touch with a subject.

* **Chain-of-command undercut**—getting official info from someone other than a boss; often from someone junior which creates concern about placement on the pyramid.

* **Ad-hocracy**—putting someone in charge of an impossible project as a prelude to failure, and subsequent de-listing from the power-elite.

* **Flapping**—making sure someone who has failed is given proper notoriety for his/her flap; a means, simply, of embellishing failure.

* **Watch list**—an agenda by which the "flapper" is observed by several adversaries with the motive of finding serious fault (alcoholism, infidelities, drugs, etc.).

* **Compartmentalization**—being sequestered from mainstream activities; no longer on the team.

* **Monitoring**—a superior sits in on meetings and notes the behavior and competence of a potential flapper.

* **Leakniqued**—being on the receiving end of any number of techniques of leak information: every leaker-leakee relationship requires collaboration and it is very easy to be a target for a "reputation-making" leak (a subordinate brings a boss down by leaking info about his gambling habits); a "shortcut" leak (dissemination false info to create enough furor to finally get heard); a "back-scratch" leak (*quid pro quo* info exchanged to the benefit of both parties); and a "trial-balloon" leak (a "Spokesman" for Cause XYZ announces something, just to get attention/reaction).

* **Psywarred**—having a dose of psychological warfare administered via conflicting requests from superiors or assignment of projects inimical to the party plan.

* **Sanitized**—receipt of memos and official correspondence that has been edited to delete critical facts/figures so that the recipient is not up to speed.

* **Elsured**—being surveyed electronically via wiretap, bugging, video taping; the ultimate step in fully serving up a sacrifical lamb.

None of these power-ploys are **pleasurable**, but they are **prevalent** at almost all levels of government, business and human endeavor. That's why CYA ("cover your ass") is such a meaningful *modus operandi* in Washington.

CHAPTER XII

THE WAY WE ARE, AND WERE
(Washington Prime & Primeval)

Photo courtesy of the Washington, DC Convention and Visitors Association

**National Cathedral, the world's largest Gothic cathedral,
a tribute to man's genius and inspiration.**

360. HOW IS WASHINGTON BEST DESCRIBED?

Paradox is the operative word. It is a city of monuments, seat of power brokers, workplace of bureaucrats and the center of government. Yet only since '64 have its citizens been able to vote for President, and even now, Washington is limited to nonvoting representation in the House and none in the Senate.

The city has a **population** of over 600,000, a small part of the 3.1 million people in the metropolitan area; Blacks and Hispanics make up a large part of the population and the Adams Morgan section of Town is as mixed in culture, income and class as parts of New York City.

The **District of Columbia** (formal name, not normally used; the capital is referred to as Washington, the District or DC) is notched out of the State of Maryland at the confluence of the Anacostia and Potomac Rivers. The Potomac is at the front door of the city; the wide Anacostia cuts through the northeast and southeast sections, and a third river, Rock Creek, winds through the northwest lined with a wooded park that is the city's largest natural recreation area.

The average price of a **home** in Washington is $218,942; the median rent is $441/month and the mean household income is $44,413. Almost 300,000 cars are registered in the District and the revenue from parking tickets checks in at $268,000 per day (some 5,100 parking tickets are written each day).

By occupation, the Town is loaded with legislators (seven percent of total jobs); other jobs by category are:

Occupation	Concentration Level
Public Adminstrators	6.1
Physicists & Astronomers	6.0
Economists	5.3
Statisticians	5.0
Public Relations Specialists	4.0
Computer Scientists	3.4
Editors & Reporters	3.3
Lawyers	3.1
Authors	2.9
Biological Scientists	2.8
Computer Programmers	2.4
Electrical Engineers	2.2
Accountants & Auditors	1.7

Source: 1990 US Census; compiled by Charles Mann Associates

The term legislator usually means a **bureaucrat**, of which there are many in Town and across the country. Since government is the number one business in Washington, the area is loaded with bureaucrats; several million involved in some way with the federal government — in the courts, military, foreign service, Capitol Hill. Many are part of the permanent government in

Washington and have jobs unrelated to elections and administrations; thereby, their stability is assured.

It is estimated that over 30 million employees across the country work for some form of government — at city, county or state levels, as government contractors and suppliers, as lobbyists or in the media. The majority work at taxpayer expense.

It is interesting to note how **bureaucratic staffs** get larger; the Department of Agriculture, for example, had 32,000 persons in 1932 serving a country with one out of four families living on a farm. Today, the Department has 110,000 people with less than two percent of the population as farmers. Further, it's estimated that the government lost almost $51 million last year by selling timber from the national forests, and lost another $53 million by leasing public land to ranchers. So there is no correlation between bureaucracy and bigness and profitability.

Washington elects a **Mayor and City Council** who have authority to pass laws and draw up a budget, but Congress has full veto power over the budget and jurisdiction over a substantial amount of federal property in the District. (The District is dependent on Congress for a federal payment in lieu of taxes on federal properties.) Current members of the city council are: **Charlene Drew Jarvis, John Ray, Hilda H.M. Mason, William P. Lightfoot, Linda W. Cropp, Frank Smith, Jr., Jack Evans, James E. Nathanson, Harry L. Thomas, Sr., Harold Brazil, H. R. Crawford, Wilhemina Rolark.** The Mayor is **Sharon Pratt Kelly.**

Uptown Washington encompasses the neighborhoods of Woodley Park,

Photo courtesy of the Washington, DC Convention and Visitors Association

U.S. Capitol, home to the legislative branch of the Federal Government.

Cleveland Park and Chevy Chase; **Downtown** is the area north of the Mall bordered by Foggy Bottom and the US Capitol. As the name implies, Downtown is where most of the business action takes place with office and municipal buildings and an air of industry.

Washington is divided into four sections, **Northwest, Northeast, Southwest,** and **Southeast.** Every street address is therefore followed by the all important NW, NE, SW, or SE. The Capitol serves as the center of the grid, with North Capitol St., South Capitol St., East Capitol St., and the Mall serving as dividing lines. North-south streets are numbers. East-west streets are letters (except J, X, Y or Z) in alphabetical order. Streets with state names, such as Connecticut, New York and Pennsylvania, are diagonals. Two-syllable names in alphabetical order (Adams, Bryant, Channing) begin where the letters end. Next come three-syllable names. In a four-digit address, the first two digits indicate the lower-numbered cross street. In a three-digit address, the first digit indicates the lower-numbered cross street. For example, Washington's most famous address, 1600 Pennsylvania Ave. (The White House) is located in the northwest quadrant at 16th St. and Pennsylvania Ave. 1915 K St. NW is between 19th and 20th Sts.

361. WHY IS WASHINGTON CALLED THE "OMNISCIENT CITY"?

The federal government has about 10,000 computer installations for keeping records on everyone and everything: It's estimated that about one billion files are updated regularly in the pursuit of knowledge. Here are some major filekeepers:

• The Department of Defense has at least 16,000,000 life histories.

• The Civil Service has over 10,000,000 sizable files on individuals.

• The Internal Revenue Service has well over 100,000,000 files.

• The Social Security Administration has another 100,000,000 or so.

• The Federal Bureau of Investigation has at least 6,500,000 files on US residents, including 600,000 computerized criminal histories. It also has files on more than 100,000 residents that at some time or another were viewed as Communist sympathizers.

• The Secret Service has computerized files on hundreds of thousands of "persons of interest." You can become a "person of interest" by protesting welfare regulations, by being in a demonstration, by making harsh remarks about people in Washington, by insisting on personally seeing high government officials for the purpose of venting grievances.

362. WHAT IS SOME OF THE AFRICAN AMERICAN LORE OF THE CAPITAL?

• The **Washington Monument** was designed as an obelisk, which was originally created by Egyptian architects in Africa.

• Four **bridges** are named after famous African Americans who lived in the District of Columbia. They are the **Frederick Douglass** (South Capitol St.), **Charles Drew** (Michigan Ave. NE), **Duke Ellington** (Calvert St. NW) and **Whitney Young** (East Capitol St.) Bridges.

• **Barry's Farm** in Anacostia was settled in 1865 by African Americans who laid the roads and built their own homes.

• Several African American residences and churches in Georgetown and the home of **Anthony Bowen**, the founder of the first YMCA in the District, were stops on the Underground Railroad.

• **Addison N. Scurlock**, a photographer, opened his studio in 1911, and documented the society of the Washington African American community for over 60 years.

• African American press is still going strong in the District to include the *Afro-American* (1892), *Capital Spotlight* ('54), *Washington Informer* ('64), *The Washington New Observer* ('57), *The Metro Chronicle, Community News* ('82) and *News Dimensions* ('92).

• **True Reformers Hall**, 1200 U St. NW was constructed by African Americans in 1903. The architect was John A. Lankford, the dean of Black architects, and the construction was performed by an African American company from Lynchburg, VA.

• The cherry tree-lined pool at the **Tidal Basin,** with paddle boats, was designed by Archie Alexander, a Black architect and engineer.

• The **Metropolitan African Methodist Episcopal Church** is an outgrowth of the free African Society of Philadelphia.

• Five African American congregations dating back to the 1800s are still located in Georgetown. They are: **Mount Zion United Methodist, Jerusalem Baptist, First Baptist Church of Georgetown, Alexander Memorial**

Photo courtesy of the Washington, DC Convention and Visitors Association

Smithsonian Institution, the red brick "castle" on the National Mall.

Baptist Church and **Epiphany Roman Catholic Church**.

• **Father Patrick F. Healy** was the first Black Jesuit and only Black president of Georgetown University.

• Muralists **Al Smith, Frank Smith** and **Michael Bernard Platt** have added their signature to the Washington scene. Many of the murals painted on buildings in the District of Columbia are by African American artists. A "Tribute to Jazz Musicians" which is dedicated to Duke Ellington, Miles Davis and others is located at 11th St. and Florida Ave. NW. Maurice Jenkins is the artist of *Lord's Supper*, the powerful mural depicting African American leaders painted in the nave of the sanctuary at Union Temple Baptist Church in Anacostia.

• **Howard University** (6th St. NW), founded in 1867, is the nation's leading Black university. The Founders' Library, the centerpiece of the campus, houses one of the world's largest collections of materials relating to the history and culture of Black people in Africa, Latin America, the Caribbean and the United States.

363. WHAT ARE SOME CODE NAMES FOR CAPITAL VIPS?

The Secret Service gets its kicks by assigning special nomenclature to various nabobs in the interest of protection and privacy. Code names change frequently to further mystify the public and add to the intrigue of high office. Some names:

Clinton	Eagle
Bush	Timber Wolf, Sheepskin
Barbara Bush	Tranquility
Reagan	Rawhide
Nancy Reagan	Rainbow
Carter	Dasher, Deacon
Rosalyn Carter	Duchess, Dancer
Amy Carter	Dynamo
Ford	Pass Key
Betty Ford	Pinafore
Nixon	Searchlight
Pat Nixon	Starlight
Johnson	Volunteer
Lady Bird	Victoria
Quayle	Scorecard
Marilyn Quayle	Sunshine

As for acronyms (the dictionary of military acronyms is 400 pages long), there are no surprises:

WARS	Worldwide Ammunition Reporting System
JUMPS	Joint Uniform Military Pay System

ABC	Atomic, Biological and Chemical
DUMB	Deep Underground Mountain Basing
HADES	Hypersonic Air Data Entry System
PITS	Payload Integration Test Set
SINS	Situational Inertial Navigation System
WAMPUM	Wage and Manpower Process Utilizing Machine

OTHERS like FBI, HUD, IMF, NAACP, CIA, EPA, NASA, MCI, IBM, etc., add to the nomenclature of CapCity.

364. WHAT ARE WASHINGTON'S MOST POPULAR "SUPERLATIVES"?

The Capital is a mecca of fascinating collections, objects, monuments, buildings, antiques, art, sportslore and historical **significa**; it is one of the leading cities in the world in its ownership of "firsts" and "bests" and records of all sorts. Here's a compilation of what the Town offers as one-of-a-kind **superlatives** (note: most of the listings to follow present a sight-seer's dream, so addresses are given; for further info, check the Visitor's Guide or phone book):

WHERE IS THE OLDEST ART COLLECTION?

Corcoran Gallery of Art, which provides a view of American art, Dutch and Flemish masterpieces, impressionists and post-impressionists. 17th St. and New York Ave. NW.

Photo courtesy of the Washington, DC Convention and Visitors Association

The Lincoln Memorial, the Washington Monument and the US Capitol Building, the beginning, middle and end, respectively, of the National Mall.

WHAT IS THE COUNTRY'S FIRST MUSEUM OF MODERN ART?

Phillips Collection—the permanent collection includes Renoir's *Luncheon of the Boating Party* and works by Cezanne, Bonnard, Braque, Daumier, Dove, El Greco, Manet, Matisse, Miro, O'Keeffe and Picasso. Dupont Circle Metro, 21st and Q Sts. NW.

WHAT GALLERY HAS THE ONLY SURVIVING EXAMPLE OF JAMES McNEILL WHISTLER'S INTERIOR DESIGN?

The Freer Gallery has Whistler's famous and opulent Peacock Room (considered the finest room in an American museum). The Oriental collection features Chinese paintings, calligraphy and ancient bronzes, Japanese screens and scrolls, ceramics from China, Japan and the Near East, Near Eastern metalwork, glass and manuscripts. Jefferson Dr. and 12th St. SW.

WHERE IS THE WORLD'S FOREMOST COLLECTION OF VICTORIAN AMERICANA AND MEMORABILIA?

The Arts and Industries Building. 900 Jefferson Dr. at 9th St. SW.

WHERE IS THE ONLY PAINTING IN AMERICA BY LEONARDO DA VINCI?

In the **National Gallery of Art**. Fourth St. and Constitution Ave, NW.

WHERE IS THE LARGEST COLLECTION OF SHAKESPEARIANA IN THE WORLD?

At the **Folger Shakespeare Library**. 201 E. Capitol St. SE.

WHAT IS THE WORLD'S FIRST MUSEUM DEVOTED TO LATIN AMERICAN ART?

Museum of Modern Art of Latin America. 201 18th St. NW.

WHAT IS THE WORLD'S LARGEST MUSEUM COMPLEX?

The Smithsonian Museum Group, a far-flung complex of many museums, buildings and attractions. The most noteworthy are: The National Museum of African Art, 950 Independence Ave. SW; The National Air and Space Museum, Independence Ave. at 6th St. SW; The National Museum of American History, Constitution Ave. at 14th St. NW; The Arts and Industries Building, 900 Jefferson Dr. SW; The Freer Gallery of Art, Jefferson Drive at 12th St. SW; The Hirshhorn Museum and Sculpture Garden, Independence Ave. at 7th St. SW; The National Museum of Natural History, Constitution Ave. at 10th St. NW; The National Portrait Gallery and The National Museum of American Art, 8th at and G Sts. NW; The Arthur M. Sackler Gallery, 1050 Independence Ave. SW

(The largest single museum is the **American Museum of Natural History** in NYC; founded in 1874, it comprises 19 interconnected buildings with 23 acre of floor space. The oldest museum is the **Ashmolean Museum** in Oxford England, built in 1679.)

WHAT IS THE SMITHSONIAN'S LARGEST MUSEUM?

Air & Space Museum houses the nation's aerodynamic treasures, from the Wright Brothers' 1903 Flyer to moon rocks and rockets.

The Museum also displays *Glamorous Glennis*, the aircraft flown by Chuck Yeager when he broke the sound barrier in 1947; Apollo II's *Columbia* from which astronaut Neil Armstrong took his first steps on the moon; a German Messerschmidt Me 262, the world's first operational jet fighter (1944); the *Voyager*, the first plane to fly around the world without refueling ('86); and the Lockheed U-2C, first reconnaisance plane to fly over the Soviet Union. Independence Ave. between 4th and 7th Sts. SW.

WHAT IS THE NATION'S OLDEST NAVAL FACILITY?

The **Washington Navy Yard** featuring the Naval Memorial Museum, housed in the old Naval Gun Factory. Exhibits include the rigged fighting top from the frigate *Constitution* and a Gulf War Tomahawk land-attack missile. Marine Corps Museum—displays uniforms, historic weapons and more. Also the *USS Barry*, a decommissioned naval destroyer, built in '55. Navy Yard Visitors' Center, 9th and M Sts. SE.

WHAT IS THE LARGEST LIBRARY IN THE WORLD?

The **Library of Congress**, a research library created in 1800 to serve Congress, contains more than 100 million items and occupies three buildings. Capitol Hill.

WHERE CAN YOU FIND ONE OF THE WORLD'S PERFECT COPIES OF THE GUTENBERG BIBLE?

At **The James Madison Building** in the Library of Congress. 101 Independence Ave. SE.

WHERE IS THE WORLD'S LARGEST HOLOGRAM?

At **The Art, Science and Technology Institute**—displays 60 holograms including the world's largest. 2018 R St. NW.

WHAT IS ONE OF THE WORLD'S LARGEST OFFICE BUILDINGS?

The Pentagon, headquarters for the Secretary of Defense, the Army, Navy and Air Force covers 29 acres, with 17 miles of corridors; displays on women in the military, flags, war art and Medal of Honor heroes are featured. Arlington. (The Sears Tower in Chicago and the World Trade Center in NYC are also among the largest buildings in the world. The Sears Tower is the tallest office building with 110 stories.)

Tomb of the Unknown Soldier (Arlington National Cemetery).

WHAT IS THE COSTLIEST BUILDING EVER PUT UP BY THE PUBLIC BUILDING SERVICE?

FBI Headquarters. Pennsylvania Ave., between 9th and 10th Sts. NW.

WHAT IS THE OLDEST PUBLIC BUILDING IN CONTINUOUS USE?

The home of the **Marine Corps Commandant** at 8th and Eye Sts. SE.

WHAT IS THE CITY'S OLDEST HOUSE?

Old Stone House—226 years old, this 5-room dwelling offers demonstrations at 3551 M St. NW.

WHAT IS THE CITY'S OLDEST TOWNHOUSE?

"Wheat Row" built in 1793, 4th St. and Waterfront.

WHERE IS WASHINGTON'S ONLY LOG CABIN?

This cabin was formerly located on **Meridian Hill** (16th Street NW between Belmont and Crescent Sts.) and was occupied by Joaquin Miller, the "Poet of the Sierras." The cabin is now located on the west side of Beach Dr., 1/4 mile north of the Military Rd. overpass in Rock Creek Park.

WHERE IS THE OLDEST PUBLIC AQUARIUM IN THE US?

In the basement of the **Department of Commerce Building**. 14th St. between E St. and Constitution Ave.

WHAT IS KNOWN AS THE MOST EXPENSIVE HOUSE IN THE US?

The former site of the residence of **General Van Ness**, who married the daughter of David Burnes, original proprietor of the grounds now occupied by the White House, Treasury Building, Executive Office Building and much of downtown Washington. The Van Nesses engaged Benjamin Henry Latrobe to design an elegant mansion, which upon completion in 1816 was said to be the most costly private residence ever built in the US. Its cost then was $2.2 million, an easy $25 million today.

WHAT WAS WASHINGTON'S FIRST APARTMENT BUILDING?

The Portland Flats apartment building, built in 1879; J. Sterling Morton of New York, originator of Arbor Day and Secretary of Agriculture in Grover Cleveland's second administration (1893-1897), resided there. The building was razed in '62.

WHERE ARE THE TALLEST CORINTHIAN COLUMNS EVER RAISED?

The eight 75-ft. columns are in the **National Building Museum**, Judiciary Sq. NW.

WHAT WAS THE NATION'S OLDEST SKYSCRAPER?

The Baltimore Sun building is the nation's earliest surviving "skyscraper." A nine-story example of Romanesque Revival architecture is now restored to its original beauty at 1317 F St. NW.

WHAT IS THE AREA'S ONLY SIX-TOWERED STRUCTURE?

The Mormon Temple, a mammoth white piece of modern architecture that rises surreally from the green trees; the Temple's six towers soar upward, the highest tower stands 288 feet from the ground and is topped with the golden figure of the Angel Moroni. 9900 Stoneybrook Dr., Kensington, MD.

WHERE IS THE ONLY ASTRONOMICAL OBSERVATORY IN THE US THAT DETERMINES TIME?

The Naval Observatory grounds on Massachusetts Ave. NW.

WHAT IS THE DIAMETER OF THE WORLD'S LARGEST TELESCOPE AT THE NAVAL OBSERVATORY?

26 inches; it was acquired in 1873.

WHAT WILL BE THE TOWN'S MOST SOPHISTICATED TRADE CENTER WHEN COMPLETED?

The new **International Cultural and Trade Center** in the Federal Triangle, when completed in '95 will be world-class in every way. With some 3.1 million sq. ft., the structure will be second in size only to the Pentagon; it was designed by I.M. Pei and will house many top officials in the administration.

WHAT REOPENED LANDMARK WAS THE LARGEST RESTORATION PROJECT IN US HISTORY?

Union Station, costing about $160 million. Massachusetts Ave. NE.

WHAT IS THE HIGHEST MASONRY STRUCTURE IN THE WORLD?

The Washington Monument, a towering 555-foot marble obelisk dedicated to our first President. Many of its stones were donated by cities, states, individuals and foreign countries. It also has the country's first aluminum roof. National Mall at 15th St. NW.

WHAT WAS THE FIRST TONY AWARD-WINNING THEATRE OUTSIDE OF NEW YORK CITY?

Arena Stage, the 800-seat circular theater on 6th St. and Maine Ave. SW.

WHAT IS ONE OF THE OLDEST CONTINUALLY OPERATING THEATER ORGANIZATIONS IN AMERICA?

National Theatre, built in 1835, at 1321 Pennsylvania Ave. NW.

WHAT IS THE ONLY AMERICAN CHURCH TO BE CALLED "THE CHURCH OF THE PRESIDENTS"?

St. John's, which is located directly across Lafayette Square from the White House, is known as "The Church of the Presidents" because every US president since James Madison has taken a seat in pew 54, the President's Pew, to worship.

WHAT IS THE WORLD'S LARGEST GOTHIC CATHEDRAL?

The **National Cathedral** has intricate stone carvings, stained glass windows depicting scenes from American history, and other works of art. Wisconsin and Massachusetts Aves. NW. (The largest of all cathedrals is St. John the Divine in NYC; has a floor area of 121,000 sq. ft. and a volume of 16,822,000 cu. ft. Its cornerstone was laid in 1892.)

WHAT IS THE LARGEST ROMAN CATHOLIC CHURCH IN THE US?

The **National Shrine of the Immaculate Conception**—built of stone and masonry in a style which blends contemporary, Byzantine and Romanesque architecture. Michigan Ave. at 4th St. NE. (The largest church in the world is the basilica of St. Peter, built between 1492 and 1612 in Vatican City, Rome; its area is 162,990 sq. ft. and its length is 611 ft.)

Embassy Row on upper Massachusetts Avenue.

WHO IS THE LARGEST PRIVATE EMPLOYER IN THE WASHINGTON AREA?

The Marriott Corporation, with many different offices and locations.

AFTER THE FEDERAL GOVERNMENT, WHO IS THE LARGEST REAL ESTATE OWNER IN THE CAPITAL?

George Washington University covers 23 blocks south and east of Washington Circle in Foggy Bottom, and has the distinction of being second biggest landholder in CapCity.

WHICH AREA REAL ESTATE COMPANY HAS THE HIGHEST VALUE OF ASSETS?

The Rouse Company, a longtime developer in the area; has holdings worth $5 billion.

WHERE IS THE WORLD'S ONLY STATUE DEDICATED TO THE *TITANIC*?

Gertrude Vanderbilt Whitney sculpted a striking monument to the men who gave their lives so that women and children could escape the doomed *Titanic*. The stone bench that surrounds the draped granite figure at the center of the memorial was designed by Henry Bacon, designer of the Lincoln Memorial. 4th and P Sts. SW. Washington Channel Park next to Fort McNair.

WHAT STATUE PROBABLY HAS THE HIGHEST IQ?

The Einstein Memorial, a 21-foot-high sculpture of Albert Einstein con templeting 3,000 stars in the universe (stainless steel studs embedded in blac granite) and holding a paper with his famous mathematical formula. Nea northwest corner of 22nd St. and Constitution Ave. NW.

WHAT IS THE LARGEST BRONZE STATUE EVER CAST?

The Iwo Jima Statue (Marine Corps Memorial), a 78-foot statue commemc rating Marines who died in battle since 1775. It was created from a wa photograph depicting the flag being raised on Mt. Suribachi during WWII. Rt. 5 near Arlington National Cemetery. It was sculpted by Felix de Weldon, wh recently suffered economic misfortune resulting in the auction of his Randolp Place 19th-century studio. He lives in Newport, RI.

WHAT IS THE ONLY STATUE IN TOWN WITH ITS SUBJECT HOLDING A CIGAR?

Sir Winston Churchill stands gloriously in front of the British Embass cigar in hand, one leg on Embassy property, the other on government propert 3100 Massachusetts Ave. NW.

WHAT ARE TWO OF THE UGLIEST MONUMENTS IN TOWN?

The two pair of **buffalos** guarding the Q St. Bridge at the entrance t Georgetown and **winged horses** at the east side of the Rayburn House Offic Building are among numerous menacing beasts and gruesome gargoyles adorn ing Washington architecture.

WHAT IS THE NATION'S NEWEST NATIONAL MEMORIAL?

The Law Enforcement Memorial features an oval tree-lined pathway c remembrance displaying the names of fallen officers on a granite wall. The name date back to 1794, when the first law enforcement officer was killed in the lin of duty. Judiciary Square, between E and F Sts.

The **Women in Military Service for America Memorial** is under constru tion at the gateway to Arlington National Cemetery; it honors the 1.8 millic women who served the country as pilots, soldiers, nurses, mechanics, translato and couriers.

WHERE IS THE NATION'S LARGEST FREESTANDING GLOBE?

At **Explorers Hall** in the National Geographic Society; equipment used Society-sponsored expeditions is on display, along with the world's large freestanding globe, artifacts of prehistoric cliff dwellers, and dioramas depictir various epochs in the development of mankind. 17th and M Sts. NW.

WHERE IS THE ONLY SOVIET PLAZA IN AMERICA?

A small stretch of **16th St.** near the Soviet Embassy at 1126 16th St. NW, once known as Ave. of Presidents was renamed Andrei Sakharov Plaza in the mid-'80s to protest Soviet treatment of the Nobel Prize-winning physicist and dissident.

WHAT 75-YEAR-OLD INSTITUTE IS CONSIDERED THE WORLD'S FOREMOST "THINK TANK"?

The Brookings Institution is the **grande dame** of think tanks and has served administrations and presidents for many decades. 1775 Massachusetts Ave. NW.

WHO WERE THE ONLY PRESIDENTS TO LIVE BEYOND THEIR 90TH BIRTHDAYS?

John Adams and **Herbert Hoover** (both died at 90); Ronald Reagan may make it!

WHO WAS THE YOUNGEST US NAVAL AVIATOR (TO BECOME PRESIDENT) WHEN HE GOT HIS WINGS IN 1942?

George Bush, who had joined the Navy the year before on his 18th birthday.

WHO WAS THE ONLY PRESIDENT TO GRADUATE FROM THE US NAVAL ACADEMY?

James Earl Carter in 1946.

Union Station, dazzling home to the railroads and worldwide visitors.

WHO WAS THE ONLY CALIFORNIA-BORN PRESIDENT?
Richard M. Nixon.

WHO WAS THE FIRST PRESIDENT TO APPEAR ON TELEVISION?
Franklin D. Roosevelt (1939) in New York City at the RCA Building.

WHO WAS THE FIRST VICE-PRESIDENT TO MOVE INTO THE
VEEP'S NEW OFFICIAL RESIDENCE AT US NAVAL
OBSERVATORY?

Nelson Rockefeller; 10 acres of land in the complex are designated for
vice-presidents. "Rocky" never officially lived at the Observatory; he and
"Happy" (his wife) had a bigger house on 11acres off Foxhall Road.

Rockefeller did officiate at parties in the Observatory and often showed
guests the $35,000 double bed (on the second floor) designed by artist Max
Ernst, which Rocky donated to the government.

WHAT ARE SOME AMERICAN FIRSTS?

The first Black elected Governor of a state was **L. Douglas Wilder**, VA,
'90; first Black elected to the Senate was **Hiram Revels**, MS, 1870; first
Black to House was **Jefferson Long**, GA, 1870; first Black Associate Justice
of the Supreme Court was **Thurgood Marshall**, '67; first Black Cabinet
Minister was **Robert C. Weaver**, HUD Secretary, '66.

The first woman Cabinet Member was **Frances Perkins**, Secretary of
Labor, 1933; first woman candidate for President was **Victoria Claflin
Woodhull**, National Radical Reformers, 1872; first woman candidate for VP
was **Geraldine A. Ferraro**, Democratic Party, '84; first woman Governor,
Nellie Tayloe Ross, WY, 1925; first woman Senator, **Hattie Caraway**, AR,
1932; first woman Congressperson, **Jeanette Rankin**, MO, 1916; first
woman member of US Supreme Court, **Sandra Day O'Connor**, '81.

WHO WAS THE ONLY PRESIDENT SWORN INTO OFFICE
ABOARD AN AIRCRAFT?

Lyndon Johnson on the occasion of JFK's death, flying back to Washington
from Dallas in '63.

WHAT WAS THE WAIST MEASUREMENT OF THE HEAVIEST U.S.
PRESIDENT?

54"—**William Howard Taft**.

WHO WAS THE SHORTEST PRESIDENT? THE TALLEST?

At 5'4" **James Madison** was the shortest resident of the White House; **George
Bush** at 6'3" was the most elevated.

Pageant of Peace, highlight of the Christmas season.

WHAT IS THE AGE OF THE OLDEST PERSON EVER TO SIT IN CONGRESS?

Senator Theodore Green (RI) was 93 when he retired in '61.

WHO REMAINS THE ONLY WOMAN TO HAVE HAD A HUSBAND AND A SON WHO WERE PRESIDENTS?

Abigail Adams; husband John was second President, son John Quincy was sixth President of the US,

WHO WAS THE YOUNGEST MAN EVER TO SERVE AS PRESIDENT?

Theodore Roosevelt at 42 years of age.

WHO WAS THE YOUNGEST MAN EVER ELECTED PRESIDENT?

John F. Kennedy at 43 years of age.

WHERE IS A COMPLETE LIST OF MORE THAN 3,000 WINNERS OF THE CONGRESSIONAL MEDAL OF HONOR?

In the **Hall of Heroes** at the Pentagon in Arlington.

WHAT TWO CAPITOL HILL EMPLOYEES ARE EMPOWERED TO ARREST THE PRESIDENT?

The **US Senate Sergeant-at-Arms** and his **deputy**.

WHO HOLDS THE RECORD FOR THE MOST PRESIDENTIAL NEWS CONFERENCES?

Franklin Roosevelt held 998 in 12 years; it is unlikely the record will ever be broken even with mass communication.

WHAT PRESIDENT HAD THE MOST CHILDREN?

W.H. Harrison, the ninth US President had six sons and four daughters; he was also the oldest president at age 68 to be inaugurated.

WHO REMAINS THE ONLY NON-US BORN FIRST LADY?

Louisa Catherine Johnson Adams (1775-1852) was born in London, England, to a British mother and an American father.

WHO WAS THE YOUNGEST FIRST LADY?

Frances Cleveland, aged 21, wife of Grover Cleveland.

WHICH FIRST LADY LIVED THE LONGEST?

Bess Truman, who was 97; Harry Truman died at age 93.

WHO WAS THE FIRST POPE TO VISIT WASHINGTON?

John Paul II.

WHAT IS THE OLDEST STREET IN DC?

Existing before the American Revolution, **Water St.** is the oldest street inside the limits of the District.

WHAT IS THE HIGHEST NUMBERED STREET IN THE DISTRICT?

63rd St. NE.

WHAT ARE THE SHORTEST STREETS? THE LONGEST?

Henry Bacon Dr. and **Daniel Chester French Dr.** Henry Bacon Drive which slants off Constitution Ave. NW between 21st and 23rd Sts. NW is only one block long, as is Daniel Chester French Dr. the mirror image of Henry Bacon Dr. leading to Independence Ave.

The longest avenue is **Massachusetts** which starts at Westmoreland Circle at the Montgomery County line, cuts through the residential Northwest and across downtown, is interrupted by the Anancostia River but resumes at Minnesota Avenue and continues all the way to the Prince George's County line. MassAve is best known for its numerous embassies between Scott Circle and the Naval Observatory.

Connecticut Avenue runs from the edge of downtown to Chevy Chase where it encounters the redoubtable Chevy Chase Circle (most famous of the "circles" in Town—Dupont, Washington, Tenley and Thomas), connecting point for District and Maryland and well-known for its confusing traffic patterns.

Another major artery is **Wisconsin Avenue** which dates back to colonial times and was once called River Street because it extended from the Potomac River up to a reservoir near the current site of Dumbarton Oaks. Today, WisAve is an important thoroughfare and runs from the Georgetown area into Maryland.

WHERE WAS THE FIRST ROOFTOP PARKING IN WASHINGTON?

The locally-established **Giant Supermarket** company opened an innovative store at 4555 Wisconsin Ave. NW in 1939 with parking on the roof. Today that building still has parking on the roof, but is owned by Hechinger's.

WHAT WAS THE FIRST PROTOTYPE OF SHOPPING CENTERS?

Park and Shop, located at Connecticut Ave. and Ordway St. NW was designed by Arthur B. Heaton in 1930; it was the first influential establishment to combine an integrated group of separate businesses with off-street parking.

WHERE WAS THE CITY'S FIRST ZOO AND WHAT IS IT NOW?

Today the **Enid A. Haupt Gardens** occupy the site between the Smithsonian "Castle" and Independence Ave. SW; in 1887 the city's first zoo was established by William Temple Hornaday, the Smithsonian's chief taxidermist, at that location.

Washington Harbour, spectacular enclave of shops and restaurants on the Potomac River.

373

WHERE IS THE ORIGINAL STAR-SPANGLED BANNER?

The Museum of American History displays the flag that inspired "T
Star Spangled Banner" and other political and cultural artifacts and t
manuscript. 14th St. and Constitution Ave. NW.

WHAT IS THE HIGHEST POINT IN TOWN?

The pinnacle of the Gloria in Excelsis Tower of the **Washingtc
National Cathedral** rates highest at 676 feet above sea level; naturally, t
Washington Monument is up there too. Downtown, the Old Post Offi
Tower hits significant highs with a glass elevator lifting guests to its 315-
high Tower Clock.

WHERE IS THE LONGEST ESCALATOR IN THE WESTERN HEMISPHERE?

At **Metrorail's Wheaton station**. (270 ft.)

WHERE WAS THE COLUMBIA RECORD COMPANY FOUNDED?

In 1889 a group of court reporters formed the **Columbia Phonograph
Company** to take dictation of the human voice. The firm (in 1890) produc
the world's first musical recordings—phonographic cylinders containing t
marches of the US Marine Band; it was located at 919 Pennsylvania Ave. N
in 1893 and later in Bridgeport where it finally evolved into Columb
Records. The building stands at 623-627 E St. NW.

WHERE IS THE OLDEST OPERATING ELEVATOR IN THE US?

The **Litwin Furniture Company**, 637 Indiana Ave. NW dates back
1826 when Elisha Graves Otis demonstrated the need for lifting devices
a era of new four-story buildings. His first elevator was presented at t
Crystal Palace Exposition in New York, 1854; from that point on h
invention took off and today is a worldwide fixture. The 1826 version st
functions at Litwin Furniture, hasn't needed repairs in 130 years and pass
inspection every six months!

WHAT IS THE OLDEST POTOMAC RIVER BRIDGE?

Chain Bridge at Little Falls; it is one of seven bridges that cross t
Potomac into DC; they are **Arlington Memorial, Theodore Rooseve
Woodrow Willson, 14th Street, Key, Cabin John** and **Chain** Bridges.

WHAT IS THE "MOST FAMOUS MILE" IN THE WORLD?

Pennsylvania Ave. from the Capitol to the White House is the mc
legendary 1,875 yards in the world. Pennsylvania is also the major artery
Town running from one end of the District to the other and center stage
any and all official processions.

WHAT ARE THE FIVE MOST BIZARRE STONE CARVINGS IN THE WASHINGTON NATIONAL CATHEDRAL?

(1) The distinctive **hubcap** and radiator of the once-famous Packard auto on the Churchill Porch; (2) the head of a **serpent** featuring the face of Hitler at a choir stall near the high altar; (3) a **dentist** working on a molar; (4) the cathedral's master carver **blowing his hat**—the hat being lifted into the air; and (5) the world's most **grotesque collection** of gargoyles, practically everywhere inside/outside the cathedral.

WHERE IS THE WORLD'S GREATEST CONCENTRATION OF EMBASSIES AND CHANCERIES?

Embassy Row, Massachusetts Ave., between Sheridan and Observatory Circles, where 150 foreign governments are headquartered.

65. WHAT IS KNOWN AS "SUICIDE POINT" IN THE US CAPITOL?

Too much talk can bring a certain suicide to a political career; on the floor of the **House Chambers** is a designated spot where Members of the House can make/break careers via their speeches; thus the "suicide" potential.

66. WHEN WAS THE GREAT ROTUNDA USED AS THE SITE FOR AN INAUGURATION?

Abe Lincoln was the first President to lie in state in the Great Rotunda, followed by many state funerals (most notable was JFK's). On **January 21, 1985** Ronald Reagan became the first President to take the oath of office in the Rotunda due to a blizzard outside.

67. OUTSIDE POWDER ROOMS, WHERE IN THE CAPITOL BUILDING IS THERE A "LADIES ONLY" ROOM?

In the **Congressional Suite**, a room is reserved for female members of Congress and select aides and lady officials; men are only allowed after hours as a clean-up detail!

68. WHERE IS THE DESK USED BY PRESIDENT LINCOLN?

When the President of the United States visits Capitol Hill, he is assigned to the **President's Room,** where the desk of Abraham Lincoln is majestically located; it's the desk used by Lincoln when he signed the Emancipation Proclamation.

69. WHERE ON CAPITOL HILL IS SEGREGATED SEATING ADVOCATED?

In the **Senator's Private Dining Room**, Democrats and Republicans take assigned seating in areas designated by political party affiliation; it's a matter of who blinks first as Senators glare across the room at the opposition.

Yet, members of both parties agree that the white Michigan "Navy" bean soup, served as a favorite for 60 years, hits the palate just right; it is a sober (but tasteful) reminder of the poverty of the depression years

370. IN THE SENATE WING, HOW IS THE AUDUBON SOCIETY EMBELLISHED?

As a presentation of native American birds — over 150 varieties — the walls of the **Senate Wing corridor** (south) are extensive enough to make an Audubonophile soar and twitter with glee.

371. WHAT FIVE-SQUARE-FOOT AREA HAS BEEN THE SITE OF SPEECHES BY THE MOST IMPORTANT OFFICIALS IN HISTORY?

At **The Rostrum** in the House Chambers more important personages have declared their intentions and enunciated their beliefs than at any similar location in the world. Our presidents and famous international visitors (foreign ministers, heads of state, etc.) make their peace (or their war) at The Rostrum.

372. WHAT IS TIFFANY'S CONNECTION TO THE AMERICAN RED CROSS?

At a dedication of the American Red Cross Building (Constitution Ave at 23rd St.) in 1917, three 10-feet tall theme windows were installed; the

National Mall, *locus* for all good and historic DC activities.

were fashioned in the Tiffany Studios in New York and given as a gift to the Red Cross.

The three windows tell the story of ministry to the sick and wounded. Tiffany portrays figures in flowing robes and knights in armor, set against a backround of luminous, cloud-filled skies.

In the central panel, a fallen warrior receives food and aid from a faithful comrade; in the left (north) panel, female warriors carry banners as Charity offers a healing draught; in the right (south) panel, noblewomen do good deeds. Of particular note in the central panel is the white steed bedecked with jeweled trappings; the jewels are embedded colored glass stones, an example of one of Tiffany's innovations. Also of interest for its extraordinary beauty is the right panel, which features Una from Spenser's *Faerie Queene*. With a crown atop her long ribbon-entwined hair, and wearing a flowing robe, she carries a basket of flowers.

373. **WHAT ARE THE MOST FAMOUS CEMETERIES IN THE AREA?**

Arlington National is the nation's most hallowed shrine; the former property of General Robert E. Lee (it was taken by the Union Army at the outbreak of the Civil War, when Lee left to join the Confederacy), the cemetery marks the graves of soldiers and patriots, best known of which is President John F. Kennedy's.

Oak Hill was established by Washington's premier merchant, banker and philanthropist, W.W. Corcoran, in the Georgetown area; about17,000 graves are there, mostly the resting sites of prominent Washington pioneers.

Rock Creek is the oldest in the district, established in 1712 (it adjoins the oldest church—St.Paul's); located on Rock Creek Church Rd., it is the grave-site for about 8,000 deceased persons. One such person is Clover Adams, a widely loved, high-profile Washington wife to Henry Adams, the grandson of a president. She committed suicide in 1885 and is buried in the park; a sculpture was erected over her grave by noted artist Augustus Saint-Gaudens. Her life and the intrigue of her death was recently treated in a book by Sarah Booth Conroy of the *Washington Post* called *Refinements of Love*. The gravesite continues to attract visitors and calls attention to the mysterious death of this then popular city leader.

Glenwood is just south of Catholic University of America; dedicated in 1854, it is the fourth oldest major cemetery in the area. It originally consisted of 90 acres but 38 of those acres now house prestigious Trinity College.

Battleground National is the smallest national cemetery in the US; it is a one-acre plot at 6625 Georgia Ave. NW and holds the bodies of 41 Union soldiers who died at the battle of Fort Stevens (1864).

Mount Olivet is on Bladensburg Road opposite the National Arboretum; the 75-acre tract dates back to 1858 as a cemetery for Catholics and other military notables (Arlington was not yet open); over 8,500 patriots are interred there.

Congressional at 1801 E St. SE is the final resting place of many statesmen (at this count—19 Senators and 43 Representatives) and other legends, most notably J. Edgar Hoover, John Philip Sousa and John Payne Todd (son of Dolley Madison). The site was founded in 1847.

Mt. Zion at 27th and Q Sts. NW dates back to 1773 and is the historical burial site of Blacks in Washington.

374. WHAT FAMOUS MILITARY MEN ARE BURIED IN ARLINGTON NATIONAL CEMETERY?

Over 225,000 servicemen and their families rest on the 612 acres of Virginia land called Arlington, the US's most celebrated cemetery; it is the home of the **Tomb of the Unknown Soldier** and the site of the eternal flame at the grave of **JFK**. Additionally, it is the final resting place of many great patriots: **Claire Lee Chennault**, Commander of the Flying Tigers of WWII; **Jacob Loucks Devers; "Wild Bill" Donovan**, WWII spymaster; **William Frederick Halsey, Jr.**, Fleet Admiral of the Navy; **William D. Leahy**, five-star Fleet Admiral of the Navy during WWI; **John Archer Lejeune**, WWI Field Commander; **George C. Marshall**, five-star General; **Audie Murphy**, WWII's most decorated soldier; **John J. "Blackjack" Pershing**, General of the Armies, the only man besides George Washington to hold the rank; and **Hyman G. Rickover**, Admiral and "Father of the Nuclear Navy."

John F. Kennedy Center for the Performing Arts, an expansive mixture of marble and glass, home to the performing arts.

375. WHAT VERY VISIBLE WASHINGTON WOMAN RECENTLY GOT A PUBLIC BATH?

The bronze **Statue of Freedom** that adorns the Capital Dome (since 1863) was given a pamper treatment for the first time in her 120 years. Removed from her heavenly perch in May '93, the 19 ft., 6 in. classic figure (she scales in at 14,985 lbs.) was on view on the East Plaza where walnut shells and special chemicals (not from Estee Lauder) were applied to her voluptuous body. She was acrylic, lacquered and waxed before gracing her lofty position in fall '93. Her "restoration" was performed by Linda Merk-Gould.

The huge crayola-colored mural of another famous woman—**Marilyn Monroe**—which greets visitors upon entering Woodley Park, gets regular baths via nature's own rainwater.

76. HOW IS GENERAL DOUGLAS MacARTHUR MEMORIALIZED IN WASHINGTON?

Surprisingly, the WWII Army hero and Governor of Japan after the surrender has a modest legacy—a **boulevard** bearing his name and some rows of **stone planters** leading from the north steps of the Executive Office Building to Pennsylvania Ave. Called "MacArthur's Planters," the containers are filled with flowers and ornamental shrubs. There is also a **corridor** in the Pentagon depicting his life and times.

MacArthur had one of the most extraordinary military careers in history. He graduated from the US Military Academy in 1903, served in the Philippines (1903-1904) and in Japan (1905-1906), was aide-de-camp to President Theodore Roosevelt (1906-1907), commanded the 42nd (Rainbow) Division in WWI and was twice wounded in action. He became Superintendent of West Point as Brigadier General in 1920. He served in the Philippines (1922-1930), was Chief of Staff (1930-1935), retired from the US Army (1937) but was recalled for active duty (July 1941) as Commander of US forces in the Far East. He resisted the Japanese in the Philippines. He was ordered to escape to Australia, saying "I shall return," which he did as Supreme Allied Commander of forces in the Southwest Pacific. As a five-star General, he accepted the surrender of the Japanese forces on the deck of the battleship *Missouri* on September 2, 1945. He commanded the occupational forces in Japan (1945-'51) and was Supreme Commander of US forces in the Korean War ('50-'51) until he was removed by President Truman on April 10, '51.

77. WHAT CAPITAL BUILDING HAS MORE FLAGS, BATHROOMS AND PARKING SPACE THAN ANY OTHER?

Considered one of the largest office buildings in the world, the **Pentagon** is "first" in many categories especially in the amount of money spent by its inhabitants (about $300 billion yearly) and the number of people it has on various payrolls (two million).

But it also has the most bathrooms (284), parking spaces (11,000), and flags (about 2,000) of any building known to man. In the building, additionally, is "the Tank," the National Military Command Center in which members of the Joint Chiefs of Staff plan global srategy.

378. WHAT IS THE CAPITAL'S MOST FAMOUS ISLAND?

When Theodore Roosevelt came into office in 1901, four-fifths of America's prime forests had been leveled. More than one-third of the wild population had been destroyed. With a belief in conservation that had grown from his boyhood enthusiasm for outdoor life, the new President set about rescuing the public domain. During his administration, more than 23 million acres were reserved for conservation; the US Forest Service was created; five national parks, 51 bird refuges, and four game refuges were established.

A historic island in the Potomac, which has had many owners since it was granted by Charles I to Lord Baltimore, was purchased by the Theodore Roosevelt Memorial Association in 1931 and **"Theodore Roosevelt Island"** was established. Paul Manship created a 17-ft. bronze statue of the nation's 26th President; set on an oval terrace in front of a 30-ft. shaft of granite, the statue is surrounded by a terrace, where a water-filled moat reflects the sky. Four granite tablets inscribed with quotes from Roosevelt' philosophy of citizenship complete the memorial.

379. WHERE CAN ONE SEE THE REVOLUTIONARY WAR FOUGHT AGAIN IN MINIATURE?

At the **Anderson House Museum**, one of the country's finest collection of miniature soldiers continues to play out the most dramatic moments of the Revolutionary War. Over 2,000 pieces are displayed in dioramas in the Reception Hall of the opulent old house. Collected from many sources over a 40-year period, the individual pieces were made by the best American English, and French craftsmen in the field.

A national museum of relics of the American Revolution, the Anderson House also displays an outstanding collection of portraits. Among these are paintings by Gilbert Stuart, including his portrait of Captain Jacob Shubert and John Trumbull's portrait of George Washington. Related artifacts on display include swords, medals and historically important works of glass, silver and porcelain. 2118 Massachusetts Ave. NW. (Note: Anderson House is headquarters for the patriotic Society of Cincinnati.)

380. WHAT IS THE COST OF WAGING WAR?

Quite beyond the human sacrifice of a war and the devastation of entir cultures and societies, the price tag of conducting a military offensive i

Georgetown, vibrant hub of restaurants, stores, restored homes.

staggering. Here's the total expense racked up in recent wars (including cost of goods/weapons, service connected veteran's benefits, interest on war loans; in millions of dollars):

Civil War	$ 6,790
WWI	62,973
WWII	447,629
Korean Conflict	67,024
Vietnam	166,775

Despite the awesome cost of war at whatever level, the US continues to be the #1 weapons merchant in the world (according to the Congressional Research Service), accounting for 57 percent of arm sales with the Third World in '92. Sale of about $13.6 were tallied with Taiwan, Saudi Arabia and Kuwait as the biggest buyers; France was next with $3.8 billion in purchases.

81. WHAT IS THE COST OF A TYPICAL "INDEPENDENT COUNSEL'S" INVESTIGATION?

There is probably no "typical" investigation, but there generally is a high price tag for any discovery of the facts surrounding a celebrated case of the federal government vs. any legal opponent (company, individual, foreign country, terrorist, etc.). Independent counsel is appointed by a judge (or judges) representing the government, with the hope that expenses will be low (taxpayers foot the bill) and justice will be served.

In the recent 6 1/2 year long Iran-Contra investigation, the expenses of independent counsel Lawrence Walsh totaled about $36 million and the results were minimal. Oklahoma City-based Walsh used the airline, Watergate Hotel, various limo services, new offices on M Street, services of the Department of Justice, printing and graphic facilities, security and secretarial services with the cool detachment of a billionaire business tycoon.

Here's a rough cost breakdown (Source: Administrative Office of the U Courts):

Parking Facilities	$ 124,835
Security Guards	1,119,495
Printing/Graphics	25,256
Office Supplies	519,075
Travel	739,441
Utilities	256,220
Office Space	5,987,352
Postage	46,064
Witness Fees	6,878
Transcripts	100,132
Salaries	17,733,206
(30 lawyers and 50 investigators)	

Total is about $27 million, but fails to include incidental expenses and special fees that escalate the total to the mid-30s (millions) range.

Any way it's measured, the Iran-Contra legal hassle was expensive; and although it may have been in the extra-pricey range, no independent counsel investigation is inexpensive, simply because humankind has just enough greed to take advantage of circumstance, and when Uncle Sam is the bursar, budgets for special services are often sky high!

382. WHAT WASHINGTON MUSEUM IS A TESTAMENT TO THE DEAD?

The **US Holocaust Memorial Museum** stands on a 1.9-acre plot between 14th and 17th Sts. and Independence Ave.; its 265,000 sq. ft. features several hundred thousand artifacts, books, souvenirs and "reminders" of the dread Holocaust.

Mandated by Congress in '80, the five-story property houses a library, archives, movie studio, chambers, photo and art gallery. In the $200 million structure, special sections like the "Hall of Remembrance" where paintings and photos recall the Holocaust or the "Children's Wall of Remembrance" (3,500 ceramic tiles painted by American schoolchildren in memory of the 1.5 million children lost) vividly depict the horrors of the years between 1942-1945.

383. WHERE DID SOME FORMER PRESIDENTS LIVE BEFORE RESIDING IN THE WHITE HOUSE?

While in play as junior whatevers in the political system, many Presidents spent long months in less than desirable homes and neighborhoods (by comparison to the White House); here are some of their early-on abodes:

Harry S Truman apartment-hopped a half-dozen times between 1935 and 1945 before finally moving into the White House—his first Washington house. The Trumans were living at **4701 Connecticut Ave. NW** when he became President.

Dwight D. Eisenhower moved in and out of Washington regularly, starting in 1919 when he was a young army officer on his way up. He lived at the **Wyoming Apartments, 2022 Columbia Rd. NW** in 1927-1928 and 1929-1936.

Before going to Europe in 1942 as Commander of US forces, Ike lived briefly with his brother Milton at **708 E. Broad St.** in Falls Church and after the war, he and Mamie lived in **Quarters One at Fort Myer**, where, in 1948, he wrote *Crusade in Europe*.

John F. Kennedy shared an apartment and houses with two of his sisters before and after WWII. He and Kathleen Kennedy lived in **Apartment No. 542** at **Dorchester House, 2480 16th St. NW** when he was in naval intelligence at the Pentagon; Kenney's Washington homes after the war included one at **1528 31st St NW** with another sister, Eunice; at **1400 34th St. NW;** at **3260 N St. NW** until he was elected to the Senate in '51; **3271 P**

U.S. Capitol, resting place for the 19-foot bronze statue "Freedom" atop the Capitol.

383

St. NW where he lived until he and Jacqueline were married in '53 Merrywood, her family home on **Chain Bridge Rd.** in McLean; **3321 Den Pl. NW** which he and Jackie rented from May '53 to December '54; **Hickory Hill** at **1147 Chain Bridge Rd.**, McLean, which later became home to brother Robert; **2808 P St. NW** for five months in '57; and finally, an 181 red-brick Federal home at **3307 N St. NW** which JFK bought while Jackie was in the hospital with their firstborn, Caroline. They sold the N Street home after moving to the White House, but rented an estate, **Glen Ora,** in Middleburg as a weekend retreat. Subsequently, they built **Wexford,** near Atoka, VA, but had stayed there a few times before Kennedy was assassinated in November '63.

Lyndon Baines Johnson, a bachelor, arrived in Washington as a congressional aide in 1932. He rented a modest apartment in **Dodge House** at N Capitol and E Sts. NW. After he married Lady Bird, the Johnsons lived in a $42-a-month, one bedroom apartment at **1910 Kalorama Rd NW**, the first of their many Washington and Texas homes. They then moved to a house at **4921 30th Pl. NW**, where they were living when Lynda Bird and Luci were born.

Before returning to Texas in '69, the Johnsons had had some of the best addresses in town, including **The Elms**, the mansion he as Vice-President bought from Perle (*Call Me Madam*) Mesta, at **4040 52nd St. NW**. The house is now the residence of the Ambassador of Algeria.

Richard M. Nixon and **Gerald R. Ford Jr.** lived in row houses in a section of Alexandria called Park Fairfax when they were young Congressmen. The Nixons lived at **3538 Gunston Rd.**, the Fords at **1521 Mount Eagle Pl.** From Alexandria, the Nixons moved into a $41,000 two-story house at **4801 Tilden St. NW,** in Washington's Spring Valley area. In '57, by then Vice-President with a $35,000-a-year salary, Nixon bought a 21-room Tudor-style stone house at **4308 Forest Ln.** in Washington's Wesley Heights district.

The Fords lived in a one-bedroom apartment at **2500 Q St. NW** in Georgetown when Gerald Ford was a freshman Congressman. Later, while living at Park Fairfax, they bought a building lot at **514 Crown View Dr.** in Alexandria, where they built a house surrounded by "empty lots and trees and mounds of red Virginia clay. From there, the Fords moved to the White House in August of '74.

Ronald Reagan like **Jimmy Carter** lived near but never in Washington before becoming President. As a midshipman, Carter lived at **Bancroft Hall** in Annapolis at the US Naval Academy from 1943 to 1946. While campaigning for the presidency in '80, Reagan and his wife Nancy rented **Wexford** the Kennedys' one-story hunt country stucco rambler which Jacqueline Kennedy sold in '64.

As a freshman Congressman from Texas, **George Bush**, with his wife Barbara, lived at **4910 Hillbrook Ln.** in Washington's Spring Valley area for a brief time. In 1969, they bought a new house on a cul-de-sac at **5161 Palisade Ln.** where their neighbors included the late Supreme Court Associate Justice Potter Stewart. The Bushes rented out the house when he became US Ambassador to the UN and US liaison officer to the People's Republic of China, but lived there while he was chairman of the Republican National Committee and director of the Central Intelligence Agency. They sold the house in the spring of '77 and returned to Texas to live. In January '81, when he was sworn in as Vice-President, Bush and his wife moved into the Vice-President's official residence (called "Admiralty House") on the grounds of the **US Naval Observatory.**

384. WHO WAS THE FIRST KENNEDY IN THE WHITE HOUSE?

During the JFK days, there was a standing joke that the President (John F. Kennedy) was an also ran as to rights of "first come-first served." Duke Ellington's father—**Edward Kennedy Ellington**—had been a butler in the White House for most of his adult years and had always been called "Kennedy." The Duke got a big kick out of citing some minutia-history re his father's presence in the Executive Mansion long before the arrival of the Kennedy Clan; and, in lighter moments, JFK would tease the elder Ellington by calling him "Master" Kennedy. In the early '70s, the Nixons held several major events in the White House honoring prominent Blacks; the biggest being a state-size dinner honoring Duke Ellington himself.

385. WHERE IS "BLACKJACK" BURIED?

"Blackjack" John J. Pershing is buried in **Arlington National Cemetary**; he was Commander of the Allied Expeditionary Forces in WW I and is buried near deceased troops who served with him in the war.

One of the **most famous horses** of the era, another "Blackjack"—the riderless horse that led the funeral procession of President John F. Kennedy—is buried on the parade grounds of Fort Myer, the prestigious Army post across the Potomac in Virginia. "Blackjack" was the last quartermaster horse issued by the Army and the last to be branded US. He served, also, at the funerals of Presidents Herbert Hoover and Lyndon Johnson, and for General Douglas MacArthur. The horse died in '76.

Incidentally, Fort Myer was also the focus of the first military test flight in 1908 when Orville Wright kept his simplistic aircraft aloft for just over one minute.

386. WHAT IS "2101"?

An **elegant apartment** located at 2101 Connecticut Ave. NW, built in 1908—with gargoyles—has been known for decades simply as 2101. To build it, three great mansions were torn down, including the G.W. Woodward mansion. From the start, it was meant to be the best on the market, with each apartment as large as a good-sized house (minimum: three bedrooms, three baths, maid's room with bath and a heated sun porch).

387. WHAT IS KNOWN AS THE "UNOFFICIAL PALACE" OF WASHINGTON?

The **Washington Hilton**, a "gull-winged" hotel opened in '65 as the 60th hotel in the Hilton chain was dubbed "the unofficial palace" of Washington by Conrad Hilton. In '81 at the T Street lower-level entry to the hotel, John Hinckley shot President Ronald Reagan, his press secretary James Brady and FBI agent Raymond Martin. A protective portico has since been constructed at the entrance. It is located at 1919 Connecticut Ave. NW.

388. WHAT IS THE SIGNIFICANCE OF THE "CAIRO HOTEL"?

This 14-story, 165-ft. hotel was the **tallest building** in the city when constructed in 1894, and exceeded the reach of city firefighting equipment. Concern for safety and aesthetics caused regulations to be imposed limiting the height of buildings to 110 ft., except along selected wider avenues, such as Pennsylvania, where buildings to 130 ft. were allowed. The '89 Height of Buildings Act also assured that Washington would not be dominated by skyscrapers. 1613 Q St. NW.

389. WHERE IS THE "BENCH OF INSPIRATION"?

The great New York financier Bernard Baruch was often called upon by presidents to give advice on matters of government, and willingly obliged. When he'd come to the Capital, he would often sit on a bench in Lafayette Square and expound on any number of subjects. Today, next to his favorite bench is a marker commemorating it as the "Bernard Baruch Bench of Inspiration" (dedicated to him by the Boy Scouts of America).

390. WHAT IS CONSIDERED AMERICA'S MOST FAMOUS TOILET?

In '88, NASA contracted with Rockwell International and Hamilton Standard to develop a toilet (commode) for the **space shuttle to Mars** (some 35 million miles away); 2 1/2 years later the commode was delivered at a cost of $23.4 million; much wrangling at congressional levels and much publicity ensued and the pricey toilet went into the *Guinness Book of World Record* as "most expensive toilet" in the history of man (a record which probaby will stand forever).

391. WHAT IS KNOWN AS THE "DOLL HOUSE" OF WASHINGTON?

Washington Dolls' House and Toy Museum (5236 44th St. NW) is the only museum in the nation's Capital devoted entirely to dolls' houses, dolls, antique toys and miniature ships.

392. WHO ORIGINATED THE WORD "HOOKER" AS WE KNOW IT TODAY?

Prostitutes became "hookers" because of **General Joseph Hooker**, who in 1863 decided to round up the roughly 4,000 ladies of the night in Washington and concentrate them in one area (below Pennsylvania Ave. near the Treasury Department) for easy surveillance. That section of Town became known as Joe Hooker's division, and its occupants got the moniker—hookers!

393. WHO IS "MR. FUSSBUDGET"?

Operating from a home in Greenwich, CT, a 67-year old gadfly named **Martin Gross** has been creating headaches and heady embarrassment for the Washington Establishment via his expose of massive governmental overspending and "stupid-spending." His best-selling book, *The Government Racket, Washington Waste from A to Z*, delivers karate chops at almost every agency in CapCity and provides startling proof of the gross inefficiency of most spending practices by bureaucrats. Examples: $3 billion for 1,300 private government airplanes—200 of which don't exist; $1 billion to buy unwanted honey from beekeepers; $150,000 to study the Hatfield-McCoy feud; $2 billion (equal to the budget of North Dakota) on new office furniture for Congress and government employees; $1 billion worth of helium gas reserves (enough to last over 100 years) stored underground in Texas at a cost

White House (South Lawn), domicile to every president except George Washington.

of $100 million annually; $19 million to examine gas emissions from cow flatulence, and $57,000 for gold-embossed playing cards on Air Force One.

Gross and a partner founded the Book Digest in '73 and marketed it up to a circulation of one million before selling it in '78 for $10 million. With plenty of cash and leisure time, he began digging into government spending and became the darling of the talkshow circuit, **Mr. Fussbudget** as he lambasted federal agency after agency for their bizarre spending. Says Gross, "Our government is the most crackpot organization in the world."

394. WHAT CAPITAL BUILDING WAS HIT BY GUNFIRE IN WWII?

After the initial fear of bomb attacks in Washington, soon after WWII commenced, anti-aircraft guns were placed in strategic locations around the city. One such gun was mounted on the roof of the Department of Interior building (18th and C St. NW). While a bored crew snoozed, an unnamed person absent-mindedly pulled the lanyard and the gun hurled a projectile at the **Lincoln Memorial**; it hit the top level and dislodged some marble on the panel bearing the Seal of the state of Maryland. Naturally, the city was on fierce alert for several hours until the cause of the mishap was understood; the errant warrior was never found in the chaos that followed.

395. WHAT WAS WASHINGTON'S MOST FAMOUS "MASSACRE"?

President Nixon appointed Archibald Cox, a Harvard law professor, in May '73 and assured him a free hand as special prosecutor in the Watergate break-in affair. When Cox attempted to secure the White House tapes, Nixon ordered Attorney General Richardson to fire Cox. Richardson refused and resigned. Deputy Attorney General Ruckelshaus refused to fire Cox and was fired. Solicitor General Robert Bork, third-in-line, agreed to perform as requested, was appointed acting Attorney General, and fired Cox. These events, known as the **Saturday Night Massacre**, occurred on October 20, '73. On June 24, '74, the Supreme Court ruled, in a unanimous decision, that Nixon was obliged by law to deliver the tapes to the new special prosecutor. On August 9, '74 Nixon resigned as President.

396. WHO IS CONSIDERED THE ULTIMATE FIRST LADY?

Since the time of **Martha Washington**, the wives of American presidents have been the subject of endless examination and relentless pressure, but none has made more news, done more for the welfare of society and been more beloved than **Eleanor Roosevelt**.

Historian Arthur M. Schlesinger, Jr. called Mrs. Roosevelt "the most liberated American woman of this century." She had been called "First Lady of the World" and even in death ('62) she is a model for humankind.

Pundits have labeled her most active First Lady in history; each year she traveled hundreds of thousands of miles carrying FDR's message and visiting coal mines, military bases, sharecropper camps and welfare villages across the country. Socially, she entertained with gusto and dignity; in her 13 years in the White House, she hosted over 2,000 parties for heads of state, Democratic friends and advocates, members of the armed forces and associates. Her daily column "My Day" was syndicated in almost 300 newspapers and she was faithful in helping the under-privileged.

She served as Assistant Director of the US Office of Civilian Defense in the early 1940s and after FDR's death, she became US Delegate to the UN (1945-'53) and a spokesman for the Voice of America.

Other First Ladies impacted their times, too: **Abigail Adams** was an early feminist and activist; **Mary Todd Lincoln** attended political rallies and urged her shy husband on; **Helen "Nelly" Taft** was a powerful political broker and sat in on cabinet meetings; **Edith Wilson** monitored her husband's policies closely and was a clandestine president during his stroke; **Florence Harding** moved the cause of women's suffrage forward; **Bess Truman supported** Harry in every way and was the perfect "woman behind" a successful man. Other First Ladies—**Mamie Eisenhower, Jacqueline Kennedy, Lady Bird Johnson, Pat Nixon, Betty Ford, Rosalyn Carter, Nancy Reagan, Barbara Bush** and now, **Hillary Rodham Clinton**, have all been positive forces in the White House and have helped their husbands and the Administration serve the country well.

But, for now, history has selected **Eleanor Roosevelt** as the most renowned and remarkable of all the American First Ladies.

397. WHO IS AMERICA'S FOREMOST HISTORIC PRESERVATIONIST?

The National Trust for Historic Preservation, a nonprofit organization chartered by Congress in 1949 to preserve the culture and sanctity of America through the ages, has a new man-on-the-run to fill the $225,000/year job as President—**Richard Moe**, former chauffeur to Hubert Humphrey, administrative assistant to then-Senator Walter Mondale and later chief-of-staff for Mondale in his losing candidacy for President in '84.

Moe is a preservationist by instinct; his recently published book—*The Last Full Measure* recounts the plight of The First Minnesota Volunteers (in the Civil War) which lost more than 80 percent of its manpower in the Battle of Gettysburg. While visiting the battleground, researching the book, Moe was appalled at the "commercial encroachment" on consecrated grounds and dedicated himself to protecting sacred areas and monuments as part of history.

At this point, National Trust manages about 20 historic properties, mostly old mansions; the group was instrumental in the revitalization of NYC's Grand Central Terminal and the Devil's Island Lighthouse in Wisconsin. Contact with its supporters is through a publication—*Historic Preservation.*

Moe suggests a tax break to generate additional funds for preservation (actually between '78 and '86 the movement prospered due to laws which made donations effective for rich people) and is working with the Clinton Administration to assure a sense of continuity with the past as new future-oriented projects are legislated.

For the moment, Moe's mandate is to keep us "the way we were."

398. WHAT IS WASHINGTON'S NEWEST MUSEUM?

The significant role played by the mail service in America's social, cultural, political and commercial growth is vividly presented in the Smithsonian Institute's newest museum—**The National Postal Museum**, located in the historic, renovated Washington City Post Office Building on Capitol Hill.

Built between 1911 and 1914, the City Post Office Building was designed by D.H. Burnham & Co. (Chicago) and was the Town's central post office until 1986. The building recently won the D.C. Preservation League's Building of the Year award for "preservation excellence."

The "Stamps and Stories" gallery exhibits 55,000 of the museum's 16 million stamps and offers a chronological history of postal service starting in 1673.

The US Postal Service is the largest civilian employer in the country with 680,000 career employees working in some 40,000 post offices; its annual budget is $50 billion, roughly one percent of the total US economy and if it were a private company, it would be the eighth largest corporation in America. The postal service delivers about a half-billion pieces of mail each day—about two pieces for every person; the customer base is almost 250 million people. Current Postmaster General is Marvin Runyon.

399. WHAT ARE THE MOST IMPORTANT TELEPHONE NUMBERS IN TOWN?

THE WHITE HOUSE	202)+
The President—William J. Clinton	456-1414
The Vice-President—Albert Gore, Jr.	456-1414
VP's Chief of Staff—Roy Neel	456-6606
Chief of Staff—Thomas F. "Mack" McLarty	456-6797
The First Lady—Hillary Rodham Clinton	456-6266
Administration—David Watkins	456-2861
Cabinet Affairs—Christine Varney	456-2174
Central Intelligence Agency—R. James Woolsey	703 - 482-1100
Communications Director—George Stephanopoulos	456-2100
Counsel to the President—Bernard Nussbaum	456-2632
Domestic Policy Council—Carol Rasco	456-2705
Intergovernmental Affairs—Regina Montoya	456-7060
Legislative Affairs—Howard Pastor	456-2230

Management and Budget—Leon Panetta	395-4840
Military Office—John Gaughn	456-2150
National Economic Council—Robert E. Rubin	456-2175
National Security Council—Anthony Lake	456-2255
Policy Development—Ira Magaziner	456-6406
Political Affairs—Rahm Emanuel	456-1125
Presidential Scheduling & Advance—Marcia Hale	456-7560
Presidential Personnel—Bruce Lindsey	456-6676
Press Secretary—Dee Dee Myers	456-2100
Public Liaison—Alexis Herman	456-2930
Science and Technology Policy—John H. Gibbons	456-7116
US Trade Representative—Mickey Kantor	395-3204

THE CABINET

Department of Agriculture Secretary—Mike Espy	720-3631
Department of Commerce	
Secretary—Ronald H. Brown	482-2112
Department of Defense Secretary—Les Aspin	703-695-5261
Department of Education Secretary—Richard Riley	401-3000
Department of Energy Secretary—Hazel O'Leary	586-6210
Department of Health and Human Services	
Secretary—Donna Shalala	690-7000
Department of Housing and Urban Development	
Secretary—Henry Cisneros	708-0417
Department of Interior Secretary—Bruce Babbitt	208-7351
Department of Justice	
Attorney General—Janet Reno	514-2001
Department of Labor Secretary—Robert Reich	219-8271
Department of State Secretary—Warren Christopher	647-5298
Department of Transportation	
Secretary—Federico Pena	366-1111
Department of the Treasury	
Secretary—Lloyd Bentsen	622-5300
Department of Veterans Affairs	
Secretary—Jesse Brown	535-8900

400. WHAT IS THE WASHINGTON CREDO?

Dreamers, optimists, pretenders, negativists, promoters, believers, whatever, invariably come to certain conclusions about life, founded on their own experiences; we hope this book has contributed to that self-discovery and will be an ongoing source of knowledge about Washington, and yourself, for some time.

ABOUT LIFE:

Life is more than just being **alive**.

Life is not based on the **way things are**, but on the way people think things are.

Life is like a **maze** in which you try to avoid the exit.

Life is **colorful** — there's red tape, red alerts and rednecks, gray matter, blue laws, blue notes, blue chips and blue bloods, backmail and blackballing, green thumbs, green backs and greenhorns, whitewash and white papers, pink elephants, yellow streaks, golden rules, and best of all silver linings and rainbows.

Life is a room full of **doors**, which close with time.

In **life**, never play poker with a guy named Doc; never eat at a restaurant called Mom's; and never play house with someone more neurotic than you.

Life in **reverse**: You get your gold watch after 40 years of hard work at the State Department; you come out of college after four years of hard play; you spin through high-school and play through grammar school ; you become a kid with toys and no responsibility, then a child and a little baby, you go back into the womb and spend your last nine months floating, and you finish off as a gleam in somebody's eye!

No one appreciates life more than those who are growing **old**.

Life's **reciprocity**—my turn today, yours tomorrow.

Life is **tough**—it takes up a lot of your time, all your days and nights, all your weekends, and what do you get in the end? **Death.**

ABOUT YOU:

To seize **opportunity** may be to die; to ignore it is never to be born.

The brightest talent grows dim with **inactivity**.

To **befriend** yourself, do good for someone else.

Vanity plays very creative tricks on our memory.

You don't need a weatherman to know which way the wind **blows.**

Take away your **life-illusion**, and you limit happiness.

There is a major **difference** between doing things that make you feel good, and doing things that make you feel good about yourself.

The greatest **aphrodisiac** is being in charge of yourself.

When you are in full possession of yourself, when you **know who you are, and are who you are**, the world is a trinket in your hand.

ABOUT OTHERS:

Beware of **H&P** people; they huff & puff their way through life, always going nowhere.

Avoid those who like the song — *Down is Up Enough!*

Songwriters have the most vivid obituaries; memories never die.

A person of **excellence** is as difficult as she is rare.

The man who **blushes** easily can hardly be a brute.

A **fool** at 40 remains a fool the next 40.

When a **general** makes a mistake, all the troops suffer.

Every **madman** thinks everybody else is mad.

A man should make at least one bet each day; otherwise he could be walking around **lucky** and never know it.

Beware of the man who brags he has the world's best **inferiority complex.**

Those who **enjoy life** the most don't talk about it; they're busy doing it.

The **ruler** of a territory chooses its religion.

A **learned** man always has wealth within himself.

He who builds no **castles in the air**, builds no castles anywhere.

ABOUT THE GAME:

The **sun** shines for everyone.

In a **junkyard**, you see the ultimate destruction of everything we once desired.

Foundations keep shifting.

Order may breed habit, but chaos breeds life.

Hunger makes everything taste good.

Never praise the day until the **twilight** comes.

Fortune **favors** the **bold.**

The **descent** to hell is easy.

Speak kindly of the dead; they have no rebuttal.

He lives twice who **lives well.**

The best **mirror** is an old and true friend.

There is no **leisure** if it's not used well.

Between grief and **nothing**, I'll take nothing (Faulkner) ; the hardest thing is to give something up and not know what you'll get in return.

Laughter is a good beginning for a friendship; and the best ending for it.

It's this simple: Love thy neighbor **as** thyself; not better than or instead of thyself. **AS** thyself.

Don't treat people (and yourself) as they are, but as they **ought** to be.

"To love" is the **greatest verb** in the world; "To help" is a close second.

FINALLY, I SUSPECT THAT EVEN BEING GOD ISN'T A BED OF ROSES.

INDEX

400

404

406

410

CONTRIBUTORS

Applause for these contributors who gave so freely of their "Facts & Fancies" knowledge:

A standing ovation for:
Pat Dixson, Garnett Stackelberg, J.R. Black, Meliss M. Posey, Herbert Jensen and Margaret Wiederhold, ir whom uncommon dedication was a common virtue.

And to our publishing company staff members—Eri Friedheim, Judith Clemence, Ariane Comstock, Tamar Newell, Sugar Rautbord, Celia Lipton Farris, Browni McLean, Robert M. Montgomery, Jr., Sally Jess Raphael, Arnold Scaasi, Judy Schrafft, Herbert Bayar Swope, Jr., and Marylou Whitney, for continued an enlightened encouragement.

For editorial inspiration, special **plaudits** to:
Betty Beale, Tom McNichol, Diana McLellan, Michae Gross, David Berger, Barbara Wainscott, Letiti Baldrige, Charles Mathias, Jr., Sally Quinn, Am Cunningham, Susan Schmidt, John White, Harry Jaffe Frank O'Donnell, Victor Gold, Larry Van Dyne, Alm Viator, Wayne Nelson, Charlotte Hays, Drew Lindsa Carla Koehl, Chuck Conconi, Irvin Molotsky, Barbar Matusow, Kim Eisler, Vernon Walters, Ken Adelma Michael Dolan, Amy Kolczak, Maureen Dodd, Joh Sedgwick, Bill Heavey, Alan Pell Crawford, Joh Flinn, Kitty Kelley, Evan Thomas, Randall Bloomquis Bob Mondello, Stephen Rosenfeld, Brooke Runnette Andrew Martin, Daphne White, Andrea Rider, Sherr Dalphonse, Craig Stoltz, Lois Romano, Jennifer Mose Tim Wells, Janis Johnson, John F. Kelly, Laur Goldstein, Susan Watters, Kevin Chaffee, Jeffre Staggs, Patrick Butters, Carrie Harper, Jeanette Wall Elise Ford, Donnie Radcliffe, Susannah Cassedy, Kare Feld, Richard Krolik, Maureen O'Sullivan, S. Cla Conroy, Lisa De Paulo, Charles Peters, Wayne Nelso

Contributors cont.

Emily Couric, Jerry Knight, Richard Harwood, Joanne Kaufman, Tim Wells, Patrick Anderson, Mark Baechtel, Joseph Amodio, Keith Girard, Andrew Ferguson, Rita McWilliams, Amy Parker, Mitch Gerber, Howard Means, Diane Lazarus, Michael Dirda, Franklyn de Marco, Donald Flamm, Jack Wetenhall, Jacqui Levitz, Nancy Sharigan, Danielle Davidson, Clement Conger, Nell Henderson, Linda Wheeler, Joel Garreau, Jan Leslie Cook, Martha Sherrill, Carol L. Anderson, Lisa Wolcott, Peter Baker, Michael Leccese, Sara L. Nagelvoort, Leslie Milk, Janet Gibson, Woody Hochswender, Vicky Moon, Godfrey Barker, Ginger Danto, Jeannette Walls, W. Hampton Sides, Ina Ginsburg, Kathy Kemper, William H. Webster, Sarah Grusin, Kevin and Alexander Bailey, Larry King, Fred Fielding, James Grafton Gore, Mary Jordan, Richard Berman, Janey Gibson, Stephen Dolainski, Jack Valenti, Adrian Havill, James M. Perry, Michael Duffy, Stephen Sherrill, Jeffrey Toobin, Owen Ullman, Lloyd Grove, Anne Crittenden, Margaret Carlson, David Ellis, Edwin Diamond, Sidney Blumenthal, Walter Shapiro, Jeffrey Slonim, David Rogers, John Harwood, Charles Kaiser, Jeff Gordinier, Mike Causey, James M. Perry, Albert R. Hunt, Jack Anderson, Michael Binstein, Bernard S. Redmont, M.B. Howard, Scott Eyman, Molly Moore, Michael Kernan, Phyllis C. Richman, David Gollan, E. Raymond Kinstler, Dianne Denise Werner.

REFERENCES

Primary sources were the many friends and associates interviewed in the Capital area; from professionals to socialites to "Chairmen" to administration officials, they were cooperative and informative to a person.

Secondary sources included dozens of books, newspapers and magazines and library staffs (most notably at the National Geographic Library, the Smithsonian Institution Archives and the US Capitol Historical Society) as follows:

BOOKS:
Bryson B. Rash, FOOTNOTE WASHINGTON,
    EPM Publications, Inc.1983
Benjamin C. Bradlee, CONVERSATIONS WITH KENNEDY,
    Pocket Books,1975
Charles Peters, HOW WASHINGTON REALLY WORKS, Addison-Wesley
    Publishing Company,1992
Robert L. Price, THE WASHINGTON POST GUIDE TO WASHINGTON,
    McGraw-Hill Publishing Company, 1989
Kitty Kelley, JACKIE OH! Ballantine Books,1978
Sam Donaldson, HOLD ON, MR. PRESIDENT, Random House,1987
McDowell Bryson and Adele Ziminski, THE CONCIERGE'S GUIDE TO
    WASHINGTON, DC, John Wiley & Sons, Inc.,1991
David Cutler, LITERARY WASHINGTON, Madison Books,1989
Spade & Archer's 50 MAPS OF WASHINGTON DC, H.M. Gousha,
    a Division of Simon & Schuster, Inc., 1991
Douglas E. Evelyn and Paul Dixon, ON THIS SPOT, Farragut Publishing
    Company, 1992
Maxine H. Atwater, WASHINGTON REVEALED,
    John Wiley & Sons, Inc.,1992
Stephen Hess, THE ULTIMATE INSIDERS, The Brookings Institution, 1986
David Brinkley, WASHINGTON GOES TO WAR, Ballantine Books,1988
Roberta Gottesman, FINDING FUN & FRIENDS IN WASHINGTON,
    Piccolo Press,1992
Thomas J. Murray, THE SOCIAL LIST OF WASHINGTON, DC, 1992
Anthony S. Pitch, WASHINGTON TRIVIA, PRESIDENTIAL TRIVIA, FIRST
    LADIES TRIVIA, Mino Publications, 1989,1991
Kevin Delany, A WALK THROUGH GEORGETOWN,
    Kevin Delany Publications,1989
Kenneth O'Donnell and David F. Powers, JOHNNY, WE HARDLY KNEW YE,
    Pocket Books,1973

References cont.

Betty Beale, POWER AT PLAY, Regnery Gateway, 1993

David Halberstam, THE FIFTIES, THE BEST AND THE BRIGHTEST, THE POWERS THAT BE, THE RECKONING, Villard Books, 1970, 1975, 1982,1993

Joseph A. Califano, Jr., THE TRIUMPH AND TRAGEDY OF LYNDON JOHNSON, Simon & Schuster,1991

Carol M. Highsmith and Ted Landphair, Inc. EMBASSIES OF WASHINGTON, The Preservation Press, 1992

Ira Gershkoff and Richard Trachtman, THE WASHINGTON DRIVER'S HANDBOOK, Addison-Wesley Publishing Company, 1984

Jane Ockershausen Smith, THE WASHINGTON ONE-DAY TRIP BOOK, EPM Publications, 1984

Adrian Havill, THE LAST MOGUL (THE UNAUTHORIZED BIOGRAPHY OF JACK KENT COOKE), St. Martin's Press, 1992

Larry King (with Peter Occhiogrosso), TELL ME MORE, St. Martin's Paperbacks, 1990

Howard Kurtz, MEDIA CIRCUS, Times Books (Random House), 1993

Jane McCaffree and Pauline Innis, PROTOCOL: THE HANDBOOK OF DIPLOMATIC, OFFICIAL AND SOCIAL USAGE, Devon Books, 1991

OTHER: *The Washington Post, Washington Times, The New York Times, Time, Newsweek, US News and World Report, Life, Fortune, The New Republic, New Yorker, Atlantic, Time, People, Vogue, Esquire, Unique Homes, Travel Agent, Spy, Elle, The New Republic, National Geographic, Congressional Record, Congressional Quarterly, Regardie* and *Washington Dossier* (both have ceased publication), *Washington Life* and *The Washingtonian* (one of the best city magazines in America), *Visitor's Guide* (Bell Atlantic); *Discover Washington, DC!* (Washington, DC Convention & Visitors Association), *Washington Portfolio* (J.B. Publishing Co. Inc.), *Guest Informant* (Lin Cellular Communications Corporation), *Guest Quick Guide* (Guest Informant, Lin Cellular Communications Corporation), *The Georgetowner, Washington CityPaper, Forbes, Vanity Fair, Where.*

ABOUT THE AUTHOR

James Jennings Sheeran is Chairman of a New York-based holding company with international interests in the travel, communication and publishing fields; he is Publisher of *Palm Beach Society* and *New York Society* Magazines and his books of *Facts & Fancies* are also published in Palm Beach, Chicago and San Francisco. He is a nationally syndicated columnist, the author of eight books, and his "sculptured canvas" artform is shown in many galleries in the US. He lives in NYC, Southampton and Palm Beach.

DATELINE: If you've enjoyed *The Washington Book of Facts & Fancies, Caprices & Curiosities* and would like to contribute information for future editions, send your comments to us at *Palm Beach Society* Magazine, c/o Washington Facts/Fancies, 240 Worth Avenue, Palm Beach, FL 33480. For additional copies of Facts/Fancies, send $18.95 plus $3 (for shipping) to the same address.